The Idle Man (1821/2)	Ric...
The Progress of Literature in America (1824)	Edw...
On the Value and Uses of Poetry (1825)	Will...
Dreams and Reveries of a Quiet Man (1832)	Theodore Sedgwick Fay (1807-1898)
Swallow Barn (1832)	John Pendleton Kennedy (1795-1870)
Outre Mer (1833/4)	Henry Wadsworth Longfellow (1807-1882)
Georgia Scenes, Characters, and Incidents (1835)	Augustus Longstreet (1790-1870)
National Literature (1835)	James Kirke Paulding (1778-1860)
The Romance as Epic (1835)	William Gilmore Simms (1806-1870)
A l'Abri (1839)	Nathaniel Parker Willis (1806-1867)
Essays (1841) *Representative Men* (1850)	Ralph Waldo Emerson (1803-1882)
Seven Lectures to Young Men (1844)	Henry Ward Beecher (1813-1887)
Papers on Literature and Art (1846)	Margaret Fuller (1810-1850)
The Philosophy of Composition (1846) The Poetic Principle (1848/9)	Edgar Allan Poe (1809-1849)
Thoughts on the Poets (1846)	Henry Theodore Tuckerman (1813-1871)
Biglow Papers (1848), 2d series (1867) *Among My Books* (1870)	James Russell Lowell (1819-1891)
Essays and Reviews (1848)	E. P. Whipple (1819-1886)
Hawthorne and His Mosses (1850)	Herman Melville (1819-1891)
Lectures on Art and Poems (1850)	Washington Allston (1779-1843)
Reveries of a Bachelor (1850)	Ik Marvel [Donald G. Mitchell] (1822-1908)
Potiphar Papers (1853)	George William Curtis (1824-1892)
Walden (1854) *Excursions* (1863)	Henry David Thoreau (1817-1862)
The Gettysburg Address (1863)	Abraham Lincoln (1809-1865)
Our Old Home (1863)	Nathaniel Hawthorne (1804-1864)
Ten Times One Is Ten (1870)	Edward Everett Hale (1822-1909)
Democratic Vistas (1871)	Walt Whitman (1819-1892)

See back cover for continuation of this chart.

AMERICAN LITERARY ESSAYS

Reader's Bookshelf of American Literature

American Drama, edited by Alan S. Downer

American Literary Essays, edited by Lewis Leary

American Poetry, edited by Karl Shapiro

American Short Novels, edited by R. P. Blackmur

American Short Stories, edited by Ray B. West, Jr.

GENERAL EDITOR: WILLIAM VAN O'CONNOR

American Literary Essays

❋ *Edited by Lewis Leary*

Thomas Y. Crowell Company · New York · Established 1834

Acknowledgments

Acknowledgment is gratefully made as follows for permission to reprint copyrighted essays.

Henry Adams, from *The Education of Henry Adams.* Copyright 1918 Massachusetts Historical Society, and 1946 Charles Francis Adams. Reprinted by permission of and arrangement with Houghton Mifflin Company, the authorized publishers.

W. H. Auden, "The Anglo-American Difference." From the 1955 *Anchor Review.* New York: Doubleday & Company, Inc., 1955. Copyright © 1955, by Doubleday & Company, Inc. Reprinted by permission of the author.

Willliam Barrett, "We're on the Road." From *The New York Times Book Review,* May 10, 1959. Reprinted by permission of the author and *The New York Times Book Review.*

Richard P. Blackmur, "The Craft of Herman Melville." Copyright © 1955, by Richard P. Blackmur. Reprinted from his volume, *The Lion and the Honeycomb,* by permission of Harcourt, Brace and Company, Inc.

Van Wyck Brooks, "On Literature Today." Copyright, 1941, by Van Wyck Brooks. Reprinted by permission of E. P. Dutton & Co., Inc.

Richard Chase, "The Broken Circuit: Romance and the American Novel." From the *Anchor Review,* 1957. © 1957 by Richard Chase. Reprinted by permission of the author. This essay appeared in 1959 in a slightly revised and expanded form as the first chapter of *The American Novel and Its Tradition* (Gloucester, Mass., Peter Smith.)

John Jay Chapman, "Emerson." From *The Selected Writings of John Jay Chap-*

man, edited by Jacques Barzun and copyright 1957 by Farrar, Straus and Cudahy, Inc. It is used by permission of the publisher, Farrar, Straus and Cudahy, Inc.

T. S. Eliot, "Tradition and the Individual Talent." From *Selected Essays 1917–1932* by T. S. Eliot, copyright, 1932, by Harcourt, Brace and Company, Inc.

James T. Farrell, "Social Themes in American Realism." Reprinted by permission of the publishers, Vanguard Press, from *Literature and Morality* by James T. Farrell. Copyright 1946, 1947 by James T. Farrell.

William Faulkner, "Nobel Prize Acceptance Speech." Reprinted by courtesy of Random House, Inc.

William Faulkner, "To the Youth of Japan." From *Faulkner at Nagano.* Tokyo: Kenkyusha Ltd., 1956. Copyright © AI 5283, 12/6/56 by William Faulkner. Reprinted by permission of Harold Ober Associates Incorporated.

Robert Frost, "The Figure a Poem Makes." From *Complete Poems of Robert Frost.* Copyright, 1930, 1949, by Henry Holt and Company, Inc. By permission of the publishers.

Donald Hall, "The New Poetry." From *New World Writing, No. 7,* April 1955. Copyright © 1955 by New American Library for World Literature, Inc. Reprinted by permission of the author. Acknowledgment is gratefully made for permission to quote the following: lines from *Lord Weary's Castle,* Copyright, 1944, 1946, by Robert Lowell. Harcourt, Brace and Company, Inc. (New York), Faber & Faber, Ltd. (London). Lines from *The Beautiful Changes and Other Poems,* Copyright, 1947, by Richard Wilbur, and *Ceremony and Other Poems,* Copyright, 1950, by Richard Wilbur, Harcourt, Brace and Company, Inc. Lines from *My Papa's Waltz* and *The Lost Son and Other Poems,* by Theodore Roethke, Copyright, 1942, by Hearst

Magazines, Inc., *Cuttings (Later)* from *The Lost Son and Other Poems,* by Theodore Roethke, Copyright, 1948, by Theodore Roethke, and *The Adamant* from *Open House,* by Theodore Roethke, Copyright, 1938, by Theodore Roethke, by permission of Doubleday & Company, Inc. Lines from *The Judge is Fury,* Copyright, 1947, by J. V. Cunningham, by permission of the publisher, Alan Swallow. Lines from *The Fly* and *Glass Poem* from *Poems 1940–1953* by Karl Shapiro, Copyright, 1946, by Karl Shapiro, by permission of Random House, Inc. Lines from *A Balcony with Birds* from *The Toy Fair,* by Howard Moss, Copyright, 1954, by Howard Moss, by permission of the publishers, Charles Scribner's Sons. Lines from *The Dancing Bears* by W. S. Merwin, by permission of Yale University Press.

John A. Kouwenhoven, "What Is American about America?" from *Harper's Magazine,* July, 1956. Reprinted by permission of the author.

H. L. Mencken, "American Culture." Reprinted from *A Mencken Chrestomathy* by H. L. Mencken, by permission of Alfred A. Knopf, Inc. First printed in the *Yale Review.* Copyright 1920, 1949 by Alfred A. Knopf, Inc.

H. L. Mencken, "Poetry in America." Reprinted from *Prejudices: Sixth Series* by H. L. Mencken, by permission of Alfred A. Knopf, Inc. Copyright 1027 by Alfred A. Knopf, Inc.

Frank Norris, "The Novel with a Purpose." From *The Responsibilities of the Novelist,* by Frank Norris. Reprinted by permission of Doubleday & Company, Inc.

William Van O'Connor, "Traditions in American Literature." From *The Times Literary Supplement,* September 17, 1954. Reprinted by permission of the author and *The Times Literary Supplement.*

Philip Rahv, "Attitudes toward Henry James." From *The Question of Henry James*, F. W. Dupee, ed. New York: Henry Holt and Company, Inc., 1945. Reprinted by permission of the author.

Constance Rourke, "Humor in America." From *American Humor* by Constance Rourke, copyright, 1931, by Harcourt, Brace and Company, Inc.; renewed by Alice D. Fore. Reprinted by permission of the publishers.

George Santayana, "The Elements and Function of Poetry." From *Interpretations of Poetry and Religion* by George Santayana. Reprinted by permission of Charles Scribner's Sons.

Logan Pearsall Smith, *The Prospects of Literature*. London: The Hogarth Press Ltd., 1927. Reprinted by permission of The Hogarth Press Ltd.

Allen Tate, "Emily Dickinson." From *Collected Essays* by Allen Tate by permission of the publishers, Alan Swallow. Copyright 1941, 1948, by Allen Tate.

Lionel Trilling, "Part I of Reality in America." From *The Liberal Imagination* by Lionel Trilling. Copyright 1940 by Lionel Trilling. Reprinted by permission of The Viking Press, Inc.

Mark Twain, "Fenimore Cooper's Literary Offenses." Reprinted by permission of Harper & Brothers.

Mark Twain, from *How to Tell a Story and Other Essays* by Mark Twain, and from *Mark Twain's Autobiography*. Copyright 1924 by Clara Gabrilowitsch. Copyright 1952 by Clara Clemens Samossoud.

E. B. White, "Poetry." From *One Man's Meat* by E. B. White. Copyright 1939 by E. B. White.

Contents

x   *Contents*

Introduction

Cassandra voices plead that the essay, like the novel or the poem which anyone can read, is dead or ill unto death. But this is not true, for change which timid people fear as death is not death. As Mark Twain was fond of explaining, rumors of this kind are likely to be exaggerated.

An essay is an attempt to express a mood or explain an attitude. Most simply, it is man speaking about what seems to him important or true or at the moment worth saying. Your dictionary will tell you that it is a literary composition, analytical or interpretative, dealing with a subject from a more or less limited or personal standpoint. That, we may say, gives the essayist plenty of room to move around in. And he has moved, in all directions, using the word to describe almost anything from a tenuously charming account of a walk in the rain to a philosophical treatise like John Locke's *Essay on the Human Understanding*, a long moralistic poem like Alexander Pope's *Essay on Man*, or a versified disquisition on the nature of poetry like Karl Shapiro's *Essay on Rime*.

But traditionally the essay has been of moderate length, has been written in prose with intention other than narrative, and has presented a view based on the writer's thought and experience rather than on formal study. Thus, the essay is different from the treatise, which is a systematic exposition or argument, presumed to be written objectively. It is usually different from the editorial, which is likely to be impersonal and formally reasoned. An article may be an essay when it deals with a subject from a particular and individualized viewpoint. Some sermons are essays, and some student themes, when they are seriously expressive of the people who wrote them. But all these forms so merge one with another that finally all one can say with assurance is that essays are more than dispassionate reports. Whatever its length or manner, the essay is personal. No one but its writer could have written it.

Yet, however personal, the essay does define and is defined by the age in which it is written. We can suppose that essayists have always existed, wherever man has had opportunity to sit quietly and write. The authors of Ecclesiastes can be thought of as essayists, and so can St. Paul. Herodotus and Plato were essayists, and essays have been discovered, it is said, among the iambics of Euripides. Some of Seneca's epistles were identified by Lord Bacon as essays, for though the word, he explained, was new, the form was old. Chaucer, Rabelais, and Cervantes might sometimes have called themselves essayists, if they had known our modern use of that word. For it was Michel de Montaigne in France in the late sixteenth century who first presented what he called *Essaies*, wherein, he said, "I desire to be delineated in mine owne genuine, simple and ordinarie fashion, without contention, art or study; for it is my selfe that I pourtray." He was occupied, he said, with the thoughts of one man sitting on his "owne taile," and that man was himself, which is about as con-

1

venient a brief description of the essay as we are likely to come on: "my selfe am the ground worke of my booke."

The essays of Montaigne, written on whatever subject at the moment pleased him—on "Vanity," "Solitude," or "Repentance"—and written with the nonchalant grace of a man at ease with himself and his thinking, set the model and tone for what seemed a new literary genre. In England, Francis Bacon followed him, not in imitation, for it was his own more formally rhetorical and less relaxed self that he portrayed, without the spacious freedom and intimate candor of his French predecessor, but in prose so incisive and sensible that he stands with honor as the first recognized essayist in our language. And after Bacon, the floodgates opened, as aphoristic or plain-spoken opinion flowed from the pens of many seventeenth-century gentlemen. None did better than he on the model he established, though the tenderness of some of Abraham Cowley's *Discourses*, the questioning of contemporary notions in the quirky prose of John Donne, and the later bluff assurance of John Milton and John Dryden, both of whom did better in other forms, place them also among England's early best.

But as times changed and men changed, the essay changed also, to mirror man's concern, not less with himself and his personal revelations, but more with other men and upstart men, and the society they made, and its need for correction. Because it was man speaking his own mind, it inevitably absorbed other forms in which he had been accustomed to speak, like the sermon, the parable, the satirical character sketch, and the moralistic dialogue. Witty and ironic portraits of men and manners built on the framework of narrative, like the Sir Roger de Coverley papers, tempted readers by the lure of story to consideration of contemporary foibles. The talk of talented men around a table or be-

fore a fire was reproduced or invented to point up a moral, indicate a direction to be followed, or simply to display the brilliance of men's minds at work. Lay sermons appeared, to chasten or chastize those who thought or acted differently from the way the writer thought men should think or act.

The tone was usually lightly humorous, as fops, pedants, politicians, or coquettes were held to ridicule or scorn, but sometimes it was bitter, as men like Jonathan Swift or Daniel Defoe used their pens as scalpels to expose religious, political, or moral ills. Men like Sir Richard Steele and Joseph Addison established periodicals, in some ways not unlike the *New Yorker* today, but called the *Tatler*, the *Spectator*, or the *Guardian* in reminder of their intention to expose, observe, or protect. The serial essay became popular, in which such characters as Isaac Bickerstaff or Will Honeycomb spoke through many appearances. A favorite device was the introduction of a commentator from another civilization, like an American Indian or the Chinese gentleman in Oliver Goldsmith's *The Citizen of the World*, who reported in amusement or dismay about the eccentric habits of Englishmen. Sometimes, as in Steele's "Recollections of Childhood," the essay spoke in the relaxed, personal accent of Montaigne or Cowley. More often it was didactic and direct, intended, explained Samuel Johnson, "to inculcate wisdom and piety," with few words wasted on "idle sports of imagination."

As much as any other kind of composition, the essay depends for its excellence on the force and wit of the men who write it. Dull men write dull essays, pretentious men are pretentious and imitative men imitative, even in prose. So after its bright days in the time of Addison, Steele, and Swift, and then Johnson and Goldsmith, the essay declined to imitation of their manner by men of less vigor who had less to say, used often as a vehicle of platitude rather than of experience. So widely dispersed did it become, so variously patterned, and sometimes so badly written that Dr. Johnson finally dismissed it as only "a loose sally of the mind: an irregular, undigested piece; not a regular and orderly composition."

But when what we remember for convenience as the Romantic Movement drove men back into themselves and away from patterns set by other men, the essay rose again, with Charles Lamb, whose quiet whimsies have delighted readers ever since, with William Hazlitt, who wrote with equally infectious gusto on boxing, literature, or the state of morals, with Samuel Taylor Coleridge, Leigh Hunt, and Thomas De Quincey. In their hands, the essay turned from didacticism and dissection of the deportment of men to more personal consideration of man's relation as an individual to the world around him. It became more simply direct, in language which avoided stereotypes. The tone again became intimate, the humor more subtle, the temper more kindly. Admonition was still needed, but encouragement was needed also if man was to keep up with new thinking imported from Germany and France and cultivated with vigor at home. Literature became more prominently a subject, as Shakespeare was rediscovered, and other writers who found the spirit of man more interesting than the social matrix in which or against which it struggled.

Later in the nineteenth century, Thomas Carlyle, John Ruskin, Thomas Babington Macaulay, and Matthew Arnold wrote seriously and at length about the conduct and responsibilities of men. The essay became graver now, addressed more often to the state of man's mind than to his manners. The world seemed to these eminent Victorians less a light and frolicsome, friendly place at which men might jest and by jest correct, and the essay lost some of its light-heartedness as men struggled to make something sensible of their place in a universe which seemed increasingly in opposition to their good intentions.

It has often been said that the eighteenth century was the golden day of the essay, and this is in some sense true, for Addison, Swift, and Goldsmith wrote wittily and well. But it is from the nineteenth century of Hazlitt and Coleridge, especially of Ruskin, Macaulay, and Arnold, that the essay as we know it best today is derived. It stretched itself then to confront a world more like the world we have learned to know. It expressed itself at greater length, with less delight and considerable less flippancy, often more puzzled than charmed, sometimes more puzzling than charming. Something of the spirit of meditation was lost, so that the essay became less personal and more learned: it treated in greater depth of history and literature and politics; it engaged in controversy and unashamedly took sides; more often than not, it was a lecture, in spirit or reality. Beside it, the less vigorous but patiently intimate essays of Robert Louis Stevenson, the bitter caricaturing wit of a modern like Max Beerbohm, or the tremendous trifling of G. K. Chesterton, however pleasantly they soothe or lightly stimulate, seem inappropriate and anachronistic.

The tradition of the cursory essay, which pleases as much by its manner as its matter, has lasted longer in England than in the United States. British readers still enjoy an occasional quiet chuckle over light ruminations on cricket, the pleasures of boating, or their own, strange British behavior. We are likely to prefer writings more solidly informative, even to discussions on the practicality of home-made bomb shelters or somber explanations of the profundity or precision with which favorite authors confront disturbances of our time or nature. Our most consistently popular essayists do not write comfortably in dressing gown and slippers. American tradition urges participation, and the traditional essayist is an observer, a contemplative bystander who does not become involved, and therefore he subverts our intention. Nevertheless, the essay as written in the United States has followed patterns set by the essay in England, though with differences in tone and content, and even language, which suggest an increasingly distinctive way of looking at the world.

Even Benjamin Franklin, whose early essays were written consciously in imitation of essayists abroad, developed an idiom and point of view which was so unmistakably native that fastidious contemporaries accused him of vulgarizing language and thought. His contributions over the signature of Silence Dogood to his brother's *New England Courant* in 1722 were quizzical commentaries on Boston manners, not unlike those which appeared in English periodicals on London manners, except that Mistress Dogood was a New England countrywoman who spoke in native accent about local idiosyncracies. In the Busybody essays which he contributed six years later to a Philadelphia paper and in the prose admonitions which he provided for one or another of his Poor Richard's almanacs, Franklin effectively followed traditions established by transatlantic wits, but with homespun flavor of humor and seasoning of pragmatic common sense. When he turned to serious topics of the times during the argumentative years which preceded the American Revolution, he did not hesitate to borrow the acid manner of Swift or the indirection of Defoe as he wrote of the need for practical rather than traditional education, for a sound money policy among the colonies, or of indignities forced on them by Britain. One of America's first self-made men, a scientist, philosopher, diplomat, inventor, and more besides, Franklin is also America's first distinguished essayist. He could be bitter or rollickingly funny; he wrote sketches like "Advice to a Young Man on the Choice of a Mistress" and "The Trial of Polly Baker," which have become part of our national lore; he wrote charmingly of his gout, of playing chess, or of insects whose busy life lasts only a day. His moods were various, in borrowing from other men he paid interest with originality, and he was seldom dull.

This was not true of most of his colonial countrymen, who cut more flimsy cloth to borrowed patterns. Hundreds of young Americans rushed essays into print during the eighteenth century, pretending to be hermits who viewed urban busyness from the sanctuary of a woodland retreat, observers who commented with mock alarm on the oddities of native beaux and belles, or reformers who put together sober sermons on the iniquities of their neighbors. When the subject was political and the pen held by people like Thomas Paine, John Adams, or Alexander Hamilton, then the writing came vividly alive, for these men in anger or resolution had something to say. But in traditional forms, only Philip Freneau and Benjamin Rush, and such dedicated aspirants from New England as John Trumbull, Timothy Dwight, and Noah Webster, wrote on a consistent level of competence. They were painstakingly American, and they were not always dull, but the shadow of the way other men had said many of the same things darkens even their best work. As the century ended, Joseph Dennie. who was proud to be known as the Addison of the United States, pleaded that imitation was to be preferred to puerile originality.

In the eyes of contemporaries, here and abroad, Washington Irving seemed to present adequate proof that writing by an American could be as charming as writing by anyone else. Gentle, reminiscent, and unashamed in his admiration for English stylists, he spoke of the evanescence of mortal fame and the goodness of old things with such well-mannered amiability that he was accepted on both sides of the Atlantic as a man of letters whose books could be displayed without shame on the same parlor table with those of Goldsmith or Lamb. So light was his touch that he seldom disturbed any surface, content, he said "if I can by any lucky chance, in these days of evil, rub out one wrinkle from the brow of care, or beguile the heavy heart of one moment of sorrow." In *Salmagundi*, a dozen years before, he had been tentatively Addisonian, but his *Sketch Book* in 1820, followed by *Bracebridge Hall* and *Tales of a Traveller* within the next four years, revealed a new literary vein which he mined with profit for the rest of his life. Brief, often colored by sentiment, sometimes only descriptive of quaint custom or scene, occasionally in narrative which viewed man and his actions with bemused benevolence, Irving's essay-sketches tempted many imitators, some of whom, like Longfellow in *Outre Mer*, blurred the outline with pretension or an embarrassingly fervid overflow of feeling, though others, like Augustus Longstreet in *Georgia Scenes* and John Pendleton Kennedy in *Swallow Barn*, extended the method to present authentic pictures of native localities. With Irving, the United States learned the advantage of writing with care. She might also have learned that literature does not have to be solemn in order to be superior.

It is surprising that Irving should have fared so well among his countrymen, for this has not been a characteristic American notion. It is probably true that few countries have been more enmeshed in seriousness than the United States. It is a great part of our virtue and some part of our vice that we have often thought of ourselves as a committed people, even when we have not been sure of all the implications of our commitment. Uncle

Sam, we can say, seldom smiles. Partly because of his background, perhaps in Puritanism, partly because of conditions of life on a wilderness frontier or the opportunities for success in economic competition, he agrees with Longfellow in this, if in little else, that life is real and life is earnest. And he has fathered a people with a mission, who are sometimes messianic, happiest when busied with reform, of other people or themselves. Having learned something good, their liveliest incentive has often been to teach it to someone else. Whether the conviction has had to do with diet, body-building, or the construction of hi-fi sets, the support of missionaries or the extension of civil rights, they seem committed to the proposition that other people are better when converted to their way. For this reason, they have sometimes turned from Edgar Allan Poe, whose insistence that literature should please before it instructs makes him seem alien. They understand why Oliver Wendell Holmes was not always taken seriously as a physician because he was fond of quipping that "Small fevers are gratefully accepted."

The light touch has not been among us the popular touch. It is difficult, for example, to remember that in his frolicsome way Dr. Holmes played about many of the same subjects that Emerson spoke of more seriously at length. Our humor, when most characteristic, has been heavy-handed, and best when leveled to a not always delicate popular taste. It has depended on exaggeration or burlesque, has fed on gross manifestations of racial or sectional differences among us, and has been answered in appreciation more often by the guffaw than the quiet smile. It has sometimes been riotously funny, and we have slapped our thighs in appreciation, especially when entertained by a master like Mark Twain, whose genius was so great that he could lure an audience to laughing at itself without tempting it to do much about mending the flaws to which he pointed and at which it laughed. Mark Twain can depress us because we agree with him that the world is insane, or he may build our self-esteem because we recognize ourselves superior to the piteous or hilariously naive people he pictures, but he is not the man we turn to for materials when we begin to build our own edifices of reform. It was one of his sorrows as well as his triumph that hardly anyone took him seriously.

This distrust of levity has determined the kind of essay which we have preferred. Each generation has enjoyed its whimsical observers and quizzical commentators. Just as Irving and James Kirk Paulding spoke pertinently to their time, so Oliver Wendell Holmes and George William Curtis spoke to theirs. But the fragile insights of Holmes's *The Autocrat of the Breakfast Table,* then *The Professor at the Breakfast Table* and *The Poet at the Breakfast Table,* do not attract readers today as they did during the late nineteenth-century years when they commanded a privileged place in the pages of the *Atlantic Monthly* and on every well-read man's bookshelf. The humor of Curtis's *Potiphar Papers,* which was greeted by contemporaries as a side-splitting native adaptation of the *Pickwick Papers* of Charles Dickens, provokes few smiles, and Ik Marvel's once popular *Reveries of a Bachelor,* which even Emily Dickinson adored, embarrasses us now. We do remember that Agnes Repplier once filled volume after volume with essays—it was the touchstone of taste among our fathers to appreciate the gracious simplicity of her style—and that Logan Pearsall Smith wrote jewelled fragments whose lustre is not wholly dimmed.

In truth, our magazines and libraries contain a fair proportion of essayists who have written in the old manner, most of them quickly forgotten except by the generation for whom they wrote. Nothing, we recall, is so old as a delapidated charm. The once honored names of E. P. Whipple and B. O. Flowers may make us think more of comic strip characters than of essayists who wrote with distinction. Yesterday we read Clarence Day and Christopher Morley; today we can read E. B. White and Joseph Wood Krutch, and many more, each the favorite of a small, delighted following. These were or are our Bacons, Hazlitts, and Lambs—the masters, we can say, of our revels, though we have been too occupied with other things to revel with them long.

But we need not therefore agree with critics who tell us that the essay is a lavender scented little old lady of literature, and that she has passed away. The essay is sturdily with us still—only its tone has changed as man's focus has changed. Readers now seem less happily impressed by gentility in phrase or light pattering of thought. Roots must reach deeper and branches spread wider to provide sustenance and refreshment. However beguiling Miss Repplier's admonition that "an appreciation of the essay is the natural result of reading it," that like virtue, it is its own reward, most Americans in every generation have required something more.

Our best continuing allegiance has been given to voices which speak seriously on matters to which we are prepared to listen. For more than a hundred years the essays of Ralph Waldo Emerson have served as charts for man's compulsive quest to discover himself. Their seriousness is compressed to words which explode to private meaning, for each reader makes them his own, and they rouse him to resolution and conviction that life can be lived on the level of spirit and aspiration at the same time that it is real and earnest. With Carlyle and Matthew Arnold, he challenges men of intelligence to plunge beneath the frivolous welter of surface in search, not of a unity which is not there, but of poles between which life can be managed with satisfactory illusion of success. The view of Emerson which puts man where we have been taught he should be, at the center of the universe, has been, even in the reaction against it, both culmination and starting point of much of our serious consideration. Few readers have lingered long over his quietly pervasive humor.

Much of the most compelling literature of the United States has been a continuing dialogue concerning possibilities for maintaining the view which Emerson put forth, as friend and comforter, Matthew Arnold said, of those who live or would live in the spirit. Some who take him most seriously forget that a fine qualification for being Emersonian is to discover faults in Emerson, for he looked with scorn on people who built, he said, on the sepulchres of their fathers. What he wrote about man thinking, about the superiority of thinking to thought, and of a world in such continual change that the man who stops thinking must go mad, has spurred some of our best as well as some of our more irresponsible writing. Whether he is demigod or, as has recently been suggested, antichrist, Emerson continues to live, our most continually provocative essayist, because he speaks with skill of matters which disturb us still. He requires personal fulfillment, for he insists that there is no greater sin than any man's failure to realize the best which his qualifications allow, but he warns also of the terror of life and its unremitting menace. Concentration, he counsels, is the only virtue; dissipation the only vice.

To most readers it is as if their own voice spoke, and they answer even when they cannot find the words. Most vocal among Emerson's early answerers were Henry David Thoreau and Walt Whitman, each of whom extended, modified, or clarified some area of his thought. Men allowed themselves to become so bewildered by desire for things that their lives were lived in quiet desperation, responded Thoreau. They had lost unashamed admission of their manliness or womanliness, echoed Whitman. Each of these writers demonstrated through revelation of himself that living could be enjoyed on different terms, with discrimination between what is worthwhile and good and what is dissipating and bad. Whitman wrote in prose of the possibilities for truer literature and saner existence in *Democratic Vistas;* he wrote of his experience among men in *Specimen Days* and in his reminiscent *A Backward Glance O'er Travel'd Roads.* Thoreau wrote, some think with more skill than anyone, of man alone, confronted by nature and searching through nature for elusive hints which might suggest the proper responsibilities of man. *Walden* best dramatized his quest, and "Civil Disobedience" made plain his conviction that each man must resist whatever seems to that man wrong, but he wrote with insight also in discursive essays like "Walking," which are not so familiarly remembered because they center more elusively on his theme and are less overtly serious. Many of us have difficulty in following explanations of Whitman as a comic poet or of Thoreau as our most subtle humorist.

Later in the nineteenth century writers like William James and Henry Adams moved through and beyond paths which Emerson opened. William Dean Howells and Henry James wrote with new discernment of literature and its relation to life or its function as art. The old question of what was distinctive or could be distinctive about American literature, never completely closed, was opened wide again as Hamlin Garland and Frank Norris took readers earnestly into their confidence about matters which seemed to relate to problems of intimate concern. That is one reason why they continue occasionally to converse with us, while the voices of other men, like that of James Russell Lowell who wrote with satisfaction to himself and many readers about books he admired or about the world as seen from his study windows, fail to carry across very many years.

Perhaps our disposition toward somber soliloquys reveals more of ourselves, our taste or imagination, than of the excellence of our favorite writers. Like many people anywhere, we do not apologize because the ills which disturb our generation seem infinitely large for the reason that they are our own. They are with us and part of us, and our entanglement among them makes it necessary to understand them, for we do not think that cures are effected through derision. No writer of our century found more faults in contemporary notions of morality or taste than H. L. Mencken, whose blunt attacks on the *boobus Americanus* delighted readers of the 1920s and 1930s, but we turn to him less often in our day. His lustiest blows land now with little force. The humor is too self-consciously pert. His facts, we think, are not always right, and prejudice too plainly shows. Favorite essayists speak more reasonably now, less intolerant because they seem to reach toward radical distinctions. They talk more often of politics, and less of party. They consider the reaches of science or the possibility that people can remain people.

If our favorites seldom smile, even in derision, they correct no less than Addison who with lighter touch discovered society imperfect two hundred years ago. Where Mencken was bellicose, Lionel Trilling is compassionate in his equally relentless probings to the contemporary psyche, engaging us in such collections of essays as *The Liberal Imagination* and *The Opposing Self* as intimately as Emerson and Matthew Arnold do, because it is our imagination and our self which

he explores. If his voice palls, there is another which corrects or extends the patient examination in tones equally compelling. Critics like Allen Tate and Edmund Wilson express our concern with more than the literary topics they discuss, as they remind us that richness in literature requires answering richness among those who read. When the best among them such as R. P. Blackmur examines a text or speaks of the responsibilities or expense of greatness, we move by his side to territories we might not have found before. Their function, we think, is not only to codify or analyze what is known, but to move beyond toward what can be discovered, not content with tidying what has been called the house of intellect, but deepening its foundations and extending its walls.

But writing is a two-way street. Not only do we respond most urgently to words spoken in our own mood; most men write best when they say what they mean. Often that best is not good enough, for meaning well is no guarantee that what is said will be heard or understood. Words are provokingly stubborn, and are fond of stepping between a man and his thought. When we remember all the men of that generation who tried to express what one of them, who was Emerson, expressed so well, we are tempted to say of every writer that his ideas are the least important thing about him, because they are what he shares with most men of his time. When he speaks with authority, he speaks well, with something which we recognize but usually fail to define, and which we call style. His ultimate distinction is in language, in adjusting words to precise requirements.

For language is finally the essayist's single tool, that and a mind acute enough to discover the right words. He cannot depend on situation, plot, or character. Spirited action does not atone for deficiencies in style. Mystery or suspense is not often useful. One reason that I have suggested why essays in the United States are not often written in the traditional manner of Bacon or Lamb is that Americans care to speak about subjects which are different from those about which Englishmen care. Another is that Americans talk differently from Englishmen. Not only are some words different, like calling an elevator a lift or an undershirt a vest, and some idioms, like a white-collar job being in London a black-suit position; there are differences in rhythm and tone which are difficult to point out, but which are unmistakably present. That is not to say that good English is un-American, only that it is not always good American, though good American is nearer to good English than are the many varieties of bad American or bad English.

Probably because we are closer and therefore notice differences, there seem to be more varieties of American writing than there are of English. There is the terse and compelling style of the news magazine, leveled to readers who have neither time nor disposition for thinking. There is the smoothly limpid language of the magazine digests, so clear and uninvolved with subtlety that it has been said that a sure-fire subject for acceptance among them would be the story of a man who made love to a bear in an iron lung for the F.B.I. and found Christianity. There is the slick patter of the copywriter which hammers slogans home with relaxed regard for grammar. And there are several more, the most natively distinctive of which is perhaps the familiar drawl of American humor, folksy and emphatic by understatement. At another extreme is the equally familiar cliche-driven prose of the physical or social scientist who achieves a kind of intellectual status by inventing a language of his own, and close linked to that is the parrot language of the critic of politics or literature, in which polysyllabic clusters are soberly moved about in patterns which simulate thought.

This is not as these things should be; it is only as they are. A more richly complex culture will inevitably find richer methods of expressing itself. We are reminded by them that it was an English writer who explained that of all forms of literature the essay has least use for long words. Language in America does seem often reduced to the generalizing simplicity of the journalist and pitchman or swollen to polysyllabic pretension by pundits. Between these extremes lies the difficult ideal of language, seldom attained, but joyously welcomed wherever found. American writers seem adept in finding words to tell a story, especially when it is a parable, but few have expressed subtly penetrating ideas with persuasive directness. Thomas Jefferson did, and Lincoln, Emerson and Thoreau, and George Santayana, but few more. Our present delight in the explanations of R. P. Blackmur, T. S. Eliot, or Lionel Trilling and the less strenuous insight of E. B. White results from their ability to say complicated things simply, without posturing in any attitude but their own. They are among those few who, in Leslie Fiedler's words, "have discovered a new way to translate the speaking voice and living self into printed prose; to achieve on the page, the lucid, direct, orderly and vivid flow of conversation, which conversation itself, interrupted and half-heard, seldom attains."

The essayist then is a personality, a man speaking his mind. His first claim to our attention is just that, but he becomes inevitably also a guide, discovering directions for the minds of other men. Next to lyric poetry, which it in some manner resembles, the essay is the most personal kind of writing, both in expression of the person who writes it and in reception by the person who reads. Its dependence on fact is less important than its revelation of point of view. Its relation to truth is only to that portion of truth glimpsed by the particularized and therefore imperfect vision of the essayist. Neither historian nor philosopher, and not limited to the findings of what we call scholarship, the essayist is finally only essayist, not oracle. His footsteps never quite fit feet which attempt to follow. When he has disclosed something of attitude which might not have been so clearly known before, or of mood which is attractive, he has done his work. We do him disservice when we expect more.

American essayists do speak to us in many voices. Some bully, some cajole, and a few still smile. And each reader inevitably makes his own choice among them, discovering accents and attitudes which most closely approximate his own. To collect all which are best, or even best representative, is a task beyond any anthologist's ability, for his mood changes, and with it his choosing. The present collection is centered about a single broad theme, which is what native men of letters have thought of the prospects for and the accomplishment of literature in the United States. For each essay reprinted, a dozen more

might be found which speak perceptively and perhaps as well. Some indication of further riches available is supplied by an appended list of additional essay collections, many of them in paperback editions, From it private anthologies can be made, for each reader's own is his best.

The essays which have been included speak, first, about the multiple problem of what characterizes an American and what are the chances for and the distinguishing features of a literature which is distinctively native. Then writers speak of other writers and themselves or sketch the influence of place or attitude on their contemporaries. Next appear some of those who have spoken of poetry, its nature and function, and its place among us; and next those who have spoken of prose fiction. Finally, a smaller group of essayists talks of opportunities for progress, says something of the qualities and conditions necessary for continued effective expression on matters which it is the responsibility of literature to examine. Effort has been made to present as many tones and varieties as possible, hoping that they may blend to a chorus which will suggest more than any single voice can say.

POSSIBILITIES

Hector St. John de Crèvecoeur

❊ 1735-1813

Michel-Guillaume Jean de Crèvecoeur, better known by the name he signed to his writings in English, Hector St. John de Crèvecoeur, was born in France and died in France, but spent much of his active adult life in the New World, as soldier, cartographer, frontier farmer, or diplomat. His LETTERS FROM AN AMERI-CAN FARMER, *from which the following essay is extracted, was published in London in 1782 just as the American Revolution was drawing to a close. Its optimistic justification of the future of America is balanced by more realistic essays which Crèvecoeur did not publish in English during his lifetime but which lay in manuscript until gathered together in 1925 as* SKETCHES OF EIGHTEENTH-CENTURY AMERICA. *But in all of his writings, the clear directness of Crèvecoeur's prose never quite conceals his tendency to idealize the natural and the primitive in the manner of his French contemporaries, Rousseau and Chateaubriand. His conception of the American, though derived as much from romantic idealization as direct observation, has formed the basis for many a subsequent account.*

What Is an American?

I wish I could be acquainted with the feelings and thoughts which must agitate the heart and present themselves to the mind of an enlightened Englishman, when he first lands on this continent. He must greatly rejoice, that he lived at a time to see this fair country discovered and settled; he must necessarily feel a share of national pride, when he views the chain of settlements which embellishes these extended shores. When he says to himself, this is the work of my countrymen, who, when convulsed by factions, afflicted by a variety of miseries and wants, restless and impatient, took refuge here. They brought along with them their national genius, to which they principally owe what liberty they enjoy, and what substance they possess. Here he sees the industry of his native country, displayed in a new manner, and traces in their works the embryos of all the arts, sciences, and ingenuity which flourish in Europe. Here he beholds fair cities, substantial villages, extensive fields, an immense country filled with decent houses, good roads, orchards, meadows, and bridges, where an hundred years ago all was wild, woody, and uncultivated!

What a train of pleasing ideas this fair spectacle must suggest! it is a prospect which must inspire a good citizen with the most heartfelt pleasure. The difficulty consists in the manner of viewing so extensive a scene. He is arrived on a new continent; a modern society offers itself to his contemplation, different from what he had hitherto seen. It is not composed, as in Europe, of great lords who possess everything, and of a herd of people who have nothing. Here are no aristocratical families, no courts, no kings, no bishops, no ecclesiastical dominion, no invisible power giving to a few a very visible one; no great manufacturers employing thousands, no

13

great refinements of luxury. The rich and the poor are not so far removed from each other as they are in Europe. Some few towns excepted, we are all tillers of the earth, from Nova Scotia to West Florida. We are a people of cultivators, scattered over an immense territory, communicating with each other by means of good roads and navigable rivers, united by the silken bands of mild government, all respecting the laws, without dreading their power, because they are equitable. We are all animated with the spirit of an industry which is unfettered and unrestrained, because each person works for himself. If he travels through our rural districts he views not the hostile castle, and the haughty mansion, contrasted with the clay-built hut and miserable cabin, where cattle and men help to keep each other warm, and dwell in meanness, smoke, and indigence.

A pleasing uniformity of decent competence appears throughout our habitations. The meanest of our log-houses is a dry and comfortable habitation. Lawyer or merchant are the fairest titles our towns afford; that of a farmer is the only appellation of the rural inhabitants of our country. It must take some time ere he can reconcile himself to our dictionary, which is but short in words of dignity, and names of honor. There, on a Sunday, he sees a congregation of respectable farmers and their wives, all clad in neat homespun, well mounted, or riding in their own humble wagons. There is not among them an esquire, saving the unlettered magistrate. There he sees a parson as simple as his flock, a farmer who does not riot on the labor of others. We have no princes, for whom we toil, starve, and bleed: we are the most perfect society now existing in the world. Here man is free as he ought to be; nor is this pleasing equality so transitory as many others are. Many ages will not see the shores of our great lakes replenished with inland nations, nor the

unknown bounds of North America entirely peopled. Who can tell how far it extends? Who can tell the millions of men whom it will feed and contain? for no European foot has as yet travelled half the extent of this mighty continent!

The next wish of this traveller will be to know whence came all these people? they are a mixture of English, Scotch, Irish, French, Dutch, Germans, and Swedes. From this promiscuous breed, that race now called Americans have arisen. The eastern provinces must indeed be expected, as being the unmixed descendants of Englishmen. I have heard many wish that they had been more intermixed also: for my part, I am no wisher, and think it much better as it has happened. They exhibit a most conspicuous figure in this great and variegated picture; they too enter for a great share in the pleasing perspective displayed in these thirteen provinces. I know it is fashionable to reflect on them, but I respect them for what they have done; for the accuracy and wisdom with which they have settled their territory, for the decency of their manners; for their early love of letters; their ancient college, the first in this hemisphere; for their industry; which to me who am but a farmer, is the criterion of everything. There never was a people, situated as they are, who with so ungrateful a soil have done more in so short a time. Do you think that the monarchical ingredients which are more prevalent in other governments, have purged them from all foul stains? Their histories assert the contrary.

In this great American asylum, the poor of Europe have by some means met together, and in consequence of various causes; to what purpose should they ask one another what countrymen they are? Alas, two thirds of them had no country. Can a wretch who wanders about, who works and starves, whose life is a continual scene of sore affliction or pinching penury; can that man call England or any other kingdom his country? A country that had no bread for him, whose fields procured him no harvest, who met with nothing but the frowns of the rich, the severity of the laws, with jails and punishments; who owned not a single foot of the extensive surface of this planet? No! urged by a variety of motives, here they came. Every thing has tended to regenerate them; new laws, a new mode of living, a new social system; here they are become men: in Europe they were as so many useless plants, wanting vegetative mould, and refreshing showers; they withered, and were mowed down by want, hunger, and war; but now by the power of transplantation, like all other plants they have taken root and flourished! Formerly they were not numbered in any civil list of their country, except in those of the poor; here they rank as citizens.

By what invisible power has this surprizing metamorphosis been performed? By that of the laws and that of their industry. The laws, the indulgent laws, protect them as they arrive, stamping on them the symbol of adoption; they receive ample rewards for their labors; these accumulated rewards procure them lands; those lands confer on them the title of freemen; and to that title every benefit is affixed which men can possibly require. This is the great operation daily performed by our laws. From whence proceed these laws? From our government. Whence that government? It is derived from the original genius and strong desire of the people, ratified and confirmed by government. This is the great chain which links us all, this is the picture which every province exhibits, Nova Scotia excepted. There the crown has done all; either there were no people who had genius, or it was not much attended to: the consequence is, that the province is very thinly inhabited indeed; the power of the crown, in conjunction

with the mosquitoes, has prevented men from settling there. Yet some part of it flourished once, and it contained a mild harmless set of people. But for the fault of a few leaders the whole were banished. The greatest political error the crown ever committed in America, was to cut off men from a country which wanted nothing but men! What attachment can a poor European emigrant have for a country where he had nothing? The knowledge of the language, the love of a few kindred as poor as himself, were the only cords that tied him: his country is now that which gives him land, bread, protection, and consequence: *Ubi panis ibi patri*, is the motto of all emigrants.

What then is the American, this new man? He is either an European, or the descendant of an European; hence that strange mixture of blood, which you will find in no other country. I could point out to you a man, whose grandfather was an Englishman, whose wife was Dutch, whose son married a French woman, and whose present four sons have now four wives of different nations. *He* is an American, who, leaving behind him all his ancient prejudices and manners, receives new ones from the new mode of life he has embraced, the new government he obeys, and the new rank he holds. He becomes an American by being received in the broad lap of our great *Alma Mater.*

Here individuals of all nations are melted into a new race of men, whose labors and posterity will one day cause great change in the world. Americans are the western pilgrims, who are carrying along with them that great mass of arts, sciences, vigor, and industry, which began long since in the east; they will finish the great circle. The Americans were once scattered all over Europe; here they are incorporated into one of the finest systems of population which has ever appeared, and which will hereafter become distinct by the power of the different climates they inhabit. The American ought, therefore, to love his country much better than that wherein either he or his forefathers were born. Here the rewards of his industry follow with equal steps the progress of his labor; his labor is founded on the basis of nature, *self-interest;* can it want a stronger allurement? Wives and children, who before in vain demanded of him a morsel of bread, now, fat and frolicsome, gladly help their father to clear those fields whence exuberant crops are to arise to feed and clothe them all; without any part being claimed, either by a despotic prince, a rich abbot, or a mighty lord. Here religion demands but little of him; a small voluntary salary to the minister, and gratitude to God; can he refuse these?

The American is a new man, who acts upon new principles; he must therefore entertain new ideas, and form new opinions. From voluntary idleness, servile dependence, penury, and useless labor, he has passed to toils of a very different nature.

This is an American.

Washington Irving

✳ 1783-1859

Beloved among his contemporaries as Diedrich Knickerbocker or Geoffrey Crayon, Washington Irving is our first successful professional author and the first literary ambassador from the United States to England. Writing at a time when tempers on both sides were strained, irritated by the memory of two wars between them, and when acid debate abounded concerning the cultural inferiority of the one, the arrogance of the other, Irving wrote with graceful charm of both the old world and the new, providing a style which England could admire and his own countrymen take pride in. He could be jocularly satirical, as in his early burlesque HISTORY OF NEW YORK (1809), *but gentleness was his most effective mood, particularly in reminiscence of old customs or in retelling old tales.* THE SKETCH BOOK (1820), *where the following essay appears, was the first of many similar volumes in which he gathered his thoughts on a variety of subjects. His later romantic histories and sentimentalized biographies have not lasted so well, perhaps because they are so weighted with subject matter that the suave gentility of Washington Irving is not able to shine unrestricted through, for that manner seems, in truth, to have been his single literary virtue. And to the ears of many readers, it is enough.*

English Writers on America

"Methinks I see in my mind a noble and puissant nation, rousing herself like a strong man after sleep, and shaking her invincible locks: methinks I see her as an eagle, mewing her mighty youth, and kindling her endazzled eyes at the full mid-day beam."

MILTON ON THE LIBERTY OF THE PRESS

It is with feelings of deep regret that I observe the literary animosity daily growing up between England and America. Great curiosity has been awakened of late with respect to the United States, and the London press has teemed with volumes of travels through the Republic; but they seem intended to diffuse error rather than knowledge; and so successful have they been, that, notwithstanding the constant intercourse between the nations, there is no people concerning whom the great mass of the British public have less pure information or entertain more numerous prejudices.

English travellers are the best and the worst in the world. Where no motives of pride or interest intervene, none can equal them for profound and philosophical views of society, or faithful and graphical descriptions of external objects; but when either the interest or reputation of their own country comes in collision with that of another, they go to the opposite extreme, and forget their usual probity and candor, in the indulgence of splenetic remark, and an illiberal spirit of ridicule.

Hence, their travels are more honest and accurate, the more remote the country described. I would place implicit confidence in an Englishman's description of the regions beyond the cataracts of the Nile; of unknown islands in the Yellow Sea; of the interior of India; or of any other tract which other travellers might be apt to picture out with the illusions of their fancies; but I would cautiously receive his account of his immediate neighbors, and of those nations with which he is in habits of most frequent intercourse. However I might be disposed to trust his probity, I dare not trust his prejudices.

It has been also the peculiar lot of our country to be visited by the worst kind of English travellers. While men of philosophical spirit and cultivated minds have been sent from England to ransack the poles, to penetrate the deserts, and to study the manners and customs of barbarous nations, with which she can have no permanent intercourse of profit or pleasure; it has been left to the broken-down tradesman, the scheming adventurer, the wandering mechanic, the Manchester and Birmingham agent, to be her oracles respecting America. From such sources she is content to receive her information respecting a country in a singular state of moral and physical development; a country in which one

of the greatest political experiments in the history of the world is now performing; and which presents the most profound and momentous studies to the statesman and the philosopher.

That such men should give prejudicial accounts of America is not a matter of surprise. The themes it offers for contemplation are too vast and elevated for their capacities. The national character is yet in a state of fermentation; it may have its frothiness and sediment, but its ingredients are sound and wholesome; it has already given proofs of powerful and generous qualities; and the whole promises to settle down into something substantially excellent. But the causes which are operating to strengthen and ennoble it, and its daily indications of admirable properties, are all lost upon these purblind observers; who are only affected by the little asperities incident to its present situation. They are capable of judging only of the surface of things; of those matters which come in contact with their private interests and personal gratifications. They miss some of the snug conveniences and petty comforts which belong to an old, highly-finished, and over-populous state of society; where the ranks of useful labor are crowded, and many earn a painful and servile subsistence by studying the very caprices of appetite and self-indulgence. These minor comforts, however, are all-important in the estimation of narrow minds; which either do not perceive, or will not acknowledge, that they are more than counterbalanced among us by great and generally diffused blessings.

They may, perhaps, have been disappointed in some unreasonable expectation of sudden gain. They may have pictured America to themselves an El Dorado, where gold and silver abounded, and the natives were lacking in sagacity; and where they were to become strangely and suddenly rich, in some unforeseen, but easy manner. The same weakness of mind that indulges absurd expectations produces petulance in disappointment. Such persons become embittered against the country on finding that there, as everywhere else, a man must sow before he can reap; must win wealth by industry and talent; and must contend with the common difficulties of nature, and the shrewdness of an intelligent and enterprising people.

Perhaps, through mistaken, or ill-directed hospitality, or from the prompt disposition to cheer and countenance the stranger, prevalent among my countrymen, they may have been treated with unwonted respect in America; and having been accustomed all their lives to consider themselves below the surface of good society, and brought up in a servile feeling of inferiority, they become arrogant on the common boon of civility: they attribute to the lowliness of others their own elevation; and underrate a society where there are no artificial distinctions, and where, by any chance, such individuals as themselves can rise to consequence.

One would suppose, however, that information coming from such sources, on a subject where the truth is so desirable, would be received with caution by the censors of the press; that the motives of these men, their veracity, their opportunities of inquiry and observation, and their capacities for judging correctly, would be rigorously scrutinized before their evidence was admitted, in such sweeping extent, against a kindred nation. The very reverse, however, is the case, and it furnishes a striking instance of human inconsistency. Nothing can surpass the vigilance with which English critics will examine the credibility of the traveller who publishes an account of some distant, and comparatively unimportant, country. How warily will they compare the measurements of a pyramid, or the description of a ruin; and how sternly will they censure any inaccuracy

in these contributions of merely curious knowledge: while they will receive, with eagerness and unhesitating faith, the gross misrepresentations of coarse and obscure writers, concerning a country with which their own is placed in the most important and delicate relations. Nay, they will even make these apocryphal volumes textbooks, on which to enlarge with a zeal and an ability worthy of a more generous cause.

I shall not, however, dwell on this irksome and hackneyed topic; nor should I have adverted to it, but for the undue interest apparently taken in it by my countrymen, and certain injurious effects which I apprehend it might produce upon the national feeling. We attach too much consequence to these attacks. They cannot do us any essential injury. The tissue of misrepresentations attempted to be woven round us are like cobwebs woven round the limbs of an infant giant. Our country continually outgrows them. One falsehood after another falls off of itself. We have but to live on, and every day we live a whole volume of refutation. All the writers of England united, if we could for a moment suppose their great minds stooping to so unworthy a combination, could not conceal our rapidly growing importance, and matchless prosperity. They could not conceal that these are owing, not merely to physical and local, but also to moral causes—to the political liberty, the general diffusion of knowledge, the prevalence of sound moral and religious principles, which give force and sustained energy to the character of a people; and which, in fact, have been the acknowledged and wonderful supporters of their own national power and glory.

But why are we so exquisitely alive to the aspersions of England? Why do we suffer ourselves to be so affected by the contumely she has endeavored to cast upon us? It is not in the opinion of England alone that honor lives, and reputation has its being. The world at large is the arbiter of a nation's fame; with its thousand eyes it witnesses a nation's deeds, and from their collective testimony is national glory or national disgrace established.

For ourselves, therefore, it is comparatively of but little importance whether England does us justice or not; it is, perhaps, of far more importance to herself. She is instilling anger and resentment into the bosom of a youthful nation, to grow with its growth and strengthen with its strength. If in America, as some of her writers are laboring to convince her, she is hereafter to find an invidious rival, and a gigantic foe, she may thank those very writers for having provoked rivalship and irritated hostility. Every one knows the all-pervading influence of literature at the present day, and how much the opinions and passions of mankind are under its control. The mere contests of the sword are temporary; their wounds are but in the flesh, and it is the pride of the generous to forgive and forget them; but the slanders of the pen pierce to the heart; they rankle longest in the noblest spirits; they dwell ever present in the mind, and render it morbidly sensitive to the most trifling collision. It is but seldom that any one overt act produces hostilities between two nations; there exists, most commonly, a previous jealousy and ill-will; a predisposition to take offence. Trace these to their cause, and how often will they be found to originate in the mischievous effusions of mercenary writers; who, secure in their closets, and for ignominious bread, concoct and circulate the venom that is to inflame the generous and the brave.

I am not laying too much stress upon this point; for it applies most emphatically to our particular case. Over no nation does the press hold a more absolute control than over the people of America; for the universal education of the poorest classes makes every individual a reader. There is nothing published in England on the subject of our country that does not circulate through every part of it. There is not a calumny dropped from English pen, nor an unworthy sarcasm uttered by an English statesman, that does not go to blight good-will, and add to the mass of latent resentment. Possessing, then, as England does, the fountainhead whence the literature of the language flows, how completely is it in her power, and how truly is it her duty, to make it the medium of amiable and magnanimous feeling—a stream where the two nations might meet together, and drink in peace and kindness. Should she, however, persist in turning it to waters of bitterness, the time may come when she may repent her folly. The present friendship of America may be of but little moment to her; but the future destinies of that country do not admit of a doubt; over those of England there lower some shadows of uncertainty. Should, then, a day of gloom arrive; should those reverses overtake her, from which the proudest empires have not been exempt; she may look back with regret at her infatuation, in repulsing from her side a nation she might have grappled to her bosom, and thus destroying her only chance for real friendship beyond the boundaries of her own dominions.

There is a general impression in England, that the people of the United States are inimical to the parent country. It is one of the errors which have been diligently propagated by designing writers. There is, doubtless, considerable political hostility, and a general soreness at the illiberality of the English press; but, generally speaking, the prepossessions of the people are strongly in favor of England. Indeed, at one time they amounted, in many parts of the Union, to an absurd degree of bigotry. The bare name of Englishman was a passport to the confidence and hospitality of every family, and too often gave a transient currency to the worthless and the ungrateful. Throughout the country there was something of enthusiasm connected with the idea of England. We looked to it with a hallowed feeling of tenderness and veneration, as the land of our forefathers—the august repository of the monuments and antiquities of our race—the birthplace and mausoleum of the sages and heroes of our paternal history. After our own country, there was none in whose glory we more delighted—none whose good opinion we were more anxious to possess—none toward which our hearts yearned with such throbbings of warm consanguinity. Even during the late war, whenever there was the least opportunity for kind feelings to spring forth, it was the delight of the generous spirits of our country to show that, in the midst of hostilities, they still kept alive the sparks of future friendship.

Is all this to be at an end? Is this golden band of kindred sympathies, so rare between nations, to be broken forever?—Perhaps it is for the best—it may dispel an illusion which might have kept us in mental vassalage; which might have interfered occasionally with our true interests, and prevented the growth of proper national pride. But it is hard to give up the kindred tie! and there are feelings dearer than interest—closer to the heart than pride—that will still make us cast back a look of regret, as we wander farther and farther from the paternal roof, and lament the waywardness of the parent that would repel the affections of the child.

Short-sighted and injudicious, however, as the conduct of England may be in this system of aspersion, recrimination on our part would be equally ill-judged. I speak not of a prompt and spirited vindication of our country, nor the keenest castigation of her slanderers—but I allude to a disposition to retaliate in kind; to retort sarcasm, and inspire prejudice; which seems to be spreading widely among our writers. Let us guard particularly against such a temper, for it would double the evil instead of redressing the wrong. Nothing is so easy and inviting as the retort of abuse and sarcasm; but it is a paltry and an unprofitable contest. It is the alternative of a morbid mind, fretted into petulance, rather than warmed into indignation. If England is willing to permit the mean jealousies of trade, or the rancorous animosities of politics, to deprave the integrity of her press, and poison the fountain of public opinion, let us beware of her example. She may deem it her interest to diffuse error, and engender antipathy, for the purpose of checking emigration; we have no purpose of the kind to serve. Neither have we any spirit of national jealousy to gratify, for as yet, in all our rivalships with England, we are the rising and the gaining party. There can be no end to answer, therefore, but the gratification of resentment—a mere spirit of retaliation; and even that is impotent. Our retorts are never republished in England; they fall short, therefore, of their aim; but they foster a querulous and peevish temper among our writers; they sour the sweet flow of our early literature, and sow thorns and brambles among its blossoms. What is still worse, they circulate through our own country, and, as far as they have effect, excite virulent national prejudices. This last is the evil most especially to be deprecated. Governed, as we are, entirely by public opinion, the utmost care should be taken to preserve the purity of the public mind. Knowledge is power, and truth is knowledge; whoever, therefore, knowingly propagates a prejudice, wilfully saps the foundation of his country's strength.

The members of a republic, above all other men, should be candid and dispassionate. They are, individually, portions of the sovereign mind and sovereign will, and should be enabled to come to all questions of national concern with calm and unbiased judgments. From the peculiar nature of our relations with England, we must have more frequent questions of a difficult and delicate character with her than with any other nation; questions that affect the most acute and excitable feelings; and as, in the adjustment of these, our national measures must ultimately be determined by popular sentiment, we cannot be too anxiously attentive to purify it from all latent passion or prepossession.

Opening, too, as we do, an asylum for strangers from every portion of the earth, we should receive all with impartiality. It should be our pride to exhibit an example of one nation, at least, destitute of national antipathies, and exercising not merely the overt acts of hospitality, but those more rare and noble courtesies which spring from liberality of opinion.

What have we to do with national prejudices? They are the inveterate diseases of old countries, contracted in rude and ignorant ages, when nations knew but little of each other, and looked beyond their own boundaries with distrust and hostility. We, on the contrary, have sprung into national existence in an enlightened and philosophic age, when the different parts of the habitable world, and the various branches of the human family, have been indefatigably studied and made known to each other; and we forego the advantages of our birth, if we do not shake off the national prejudices, as we would the local superstitions, of the old world.

But above all let us not be influenced by any angry feelings, so far as to shut our eyes to the perception of what is really excellent and amiable in the English character. We are a young people, necessarily an imitative one, and must take our examples and models, in a great degree, from the existing nations of Europe. There is no country more worthy of our study than England. The spirit of her constitution is most analogous to ours. The manners of her people—their intellectual activity—their freedom of opinion—their habits of thinking on those subjects which concern the dearest interests and most sacred charities of private life, are all congenial to the American character; and, in fact, are all intrinsically excellent; for it is in the moral feeling of the people that the deep foundations of British prosperity are laid; and however the superstructure may be time-worn, or overrun by abuses, there must be something solid in the basis, admirable in the materials, and stable in the structure of an edifice that so long has towered unshaken amidst the tempests of the world.

Let it be the pride of our writers, therefore, discarding all feelings of irritation, and disdaining to retaliate the illiberality of British authors, to speak of the English nation without prejudice, and with determined candor. While they rebuke the indiscriminating bigotry with which some of our countrymen admire and imitate everything English, merely because it is English, let them frankly point out what is really worthy of approbation. We may thus place England before us as a perpetual volume of reference, wherein are recorded sound deductions from ages of experience; and while we avoid the errors and absurdities which may have crept into the page, we may draw thence golden maxims of practical wisdom, wherewith to strengthen and to embellish our national character.

Ralph Waldo Emerson
✳ 1803-1882

Not only was the generation of Ralph Waldo Emerson set to fresh resolution by this address delivered at his Alma Mater sixteen years after his graduation; many men since have found it to contain fundamental statements about the importance and responsibilities of man thinking. A year later, Emerson created what has been called a "tempest in the Boston teapot" by another address, to the graduates of the Divinity School at Harvard, in which he counselled them to forget codified tradition, even when urged on them by the greatest of books or teachers, and to look at the world about them with their own eyes and to the truth revealed by their own hearts. But the germ of what he said then and of much that he would say afterwards, in a long career as essayist and lecturer, was in "The American Scholar" or, most completely sketched in the essay NATURE *which he had published two years before and which is too long for an anthology like this, but which everyone who would understand important fundamentals of American thought will read.*

The American Scholar

PHI BETA KAPPA ADDRESS, HARVARD, 1837

MR. PRESIDENT AND GENTLEMEN:

I greet you on the recommencement of our literary year. Our anniversary is one of hope, and, perhaps, not enough of labor. We do not meet for games of strength or skill, for the recitation of histories, tragedies, and odes, like the ancient Greeks; for parliaments of love and poesy, like the Troubadours; nor for the advancement of science, like our contemporaries in the British and European capitals. Thus far, our holiday has been simply a friendly sign of the survival of the love of letters amongst a people too busy to give to letters any more. As such it is precious as the sign of an indestructible instinct. Perhaps the time is already come when it ought to be, and will be, something else; when the sluggard intellect of this continent will look

from under its iron lids and fill the postponed expectation of the world with something better than the exertions of mechanical skill. Our day of dependence, our long apprenticeship to the learning of other lands, draws to a close. The millions that around us are rushing into life, cannot always be fed on the sere remains of foreign harvests. Events, actions arise, that must be sung, that will sing themselves. Who can doubt that poetry will revive and lead in a new age, as the star in the constellation Harp, which now flames in our zenith, astronomers announce, shall one day be the pole-star for a thousand years?

In this hope I accept the topic which not only usage but the nature of our association seem to prescribe to this day—the AMERICAN SCHOLAR. Year by year we come up hither to read one more chapter of his biography. Let us inquire what light new days and events have thrown on his character and his hopes.

It is one of those fables which out of an unknown antiquity convey an unlooked-for wisdom, that the gods, in the beginning, divided Man into men, that he might be more helpful to himself; just as the hand was divided into fingers, the better to answer its end.

The old fable covers a doctrine ever new and sublime; that there is One Man —present to all particular men only partially, or through one faculty; and that you must take the whole society to find the whole man. Man is not a farmer, or a professor, or an engineer, but he is all. Man is priest, and scholar, and statesman, and producer, and soldier. In the *divided* or social state these functions are parcelled out to individuals, each of whom aims to do his stint of the joint work, whilst each other performs his. The fable implies that the individual, to possess himself, must sometimes return from his own labor to embrace all the other laborers. But, unfortunately, this original unit, this fountain of power, has been so distributed to multitudes, has been so minutely subdivided and peddled out, that it is spilled into drops, and cannot be gathered. The state of society is one in which the members have suffered amputation from the trunk, and strut about so many walking monsters— a good finger, a neck, a stomach, an elbow, but never a man.

Man is thus metamorphosed into a thing, into many things. The planter, who is Man sent out into the field to gather food, is seldom cheered by any idea of the true dignity of his ministry. He sees his bushel and his cart, and nothing beyond, and sinks into the farmer, instead of Man on the farm. The tradesman scarcely ever gives an ideal worth to his work, but is ridden by the routine of his craft, and the soul is subject to dollars. The priest becomes a form; the attorney a statute-book; the mechanic a machine; the sailor a rope of the ship.

In this distribution of functions the scholar is the delegated intellect. In the right state he is *Man Thinking*. In the degenerate state, when the victim of society, he tends to become a mere thinker, or still worse, the parrot of other men's thinking.

In this view of him, as Man Thinking, the theory of his office is contained. Him Nature solicits with all her placid, all her monitory pictures; him the past instructs; him the future invites. Is not indeed every man a student, and do not all things exist for the student's behoof? And, finally, is not the true scholar the only true master? But the old oracle said, "All things have two handles: beware of the wrong one." In life, too often, the scholar errs with mankind and forfeits his privilege. Let us see him in his school, and consider him in reference to the main influences he receives.

I. The first in time and the first in importance of the influences upon the mind is that of nature. Every day, the sun; and, after sunset, Night and her stars. Ever the winds blow; ever the grass grows. Every day, men and women, conversing—beholding and beholden. The scholar is he of all men whom this spectacle most engages. He must settle its value in his mind. What is nature to him? There is never a beginning, there is never an end, to the inexplicable continuity of this web of God, but always circular power returning into itself. Therein it resembles his own spirit, whose beginning, whose ending, he never can find—so entire, so boundless. Far too as her splendors shine, system on system shooting like rays, upward, downward, without centre, without circumference—in the mass and in the particle, Nature hastens to render account of herself to the mind. Classification begins. To the young mind every thing is individual, stands by itself. By and by, it finds how to join two things and see in them one nature; then three, then three thousand; and so, tyrannized over by its own unifying instinct, it goes on tying things together, diminishing anomalies, discovering roots running under ground whereby contrary and remote things cohere and flower out from one stem. It presently learns that since the dawn of history there has been a constant accumulation and classifying of facts. But what is classification but the perceiving that these objects are not chaotic, and are not foreign, but have a law which is also a law of the human mind? The astronomer discovers that geometry, a pure abstraction of the human mind, is the measure of planetary motion. The chemist finds proportions and intelligible method throughout matter; and science is nothing but the finding of analogy, identity, in the most remote parts. The ambitious soul sits down before each refractory fact; one after another reduces all strange constitutions, all new powers, to their class and their law, and goes on forever to animate the last fibre of organization, the outskirts of nature, by insight.

Thus to him, to this schoolboy under the bending dome of day, is suggested that he and it proceed from one root; one is leaf and one is flower; relation, sympathy, stirring in every vein. And what is that root? Is not that the soul of his soul? A thought too bold; a dream too wild. Yet when this spiritual light shall have revealed the law of more earthly natures—when he has learned to worship the soul, and to see that the natural philosophy that now is, is only the first gropings of its gigantic hand, he shall look forward to an ever expanding knowledge as to a becoming creator. He shall see that nature is the opposite of the soul, answering to it part for part. One is seal and one is print. Its beauty is the beauty of his own mind. Its laws are the laws of his own mind. Nature then becomes to him the measure of his attainments. So much of nature as he is ignorant of, so much of his own mind does he not yet possess. And, in fine, the ancient precept, "Know thyself," and the modern precept, "Study nature," become at last one maxim.

II. The next great influence into the spirit of the scholar is the mind of the Past—in whatever form, whether of literature, of art, of institutions, that mind is inscribed. Books are the best type of the influence of the past, and perhaps we shall get at the truth—learn the amount of this influence more conveniently—by considering their value alone.

The theory of books is noble. The scholar of the first age received into him the world around; brooded thereon; gave it the new arrangement of his own mind, and uttered it again. It came into him life; it went out from him truth. It came to him short-lived actions; it went out from him immortal thoughts. It came to him business; it went from him po-etry. It was dead fact; now, it is quick thought. It can stand, and it can go. It now endures, it now flies, it now inspires. Precisely in proportion to the depth of mind from which it issued, so high does it soar, so long does it sing.

Or, I might say, it depends on how far the process had gone, of transmuting life into truth. In proportion to the completeness of the distillation, so will the purity and imperishableness of the product be. But none is quite perfect. As no air-pump can by any means make a perfect vacuum, so neither can any artist entirely exclude the conventional, the local, the perishable from his book, or write a book of pure thought, that shall be as efficient, in all respects, to a remote posterity, as to contemporaries, or rather to the second age. Each age, it is found, must write its own books; or rather, each generation for the next succeeding. The books of an older period will not fit this.

Yet hence arises a grave mischief. The sacredness which attaches to the act of creation, the act of thought, is transferred to the record. The poet chanting was felt to be a divine man: henceforth the chant is divine also. The writer was a just and wise spirit: henceforward it is settled the book is perfect; as love of the hero corrupts into worship of his statue. Instantly the book becomes noxious: the guide is a tyrant. The sluggish and perverted mind of the multitude, slow to open to the incursions of Reason, having once so opened, having once received this book, stands upon it, and makes an outcry if it is disparaged. Colleges are built on it. Books are written on it by thinkers, not by Man Thinking; by men of talent, that is, who start wrong, who set out from accepted dogmas, not from their own sight of principles. Meek young men grow up in libraries, believing it their duty to accept the views which Cicero, which Locke, which Bacon, have given; forgetful that Cicero, Locke, and Bacon were only young men in libraries when they wrote these books.

Hence, instead of Man Thinking, we have the bookworm. Hence the book-learned class, who value books, as such; not as related to nature and the human constitution, but as making a sort of Third Estate with the world and the soul. Hence the restorers of readings, the emendators, the bibliomaniacs of all degrees.

Books are the best of things, well used; abused, among the worst. What is the right use? What is the one end which all means go to effect? They are for nothing but to inspire. I had better never see a book than to be warped by its attraction clean out of my own orbit, and made a satellite instead of a system. The one thing in the world, of value, is the active soul. This every man is entitled to; this every man contains within him, although in almost all men obstructed and as yet unborn. The soul active sees absolute truth and utters truth, or creates. In this action it is genius; not the privilege of here and there a favorite, but the sound estate of every man. In its essence it is progressive. The book, the college, the school of art, the institution of any kind, stop with some past utterance of genius. This is good, say they—let us hold by this. They pin me down. They look backward and not forward. But genius looks forward: the eyes of man are set in his forehead, not in his hindhead: man hopes: genius creates. Whatever talents may be, if the man create not, the pure efflux of the Deity is not his; cinders and smoke there may be, but not yet flame. There are creative manners, there are creative actions, and creative words; manners, actions, words, that is, indicative of no custom or authority, but springing spontaneous from the mind's own sense of good and fair.

On the other part, instead of being its own seer, let it receive from another mind its truth, though it were in torrents of light, without periods of solitude, inquest, and self-discovery, and a fatal disservice is done. Genius is always sufficiently the enemy of genius by over-influence. The literature of every nation bears me witness. The English dramatic poets have Shakespearized now for two hundred years.

Undoubtedly there is a right way of reading, so it be sternly subordinated. Man Thinking must not be subdued by his instruments. Books are for the scholar's idle times. When he can read God directly, the hour is too precious to be wasted in other men's transcripts of their readings. But when the intervals of darkness come, as come they must—when the sun is hid and the stars withdraw their shining—we repair to the lamps which were kindled by their ray, to guide our steps to the East again, where the dawn is. We hear, that we may speak. The Arabian proverb says, "A fig tree, looking on a fig tree, becometh fruitful."

It is remarkable, the character of the pleasure we derive from the best books. They impress us with the conviction that one nature wrote and the same reads. We read the verses of one of the great English poets, of Chaucer, of Marvell, of Dryden, with the most modern joy—with a pleasure, I mean, which is in great part caused by the abstraction of all *time* from their verses. There is some awe mixed with the joy of our surprise, when this poet, who lived in some past world, two or three hundred years ago, says that which lies close to my own soul, that which I also had well-nigh thought and said. But for the evidence thence afforded to the philosophical doctrine of the identity of all minds, we should suppose some preëstablished harmony, some foresight of souls that were to be, and some preparation of stores for their future wants, like the fact observed in insects, who lay up food before death for the young grub they shall never see.

I would not be hurried by any love of system, by any exaggeration of instincts, to underrate the Book. We all know, that as the human body can be nourished on any food, though it were boiled grass and the broth of shoes, so the human mind can be fed by any knowledge. And great and heroic men have existed who had almost no other information than by the printed page. I only would say that it needs a strong head to bear that diet. One must be an inventor to read well. As the proverb says, "He that would bring home the wealth of the Indies, must carry out the wealth of the Indies." There is then creative reading as well as creative writing. When the mind is braced by labor and invention, the page of whatever book we read becomes luminous with manifold allusion. Every sentence is doubly significant, and the sense of our author is as broad as the world. We then see, what is always true, that as the seer's hour of vision is short and rare among heavy days and months, so is its record, perchance, the least part of his volume. The discerning will read, in his Plato or Shakespeare, only that least part—only the authentic utterances of the oracles; all the rest he rejects, were it never so many times Plato's and Shakespeare's.

Of course there is a portion of reading quite indispensable to a wise man. History and exact science he must learn by laborious reading. Colleges, in like manner, have their indispensable office—to teach elements. But they can only highly serve us when they aim not to drill, but to create; when they gather from far every ray of various genius to their hospitable halls, and by the concentrated fires, set the hearts of their youth on flame. Thought and knowledge are natures in which apparatus and pretension avail nothing. Gowns and pecuniary foundations, though of towns of gold, can never countervail the least sentence or syllable of wit. Forget this, and our American colleges will recede in their public importance, whilst they grow richer every year.

III. There goes in the world a notion that the scholar should be a recluse, a valetudinarian—as unfit for any handiwork or public labor as a penknife for an axe. The so-called "practical men" sneer at speculative men, as if, because they speculate or *see*, they could do nothing. I have heard it said that the clergy—who are always, more universally than any other class, the scholars of their day—are addressed as women; that the rough, spontaneous conversation of men they do not hear, but only a mincing and diluted speech. They are often virtually disfranchised; and indeed there are advocates for their celibacy. As far as this is true of the studious classes, it is not just and wise. Action is with the scholar subordinate, but it is essential. Without it he is not yet man. Without it thought can never ripen into truth. Whilst the world hangs before the eye as a cloud of beauty, we cannot even see its beauty. Inaction is cowardice, but there can be no scholar without the heroic mind. The preamble of thought, the transition through which it passes from the unconscious to the conscious, is action. Only so much do I know, as I have lived. Instantly we know whose words are loaded with life, and whose not.

The world—this shadow of the soul, or *other me*—lies wide around. Its attractions are the keys which unlock my thoughts and make me acquainted with myself. I run eagerly into this resounding tumult. I grasp the hands of those next me, and take my place in the ring to suffer and to work, taught by an instinct that so shall the dumb abyss be vocal with speech. I pierce its order; I dissipate its fear; I dispose of it within the circuit of my expanding life. So much only of life as I know by experience, so much of the wilderness have I vanquished and planted, or so far have

I extended my being, my dominion. I do not see how any man can afford, for the sake of his nerves and his nap, to spare any action in which he can partake. It is pearls and rubies to his discourse. Drudgery, calamity, exasperation, want, are instructors in eloquence and wisdom. The true scholar grudges every opportunity of action past by, as a loss of power. It is the raw material out of which the intellect moulds her splendid products. A strange process too, this by which experience is converted into thought, as a mulberry leaf is converted into satin. The manufacture goes forward at all hours.

The actions and events of our childhood and youth are now matters of calmest observation. They lie like fair pictures in the air. Not so with our recent actions—with the business which we now have in hand. On this we are quite unable to speculate. Our affections as yet circulate through it. We no more feel or know it than we feel the feet, or the hand, or the brain of our body. The new deed is yet a part of life—remains for a time immersed in our unconscious life. In some contemplative hour it detaches itself from the life like a ripe fruit, to become a thought of the mind. Instantly it is raised, transfigured; the corruptible has put on incorruption. Henceforth it is an object of beauty, however base its origin and neighborhood. Observe too the impossibility of antedating this act. In its grub state, it cannot fly, it cannot shine, it is a dull grub. But suddenly, without observation, the selfsame thing unfurls beautiful wings, and is an angel of wisdom. So is there no fact, no event, in our private history, which shall not, sooner or later, lose its adhesive, inert form, and astonish us by soaring from our body into the empyrean. Cradle and infancy, school and playground, the fear of boys, and dogs, and ferrules, the love of little maids and berries, and many another fact that once filled the whole sky, are gone already; friend and relative,

profession and party, town and country, nation and world, must also soar and sing.

Of course, he who has put forth his total strength in fit actions has the richest return of wisdom. I will not shut myself out of this globe of action, and transplant an oak into a flowerpot, there to hunger and pine; nor trust the revenue of some single faculty, and exhaust one vein of thought, much like those Savoyards, who, getting their livelihood by carving shepherds, shepherdesses, and smoking Dutchmen, for all Europe, went out one day to the mountain to find stock, and discovered that they had whittled up the last of their pine trees. Authors we have, in numbers, who have written out their vein, and who, moved by a commendable prudence, sail for Greece or Palestine, follow the trapper into the prairie, or ramble round Algiers, to replenish their merchantable stock.

If it were only for a vocabulary, the scholar would be covetous of action. Life is our dictionary. Years are well spent in country labors; in town; in the insight into trades and manufactures; in frank intercourse with many men and women; in science; in art; to the one end of mastering in all their facts a language by which to illustrate and embody our perceptions. I learn immediately from any speaker how much he has already lived, through the poverty or the splendor of his speech. Life lies behind us as the quarry from whence we get tiles and copestones for the masonry of to-day. This is the way to learn grammar. Colleges and books only copy the language which the field and the work-yard made.

But the final value of action, like that of books, and better than books, is that it is a resource. That great principle of Undulation in nature, that shows itself in the inspiring and expiring of the breath; in desire and satiety; in the ebb and flow of the sea; in day and night; in heat and cold; and, as yet more deeply ingrained in every atom and every fluid, is known to us under the name of Polarity—these "fits of easy transmission and reflection," as Newton called them, are the law of nature because they are the law of spirit.

The mind now thinks, now acts, and each fit reproduces the other. When the artist has exhausted his materials, when the fancy no longer paints, when thoughts are no longer apprehended and books are a weariness—he has always the resources *to live*. Character is higher than intellect. Thinking is the function. Living is the functionary. The stream retreats to its source. A great soul will be strong to live, as well as strong to think. Does he lack organ or medium to impart his truths? He can still fall back on this elemental force of living them. This is a total act. Thinking is a partial act. Let the grandeur of justice shine in his affairs. Let the beauty of affection cheer his lowly roof. Those "far from fame", who dwell and act with him, will feel the force of his constitution in the doings and passages of the day better than it can be measured by any public and designed display. Time shall teach him that the scholar loses no hour which the man lives. Herein he unfolds the sacred germ of his instinct, screened from influence. What is lost in seemliness is gained in strength. Not out of those on whom systems of education have exhausted their culture, comes the helpful giant to destroy the old or to build the new, but out of unhandselled savage nature; out of terrible Druids and Berserkers come at last Alfred and Shakespeare.

I hear therefore with joy whatever is beginning to be said of the dignity and necessity of labor to every citizen. There is virtue yet in the hoe and the spade, for learned as well as for unlearned hands. And labor is everywhere welcome; always we are invited to work; only be this limitation observed, that a man shall not for the sake of wider activity sacrifice any opinion to the popular judgments and modes of action.

I have now spoken of the education of the scholar by nature, by books, and by action. It remains to say somewhat of his duties.

They are such as become Man Thinking. They may all be comprised in self-trust. The office of the scholar is to cheer, to raise, and to guide men by showing them facts admidst appearances. He plies the slow, unhonored, and unpaid task of observation. Flamsteed and Herschel, in their glazed observatories, may catalogue the stars with the praise of all men, and the results being splendid and useful, honor is sure. But he, in his private observatory, cataloguing obscure and nebulous stars of the human mind, which as yet no man has thought of as such—watching days and months sometimes for a few facts; correcting still his old records; must relinquish display and immediate fame. In the long period of his preparation he must betray often an ignorance and shiftlessness in popular arts, incurring the disdain of the able who shoulder him aside. Long he must stammer in his speech; often forego the living for the dead. Worse yet, he must accept—how often!—poverty and solitude. For the ease and pleasure of treading the old road, accepting the fashions, the education, the religion of society, he takes the cross of making his own, and, of course, the self-accusation, the faint heart, the frequent uncertainty and loss of time, which are the nettles and tangling vines in the way of the self-relying and self-directed; and the state of virtual hostility in which he seems to stand to society, and especially to educated society. For all this loss and scorn, what offset? He is to find consolation in exercising the highest functions of human nature. He is one who raises himself from private considerations and breathes and lives on public and illustrious thoughts. He is the world's eye. He is the world's heart. He is to resist the vulgar prosperity that retrogrades ever to barbarism, by preserving and communicating heroic sentiments, noble biographies, melodious verse, and the conclusions of history. Whatsoever oracles the human heart, in all emergencies, in all solemn hours, has uttered as its commentary on the world of actions—these he shall receive and impart. And whatsoever new verdict Reason from her inviolable seat pronounces on the passing men and events of to-day—this he shall hear and promulgate.

These being his functions, it becomes him to feel all confidence in himself, and to defer never to the popular cry. He and he only knows the world. The world of any moment is the merest appearance. Some great decorum, some fetish of a government, some ephemeral trade, or war, or man, is cried up by half mankind and cried down by the other half, as if all depended on this particular up or down. The odds are that the whole question is not worth the poorest thought which the scholar has lost in listening to the controversy. Let him not quit his belief that a popgun is a popgun, though the ancient and honorable of the earth affirm it to be the crack of doom. In silence, in steadiness, in severe abstraction, let him hold by himself; add observation to observation, patient of neglect, patient of reproach, and bide his own time—happy enough if he can satisfy himself alone that this day he has seen something truly. Success treads on every right step. For the instinct is sure, that prompts him to tell his brother what he thinks. He then learns that in going down into the secrets of his own mind he has descended into the secrets of all minds. He learns that he who has mastered any law in his private thoughts, is master to that extent of all men whose language he speaks, and of all into whose language his own can be translated. The poet, in

utter solitude remembering his spontaneous thoughts and recording them, is found to have recorded that which men in crowded cities find true for them also. The orator distrusts at first the fitness of his frank confessions, his want of knowledge of the persons he addresses, until he finds that he is the complement of his hearers; that they drink his words because he fulfils for them their own nature; the deeper he dives into his privatest, secretest presentiment, to his wonder he finds this is the most acceptable, most public, and universally true. The people delight in it; the better part of every man feels, This is my music; this is myself.

In self-trust all the virtues are comprehended. Free should the scholar be—free and brave. Free even to the definition of freedom, "without any hindrance that does not arise out of his own constitution." Brave; for fear is a thing which a scholar by his very function puts behind him. Fear always springs from ignorance. It is a shame to him if his tranquillity, amid dangerous times, arise from the presumption that like children and women his is a protected class; or if he seek a temporary peace by the diversion of his thoughts from politics or vexed questions, hiding his head like an ostrich in the flowering bushes, peeping into microscopes, and turning rhymes, as a boy whistles to keep his courage up. So is the danger a danger still; so is the fear worse. Manlike let him turn and face it. Let him look into its eye and search its nature, inspect its origin—see the whelping of his lion—which lies no great way back; he will then find in himself a perfect comprehension of its nature and extent; he will have made his hands meet on the other side, and can henceforth defy it and pass on superior. The world is his who can see through its pretension. What deafness, what stone-blind custom, what overgrown error you behold is there only by sufferance—by your sufferance. See it to be a lie, and you have already dealt it its mortal blow.

Yes, we are the cowed—we the trustless. It is a mischievous notion that we are come late into nature; that the world was finished a long time ago. As the world was plastic and fluid in the hands of God, so it is ever to so much of his attributes as we bring to it. To ignorance and sin, it is flint. They adapt themselves to it as they may; but in proportion as a man has any thing in him divine, the firmament flows before him and takes his signet and form. Not he is great who can alter matter, but he who can alter my state of mind. They are the kings of the world who give the color of their present thought to all nature and all art, and persuade men by the cheerful serenity of their carrying the matter, that this thing which they do is the apple which the ages have desired to pluck, now at last ripe, and inviting nations to the harvest. The great man makes the great thing. Wherever Macdonald sits, there is the head of the table. Linnæus makes botany the most alluring of studies, and wins it from the farmer and the herb-woman; Davy, chemistry; and Cuvier, fossils. The day is always his who works in it with serenity and great aims. The unstable estimates of men crowd to him whose mind is filled with a truth, as the heaped waves of the Atlantic follow the moon.

For this self-trust, the reason is deeper than can be fathomed—darker than can be enlightened. I might not carry with me the feeling of my audience in stating my own belief. But I have already shown the ground of my hope, in adverting to the doctrine that man is one. I believe man has been wronged; he has wronged himself. He has almost lost the light that can lead him back to his prerogatives. Men are become of no account. Men in history, men in the world of to-day, are bugs, are spawn, and are called "the mass" and "the herd." In a century, in a

millennium, one or two men; that is to say, one or two approximations to the right state of every man. All the rest behold in the hero or the poet their own green and crude being—ripened; yes, and are content to be less, so *that* may attain to its full stature. What a testimony, full of grandeur, full of pity, is borne to the demands of his own nature, by the poor clansman, the poor partisan, who rejoices in the glory of his chief. The poor and the low find some amends to their immense moral capacity, for their acquiescence in a political and social inferiority. They are content to be brushed like flies from the path of a great person, so that justice shall be done by him to that common nature which it is the dearest desire of all to see enlarged and glorified. They sun themselves in the great man's light, and feel it to be their own element. They cast the dignity of man from their downtrod selves upon the shoulders of a hero, and will perish to add one drop of blood to make that great heart beat, those giant sinews combat and conquer. He lives for us, and we live in him.

Men, such as they are, very naturally seek money or power; and power because it is as good as money—the "spoils," so called, "of office." And why not? for they aspire to the highest, and this, in their sleep-walking, they dream is highest. Wake them and they shall quit the false good and leap to the true, and leave governments to clerks and desks. This revolution is to be wrought by the gradual domestication of the idea of Culture. The main enterprise of the world for splendor, for extent, is the upbuilding of a man. Here are the materials strewn along the ground. The private life of one man shall be a more illustrious monarchy, more formidable to its enemy, more sweet and serene in its influence to its friend, than any kingdom in history. For a man, rightly viewed, comprehendeth the particular natures of all men. Each philosopher, each bard, each actor has only done for me, as by a delegate, what one day I can do for myself. The books which once we valued more than the apple of the eye, we have quite exhausted. What is that but saying that we have come up with the point of view which the universal mind took through the eyes of one scribe; we have been that man, and have passed on. First, one, then another, we drain all cisterns, and waxing greater by all these supplies, we crave a better and more abundant food. The man has never lived that can feed us ever. The human mind cannot be enshrined in a person who shall set a barrier on any one side to this unbounded, unboundable empire. It is one central fire, which, flaming now out of the lips of Etna, lightens the capes of Sicily, and now out of the throat of Vesuvius, illuminates the towers and vineyards of Naples. It is one light which beams out of a thousand stars. It is one soul which animates all men.

But I have dwelt perhaps tediously upon this abstraction of the Scholar. I ought not to delay longer to add what I have to say of nearer reference to the time and to this country.

Historically, there is thought to be a difference in the ideas which predominate over successive epochs, and there are data for marking the genius of the Classic, of the Romantic, and now of the Reflective or Philosophical age. With the views I have intimated of the oneness or the identity of the mind through all individuals, I do not much dwell on these differences. In fact, I believe each individual passes through all three. The boy is a Greek; the youth, romantic; the adult, reflective. I deny not, however, that a revolution in the leading idea may be distinctly enough traced.

Our age is bewailed as the age of Introversion. Must that needs be evil? We, it seems, are critical; we are embarrassed with second thoughts; we cannot enjoy any thing for hankering to know whereof the pleasure consists; we are lined with eyes; we see with our feet; the time is infected with Hamlet's unhappiness—

Sicklied o'er with the pale cast of thought.

It is so bad then? Sight is the last thing to be pitied. Would we be blind? Do we fear lest we should outsee nature and God, and drink truth dry? I look upon the discontent of the literary class as a mere announcement of the fact that they find themselves not in the state of mind of their fathers, and regret the coming state as untried; as a boy dreads the water before he has learned that he can swim. If there is any period one would desire to be born in, is it not the age of Revolution; when the old and the new stand side by side and admit of being compared; when the energies of all men are searched by fear and by hope; when the historic glories of the old can be compensated by the rich possibilities of the new era? This time, like all times, is a very good one, if we but know what to do with it.

I read with some joy of the auspicious signs of the coming days, as they glimmer already through poetry and art, through philosophy and science, through church and state.

One of these signs is the fact that the same movement which effected the elevation of what was called the lowest class in the state, assumed in literature a very marked and as benign an aspect. Instead of the sublime and beautiful, the near, the low, the common, was explored and poetized. That which had been negligently trodden under foot by those who were harnessing and provisioning themselves for long journeys into far countries, is suddenly found to be richer than all foreign parts. The literature of the poor, the feelings of the child, the philosophy of the street, the meaning of household life, are the topics of the time. It is a great stride. It is a sign—is it not?—of new vigor when the extremities are made active, when currents of warm life run into the hands and the feet. I ask not for the great, the remote, the romantic; what is doing in Italy or Arabia; what is Greek art, or Provençal minstrelsy; I embrace the common, I explore and sit at the feet of the familiar, the low. Give me insight into to-day, and you may have the antique and future worlds. What would we really know the meaning of? The meal in the firkin; the milk in the pan; the ballad in the street; the news of the boat; the glance of the eye; the form and the gait of the body; show me the ultimate reason of these matters; show me the sublime presence of the highest spiritual cause lurking, as always it does lurk, in these suburbs and extremities of nature; let me see every trifle bristling with the polarity that ranges it instantly on an eternal law; and the shop, the plough, and the ledger referred to the like cause by which light undulates and poets sing; and the world lies no longer a dull miscellany and lumber-room, but has form and order; there is no trifle, there is no puzzle, but one design unites and animates the farthest pinnacle and the lowest trench.

This idea has inspired the genius of Goldsmith, Burns, Cowper, and, in a newer time, of Goethe, Wordsworth, and Carlyle. This idea they have differently followed and with various success. In contrast with their writing, the style of Pope, of Johnson, of Gibbon, looks cold and pedantic. This writing is blood-warm. Man is surprised to find that things near are not less beautiful and wondrous than things remote. The near explains the far. The drop is a small ocean. A man is related to all nature. This perception of the worth of the vulgar is fruitful in discoveries. Goethe, in this very thing the most modern of the

moderns, has shown us, as none ever did, the genius of the ancients.

There is one man of genius who has done much for this philosophy of life, whose literary value has never yet been rightly estimated; I mean Emanuel Swedenborg. The most imaginative of men, yet writing with the precision of a mathematician, he endeavored to engraft a purely philosophical Ethics on the popular Christianity of his time. Such an attempt of course must have difficulty which no genius could surmount. But he saw and showed the connection between nature and the affections of the soul. He pierced the emblematic or spiritual character of the visible, audible, tangible word. Especially did his shade-loving muse hover over and interpret the lower parts of nature; he showed the mysterious bond that allies moral evil to the foul material forms, and has given in epical parables a theory of insanity, of beasts, of unclean and fearful things.

Another sign of our times, also marked by an analogous political movement, is the new importance given to the single person. Every thing that tends to insulate the individual—to surround him with barriers of natural respect, so that each man shall feel the world is his, and man shall treat with man as a sovereign state with a sovereign state—tends to true union as well as greatness. "I learned," said the melancholy Pestalozzi, "that no man in God's wide earth is either willing or able to help any other man." Help must come from the bosom alone. The scholar is that man who must take up into himself all the ability of the time, all the contributions of the past, all the hopes of the future. He must be an university of knowledges. If there be one lesson more than another which should pierce his ear, it is, The world is nothing, the man is all; in yourself is the law of all nature, and you know not yet how a globule of sap ascends; in yourself slumbers the whole of Reason; it is for you to know all; it is for you to dare all. Mr. President and Gentlemen, this confidence in the unsearched might of man belongs, by all motives, by all prophecy, by all preparation, to the American Scholar. We have listened too long to the courtly muses of Europe. The spirit of the American freeman is already suspected to be timid, imitative, tame. Public and private avarice make the air we breathe thick and fat. The scholar is decent, indolent, complaisant. See already the tragic consequence. The mind of this country, taught to aim at low objects, eats upon itself. There is no work for any but the decorous and the complaisant. Young men of the fairest promise, who begin life upon our shores, inflated by the mountain winds, shined upon by all the stars of God, find the earth below not in unison with these, but are hindred from action by the disgust which the principles on which business is managed inspire, and turn drudges, or die of disgust, some of them suicides. What is the remedy? They did not yet see, and thousands of young men as hopeful now crowding to the barriers for the career do not yet see, that if the single man plant himself indomitably on his instincts, and there abide, the huge world will come round to him. Patience —patience; with the shades of all the good and great for company; and for solace the perspective of your own infinite life; and for work the study and the communication of principles, the making those instincts prevalent, the conversion of the world. Is it not the chief disgrace in the world, not to be an unit; not to be reckoned one character; not to yield that peculiar fruit which each man was created to bear, but to be reckoned in the gross, in the hundred, or the thousand, of the party, the section, to which we belong; and our opinion predicted geographically, as the north,

or the south? Not so, brothers and friends—please God, ours shall not be so. We will walk on our own feet; we will work with our own hands; we will speak our own minds. The study of letters shall be no longer a name for pity, for doubt, and for sensual indulgence. The dread of man and the love of man shall be a wall of defence and a wreath of joy around all. A nation of men will for the first time exist, because each believes himself inspired by the Divine Soul which also inspires all men.

James Kirk Paulding
✳ 1778-1860

As the following essay will indicate, James Kirk Paulding did not write very well: he used too many words in too many ways that had been used before. He was Washington Irving's collaborator in SALMAGUNDI *(1807), a serial miscellany modeled on the* TATLER *or the* SPECTATOR, *he contributed an amusing* DIVERTING HISTORY OF JOHN BULL AND BROTHER JONATHAN *(1812) to the war of words between England and the United States; he wrote several novels, perhaps the best of which is* THE DUTCHMAN'S FIRESIDE *(1832), and he was an early, not conspicuously successful, writer of short stories. Much of his active life was spent in public service, climaxed by appointment in 1838 as Secretary of the Navy by his friend Martin Van Buren. His limitations and extraliterary preoccupations make Paulding, however, an effective representative spokesman for his time. Uncompromisingly a nationalist, he was convinced that America would have a literature of her own: on that subject he could sometimes, as at the end of the present essay, mount toward eloquence. The remarks on "National Literature" appeared first in Paulding's* SALMAGUNDI: SECOND SERIES *(1820), but the text here followed is that corrected for his collected* WORKS *(1835).*

National Literature

It has been often observed by such as have attempted to account for the scarcity of romantic fiction among our native writers, that the history of the country affords few materials for such works, and offers little in its traditionary lore to warm the heart or elevate the imagination. The remark has been so often repeated that it is now pretty generally received with perfect docility, as an incontrovertible truth, though it seems to me without the shadow of a foundation.

Wherever there are men, there will be materials for romantic adventure. In the misfortunes that befall them; in the sufferings and vicissitudes which are everywhere the lot of human beings in the struggles to counteract fortune, and in the conflicts of the passions, in every situation of life, he who studies nature and draws his pictures from her rich and inexhaustible sources of variety, will always find enough of those characters and incidents which give relish to works of fancy. The aid of superstition, the agency of ghosts, fairies, goblins, and all that antiquated machinery which till lately was confined to the nursery, is not necessary to excite our wonder or interest our feelings; although it is not the least of incongruities, that in an age which boasts of having by its scientific discoveries dissipated almost all the materials of superstition, some of the most popular fictions should be founded upon a superstition which is now become entirely ridiculous, even among the ignorant.

The best and most perfect works of imagination appear to me to be those which are founded upon a combination of such characters as every generation of men exhibits, and such events as have often taken place in the world, and will again. Such works are only fictions, because the tissue of events which they record never perhaps happened in precisely the same train, and to the same number of persons, as are exhibited and associated in the relation. Real life is fraught with adventures, to which the wildest fictions scarcely afford a parallel; and it has this special advantage over its rival, that these events, however extraordinary, can always be traced to motives, actions and passions, arising out of circumstances no way unnatural, and partaking of no impossible or supernatural agency. . . .

That these materials have as yet been little more than partially interwoven into the few fictions which this country has given birth to, is not owing to their being inapplicable to that purpose, but to another cause entirely. We have been misled by bad models, or the suffrages of docile critics, who have bowed to the influence of rank and fashion, and given testimony in favor of works which their better judgment must have condemned. We have cherished a habit of looking to other nations for examples of every kind, and debased the genius of this new world by making it the ape and the tributary of that of the old. We have imitated where we might often have excelled; we have overlooked our own rich resources, and sponged upon the exhausted treasury of our impoverished neighbors; we were born rich, and yet have all our lives subsisted by borrowing. Hence it has continually occurred, that those who might have gone before had they chosen a new path, have been content to come last, merely by following the old track. Many a genius that could and would have attained an equal height, in some new and unexplored region of fancy, has dwindled into insignificance and contempt by stooping to track some inferior spirit, to whom fashion had assigned a temporary elevation. They ought to be told, that though fashion may give a momentary popularity to works that neither appeal to national attachments, domestic habits, or those feelings which are the same yesterday, today, and forever, and everywhere, still it is not by imitation that they can hope to equal any thing great. . . .

By freeing himself from a habit of servile imitation; by daring to think and feel, and express his feelings; by dwelling on scenes and events connected with our pride and our affections; by indulging in those little peculiarities of thought, feeling, and expression which belong to every nation; by borrowing from nature, and not from those who disfigure or burlesque her—he may and will in time destroy the ascendancy of foreign taste and opinions, and elevate his own in the place of them. These causes lead to the final establishment of a national literature, and give that air and character of originality which it is sure to acquire, unless it is debased and expatriated by a habit of servile imitation. . . . This country is not destined to be always behind in the race of literary glory. The time will assuredly come, when that same freedom of thought and action which has given such a spur to our genius in other respects, will achieve similar wonders in literature. It is then that our early specimens will be sought after with avidity, and that those who led the way in the rugged discouraging path will be honored, as we begin to honor the adventurous spirits who first sought, explored, and cleared this western wilderness.

Edgar Allan Poe
✳ 1809-1849

The first claim that Edgar Allan Poe has to our remembrance is as a literary artist, poet and creator of unforgettable tales. His essays in criticism stand high because hardly anyone of his time did as well; but as critic Poe is uneven, prejudiced, and delightedly controversial. He said, as we shall see, some sensible things about poetry, and he defined, if he did not invent, the short story, but personal feelings seem often to have distorted his vision when he examined most of his literary contemporaries or spoke on subjects of contemporary importance. As artist, he knew that art owes no political allegiance, and that true art transcends national boundaries, and he spoke sharply against claims made for American writers on the single ground of their nativeness in language or theme. The following remarks appeared untitled among Poe's "Marginalia" in the DEMOCRATIC REVIEW *in 1845.*

Nationality in American Letters

Much has been said, of late, about the necessity of maintaining a proper *nationality* in American Letters; but what this nationality *is*, or what is to be gained by it, has never been distinctly understood. That an American should confine himself to American themes, or even prefer them, is rather a political than a literary idea—and at best is a questionable point. We would do well to bear in mind that "distance lends enchantment to the view." *Ceteris paribus*, a foreign theme is, in a strictly literary sense, to be preferred. After all, the world at large is the only legitimate stage for the autorial *histrio*.

But of the need of *that* nationality which defends our own literature, sustains our own men of letters, upholds our own dignity, and depends upon our own resources, there cannot be the shadow of a doubt. Yet here is the very point at which we are most supine. We complain of our want of an International Copyright, on the ground that this want justifies our publishers in inundating us with British opinion in British books; and yet when these very publishers, at their own obvious risk, and even obvious loss, do publish an American book, we turn up our noses at it with supreme contempt (this is the general thing) until it (the American book) has been dubbed "readable" by some illiterate Cockney critic. Is it too much to say that, with us, the opinion of Washington Irving—of Prescott—of Bryant—is a mere nullity in comparison with that of any anonymous sub-sub-editor of the "Spectator," the "Athenæum," or the "London Punch"? It is *not* saying too much, to say this. It is a solemn—an absolutely awful act. Every publisher in the country will admit it to be a fact. There is not a more disgusting spectacle under the sun than our subserviency to British criticism. It is disgusting, first, because it is trucking, servile, pusillanimous—secondly, because of its gross irrationality. We *know* the British to bear us little but ill will—we know that, in no case, do they utter unbiassed opinions of American books—we know that in the few instances in which our writers have been treated with common decency in England, these writers have either openly paid homage to English institutions, or have had lurking at the bottom of their hearts a secret principle at war with Democracy: we *know* all this, and yet, day after day, submit our necks to the degrading yoke of the crudest opin-

ion that emanates from the fatherland. Now if we *must* have nationality, let it be a nationality that will throw off this yoke.

Walt Whitman
✳ 1819-1892

Walt Whitman was as ejaculatory and oracular in prose as he was, with more effect, in verse. Devotedly native, to him America was itself a poem, and the strivings and strength of the American freeman the subject of poetry. Because he was a poet, he sometimes said things indirectly, but he suggested them so often and so well that many other writers have attempted to say the same things since. The paragraphs on "Democratic American Genius" appear without title in the Preface to the first edition of LEAVES OF GRASS *(1855) and we are not surprised to find them reworked into verse in later editions of that work.*

Democratic American Genius

America does not repel the past or what it has produced under its forms or amid other politics or the idea of castes or the old religions . . . accepts the lesson with calmness . . . is not so impatient as has been supposed that the slough still sticks to opinions and manners and literature while the life which served its requirements has passed into the new life of the new forms . . . perceives that the corpse is slowly borne from the eating and sleeping rooms of the house . . . perceives that it waits a little while in the door . . . that it was fittest for its days . . . that its action has descended to the stalwart and well-shaped heir who approaches . . . and that he shall be fittest for his days.

The Americans of all nations at any time upon the earth have probably the fullest poetical nature. The United States themselves are essentially the greatest poem. In the history of the earth hitherto the largest and most stirring appear tame and orderly to their ampler largeness and stir. Here at last is something in the doings of man that corresponds with the broadcast doings of the day and night. Here is not merely a nation but a teeming nation of nations. Here is action untied from strings necessarily blind to particulars and details magnificently moving in vast masses. Here is the hospitality which forever indicates heroes. . . . Here are the roughs and beards and space and ruggedness and nonchalance that the soul loves. Here the performance disdaining the trivial unapproached in the tremendous audacity of its crowds and groupings and the push of its perspective spreads with crampless and flowing breadth and showers its prolific and splendid extravagance. One sees it must indeed own the riches of the summer and winter, and need never be bankrupt while corn grows from the ground or the orchards drop apples or the bays contain fish or men beget children upon women.

Other states indicate themselves in their deputies . . . but the genius of the United States is not best or most in its executives or legislatures, nor in its ambassadors or authors or colleges or churches or parlors, nor even in its newspapers or inventors . . . but always most in the common people. Their manners, speech, dress, friendships—the picturesque looseness of their carriage . . . their deathless attachment to freedom—their aversion to anything indecorous or soft or mean—the practical acknowledgment of the citizens of all other states—the fierceness of their roused resentment—their curiosity and welcome of novelty—their self-esteem and wonderful sympathy—their susceptibility to a slight—the air they have of persons who never knew how it felt to stand in the presence of superiors—the fluency of their speech—their delight in music, the sure symptom of manly tenderness and native elegance of soul . . . their good temper and openhandedness—the terrible significance of their elections—the President's taking off his hat to them not they to him—these too are unrhymed poetry. It awaits the gigantic and generous treatment worthy of it.

Henry James
✳ 1843-1916

Few Americans have pled for and maintained more rigorous standards for the novel than Henry James whose "The Art of Fiction," reprinted later in this volume, has become a classic statement on the subject. The present paragraph, expressive of an earlier and not completely inconsistent attitude appears in his study HAWTHORNE, *written for the English Men of Letters Series in 1879. Compare it with Hawthorne's own estimate of the American situation on pp. 231–233 below.*

Absent Things in American Life

. . . One might enumerate the items of high civilization, as it exists in other countries, which are absent from the texture of American life, until it should become a wonder to know what was left. No State, in the European sense of the word, and indeed barely a specific national name. No sovereign, no court, no personal loyalty, no aristocracy, no church, no clergy, no army, no diplomatic service, no country gentlemen, no palaces, no castles, nor manors, nor old country houses, nor parsonages, nor thatched cottages, nor ivied ruins; no cathedrals, nor abbeys, nor little Norman churches; no great universities nor public schools— no Oxford, nor Eton, nor Harrow; no literature, no novels, no museums, no pictures, no political society, no sporting class—no Epsom nor Ascot! Some such list as that might be drawn up of the absent things in American life—especially in the American life of forty years ago, the effect of which, upon an English or a French imagination, would probably as a general thing be appalling. The natural remark, in the almost lurid light of such an indictment, would be that if these things are left out, everything is left out. The American knows that a good deal remains; what it is that remains —that is his secret, his joke, as one may say. It would be cruel, in this terrible denudation, to deny him the consolation of his national gift, that "American humor" of which of late years we have heard so much.

William Dean Howells

✳ 1837-1920

With good reason William Dean Howells was known during the last decades of his long life as the dean of American letters. He probably wrote more good novels than any other American except his friend Henry James, and he perhaps wrote more commentary on the novel than any American of his time or since. His principal personal characteristic was

kindliness, his principal defect that he saw most clearly only into what he called "the smiling aspects of life." His essays appeared over many years in the ATLANTIC MONTHLY, *of which he was an editor from 1865 to 1881, in* HARPER'S, *and other periodicals. No one of them is quite as good as the cumulative effect of them all, but each is an honest, well-reasoned expression of Howells's conviction that the United States did indeed offer fair opportunities for the man of letters. The extract which follows is from* CRITICISM AND FICTION, *one of the more than a dozen volumes in which his essays are collected.*

Art and Democracy

. . . I would have our American novelists be as American as they unconsciously can. Matthew Arnold complained that he found no "distinction" in our life, and I would gladly persuade all artists intending greatness in any kind among us that the recognition of the fact pointed out by Mr. Arnold ought to be a source of inspiration to them, and not discouragement. We have been now some hundred years building up a state on the affirmation of the essential equality of men in their rights and duties, and whether we have been right or wrong the gods have taken us at our word, and have responded to us with a civilization in which there is no "distinction" perceptible to the eye that loves and values it. Such beauty and such grandeur as we have is common beauty, common grandeur, or the beauty and grandeur in which the quality of solidarity so prevails that neither distinguishes itself to the disadvantage of anything else. It seems to me that these conditions invite the artist to the study and the appreciation of the common, and to the portrayal in every art of those finer and higher aspects which unite rather than sever humanity, if he would thrive in our new order of things. The talent that is robust enough to front the every-day world and catch the charm of its work-worn, care-worn, brave, kindly face, need not fear the encounter, though it seems terrible to the sort nurtured in the superstition of the romantic, the bizarre, the heroic, the distinguished, as the things alone worthy of painting or carving or writing. The arts must become democratic, and then we shall have the expression of America in art; and the reproach which Arnold was half right in making us shall have no justice in it any longer; we shall be "distinguished."

H. L. Mencken
✳ 1880-1956

As a critic, Henry Louis Mencken was often more forceful than perspicacious, quicker in pointing to shortcomings in what he called the Great Sahara of America than in underlining its virtues. But he wrote with such vigor and skill that he became over many years an oracle, listened to with interest and usually with respect: he has been compared with dubious justification to Swift, Voltaire, and Dr. Samuel Johnson. Author of many books, not the least important of which is his giant study of THE AMERICAN LANGUAGE, *he collected his occasional writings in a series of volumes aptly called* PREJUDICES; *the present essay, which appeared first in the* YALE REVIEW *for June, 1920, was included among* PREJUDICES: SECOND SERIES *in 1924 and reprinted in* A MENCKEN CHRESTOMATHY *in 1949.*

American Culture

The capital defect in the culture of These States is the lack of a civilized aristocracy, secure in its position, animated by an intelligent curiosity, skeptical of all facile generalizations, superior to the sentimentality of the mob, and delighting in the battle of ideas for its own sake. The word I use, despite the qualifying adjective, has got itself meanings, of course, that I by no means intend to convey. Any mention of an aristocracy, to a public fed upon democratic fustian, is bound to bring up images of stock-brokers' wives lolling obscenely in opera boxes, or of haughty Englishmen slaughtering whole generations of grouse in an inordinate and incomprehensible manner, or of bogus counts coming over to work their magic upon the daughters of break-fast-food and bathtub kings. The misconception belongs to the general American tradition. Its depth and extent are constantly revealed by the naïve assumption that the so-called fashionable folk of the large cities—chiefly wealthy industrials in the interior-decorator and country-club stage of culture—constitute an aristocracy, and by the scarcely less remarkable assumption that the peerage of England is identical with the gentry—that is, that such men as Lord Northcliffe, Lord Riddel and even Lord Reading were English gentlemen.

Here, as always, the worshiper is the father of the gods, and no less when they are evil than when they are benign. The inferior man must find himself superiors, that he may marvel at his political equality with them, and in the absence of recognizable superiors *de facto* he creates superiors *de jure*. The sublime principle of one man, one vote must be translated into terms of dollars, diamonds, fashionable intelligence; the equality of all men before the law must have clear and dramatic proofs. Sometimes, perhaps, the thing goes further and is more subtle. The inferior man needs an aristocracy to demonstrate, not only his mere equality, but also his actual superiority. The society columns in the newspapers may have some such origin. They may visualize once more the accomplished journalist's understanding of the mob mind that he plays upon so skillfully, as upon some immense and cacophonous organ, always going *fortissimo*. What the inferior man and his wife see in the sinister revels of those brummagem first families, I suspect, is often a massive witness to their own higher rectitude—in brief, to their firmer grasp upon the immutable axioms of Christian virtue, the one sound boast of the nether nine-tenths of humanity in every land under the cross.

But this bugaboo aristocracy is actually bogus, and the evidence of its bogusness lies in the fact that it is insecure. One gets into it only onerously, but out of it very easily. Entrance is effected by dint of a long and bitter struggle, and the chief accidents of that struggle are almost intolerable humiliations. The aspirant must school and steel himself to sniffs and sneers; he must see the door slammed upon him a hundred times before ever it is thrown open to him. To get in at all he must show a talent for abasement—and abasement makes him timorous. Worse, that timorousness is not cured when he succeeds at last. On the contrary, it is made even more tremulous, for what he faces within the gates is a scheme of things made up almost wholly of harsh and often unintelligible taboos, and the penalty for violating even the least of them is swift and disastrous. He must exhibit exactly the the right social habits, appetites and prejudices, public and private. He must harbor exactly the right enthusiasms and indignations. He must have a hearty

taste for exactly the right sports and games. His attitude toward the fine arts must be properly tolerant and yet not a shade too eager. He must read and like exactly the right books, pamphlets and public journals. He must put up at the right hotels when he travels. His wife must patronize the right milliners. He himself must stick to the right haberdashery. He must live in the right neighborhood. He must even embrace the right doctrines of religion. It would ruin him, for all society column purposes, to move to Union Hill, N.J., or to drink coffee from his saucer, or to marry a chambermaid with a gold tooth, or to join the Seventh Day Adventists. Within the boundaries of his curious order he is worse fettered than a monk in a cell. Its obscure conception of propriety, its nebulous notion that this or that is honorable, hampers him in every direction, and very narrowly. What he resigns when he enters, even when he makes his first deprecating knock at the door, is every right to attack the ideas that happen to prevail within. Such as they are, he must accept them without question. And as they shift and change he must shift and change with them, silently and quickly.

Obviously, that order cannot constitute a genuine aristocracy, in any rational sense. A genuine aristocracy is grounded upon very much different principles. Its first and most salient character is its interior security, and the chief visible evidence of that security is the freedom that goes with it—not only freedom in act, the divine right of the aristocrat to do what he damn well pleases, so long as he does not violate the primary guarantees and obligations of his class, but also and more importantly freedom in thought, the liberty to try and err, the right to be his own man. It is the instinct of a true aristocracy, not to punish eccentricity by expulsion, but to throw a mantle of protection about it—to safeguard it from the suspicions and resentments of the lower orders. Those lower orders are inert, timid, inhospitable to ideas, hostile to changes, faithful to a few maudlin superstitions. All progress goes on on the higher levels. It is there that salient personalities, made secure by artificial immunities, may oscillate most widely from the normal track. It is within that entrenched fold, out of reach of the immemorial certainties of the mob, that extraordinary men of the lower orders may find their city of refuge, and breathe a clear air. This, indeed, is at once the hall-mark and the justification of a genuine aristocracy— that it is beyond responsibility to the general masses of men, and hence superior to both their degraded longings and their no less degraded aversions. It is nothing if it is not autonomous, curious, venturesome, courageous, and everything if it is. It is the custodian of the qualities that make for change and experiment; it is the class that organizes danger to the service of the race; it pays for its high prerogatives by standing in the forefront of the fray.

No such aristocracy, it must be plain, is now on view in the United States. The makings of one were visible in the Virginia of the Eighteenth Century, but with Jefferson and Washington the promise died. In New England, it seems to me, there was never anything of the sort, either in being or in nascency: there was only a theocracy that degenerated very quickly into a plutocracy on the one hand and a caste of sterile pedants on the other—the passion for God splitting into a lust for dollars and a weakness for mere words. Despite the common notion to the contrary—a notion generated by confusing literacy with intelligence—the New England of the great days never showed any genuine enthusiasm for ideas. It began its history as a slaughter-house of ideas, and it is today not easily distinguishable from a

cold-storage plant. Its celebrated adventures in mysticism, once apparently so bold and significant, are now seen to have been little more than an elaborate hocus-pocus—respectable Unitarians shocking the peasantry and scaring the horned cattle in the fields by masquerading in the robes of Rosicrucians. The notions that it embraced in those austere and far-off days were stale, and when it had finished with them they were dead. So in politics. Since the Civil War it has produced fewer political ideas, as political ideas run in the Republic, than any average county in Kansas or Nebraska. Appomattox seemed to be a victory for New England idealism. It was actually a victory for the New England plutocracy, and that plutocracy has dominated thought above the Housatonic ever since. The sect of professional idealists has so far dwindled that it has ceased to be of any importance, even as an opposition. When the plutocracy is challenged now, it is challenged by the proletariat.

Well, what is on view in New England is on view in all other parts of the nation, sometimes with ameliorations, but usually with the colors merely exaggerated. What one beholds, sweeping the eye over the land, is a culture that, like the national literature, is in three layers— the plutocracy on top, a vast mass of undifferentiated human blanks bossed by demagogues at the bottom, and a forlorn *intelligentsia* gasping out a precarious life between. I need not set out at any length, I hope, the intellectual deficiencies of the plutocracy—its utter failure to show anything even remotely resembling the makings of an aristocracy. It is badly educated, it is stupid, it is full of low-caste superstitions and indignations, it is without decent traditions or informing vision; above all, it is extraordinarily lacking in the most elemental independence and courage. Out of this class comes the grotesque fashionable society of our big towns, already described. It shows all the stigmata of inferiority—moral certainty, cruelty, suspicion of ideas, fear. Never does it function more revealingly than in the recurrent *pogroms* against radicalism, *i.e.*, against humorless persons who, like Andrew Jackson, take the platitudes of democracy seriously. And what is the theory at the bottom of all these proceedings? So far as it can be reduced to comprehensible terms it is much less a theory than a fear—a shivering, idiotic, discreditable fear of a mere banshee—an overpowering, paralyzing dread that some extra-eloquent Red, permitted to emit his balderdash unwhipped, may eventually convert a couple of courageous men, and that the courageous men, filled with indignation against the plutocracy, may take to the highroad, burn down a nail-factory or two, and slit the throat of some virtuous profiteer.

Obviously, it is out of reason to look for any hospitality to ideas in a class so extravagantly fearful of even the most palpably absurd of them. Its philosophy is firmly grounded upon the thesis that the existing order must stand forever free from attack, and not only from attack, but also from the mere academic criticism, and its ethics are firmly grounded upon the thesis that every attempt at any such criticism is a proof of moral turpitude. Within its own ranks, protected by what may be regarded as the privilege of the order, there is nothing to take the place of this criticism. In other countries the plutocracy has often produced men of reflective and analytical habit, eager to rationalize its instincts and to bring it into some sort of relationship to the main streams of human thought. The case of David Ricardo at once comes to mind, and there have been many others: John Bright, Richard Cobden, George Grote. But in the United States no such phenomenon has been visible. Nor has the plutocracy

ever fostered an inquiring spirit among its intellectual valets and footmen, which is to say, among the gentlemen who compose headlines and leading articles for its newspapers. What chiefly distinguishes the daily press of the United States from the press of all other countries pretending to culture is not its lack of truthfulness or even its lack of dignity and honor, for these deficiencies are common to newspapers everywhere, but its incurable fear of ideas, its constant effort to evade the discussion of fundamentals by translating all issues into a few elemental fears, its incessant reduction of all reflection to mere emotion. It is, in the true sense, never well-informed. It is seldom intelligent, save in the arts of the mob-master. It is never courageously honest. Held harshly to a rigid correctness of opinion, it sinks rapidly into formalism and feebleness. Its yellow section is perhaps its best section, for there the only vestige of the old free journalist survives. In the more respectable papers one finds only a timid and petulant animosity to all questioning of the existing order, however urbane and sincere— a pervasive and ill-concealed dread that the mob now heated up against the orthodox hobgoblins may suddenly begin to unearth hobgoblins of its own, and so run amok. . . .

Constance Rourke
✳ 1885-1941

Herself a writer of merit and a student of the folk backgrounds of our literature, Constance Rourke published in 1931 a book called AMERICAN HUMOR: A STUDY OF THE NATIONAL CHARACTER *which was acclaimed at once and has been remembered since as a brilliantly original inter-*

pretation of American cultural history. The present essay is drawn from the final, summarizing pages of that book.

Humor in America

Humor has been a fashioning instrument in America, cleaving its way through the national life, holding tenaciously to the spread elements of that life. Its mode has often been swift and coarse and ruthless, beyond art and beyond established civilization. It has engaged in warfare against the established heritage, against the bonds of pioneer existence. Its objective—the unconscious objective of a disunited people—has seemed to be that of creating fresh bonds, a new unity, the semblance of a society and the rounded completion of an American type. But a society has not been palpably defined either in life or in literature. If literature is a gauge, only among expatriates has its strong semblance existed, without genuine roots, and mixed with the tragical. The other social semblance which has come into the common view is that of Main Street.

Nor has a single unmistakable type emerged; the American character is still split into many characters. The comic upset has often relaxed rigidities which might have been more significant if taut; individualism has sometimes seemed to wear away under a prolonged common laughter. The solvent of humor has often become a jaded formula, the comic rebound automatic—"laff that off"—so that only the uneasy habit of laughter appears, with an acute sensitivity and insecurity beneath it as though too much had been laughed away. Whole phases of comedy have become empty; the comic rejoinder has become every man's tool. From the comic the American has often moved to a cult of the comic. But a characteristic humor

has emerged, quiet, explosive, competitive, often grounded in good humor, still theatrical at bottom and full of large fantasy. The note of triumph has diminished as the decades have proved that the land is not altogether an Eden and that defeat is a common human portion. Humor has moved into more difficult areas and has embraced a subtler range of feeling; exaltation of the common American as the national type has been deflated. Yet what must still be called a folk strain has been dominant; perhaps it is still uppermost; the great onset of a Negro art, the influence of Negro music, and popular responses to the more primitive aspects of Negro expression suggest that the older absorption in such elements is unbroken. If the American character is split and many-sided at least a large and shadowy outline has been drawn by the many ventures in comedy.

A consistent native tradition has been formed, spreading over the country, surviving cleavages and dispersals, often growing underground, but rising to the surface like some rough vine. This ruthless effort has produced poetry, not only in the sense that primitive concepts are often poetic, but keeping the poetic strain as a domininant strain. Not the realistic sense, which might have been expected of a people who call themselves practical, but the poetic sense of life and of character has prevailed. With all the hasty experiment this tradition has revealed beauty, and wry engaging human twists. It has used subtle idioms, like the quieter Yankee idiom; it has contained the dynamic serenity of Whitman and the sensitive discovering genius of Henry James. With all the explosions its key has often remained low; this tradition has shown an effect of reserve, as if in immediate expression and in its large elements something were withheld, to be drawn upon again. It has produced two major patterns, the rhapsodic and the understated, whose outlines may be traced through the many sequences of popular comedy and through American literature; regional at first, they have passed far beyond the regional.

Clear courses have been drawn, yet these have been full of the vagaries that come from complex experiment. New themes have often been upturned and penetrated only in part. The epical promise has never been completely fulfilled. Though extravagance has been a major element in all American comedy, though extravagance may have its incomparable uses with flights and inclusions denied the more equable view, the extravagant vein in American humor has reached no ultimate expression. The comedy of Rabelais provides a gauge, or that of *Ulysses*. On the other hand little equability has appeared, only a few aspects of social comedy; and emotion remains, as earlier, submerged, or shaded and subtle and indwelling. T. S. Eliot has voiced an insistent mood.

Well! and what if she should die some afternoon,
Afternoon gray and smoky, evening yellow and rose;
Should die and leave me sitting pen in hand
With the smoke coming down above the housetops;
Doubtful, for quite a while
Not knowing what to feel or if I understand. . . .

Set against this self-consciousness and disillusionment are further primitive elements of American life, showing themselves in the continuance of the cults, in lodges, parades, masquerades, as in earlier years, in shouts like "Hallelujah! I'm a bum!" and in a simple persistent self-portraiture not unlike that to which the American was first given. He still envisages himself as an innocent in relation to other peoples; he showed the enduring conviction during the Great War. He is still given to the rhapsody, the monologue, the tale, in life as in literature. Of late has come one of those absorptions in homely retrospect to which the American mind has periodically been devoted; common and comic characters, pioneers, orators, evangelists, hoboes, hold-up men, have come to the fore with a stream of old story and song, often engaging the same Americans who turn to Eliot or Robinson or Henry James.

These oddly matched aspects of the American character are often at variance. Together or separated, they have found no full and complete expression. Who can say what will bring fulfillment? If this comes it may be conditioned by many undetermined elements in the national life and character, by outside impingements even—since Americans are acutely aware of these—like that which weighed heavily in earlier years, the burden of British opinion. Its effects are still not altogether resolved; it has been noted that the sharp critiques offered in an earlier day by visiting foreigners are now defined by Americans, often as though they had merely borrowed the attitude. The involvement with the older countries is genuine; and the task looms for literature of absorbing traditions of the older world as part of the natural American heritage. The alliances must be instinctive or the fabric will be seamy. In general the American creative mind has lacked the patience and humility to acquire them, or it has been fearful of alienation from American sources.

Against full use of the native tradition many factors are set. That nomadic strain which has run through all American life, deeply influencing the American character, is now accented by the conditions of modern life; and the native character seems to grow more generalized, less specially American. Within the space of a lifetime Henry James saw something of the kind happen; in later years he remarked of the heroine of

Pandora's Box that she could no longer "pass for quaint or fresh or for exclusively native to any one tract of Anglo-Saxon soil." Yet the main outlines of the American character still persist; American types can be found far from their native habitat and unmistakable in outline, homeless Yankees in Nebraska or frontiersmen in Monte Carlo, and others who may show an erosion due to alien places so that the original grain has grown dim, but who show that grain.

For the creative writer the major problem seems to be to know the patternings of the grain; and these can hardly be discovered in rich color without understanding of the many sequences of the American tradition on the popular side as well as on purely literary levels. The writer must know, as Eliot has said, "the mind of his own country—a mind which he learns in time to be much more important than his own private mind." A favored explanation for the slow and spare development of the arts in America has lain in stress upon the forces of materialism. But these have existed in every civilization; they have even at times seemed to assist the processes of art. The American failure to value the productions of the artist has likewise been cited; but the artist often seems to need less of critical persuasion and sympathy than an unstudied association with his natural inheritance. Many artists have worked supremely well with little encouragement; few have worked without a rich traditional store from which consciously or unconsciously they have drawn. The difficult task of discovering and diffusing the materials of the American tradition—many of them still buried —belongs for the most part to criticism; the artist will steep himself in the gathered light. In the end he may use native sources as a point of radical departure; he may seldom be intent upon early materials; but he will discover a relationship with the many streams of native character and feeling. The single writer—the single production—will no longer stand solitary or aggressive but within a natural sequence.

Lionel Trilling
✳ 1905-

Perhaps no commentator on native culture has more firmly imprinted his personality on critical readers of our time than Lionel Trilling, critic, novelist, and teacher at Columbia University, who may be said to represent something of America's brooding conscience, committed to a search not only for the characteristic but the best. In addition to essays in various periodicals, he has written studies of Matthew Arnold, E. M. Forster, and Sigmund Freud, and a novel, THE MIDDLE OF THE JOURNEY *(1947), all of which have had wide influence. His definition of culture as a dialectic rather than a flow, first suggested in his book on Arnold, but repeated in the penultimate paragraph of "Reality in America," has provided him and other critics with an effective, fresh approach to literary interpretation. The essay first appeared in the* PARTISAN REVIEW *in 1940; it is reprinted in* THE LIBERAL IMAGINATION *(1950), which contains much of Mr. Trilling's early and most influential critical comment. Later essays are collected in* THE OPPOSING SELF *(1955) and* A GATHERING OF FUGITIVES *(1956).*

Reality in America

It is possible to say of V. L. Parrington that with his *Main Currents in American Thought* he has had an influence on our conception of American culture which is not equaled by that of any other writer of the last two decades. His ideas are now the accepted ones wherever the college course in American literature is given by a teacher who conceives himself to be opposed to the genteel and the academic and in alliance with the vigorous and the actual. And whenever the liberal historian of America finds occasion to take account of the national literature, as nowadays he feels it proper to do, it is Parrington who is his standard and guide. Parrington's ideas are the more firmly established because they do not have to be imposed—the teacher or the critic who presents them is likely to find that his task is merely to make articulate for his audience what it has always believed, for Parrington formulated in a classic way the suppositions about our culture which are held by the American middle class so far as that class is at all liberal in its social thought and so far as it begins to understand that literature has anything to do with society.

Parrington was not a great mind; he was not a precise thinker or, except when measured by the low eminences that were about him, an impressive one. Separate Parrington from his informing idea of the economic and social determination of thought and what is left is a simple intelligence, notable for its generosity and enthusiasm but certainly not for its accuracy or originality. Take him even with his idea and he is, once its direction is established, rather too predictable to be continuously interesting; and, indeed, what we dignify with the name of economic and social determinism amounts in his use of it to not much more than the demonstration that most writers incline to stick to their own social class. But his best virtue was real and important—he had what we like to think of as the saving salt of the American mind, the lively sense of the practical, workaday world, of the

welter of ordinary undistinguished things and people, of the tangible, quirky, unrefined elements of life. He knew what so many literary historians do not know, that emotions and ideas are the sparks that fly when the mind meets difficulties.

Yet he had after all but a limited sense of what constitutes a difficulty. Whenever he was confronted with a work of art that was complex, personal and not liberal, that was not, as it were, a public document, Parrington was at a loss. Difficulties that were complicated by personality or that were expressed in the language of successful art did not seem quite real to him and he was inclined to treat them as aberrations, which is one way of saying what everybody admits, that the weakest part of Parrington's talent was his aesthetic judgment. His admirers and disciples like to imply that his errors of aesthetic judgment are merely lapses of taste, but this is not so. Despite such mistakes as his notorious praise of Cabell, to whom in a remarkable passage he compares Melville, Parrington's taste was by no means bad. His errors are the errors of understanding which arise from his assumptions about the nature of reality.

Parrington does not often deal with abstract philosophical ideas, but whenever he approaches a work of art we are made aware of the metaphysics on which his aesthetics is based. There exits, he believes, a thing called *reality;* it is one and immutable, it is wholly external, it is irreducible. Men's minds may waver, but reality is always reliable, always the same, always easily to be known. And the artist's relation to reality he conceives as a simple one. Reality being fixed and given, the artist has but to let it pass through him, he is the lens in the first diagram of an elementary book on optics: Fig. 1, Reality: Fig. 2, Artist; Fig. 1', Work of Art. Figs. 1 and 1' are normally in virtual correspondence with each other. Sometimes the artist spoils this ideal relation by "turning away from" reality. This results in certain fantastic works, unreal and ultimately useless. It does not occur to Parrington that there is any other relation possible between the artist and reality than this passage of reality through the transparent artist; he meets evidence of imagination and creativeness with a settled hostility the expression of which suggests that he regards them as the natural enemies of democracy.

In this view of things, reality, although it is always reliable, is always rather sober-sided, even grim. Parrington, a genial and enthusiastic man, can understand how the generosity of man's hopes and desires may leap beyond reality; he admires will in the degree that he suspects mind. To an excess of desire and energy which blinds a man to the limitations of reality he can indeed be very tender. This is one of the many meanings he gives to *romance* or *romanticism*, and in spite of himself it appeals to something in his own nature. The praise of Cabell is Parrington's response not only to Cabell's elegance—for Parrington loved elegance—but also to Cabell's insistence on the part which a beneficent self-deception may and even should play in the disappointing fact-bound life of man, particularly in the private and erotic part of his life.[1]

The second volume of *Main Currents* is called *The Romantic Revolution in America* and it is natural to expect that the word romantic should appear in it frequently. So it does, more frequently than one can count, and seldom with the same meaning, seldom with the sense that the word, although scandalously vague as it has been used by the literary historians, is still full of

[1] See, for example, how Parrington accounts for the "idealizing mind"—Melville's —by the discrepancy between "a wife in her morning kimono" and "the Helen of his dreams." Vol. II, p. 259.

complicated but not wholly pointless ideas, that it involves many contrary but definable things; all too often Parrington uses the word romantic with the word romance close at hand, meaning *a* romance, in the sense that *Graustark* or *Treasure Island* is a romance, as though it signified chiefly a gay disregard of the limitations of everyday fact. Romance is refusing to heed the counsels of experience (p. iii); it is ebullience (p. iv); it is utopianism (p. iv); it is individualism (p. vi); it is self-deception (p. 59)—"romantic faith . . . in the beneficent processes of trade and industry" (as held, we inevitably ask, by the romantic Adam Smith?); it is the love of the picturesque (p. 49); it is the dislike of innovation (p. 50) but also the love of change (p. iv); it is the sentimental (p. 192); it is patriotism, and then it is cheap (p. 235). It may be used to denote what is not classical, but chiefly it means that which ignores reality (pp. ix, 136, 143, 147, and *passim*); it is not critical (pp. 225, 235), although in speaking of Cooper and Melville, Parrington admits that criticism can sometimes spring from romanticism.

Whenever a man with whose ideas he disagrees wins from Parrington a reluctant measure of respect, the word romantic is likely to appear. He does not admire Henry Clay, yet something in Clay is not to be despised—his romanticism, although Clay's romanticism is made equivalent with his inability to "come to grips with reality." Romanticism is thus, in most of its significations, the venial sin of *Main Currents;* like carnal passion in the *Inferno,* it evokes not blame but tender sorrow. But it can also be the great and saving virtue which Parrington recognizes. It is ascribed to the transcendental reformers he so much admires; it is said to mark two of his most cherished heroes, Jefferson and Emerson: "they were both romantics and their idealism was only a different expression of a common spirit." Parrington held, we may say, at least two different views of romanticism which suggest two different views of reality. Sometimes he speaks of reality in an honorific way, meaning the substantial stuff of life, the ineluctable facts with which the mind must cope, but sometimes he speaks of it pejoratively and means the world of established social forms; and he speaks of realism in two ways: sometimes as the power of dealing intelligently with fact, sometimes as a cold and conservative resistance to idealism.

Just as for Parrington there is a saving grace and a venial sin, there is also a deadly sin, and this is turning away from reality, not in the excess of generous feeling, but in what he believes to be a deficiency of feeling, as with Hawthorne, or out of what amounts to sinful pride, as with Henry James. He tells us that there was too much realism in Hawthorne to allow him to give his faith to the transcendental reformers: "he was too much of a realist to change fashions in creeds"; "he remained cold to the revolutionary criticism that was eager to pull down the old temples to make room for nobler." It is this cold realism, keeping Hawthorne apart from his enthusiastic contemporaries, that alienates Parrington's sympathy—"Eager souls, mystics and revolutionaries, may propose to refashion the world in accordance with their dreams; but evil remains, and so long as it lurks in the secret places of the heart, utopia is only the shadow of a dream. And so while the Concord thinkers were proclaiming man to be the indubitable child of God, Hawthorne was critically examining the question of evil as it appeared in the light of his own experience. It was the central fascinating problem of his intellectual life, and in pursuit of a solution he probed curiously into the hidden, furtive recesses of the soul." Parrington's disapproval of the enterprise is unmistakable.

Now we might wonder whether Hawthorne's questioning of the naïve and often eccentric faiths of the transcendental reformers was not, on the face of it, a public service. But Parrington implies that it contributes nothing to democracy, and even that it stands in the way of the realization of democracy. If democracy depends wholly on a fighting faith, I suppose he is right. Yet society is after all something that exists at the moment as well as in the future, and if one man wants to probe curiously into the hidden furtive recesses of the contemporary soul, a broad democracy and especially one devoted to reality should allow him to do so without despising him. If what Hawthorne did was certainly nothing to build a party on, we ought perhaps to forgive him when we remember that he was only one man and that the future of mankind did not depend upon him alone. But this very fact serves only to irritate Parrington; he is put out by Hawthorne's loneliness and believes that part of Hawthorne's insufficiency as a writer comes from his failure to get around and meet people. Hawthorne could not, he tells us, establish contact with the "Yankee reality," and was scarcely aware of the "substantial world of Puritan reality that Samuel Sewall knew."

To turn from reality might mean to turn to romance, but Parrington tells us that Hawthorne was romantic "only in a narrow and very special sense." He was not interested in the world of, as it were, practical romance, in the Salem of the clipper ships; from this he turned away to create "a romance of ethics." This is not an illuminating phrase but it is a catching one, and it might be taken to mean that Hawthorne was in the tradition of, say, Shakespeare; but we quickly learn that, no, Hawthorne had entered a barren field, for although he himself lived in the present and had all the future to mold, he preferred to find many of his subjects in the past. We learn too that his romance of ethics is not admirable because it requires the hard, fine pressing of ideas, and we are told that "a romantic uninterested in adventure and afraid of sex is likely to become somewhat graveled for matter." In short, Hawthorne's mind was a thin one, and Parrington puts in evidence his use of allegory and symbol and the very severity and precision of his art to prove that he suffered from a sadly limited intellect, for so much fancy and so much art could scarcely be needed unless the writer were trying to exploit to the utmost the few poor ideas that he had.

Hawthorne, then, was "forever dealing with shadows, and he knew that he was dealing with shadows." Perhaps so, but shadows are also part of reality and one would not want a world without shadows, it would not even be a "real" world. But we must get beyond Parrington's metaphor. The fact is that Hawthorne was dealing beautifully with realities, with substantial things. The man who could raise those brilliant and serious doubts about the nature and possibility of moral perfection, the man who could keep himself aloof from the "Yankee reality" and who could dissent from the orthodoxies of dissent and tell us so much about the nature of moral zeal, is of course dealing exactly with reality.

Parrington's characteristic weakness as a historian is suggested by his title, for the culture of a nation is not truly figured in the image of the current. A culture is not a flow, nor even a confluence; the form of its existence is struggle, or at least debate—it is nothing if not a dialectic. And in any culture there are likely to be certain artists who contain a large part of the dialectic within themselves, their meaning and power lying in their contradictions; they contain within themselves, it may be said, the very essence of the culture, and the sign of this is that they do not submit to serve the ends of any one ideological group or tendency. It is a significant circumstance of American culture, and one which is susceptible of explanation, that an unusually large proportion of its notable writers of the nineteenth century were such repositories of the dialectic of their times—they contained both the yes and the no of their culture, and by that token they were prophetic of the future. Parrington said that he had not set up shop as a literary critic; but if a literary critic is simply a reader who has the ability to understand literature and to convey to others what he understands, it is not exactly a matter of free choice whether or not a cultural historian shall be a literary critic, nor is it open to him to let his virtuous political and social opinions do duty for percipience. To throw out Poe because he cannot be conveniently fitted into a theory of American culture, to speak of him as a biological sport and as a mind apart from the main current, to find his gloom to be merely personal and eccentric, "only the atrabilious wretchedness of a dipsomaniac," as Hawthorne's was "no more than the skeptical questioning of life by a nature that knew no fierce storms," to judge Melville's response to American life to be less noble than that of Bryant or of Crooley, to speak of Henry James as an escapist, as an artist similar to Whistler, a man characteristically afraid of stress—this is not merely to be mistaken in aesthetic judgment; rather it is to examine without attention and from the point of view of a limited and essentially arrogant conception of reality the documents which are in some respects the most suggestive testimony to what America was and is, and of course to get no answer from them.

Parrington lies twenty years behind us, and in the intervening time there has developed a body of opinion which is aware of his inadequacies and of the inadequacies of his coadjutors and disciples, who make up what might be called the literary academicism of liberalism. Yet Parrington still stands at the center of American thought about American culture because, as I say, he expressed the chronic American belief that there exists an opposition between reality and mind and that one must enlist oneself in the party of reality.

William Van O'Connor
✳ 1915-

William Van O'Connor is a critic and historian of criticism, editor, and author, who teaches literature at the University of Minnesota. He has written CLIMATES OF TRAGEDY (1943), SENSE AND SENSIBILITY IN MODERN POETRY (1948), THE SHAPING SPIRIT: A STUDY OF WALLACE STEVENS (1950), AN AGE OF CRITICISM, 1900–1950 (1952), THE TANGLED FIRE OF WILLIAM FAULKNER (1954), *and a volume of short stories entitled* CAMPUS ON THE RIVER (1960). *He is also the editor of* MODERN PROSE: FORM AND STYLE (1959) *and the co-editor of* A CASEBOOK ON EZRA POUND (1959). *"Traditions in American Literature" is reprinted, with modifications, from the September 17, 1954, issue of the London* TIMES LITERARY SUPPLEMENT *which surveyed American Writing Today.*

Traditions in American Literature

The American writer is a human being before he is an American, and he writes out of his own congenital temperament. The too simple formulation of what is or is not an American expression or attitude has first to explain away the variety in human temperament. Yet he does write inside the American milieu and that milieu influences what he feels and believes. The now standard history of American literature, the *Literary History of the United States* (1948), says in effect that a happy and forward-looking literature has been produced by a happy and forward-looking people:

It has been a literature profoundly influenced by ideals and by practices developed in democratic living. It has been intensely conscious of the aspirations of the individual in such a democracy as we have known here. It has been humanitarian. It has been, on the whole, an optimistic literature, made virile by criticism of the actual in comparison with the ideal.

It is true that America has envisioned herself as the land of new opportunities and great expectations. As a nation America has been optimistic. It does not follow that the bulk of American literature has been optimistic. Whether intentionally or not the editors of the *Literary History* have imposed a tendentiousness on American literature that it does not, except in small part, actually have. And the reason why they have done so is clear: they desire a literature in the service of democracy.

Most literature, however, is written out of the author's vision of the nature of things, a vision that is much larger and more inclusive than a political system. He may, like Melville, Hawthorne, or Faulkner, create a vision of horror and yet be a democrat. Perhaps most good writers would feel a little uneasy with the label "optimistic," and with some justice they might say that a better word for this state of mind is innocence, the state to which optimism aspires. It is the better word too because it suggests ironic overtones. They could say that many American writers have discovered the tension inherent in the doctrine of innocence, and, furthermore, that many of our best writers have been anything but optimistic.

1

Probably all American writers are influenced by their country's dream of innocence. The horrors of Poe or Bierce or those in the novel of violence may be darker than they might have been if the authors were not American. Hawthorne and Melville wrote with the ironic awareness that the received doctrine was that man is innocent. Grotesqueries as they appear in Stephen Crane, Sherwood Anderson, Nathaniel West, Carson McCullers, Truman Capote, Tennessee Williams (there is a School of the Grotesque) have lent to them a quality of pathos and shock by their American *mise en scène*. America was not supposed to be like this, to let such things happen! Their grotesqueries are like the corrupted young or the wicked act of the dedicated idealist, doubly a betrayal, doubly evil. Presumably each of these and other writers would not be what they are were it not that innocence is a part of the landscape, a part of the topographical reaches of the American mind. The desire for innocence, aside from the question of the ways it influences American conduct, is a part of the national character.

In Henry Adams' novel *Democracy* (1880) one Baron Jacobi complains bitterly about the American's vision of himself as a citizen of a nation of purity and innocence:

You Americans believe yourself to be excepted from the operation of general laws. You care not for experience. I have lived seventy-five years, and all that time in the midst of corruption. I am corrupt myself, only I do have the courage to proclaim it, and you others have not. Rome, Paris, Vienna, Petersburg, London, all are corrupt, only Washington is pure!

He goes on to say that many business men and local legislators are corrupt—and why shouldn't Americans acknowledge that evil flourishes among them as

much as it does anywhere else. A half century and more later one finds Leslie Fiedler, in the symposium *America and the Intellectuals* (1953) writing a dramatically exclamatory paragraph on the American's horrified reaction when he discovers that all is not innocent:

Among us, nothing is winked at or shrugged away; we are being eternally horrified at dope addiction or bribery or war, at things accepted in older civilizations as the facts of life, scarcely worth a tired joke. Even tax evasion dismays us! We are forever feeling our own pulses, collecting statistics to demonstrate the plight of the Negro, the prevalence of divorce, . . . the decline of family Bible reading, because we feel, we *know* that a little while ago it was in our power, new men in a new world (and even now there is hope), to make all perfect.

The student of the American temperament could collect innumerable quotations apposite in some way to America's desire for innocence. There is no doubt that the Jeffersonian heritage, among others, has helped to convince many Americans that they are not merely freer from prejudice than Europeans but infinitely freer from political tyranny. Any number of writers, regardless of nationality, have questioned these assumptions. The assumptions remain. The shocked surprise, to take a single example, provoked by exposé volumes—almost an industry in itself—suggests how deeply Americans, in intention, assent to their Jeffersonian doctrines.

The West, the frontiersman, and the cowboy have, of course, played a considerable part in the American's image of himself. The "horse-opera" and books about the cowboy, most of them third or fourth rate or worse, are to the twentieth century what pastoral poetry was to Renaissance Europe. Perhaps no small number of Americans are a little uneasy with Stephen Crane's "The Blue Hotel" or Steinbeck's *Of Mice and Men* because they seem, by the sheer fact of being set in the West, a questioning of the reassurance and hope for which the West as symbol stands.

James Fenimore Cooper's Leatherstocking, especially in *The Prairie*, affords an interesting introduction to the plainsman and to the West as symbols of American innocence. When Leatherstocking inhabits the settled land of New York State, Cooper feels obliged to give him a relatively low place in the social order—his love affairs, if they may be called that, are kept free from development by the impropriety of a woodsman courting a genteel, that is upper-class, heroine. But in *The Prairie* the social structure of the East is not greatly in evidence, and Leatherstocking is seen against the backdrop of nature. Susan Cooper said her father wished he had not introduced Captain Middleton and Inez de Certavallos, genteel aristocrats, and his reason is clear: the social hierarchies of civilization interfere with Leatherstocking: freedom and his being apotheosized as a symbol of natural wisdom. Ironically a weakness in stories of this sort is that the tensions of civilization are left behind and the resulting peacefulness, though momentarily enchanting, seems unengaging because it is undramatic.

William Faulkner's "The Bear" may well be the greatest paean to innocence in all American literature. It belongs, of course, to the latter part of the Faulkner canon, beginning with *Go Down Moses*, of which it is a section, when he turns toward a vision of innocence and hope. Ike McCaslin is a kind of Leatherstocking. He contemplates Nature as bountiful, peaceful, and moral. Civilization, with its lusts and axes and dirt, has destroyed it. Ike dreams a kind of Midsummer Night's Dream of innocence, and of America as it might have been.

The dream of innocence has also contributed to certain reputations, most notably those of Mark Twain and Walt Whitman. Their subject matter is the West and innocence, and it follows (by association though not by logic) that they are the most American writers. Twain wrote a number of declarations of independence from the Old World. He wrote about the common man. He took the tall tale, an indigenous form, and gave it literary eminence. Twain himself came from Missouri, the very heart of America, and he lived near and worked on America's mythic river, the Mississippi. He was a home product, at once comic, shrewd, and innocent. The pathetic irony of his role is that (it is the conflict of visions again) he ended his life terribly disillusioned and pessimistic.

Whitman also was a celebrant of the West as natural innocence, and it is instructive that most propaganda poetry and most "war poetry" has been written in the Whitman idiom. Karl Shapiro in *Essay on Rime* says of epics or would-be epics written by his contemporaries:

The bulk of these fall from the sanguine pens
Of Emersonian and Whitmanian bards.

Thoreau had his own version of the recovery of innocence: one sloughed off old conventions, allowing in their place new organic conventions to reveal themselves. Innocence, too, was Emerson's message: sorrow is "superficial" and varieties of evil are "the souls mumps and measles." The Sage of Concord does not speak in tones that sound very compelling to twentieth-century ears, but most certainly he was the dominant figure in his own era, and if he did not begin the Genteel Tradition he was, in part, its prophet and lawgiver.

Almost the whole history of American fiction in the late nineteenth century and the early decades of the twentieth century can be brought to focus by demonstrating ways in which it was in reaction against the Genteel Tradition. Henry James demanded that novelists be free to tell the truth as they knew it. William Dean Howells bridged the world of Emerson and the "new realism," first by insisting that God's goodness and truth are in "reality," then by showing, as in *A Hazard of New Fortunes* that the business ethics of the new industrialism seemed to have weakened or destroyed America's moral idealism. Stephen Crane wrote *Maggie* "to show people to people as they appear to me," and Richard Watson Gilder declined to publish it because, so it is said, he found it *"too honest."* Crane ridiculed sentimental fiction, demonstrated that a bad neighborhood environment and overly righteous people are equally destructive agents, and presented Nature as "alien." Theodore Dreiser's *Sister Carrie* bluntly gainsaid the belief that "virtuous conduct" is rewarded and "immoral conduct" is punished, and so on. Jack London and Frank Norris played with themes borrowed from Zola, and produced a fiction of romantic naturalism. The names in the history of "realism" are many: Edward Eggleston, Hamlin Garland, Harold Frederick, Ed Howe. . . . When Sinclair Lewis made his acceptance speech in receiving the Nobel Award in 1930 he announced the final defeat of the Genteel Tradition,—of one part of the cult of innocence.

But the tradition of innocence did not die with the rise of realism. One finds it in a variety of fiction, in Sherwood Anderson's search for the American soul and a return to some blessedness that has disappeared, in Thomas Wolfe's romantic search and his anguished cry that he cannot go home again, and in William Saroyan's discovery that people are zany and yet somehow wonderful. Perhaps the weakness in these writers is that each felt he could find or rest in a state of innocence. America's vision of innocence has not invariably passed into literature in forms that seem mature or able to resist skeptical gaze. On the other hand, some of the best of her writers have been preoccupied with it, and have found therein a play of forces, moral and intellectual, that have engaged them significantly and seriously.

2

Charles Brockden Brown, the first American novelist, wrote tales of Gothic horror. Edgar Allan Poe envisioned a universe haunted, malevolent, and in decay. Hawthorne believed in the doctrine of original sin, and he discovered his primary subject in the iron righteousness of the New England conscience. Herman Melville, his contemporary, possessed a profound sense of the human mind as the carrier of long forgotten terrors and violences, and he inclined to be contemptuous of writers who had little or no sense of man's still living in the presence of roaring Niagaras. Twentieth-century literature in America looks backward to Poe, to Hawthorne, to Melville, as much as to Emerson and to Whitman. There is a Hawthorne aspect, as well as a Henry James aspect, to T. S. Eliot's poetry (if he may still be regarded as American). There is a Hawthorne aspect to William Faulkner's *Light in August* and, in part, to *Absalom, Absalom!* There is a Melville aspect to the "Hemingway world" and to the fiction of Robert Penn Warren. In other words, there is a continuity to American literature that envisions worlds of terror or horror.

Poe had sufficient reason for imagining a world shrouded in darkness and threatening disaster. But his decaying castles, slimy tarns, and "clammy virgins" are not merely the projection of a sick mind; they are a version of the world. And it is this—that they are a version of the world—that has caused Allen Tate to speak of "Our Cousin, Mr. Poe." Ambrose Bierce and perhaps Fitzjames O'Brien are the only significant nineteenth-century American writers who seem very close to Poe, probably because it is unnatural constantly to envision the world as mad. But there are awarenesses in Poe's fiction of the world as mad or haunted or malevolent that find their echoes in twentieth century literature, American as well as European. In "Morella" the nature of human identity is discussed very explicitly, and it is clear that Poe was not satisfied with Plato's doctrine of the soul as "one everlastingly, and single." W. B. Yeats in the introduction to the *Oxford Book of Modern Verse* said modern poets are haunted by the idea of the human mind as flux. Instances might be quoted from Pound's *Cantos* or from any number of poems by Conrad Aiken. Again, Poe's generation did not have such terms as sadism, masochism, or the death wish, but Poe understood these phenomena. Gertrude Stein's Melanctha, Faulkner's Miss Emily, and Warren's Lilburne Lewis are all cousins to Mr. Poe.

Nathaniel Hawthorne continued the Gothic tradition in something like direct descent from Mrs. Radcliffe and Charles Brockden Brown. Wizards and witches hold their horrible seances in dark forests, portraits have mysterious powers, a curse hangs heavily in a family line, the wind and even flowers can be malevolent. But Hawthorne was not preeminently a teller of eerie tales. His plots were frequently an embarrasment to him. His interest was the psychology of evil, especially as he knew it, historically and contemporaneously, in New England. He believed profoundly in man's capacity for evil, and he was amused by, or contemptuous of, the doctrines of innocence proposed by his Transcendental friends. He admired moral fibre, but he was fascinated by the iron-like morality of the Puritans and the righteous persecution to which it gave rise.

William Faulkner is also preoccupied with rigidity of spirit, which he suggests by the phrase "iron New England dark" and which he develops at great length in his anti-Calvinist novel, *Light in August*. None of Hawthorne's iron men is more intent on righteous persecution than Simon McEachern, foster father of Joe Christmas, and probably no other modern novel so clearly demonstrates the evil lurking in the righteous mind. *Absalom, Absalom!* also deals with rigidity of spirit, but this time Faulkner, a master of violence, uses a Gothic form: father and brother talking on dim battlefields, brother shooting brother, the decapitation of Sutpen, the "demon," with a scythe, a once great house roaring in flames, a slack-jawed idiot seeming to hover half disembodied in the night. . . . Yet another form of horror is in his *Sanctuary*, with amoral creatures on a cooling ball in space pusuing their meaningless lusts of flesh and spirit, and coming to violent deaths or vacuous ennui. Novel after novel, until rather late in Faulkner's career, say, and in a variety of ways, that life is a condition of violence and of horror.

In Faulkner's work a vision of innocence or the desire for innocence has gradually replaced a vision of horror. In Ernest Hemingway the two visions coexist, contributing to the dramatic tension and ironic tone of his fiction. The world of childhood is used to evoke a sense of innocence, but set against it are the images of evil, of Africa, Kilimanjaro, the hyenas, the sea, the bullfight, war. There is also something that might be called the Huck Finn aspect; that is, the Hemingway hero will have nothing to do with ordinary civilization, and, like Huck, he takes off for the territory. But, and this is Hemingway's double vision, the evil is there too. If finally the truth is *Nada* it is a truth heard by innocent ears, and the hearer is horror-struck.

One reason behind the renewed interest in Melville and the acceptance of Robert Penn Warren as an important novelist is that both writers have created visions of horror that in some inevitable sense seem true. The thematic similarity between *Pierre or, the Ambiguities* and *World Enough and Time* might suggest that Robert Penn Warren's fiction in some sense derives from Herman Melville's fiction. Warren did write a sympathetic essay on the poetry of Melville, but that appeared long after Warren had established himself as a poet and novelist. The influence of Conrad or Faulkner is more easily demonstrable. More interesting than direct influences are the accidental similarities, in points of view, attitudes, and vision. Both are intensely moralistic writers who have struggled to work out a naturalistic ethic. Both attempt to reconcile profound skepticism with an equally profound idealism. Neither writer belongs to what Warren had called the Captain McWhirrs of literature, the writers who for all their good will or courage never suffer from a vision of horror, who are so lacking in imagination that terror is beyond them. Melville of course created his own Captain Mc-Whirr in the Captain Delano of *Benito Cereno,* and in his essay on Hawthorne he noted his preference for those men who dive deep. And both writers have believed profoundly that nature seems or is alien to man's spirit, that his idealistic side pulls away from nature, and, conversely, that nature exerts a pull to draw man deeply into herself. Nature is neither to be denied nor unresisted, for man is *in* nature, but not *of* it.

In Melville's "The Encatadas" there is one Oberlus who lived with the turtles on a lava island. "So warped and crooked was his strange nature, that the very handle of his hoe seemed gradually to have shrunk and twisted in his grasp, being a wretched bent stick, elbowed more like a savage's war-sickle than a civilized hoe-handle." In Warren's *All the King's Men* Jack Burden observes a row of statutes that line a road leading into a nerve sanatorium:

Between the regularly spaced oaks stood pedestals on which classical marble-draped and undraped, male and female, stained by weathers and leaf acid and encroaching lichen, looking as though they had, in fact, sprouted dully out of the clinging black-green humus below them—stared out at the passer-by with the faintly pained, heavy, incurious unamazement of cattle. The gaze of those marble eyes must have been the first stage in the treatment the neurotic got when he came out to the sanatorium. It must have been like smearing a cool unguent of time on the hot pustule and dry itch of the soul.

The "dry itch of the soul" and the conjunction of "hot pustule" and "soul" say what Warren's fiction as a whole says, that man is capable of great good and tremendous evil. He is at once in nature and above it—and his conduct, human, natural, ethical, is determined by this fact.

3

To say that literature is experience may, if it does not seem merely fatuous, seem merely another way of saying that literature is "knowledge" or "power" or "a criticism of life." But the term is useful. sometimes experience uses a vision of innocence to encourage hope, and sometimes to criticize excesses of hope; it says with Lambert Strether, "Live all you can, it's a mistake not to" discovering refinements of mind, imagination, and sense; it helps define the nature of life as quotidian.

American poets, from Anne Bradstreet to Marianne Moore, present a view of the unusual in the commonplace. In Emily Dickinson, who employed a most homely diction, New England had a poet who domesticated the Old Calvinist vision. In Robert Frost and John Crowe Ransom romantic innocence and romantic horrors are disciplined and restrained. Frost has written, "The fact is the sweetest dream that labor knows," and

Ransom, "I am shaken, but not as a leaf." (In E. E. Cummings, Kenneth Fearing, and Karl Shapiro contemporary poetry has critics of the Babbitt type of innocence.)

Henry James had a whole gallery of American innocents, Christopher Newman, Isabel Archer, Milly Theale, Daisy Miller, Lambert Strether. Perhaps Newman, of *The American* is the prototype of them all. He is the voyager into new experiences, he has great capacities for hope, and he is trusting. The story may be summarized as the conflict between Newman's artistic, social and moral innocence, and the Bellegarde's knowingness, strict forms, restraint, and guile. Newman learns the importance of self-discipline, of forms, proprieties, and the implication is that Europe could learn from him. As with so many of James' characters, Newman makes terms with necessity without falling into despondency or hopelessness.

A surprising number of modern fiction writers in America have found one of their major themes in causing characters to pursue romantic dreams and absolutes, and coming to terms with or being destroyed by the consequences. The beginnings seem to be with Henry James, but those who follow are legion: Edith Wharton, Willa Cather, Scott Fitzgerald, Glenway Wescott, Caroline Gordon, Katherine Anne Porter, James Gould Cozzens, and Lionel Trilling. Each is concerned with the phenomenon Allen Tate called "positive Platonism," that is, a "cheerful confidence in the limitless powers of man."

Edith Wharton, commonly seen as the most distinguished of the immediate followers of James, may be said to have found her major theme in explaining the need for compromise. That certainly is the theme of her *The Age of Innocence*. Mrs. Wharton ordinarily is not especially witty or humorous, but in "The Other Two" she had written a finely humorous story about compromise. It concerns the slow and ironic recognition on the part of husband number three that his wife owes her undoubted charms to having lived with her two earlier husbands; from the first, who was lower middle class in taste, she learned to appreciate delicacy, and from the other, who had had "advantages" but was a little on the libertine side, she learned to respect fidelity and loyalty. Husband number three comes finally to his discovery one afternoon when circumstances have caused all of them to be present in his drawing room. The men are embarrassed, but she, who has faced and surmounted difficulties before, is her charming self. He finds his discovery painful, but accept he does, wryly appreciative.

Willa Cather, who also learned a good deal from James, is, though less ironic, like Edith Wharton in understanding muted joys. She understands the strangeness, pain and pleasure of "obscure destinies," and the deep satisfaction in simple, unostentatious, and even hard conditions of life. Miss Cather's knowledge of frontier, village and farm life may have given her an even fuller understanding of the pretentious and the meretricious. Professor St. Peter, in her fine novel *The Professor's House*, tries to understand what had brought him to the edge of suicide, and he says to himself: "Perhaps the mistake was merely an attitude of mind. He had never learned how to live without delight."

Scott Fitzgerald provides a classic instance of romantic innocence defeated. Jay Gatsby is presented as a prototype of American innocence and hopefulness: defeat is impossible to him and even time can be brought to a standstill, or life can be relived and mistakes refined into non-existence. Each of his protagonists, like the one in "Babylon Revisited," is asked to recognize that the snow is "real snow." He is subjected to a series of tests which, at long last, force him to face the consequences of living with sentiments that were ill-understood, of having confused illusion and reality. Similar statements, modified to suit their special preoccupations and subject matters, might be made about the fiction of Glenway Wescott, Caroline Gordon, Katherine Anne Porter, James Gould Cozzens—and about still other writers who, consciously or not, write in the tradition of Henry James. However individualized their subject matter and tone, qualities they have in common are the surprise that attends failure and the pathos that attends making friends with death, time and necessity.

John A. Kouwenhoven
✳ 1909-

Formerly an editor of HARPER'S MAG-AZINE, *John A. Kouwenhoven teaches literature in its relation to allied arts at Barnard College. Known for his essays in such periodicals as* HARPER'S, *the* AT-LANTIC MONTHLY, *and the* YALE REVIEW *and for his pictorial histories,* ADVENTURES IN AMERICA, 1857–1900 *(1938) and* THE COLUMBIA HISTORICAL PORTRAIT OF NEW YORK *(1953), he is better known as a cultural historian whose* MADE IN AMERICA: THE ARTS IN MODERN CIVILIZA-TION *(1948) brought to single perspective such apparently disparate elements of our culture as technology, architecture, the fine arts, the movies, literature, and jazz. The present essay is reproduced from a paper read in 1954 at the American Civilization Seminar at Columbia University; it appeared in another version in the* COLORADO QUARTERLY *in 1955, and, slightly shortened from the form here given, in* HARPER'S MAGAZINE *in 1956.*

What Is American about America?

The discovery of America is, in our time, a very popular pastime. Universities and colleges which, a generation ago, almost ignored American literature and art, now frequently offer interdepartmental programs in American Studies, in which the student may focus his major work. The editors of *The Partisan Review* as well as the editors of *Life* devote whole issues of their magazines to explorations of our native culture. Scarcely a week goes by without someone's publishing a new book of travels in the bright continent. The anthropologists, native and foreign, have discovered that the natives of Middletown and Plainville are as amazing and as interesting as the natives of better known communities such as the Trobriand Islands and Samoa. And the magazines provide a steady flow of articles by journalists, historians, sociologists, and philosophers who want to explain America to itself, or to themselves, or to others.

The discoverers of America have, of course, been describing their experiences ever since Captain John Smith wrote his first book about America almost 350 years ago. But as Smith himself noted, not everyone "who hath bin at Virginia, understandeth or knowes what Virginia is." Indeed, just a couple of years ago the Carnegie Corporation, which contributes to the support of a number of American Studies programs, entitled its Quarterly Report "Who Knows America?," and went on to imply that nobody does, not even "our lawmakers, journalists, civic leaders, diplomats, teachers and others."

There is, of course, the possibility that some of the writers who have explored, vicariously or in person, this country's past and present may have come to understand or know what America is. But how is the lay inquirer and the student to know which accounts to trust? Especially since most of the explorers seem to have found not one but two or more antipodal and irreconcilable Americas. The Americans, we are convincingly told, are the most materialistic of peoples, and, on the other hand, they are the most idealistic; the most revolutionary, and conversely, the most conservative; the most rampantly individualistic, and, simultaneously, the most gregarious and herd-like; the most irreverent toward their elders, and, contrariwise, the most abject worshippers of "Mom." They have an unbridled admiration of everything big, from bulldozers to bosoms; and they are in love with everything diminutive, from the "small hotel" in the song to the "little woman" in the kitchen.

Maybe, as Henry James thought when he wrote *The American Scene,* it is simply that the country is "too large for any human convenience," too diverse in geography and in blood strains to make sense as any sort of unit. Whatever the reason, the conflicting evidence turns up wherever you look, and the observer has to content himself with some sort of pluralistic conception. Santayana's way out was to say that the American mind was split in half, one half symbolized by the skyscraper, the other by neat reproductions of Colonial mansions (with surreptitious modern conveniences). "The American will," he concluded, "inhabits the skyscraper; the American intellect inherits the Colonial mansion." Mark Twain also defined the split in architectural terms, but more succinctly: American houses, he said, had Queen Anne fronts and Mary Ann behinds.

And yet, for all the contrarities, for all that Henry Ford spent the millions he made out of destroying the past in an effort to revive its square dances and handicrafts, there remains something

which I think we all feel to be distinctively American, some quality or characteristic underlying the polarities which —as Henry James himself went on to say—seems to make the American way of doing things differ more from any other nation's way than the ways of any two other nations differ from each other.

I am aware of the risks in generalizing. And yet it would be silly, I am convinced, to assert that there are not certain things which are more American than others. Take the New York City skyline, for example—that ragged and glorious man-made Sierra at the eastern edge of the continent. Clearly, in the minds of immigrants and returning travellers, in the iconography of the ad-men who use it as a backdrop for the bourbon and airplane luggage they are selling, in the eyes of poets and of military strategists, it is one of the prime American symbols.

Let me start, then, with the Manhattan skyline and list a few things which occur to me as distinctively American. Then, when we have the list, let us see what, if anything, these things have in common. Here are a dozen items to consider:

1. The Manhattan skyline
2. The gridiron town plan
3. The skyscraper
4. The model-T Ford
5. Jazz
6. The constitution
7. Mark Twain's writing
8. Whitman's *Leaves of Grass*
9. Comic strips
10. Soap operas
11. Assembly-line production
12. Chewing Gum

Here we have a round dozen artifacts which are, it seems to me, recognizably American, not likely to have been produced elsewhere. Granted that some of us take more pleasure in some of them than in others—that many people vastly prefer soap opera to *Leaves of Grass,* while others think Mark Twain's storytelling is less offensive than chewing gum—all twelve items are, I believe, widely held to be indigenous to our culture. The fact that many people in other lands like them too, and that some of them are nearly as acceptable overseas as they are here at home, does not in any way detract from their obviously American character. It merely serves to remind us that to be American does not mean to be inhuman—a fact which, in certain moods of self-criticism, we are inclined to forget.

What, then, is the "American" quality which these dozen items share? And what can that quality tell us about the character of our culture, about the nature of our civilization?

2

Those engaged in discovering America often begin by discovering the Manhattan skyline, and here as well as elsewhere they discover apparently irreconcilable opposites. They notice at once that it doesn't make any sense, in human or aesthetic terms. It is the product of insane politics, greed, competitive ostentation, megalomania, the worship of false gods. Its products, in turn, are traffic jams, bad ventilation, noise, and all the other ills that metropolitan flesh is heir to. And the net result is, illogically enough, one of the most exaltedly beautiful things man has ever made.

Perhaps this paradoxical result will be less bewildering if we look for a moment at the formal and structural principles which are involved in the skyline. It may be helpful to consider the skyline as we might consider a lyric poem, or a novel, if we were trying to analyze its aesthetic quality.

Looked at in this way, it is clear that the total effect which we call "the Manhattan skyline" is made up of almost innumerable buildings, each in competition (for height, or glamor, or efficiency, or respectability) with all of the others. Each goes its own way, as it were, in a carnival of rugged architectural individualism. And yet—as witness the universal feeling of exaltation and aspiration which the skyline as a whole evokes—out of this irrational, unplanned, and often infuriating chaos, an unforeseen unity has evolved. No building ever built in New York was placed where it was, or shaped as it was, because it would contribute to the aesthetic effect of the skyline—lifting it here, giving it mass there, or lending a needed emphasis. Each was built, all those now under construction are being built, with no thought for their subordination to any over-all affect.

What, then, makes possible the fluid and ever-changing unity which does, in fact, exist? Quite simply, there are two things, both quite simple in themselves, which do the job. If they were not simple, they would not work; but they are, and they do.

One is the gridiron pattern of the city's streets—the same basic pattern which accounts for Denver, Houston, Little Rock, Birmingham and almost any American town you can name, and the same pattern which, in the form of square townships, sections, and quarter sections, was imposed by the Ordinance of 1785 on almost continental scale. Whatever its shortcomings when compared with the "discontinuous street patterns" of modern planned communities, this artificial geometric grid—imposed upon the land without regard to contours or any preconceived pattern of social zoning—had at least the quality of rational simplicity. And it is this simple gridiron street pattern which, horizontally, controls the spacing and arrangement of the rectangular shafts which go to make up the skyline.

The other thing which holds the skyline's diversity together is the structural principle of the skyscraper. When we think of individual buildings, we tend to think of details of texture, color, and form, of surface ornamentation or the lack of it. But as elements in Manhattan's skyline, these things are of little consequence. What matters there is the vertical thrust, the motion upward; and that is the product of cage or skeleton, construction in steel—a system of construction which is, in effect, merely a three dimensional variant of the gridiron street plan, extending vertically instead of horizontally.

The aesthetics of cage, or skeleton, construction have never been fully analyzed, nor am I equipped to analyze them. But as a lay-observer, I am struck by fundamental differences between the effect created by height in the RCA building at Radio City, for example, and the effect created by height in Chartres cathedral or in Giotto's Campanile. In both the latter (as in all the great architecture of the past) proportion and symmetry, the relation of height to width, are constituent to the effect. One can say of a Gothic cathedral, this tower is too high; of a Romanesque dome, this is top-heavy. But there is nothing inherent in cage construction which would invite such judgements. A true skyscraper like the RCA building could be 18 or 20 stories taller, or ten or a dozen stories shorter without changing its essential aesthetic effect. Once steel cage construction has passed a certain height, the effect of transactive upward motion has been established; from there on, the point at which you cut it off is arbitrary and makes no difference.

Those who are familiar with the history of the skyscraper will remember how slowly this fact was realized. Even Louis Sullivan—greatest of the early skyscraper architects—thought in terms of having to close off and climax the upward motion of the tall building with an "attic" or cornice. His lesser contemporaries worked for years on the blind assumption that the proportion and symmetry of masonry architecture must be preserved in the new technique. If with the steel cage one could go higher than with load-bearing masonry walls, the old aesthetic effects could be counterfeited by dressing the façade as if one or more buildings had been piled on top of one another—each retaining the illusion of being complete in itself. You can still see such buildings in New York: the first five stories perhaps a Graeco-Roman temple, the next ten a neuter warehouse, and the final five or six an Aztec pyramid. And that Aztec pyramid is simply a cheap and thoughtless equivalent of the more subtle Sullivan cornice. Both attempt to close and climax the upward thrust, to provide something similar to the *Katharsis* in Greek tragedy.

But the logic of cage construction requires no such climax. It has less to do with the inner logic of masonry forms than with that of the old Globe-Wernicke sectional bookcases, whose interchangeable units (with glass-flap fronts) anticipated by fifty years the modular unit systems of so-called modern furniture. Those bookcases were advertised in the nineties as "always complete but never finished"—a phrase which could with equal propriety have been applied to the Model-T Ford. Many of us remember with affection that admirably simple mechanism, forever susceptible to added gadgets or improved parts, each of which was interchangeable with what you already had.

Here, then, are the two things which serve to tie together the otherwise irrelevant components of the Manhattan skyline: the gridiron ground plan and the three-dimensional vertical grid of steel cage construction. And both of these are closely related to one another. Both are composed of simple and infinitely repeatable units.

3

It was the French architect, Le Corbusier, who first noted the relation between New York's skyscrapers and American jazz. The city, he said, is "hot jazz in stone and steel." At first glance this may sound as if it were merely a slick updating of Schelling's "Architecture . . . is frozen music," but it is more than that if one thinks in terms of the structural principles we have been discussing and the structural principles of jazz.

Let me begin by making clear that I am using the term jazz in its broadest significant application. There are circumstances in which it is important to define the term with considerable precision, as when you are involved in discussion with a disciple of one of the many cults, orthodox or progressive, which devote themselves to some particular sub-species of jazz. But in our present context we need to focus upon what all the sub-species (Dixieland, Bebop, Swing, or Cool Jazz) have in common; in other words, we must neglect the by no means uninteresting qualities which differentiate one from another, since it is what they have in common which can tell us most about the civilization which produced them.

There is no definition of jazz, academic or otherwise, which does not acknowledge that its essential ingredient is a particular kind of rhythm. Improvisation is also frequently mentioned as an essential; but even if it is true that jazz always involves improvisation, that would not distinguish it from a good deal of Western European music of the past. It is the distinctive rhythm which differentiates all types of jazz from all other music and which gives to all of its types a basic family resemblance.

It is not easy to define that distinctive rhythm. Winthrop Sargeant has described it as the product of two super-imposed devices: syncopation and polyrhythm, both of which have the effect of constantly upsetting rhythmical expectations. Andre Hodeir, in his recent analysis of *Jazz: Its Evolution and Essence*, speaks of "an unending alternation" of syncopations and of notes played *on* the beat, which "gives rise to a kind of expectation that is one of jazz's subtlest effects."

As you can readily hear, if you listen to any jazz performance (whether of the Louis Armstrong, Benny Goodman, or Charlie Parker variety), the rhythmical effect depends upon there being a clearly defined basic rhythmic pattern which enforces the expectations which are to be upset. That basic pattern is the 4/4 or 2/4 beat which underlies all jazz. Hence the importance of the percussive instruments in jazz: the drums, the guitar or banjo, the bull fiddle, the piano. Hence too the insistent thump, thump, thump, thump which is so boring when you only half-hear jazz—either because you are too far away, across the lake or in the next room, or simply because you will not listen attentively. But hence also the delight, the subtle effects, which good jazz provides as the melodic phrases evade, anticipate, and return to, and then again evade the steady basic four-beat pulse which persists, implicitly or explicitly, throughout the performance.

In other words, the structure of a jazz performance is, like that of the New York Skyline, a tension of cross-purposes. In jazz at its characteristic best, each player seems to be—and has the sense of being —on his own. Each goes his own way, inventing rhythmic and melodic patterns which, superficially, seem to have as little relevance to one another as the U.N. building does to the Empire State. And yet the outcome is a dazzlingly precise creative unity.

That unity of effect is, of course, the result of the very thing which each of the players is flouting: namely, the basic

4/4 beat—that simple rhythmic grid-iron of identical and infinitely extenda-ble units which holds the performance together. As Louis Armstrong once wrote, you would expect that if every man in a band "had his own way and could play as he wanted, all you would get would be a lot of jumbled up, crazy noise." But, as he goes on to say, that does not happen, because the players know "by ear and sheer musical instinct" just when to leave the underlying pat-tern and when to get back on it. What it adds up to is that jazz is the first art form to give full expression to Emerson's ideal of a union which is perfect only "when all the uniters are isolated." That Emer-son's ideal is deeply rooted in our na-tional experience need not be argued. Turner quotes a letter written by a frontier settler to friends back East, which in simple, unselfconscious words expresses the same reconciling of op-posites. "It is a universal rule here," the frontiersman wrote, "to help one another, each one keeping an eye single to his own business." One need only remember that the Constitution itself, by providing for a federation of separate units, be-came the infinitely extendable frame-work for the process of reconciling lib-erty and unity over vast areas and con-flicting interests. Its seven brief articles, providing for checks and balances be-tween interests, classes, and branches of the government establish, in effect, the underlying beat which gives momentum and direction to a political process which Richard Hofstadter has called "a har-monious system of mutual frustration"—a description which fits a jazz perform-ance as well as it fits our politics.

The aesthetic effects of jazz, as you can readily see, have as little to do with symmetry and proportion as have those of a skyscraper. Like the skyscraper, a jazz performance need not build to an organically required climax; it can sim-ply cease. The "piece" which the mu-sicians are playing may, and often does, have a rudimentary Aristotelian pattern of beginning, middle, and end; but the jazz performance need not. In tradi-tional Western European music themes are developed. In jazz they are toyed with and dismantled. There is no in-herent reason why the jazz performance should not continue for another 12 or 16 or 24 or 32 measures (for these are the rhythmic cages which in jazz correspond to the cages of a steel skeleton in archi-tecture). As in the skyscraper, the aesthetic effect is one of motion, in this case horizontal rather than vertical. Jazz rhythms create what can only be called momentum. When the rhythm of one voice (say the trumpet, off on a rhyth-mic and melodic excursion) lags behind the underlying beat, its four-beat meas-ure carries over beyond the end of the underlying beat's measure into the suc-ceeding one, which has already begun. When the trumpet anticipates the beat, it starts a new measure before the steady underlying beat has ended one. And the result is an exhilarating forward motion which the jazz trumpeter Wingy Manone once described as "feeling an increase in tempo though you're still playing at the same tempo." Hence the importance in jazz of timing, and hence the delight and amusement of the so-called "break," in which the basic 4/4 beat ceases and a soloist goes off on a flight of rhythmic and melodic fancy which nevertheless comes back surprisingly and unerringly to encounter the beat precisely where it would have been if it had kept going.

Once the momentum is established, it can continue until—after an interval dic-tated by some such external factor as the conventional length of phonograph rec-ords or the endurance of dancers—it stops. And as if to guard against any Aristotelian misconceptions about an end, it is likely to stop on an unresolved chord, so that harmonically as well as rhythmically everything is left up in the air. Even the various coda-like devices employed by jazz performers at dances, such as the corny old "without a shirt" phrase of blessed memory, are harmonically unresolved. They are merely conventional ways of saying "we quit," not, like Beethoven's insistent codas, ways of saying "There now; that ties off all the loose ends; I'm going to stop now; done; finished; concluded; signed, sealed, delivered; *hic iacet.*"

4

Thus far, in our discussion of distinctively "American" things, we have focussed chiefly upon twentieth-century items. But the references to the rectangular grid pattern of cities and townships and to the constitution should remind us that the underlying structural principles with which we are concerned are deeply embedded in our civilization. To shift the emphasis, however, let us look at item number 7 on our list: Mark Twain's writing.

Mark's writing was, of course, very largely the product of oral influences. He was a born story-teller, and he always insisted that the oral form of the humorous story was high art. Its essential tool (or weapon), he said, is the pause —which is to say, timing. "If the pause is too long the impressive point is passed," he wrote, "and the audience have had time to divine that a surprise is intended—and then you can't surprise them, of course." In other words, he saw the pause as a device for upsetting expectations, like the jazz "break."

In his essay on "How to Tell a Story," Mark differentiated between the comic story (which he said was English), the witty story (which he said was French) and the humorous story (which he said originated in America and stayed at home). The comic and witty stories, he pointed out, depended for their effect on the *matter* dealt with; the humorous story depended upon the *manner* of tell-

ing it. (That business of the pause, of course, is simply a question of manner.)

Mark, as you know, was by no means a formal perfectionist. In fact he took delight in being irreverent about literary form. Take, for example, his account of the way *Pudd'nhead Wilson* came into being.

It started out to be a story called "Those Extraordinary Twins," about a youthful freak consisting, as he said, of "a combination of two heads and four arms joined to a single body and a single pair of legs—and I thought I would write an extravagantly fantastic little story with this freak of nature for hero —or heroes—a silly young miss for heroine, and two old ladies and two boys for the minor parts."

But as he got writing the tale, it kept spreading along and other people got to intruding themselves—among them Pudd'nhead, and a woman named Roxana, and a young fellow named Tom Driscoll, who—before the book was half finished —had taken things almost entirely into their own hands and were "working the whole tale as a private venture of their own."

From this point, I want to quote Mark directly, because in the process of making fun of fiction's formal conventions he employs a technique which is the verbal equivalent of the jazz "break"— a technique of which he was a master.

When the book was finished, and I came to look round to see what had become of the team I had originally started out with— Aunt Patsy Cooper, Aunt Betsy Hale, the two boys, and Rowena the light-weight heroine—they were nowhere to be seen; they had disappeared from the story some time or other. I hunted about and found them— found them stranded, idle, forgotten, and permanently useless. It was very awkward. It was awkward all around; but more particularly in the case of Rowena, because there was a lovematch on, between her and one of the twins that constituted the freak, and I had worked it up to a blistering heat and thrown in a quite dramatic love-quarrel [Now watch Mark take off like a jazz trumpeter flying off on his own in a fantastic break] wherein Rowena scathingly denounced her betrothed for getting drunk, and scoffed at his explanation of how it had happened, and wouldn't listen to it, and had driven him from her in the usual "forever" way; and now here she sat crying and broken hearted; for she had found that he had spoken only the truth; that it was not he but the other half of the freak, that had drunk the liquor that made him drunk; that her half was a prohibitionist and had never drunk a drop in his life, and, although tight as a brick three days in the week, was wholly innocent of blame; and, indeed, when sober was constantly doing all he could to reform his brother, the other half, who never got any satisfaction out of drinking anyway, because liquor never affected him. [Now he's going to get back on the basic beat again.] Yes, here she was, stranded with that deep injustice of hers torturing her poor heart.

Now I'll have to summarize again. Mark didn't know what to do with her. He couldn't just leave her there, of course, after making such a to-do over her; he'd have to account to the reader for her somehow. So he finally decided that all he could do was "give her the grand bounce." It grieved him, because he'd come to like her after a fashion, "notwithstanding she was such an ass and said such stupid, irritating things and was so nauseatingly sentimental"; but it had to be done. So he started Chapter Seventeen with: "Rowena went out in the back yard after supper to see the fireworks and fell down the well and got drowned."

It seemed abrupt, [Mark went on] but I thought maybe the reader wouldn't notice it, because I changed the subject right away to something else. Anyway, it loosened up Rowena from where she was stuck and got her out of the way, and that was the main thing. It seemed a prompt good way of weeding out people that had got stalled, and a plenty good enough way for those others; so I hunted up the two boys and said they

went out back one night to stone the cat and fell down the well and got drowned. Next I searched around and found Aunt Patsy Cooper and Aunt Betsy Hale where they were aground, and said they went out back one night to visit the sick and fell down the well and got drowned. I was going to drown some of the others, but I gave up the idea, partly because I believed that if I kept that up it would arouse attention, . . . and partly because it was not a large well and would not hold any more anyway.

That was a long excursion—but it makes the point: that Mark didn't have much reverence for conventional story structure. Even his greatest book, which is perhaps also the greatest book written on this continent—*Huckleberry Finn*—is troublesome. One can scarcely find a criticism of the book which does not object, for instance, to the final episodes, in which Tom rejoins Huck and they go through that burlesque business of "freeing" the negro Jim—who is, it turns out, already free. But, as T. S. Eliot was, I think, the first to observe, the real structure of *Huckleberry Finn* has nothing to do with the traditional form of the novel, with exposition, climax, and resolution. Its structure is like that of the great river itself, without beginning and without end. Its structural units, or "cages," are the episodes of which it is composed. Its momentum is that of the tension between the river's steady flow and the eccentric superimposed rhythms of Huck's flights from, and near recapture by, the restricting forces of routine and convention. It is not a novel of escape, starting in confinement and culminating in long-sought freedom. Huck is free at the beginning, having "lit out" from the Widow Douglas's. He is lured back by one of Tom's fantastic schemes and is in renewed danger of being civilized, when he lights out again. And so it goes until at the very end of the book with the imminent prospect of being "civilized" by still another "Aunt," he announces he is ready to "light out" again. Looked at in this way, it is clear that *Huckleberry Finn* has as little need of a "conclusion" as has a skyscraper or a jazz performance. Questions of proportion and symmetry are as irrelevant in its structure as they are in the total effect of the New York Skyline.

There is not room here for more than brief reference to the other "literary" items on our list: Whitman's *Leaves of Grass*, comic strips, and soap opera. Perhaps it is enough to remind you that *Leaves of Grass* has discomfited many a critic by its lack of symmetry and proportion, and that Whitman himself insisted: "I round and finish little, if anything; and could not, consistently with my scheme." As for the words of true poems, Whitman said in the "Song of the Answerer" (using almost the identical phraseology he had first used in the prose preface to the 1855 edition of the *Leaves*),

They bring none to his or her terminus or to
    be content and full,
Whom they take they take into space to be-
    hold the birth of stars, to learn one of
    the meanings,
To launch off with absolute faith, to sweep
    through the ceaseless rings and never
    be quiet again.

Although this is not the place for a detailed analysis of Whitman's verse techniques, it is worth noting in passing, how the rhythm of these lines reinforces their logical meaning. The basic rhythmical unit, throughout, is a three beat phrase. (The first quoted line comprises two such units: "They bring nóne to hís or her términus / or to bé contént and fúll"; the second and third lines both comprise three.) Superimposed upon the basic three-beat measure there is a flexible, non-metrical rhythm of rhetorical phrasing. That rhythm is controlled in part by the visual effect of the

arrangement in long lines, to each of which the reader tends to give equal duration, and in part by the punctuation within the lines. For example, the comma after the second three-beat measure in line two tends, since line one also consisted of two such measures, to establish an expectation of rest which is upset by the line's continuing for another measure; then, in the final line, the placement of the comma reverses the pattern, requiring a rest after the first measure and doubling up the remaining two.

It is, therefore, the tension between the flexible, superimposed rhythms of the rhetorical patterns and the basic three-beat measure of the underlying framework which unites with the imagery and the logical meaning of the words to give the passage its restless, sweeping movement. It is this tension, and other analogous aspects of the structure of *Leaves of Grass* which give to the book that "vista" which Whitman himself claimed for it. If I may apply to it T. S. Eliot's idea about *Huckleberry Finn*, the structure of the *Leaves* is open at the end. Its key poem may well be, as D. H. Lawrence believed, the "Song of the Open Road."

As for the comics and soap opera, they too—on their own frequently humdrum level—have devised structures which provide for no ultimate climax, which come to no end demanded by symmetry or proportion. In them both there is a shift in interest away from the "How does it come out?" of traditional storytelling to "How are things going?" In a typical installment of Harold Gray's *Orphan Annie*, the final panel shows Annie walking purposefully down a path with her dog, Sandy, saying: "But if we're goin', why horse around? It's a fine night for walkin' . . . C'mon, Sandy . . . Let's go . . ." (It doesn't even end with a period, or full stop, but with the conventional three dots or suspension points, to indicate incompletion.) So too, in the soap operas, *Portia Faces Life*, in one form or another, day after day, over and over again. And the operative word is the verb *faces*. It is the process of facing that matters.

5

And here, I think, we are approaching the central quality which all the diverse items on our list have in common.

That quality I would define as a concern with process rather than with product—or, to re-use Mark Twain's words, a concern with the manner of handling experience or materials rather than with the experience or materials themselves. Emerson, a century ago, was fascinated by the way "becoming somewhat else is the perpetual game of nature." The universe, he wrote, "exists only in transit. . . . Man was made for conflict, not for rest. In action is his power; not in his goals but in his transitions man is great."

And this preoccupation with process is, of course, basic to modern science. "Matter" itself is no longer to be thought of as something fixed, but fluid and ever-changing. As Veblen observed almost forty years ago, "sciences which are in any peculiar sense modern take as an (unavowed) postulate the fact of consecutive change," and their researches cluster about the "notion of process," which is to say the notion of a sequence, or complex, of consecutive change. Similarly, modern economic theory has abandoned the "static equilibrium" analysis of the neoclassic economists, and in philosophy John Dewey's instrumentalism abandoned the classic philosophical interest in final causes for a scientific interest in "the mechanism of occurrences"—that is, process.

It is obvious, I think, that the American system of industrial mass-production reflects this same focus of interest in its concern with production rather than products. And it is the mass-production system, *not* machinery, which has been America's contribution to industry.

In that system there is an emphasis different from that which was characteristic of handicraft production or even of machine manufacture. In both of these there was an almost total disregard of the means of production. The aristocratic ideal inevitably relegated interest in the means exclusively to anonymous peasants and slaves; what mattered to those who controlled and administered production was, quite simply, the finished product. In a mass-production system, on the other hand, it is the process of production itself which becomes the center of interest, rather than the product.

If we are aware of this fact, we usually regard it as a misfortune. We hear a lot, for instance, of the notion that our system "dehumanizes" the worker, turning him into a machine and depriving him of the satisfaction of finishing anything, since he performs only some repetitive operation. It is true that the unit of work in mass-production is not a product but an operation. But the development of the system, in contrast with Charlie Chaplin's wonderful but wild phantasy of the assembly line, has shown the intermediacy of the stage in which the worker is doomed to frustrating boredom. Merely repetitive work, in the logic of mass-production, can and must be done by machine. It is unskilled work which is doomed by it, not the worker. More and more skilled workers are needed to design products, analyze jobs, cut patterns, attend complicated machines, and coordinate the increasingly complex processes which comprise the productive system.

The skills required for these jobs are different, of course, from those required to make handmade boots or to carve stone ornament, but they are not in themselves less interesting or less human. Operating a crane in a steel mill, or a turret lathe, is an infinitely more varied and stimulating job than shaping boots day after day by hand. A recent study of a group of workers on an automobile assembly line makes it clear that many of the men object, for a variety of reasons, to those monotonous, repetitive jobs which (as we have already noted) should be—but in many cases are not yet —done by machine; but those who *like* such jobs like them because they enjoy the process. As one of them said: "Repeating the same thing you can catch up and keep ahead of yourself . . . you can get in the swing of it." The report of members of a team of British workers who visited twenty American steel foundries in 1949 includes this description of the technique of "snatching" a steel casting with a magnet, maneuvered by a gantry crane running on overhead rails:

In its operation, the crane approaches a pile of castings at high speed with the magnet hanging fairly near floor level. The crane comes to a stop somewhere short of the castings, while the magnet swings forward over the pile, is dropped on to it, current switched on, and the hoist begun, at the same moment as the crane starts on its return journey. [And then, in words which might equally be applied to a jazz musician, the report adds:] The whole operation requires timing of a high order, and the impression gained is that the crane drivers derive a good deal of satisfaction from the swinging rhythm of the process.

This fascination with process has possessed Americans ever since Oliver Evans in 1785 created the first wholly automatic factory: a flour mill in Delaware in which mechanical conveyors —belt conveyors, bucket conveyors, screw conveyors—are interlinked with machines in a continuous process of production. But even if there were no other visible sign of the national preoccupation with process, it would be enough to point out that it was an Amer-

ican who invented chewing gum (in 1869) and that it is the Americans who have spread it—in all senses of the verb —throughout the world. An absolutely non-consumable confection, its sole appeal is the process of chewing it.

The apprehensions which many people feel about a civilization absorbed with process—about its mobility and wastefulness as well as about the "dehumanizing" effects of its jobs—derive, I suppose, from old habit and the persistence of values and tastes which were indigenous to a very different social and economic system. Whitman pointed out in *Democratic Vistas* more than eighty years ago that America was a stranger in her own house, that many of our social institutions, like our theories of literature and art, had been taken over almost without change from a culture which was not, like ours, the product of political democracy and the machine. Those institutions and theories are still around, though some (like collegiate gothic, of both the architectural and intellectual variety) are less widely admired than formerly.

Change, or the process of consecutive occurrences, is, we tend to feel, a bewildering and confusing and lonely thing. We talk fondly of the need for roots—as if man were a vegetable, not an animal with legs whose distinction it is that he can move and "get on with it." We would do well to make ourselves more familiar with the idea that the process of development is universal, that it is "the form and order of nature." As Lancelot Law Whyte has said:

Man shares the special form of the universal formative process which is common to all organisms, and herein lies the root of his unity with the rest of organic nature. While life is maintained, the component processes in man never attain the relative isolation and static perfection of inorganic processes . . . The individual may seek, or believe that he seeks, independence, permanence, or perfection, but that is only through his failure to recognize and accept his actual situation.

As an "organic system" man cannot, of course, expect to achieve stability or permanent harmony, though he can create (and in the great arts of the past, has created) the illusion of them. What he can achieve is a continuing development in response to his environment. The factor which gives vitality to all the component processes in the individual and in society is "not permanence but development."

To say this is not to deny the past. It is simply to recognize that for a variety of reasons people living in America have, on the whole, been better able to relish process than those who have lived under the imposing shadow of the arts and institutions which Western man created in his tragic search for permanence and perfection. The past of those who live in the United States does not, like the past of most other peoples, extend downward into the soil upon which they stand. It extends laterally backward across the plains, the mountains, or the sea to somewhere else, whence they or their families came. Our history is the process of westering and the counter-process of return; of motion into and out of cities; of motion up and down the social ladder—a long, complex, and sometimes terrifyingly rapid sequence of consecutive change.

"America" is not a synonym for the United States. It is not an artifact. It is not a fixed and immutable ideal toward which citizens of this nation strive. America has not order or proportion, but neither is it chaos, except as that is chaotic whose components no single mind can comprehend or control. America is process. And in so far as people have been "American"—as distinguished from being (as most of us, in at least some of our activities, have been) mere carriers of transplanted cultural traditions, that fact has been reflected in the work of their heads and hearts and hands.

PEOPLE

Benjamin Franklin

* 1706-1790

Though part of a longer work, this portion of the AUTOBIOGRAPHY *of Benjamin Franklin presents so candid a picture of important events and occupations of his early life and of influences which contributed to the development of his literary style that it can be considered in its own right an essay. Written at different times between 1771 and 1789 and only published in its entirety in 1868, the* AUTOBIOGRAPHY *was intended by Franklin as an illustrative guide for his grandson, who he hoped would profit by his example and also be saved from some of his mistakes. The simple directness of its diction was the result of Franklin's lifelong quest for words which would most efficiently communicate what he had to say: the use of too many words was a waste of time; the use of too few was waste also because the subject was then incompletely presented and to be understood would have to be stated again.*

Portion of an Autobiography

From a child I was fond of reading, and all the little money that came into my hands was ever laid out in books. Pleased with the *Pilgrim's Progress,* my first collection was of John Bunyan's works in separate little volumes. I afterwards sold them to enable me to buy R. Burton's *Historical Collections;* they were small chapman's books, and cheap, forty or fifty in all. My father's little library consisted chiefly of books in polemic divinity, most of which I read and have since often regretted that at a time when I had such a thirst for knowledge, more proper books had not fallen in my way, since it was now resolved I should not be a clergyman. *Plutarch's Lives* there was, in which I read abundantly, and I still think that time spent to great advantage. There was also a book of Defoe's, called an *Essay on Projects,* and another of Dr. Mather's, called *Essays to do Good,* which perhaps gave me a turn of thinking that had an influence on some of the principal future events of my life.

This bookish inclination at length determined my father to make me a printer, though he had already one son (James) of that profession. In 1717 my brother James returned from England with a press and letters to set up his business in Boston. I liked it much better than that of my father, but still had a hankering for the sea. To prevent the apprehended effect of such an inclination, my father was impatient to have me bound to my brother. I stood out some time, but at last was persuaded, and signed the indentures when I was yet but twelve years old. I was to serve as an apprentice till I was twenty-one years of age, only I was to be allowed journeyman's wages during the last year. In a little time I made great proficiency in the business and became a useful hand to my brother. I now had access to better books. An acquaintance with the apprentices of booksellers enabled me sometimes to borrow a small one, which I was careful to return soon and clean. Often I sat up in my room reading the greatest part of the night, when the book was borrowed in the evening and to be returned early in the morning, lest it should be missed or wanted.

And after some time an ingenious tradesman, Mr. Matthew Adams, who had a pretty collection of books, and who frequented our printing-house, took notice of me, invited me to his library, and very kindly lent me such books as I chose to read. I now took a fancy to poetry, and made some little pieces; my brother, thinking it might turn to account, encouraged me, and put me on composing two occasional ballads. One was called *The Lighthouse Tragedy,* and contained an account of the drowning of Captain Worthilake with his two daughters; the other was a sailor's song, on the taking of Teach (or Blackbeard), the pirate. They were wretched stuff, in the Grub-street-ballad style; and when they were printed he sent me about the town to sell them. The first sold wonderfully, the event being recent, having made a great noise. This flattered my vanity; but my father discouraged me by ridiculing my performances and telling me verse-makers were generally beggars. So I escaped being a poet, most probably a very bad one; but as prose writing has been of great use to me in the course of my life, and was a principal means of my advancement, I shall tell you how, in such a situation, I acquired what little ability I have in that way.

There was another bookish lad in the town, John Collins by name, with whom I was intimately acquainted. We sometimes disputed; and very fond we were of argument, and very desirous of confuting one another, which disputatious turn, by the way, is apt to become a very bad habit, making people often extremely disagreeable in company by the contradiction that is necessary to bring it into practice; and thence, besides souring and spoiling the conversation, is produc-

tive of disgusts and, perhaps, enmities where you may have occasion for friendship. I had caught it by reading my father's books of dispute about religion. Persons of good sense, I have since observed, seldom fall into it, except lawyers, university men, and men of all sorts that have been bred at Edinburgh.

A question was once, somehow or other, started between Collins and me of the propriety of educating the female sex in learning, and their abilities for study. He was of opinion that it was improper, and that they were naturally unequal to it. I took the contrary side, perhaps a little for dispute's sake. He was naturally more eloquent, had a ready plenty of words, and sometimes, as I thought, bore me down more by his fluency than by the strength of his reasons. As we parted without settling the point, and were not to see one another again for some time, I sat down to put my arguments in writing, which I copied fair and sent to him. He answered, and I replied. Three or four letters of a side had passed, when my father happened to find my papers and read them. Without entering into the discussion, he took occasion to talk to me about the manner of my writing; observed that, though I had the advantage of my antagonist in correct spelling and pointing (which I owed to the printing-house), I fell far short in elegance of expression, in method, and in perspicuity, of which he convinced me by several instances. I saw the justice of his remarks, and thence grew more attentive to the *manner* in writing, and determined to endeavor at improvement.

About this time I met with an odd volume of the *Spectator.* It was the third. I had never before seen any of them. I bought it, read it over and over, and was much delighted with it. I thought the writing excellent, and wished, if possible, to imitate it. With that view I took some of the papers, and, making short hints of the sentiment in each sentence, laid them by a few days, and then, without looking at the book, tried to complete the papers again by expressing each hinted sentiment at length, and as fully as it had been expressed before, in any suitable words that should come to hand. Then I compared my *Spectator* with the original, discovered some of my faults, and corrected them. But I found I wanted a stock of words, or a readiness in recollecting and using them, which I thought I should have acquired before that time if I had gone on making verses; since the continual occasion for words of the same import, but of different length to suit the measure, or of different sound for the rhyme, would have laid me under a constant necessity of searching for variety and also have tended to fix that variety in my mind and make me master of it. Therefore, I took some of the tales and turned them into verse; and, after a time, when I had pretty well forgotten the prose, turned them back again. I also sometimes jumbled my collections of hints into confusion, and after some weeks endeavored to reduce them into the best order, before I began to form the full sentences and complete the paper. This was to teach me method in the arrangement of thoughts. By comparing my work afterwards with the original, I discovered many faults and amended them; but I sometimes had the pleasure of fancying that in certain particulars of small import I had been lucky enough to improve the method or the language, and this encouraged me to think I might possibly in time come to be a tolerable English writer, of which I was extremely ambitious. My time for these exercises and for reading was at night, after work, or before it began in the morning, or on Sundays, when I contrived to be in the printing-house alone, evading as much as I could the common attendance on public worship which my father used to exact of me when I was under his care, and which indeed I still thought a duty, though I could not, as it seemed to me, afford time to practice it.

When about sixteen years of age I happened to meet with a book, written by one Tryon, recommending a vegetable diet. I determined to go into it. My brother, being yet unmarried, did not keep house, but boarded himself and his apprentices in another family. My refusing to eat flesh occasioned an inconveniency, and I was frequently chid for my singularity. I made myself acquainted with Tryon's manner of preparing some of his dishes, such as boiling potatoes or rice, making hasty pudding, and a few others, and then proposed to my brother, that if he would give me, weekly, half the money he paid for my board, I would board myself. He instantly agreed to it, and I presently found that I could save half what he paid me. This was an additional fund for buying books. But I had another advantage in it. My brother and the rest going from the printing-house to their meals, I remained there alone and dispatching presently my light repast, which often was no more than a biscuit or a slice of bread, a handful of raisins or a tart from the pastrycook's, and a glass of water, had the rest of the time till their return for study, in which I made the greater progress, from that greater clearness of head and quicker apprehension which usually attend temperance in eating and drinking.

And now it was that, being on some occasion made ashamed of my ignorance in figures, which I had twice failed in learning when at school, I took Cocker's book of arithmetic, and went through the whole by myself with great ease. I also read Seller's and Sturmy's books of navigation, and became acquainted with the little geometry they contain; but never proceeded far in that science. And

I read about this time Locke *On Human Understanding*, and the *Art of Thinking*, by Messrs. du Port Royal.

While I was intent on improving my language, I met with an English grammar (I think it was Greenwood's), at the end of which there were two little sketches of the arts of rhetoric and logic, the latter finishing with a specimen of a dispute in the Socratic method; and soon after I procured Xenophon's *Memorable Things of Socrates*, wherein there are many instances of the same method. I was charmed with it, adopted it, dropped my abrupt contradiction and positive argumentation, and put on the humble inquirer and doubter. And being then, from reading Shaftesbury and Collins, become a real doubter in many points of our religious doctrine, I found this method safest for myself and very embarrassing to those against whom I used it; therefore I took a delight in it, practiced it continually, and grew very artful and expert in drawing people, even of superior knowledge, into concessions, the consequences of which they did not foresee, entangling them in difficulties out of which they could not extricate themselves, and so obtaining victories that neither myself nor my cause always deserved. I continued this method some few years, but gradually left it, retaining only the habit of expressing myself in terms of modest diffidence; never using, when I advanced anything that may possibly be disputed, the words *certainly*, *undoubtedly*, or any others that give the air of positiveness to an opinion; but rather say, I conceive or apprehend a thing to be so or so; it appears to me, or I should think it so or so, for such and such reasons; or I imagine it to be so; or it is so, if I am not mistaken. This habit, I believe, has been a great advantage to me when I have had occasion to inculcate my opinions and persuade men into measures that I have been from time to time engaged in pro-

moting; and, as the chief ends of conversation are to *inform* or to be *informed*, to *please* or to *persuade*, I wish well-meaning, sensible men would not lessen their power of doing good by a positive, assuming manner that seldom fails to disgust, tends to create opposition and to defeat every one of those purposes for which speech was given to us, to wit, giving or receiving information or pleasure. For if you would *inform*, a positive dogmatical manner in advancing your sentiments may provoke contradiction and prevent a candid attention. If you wish information and improvement from the knowledge of others, and yet at the same time express yourself as firmly fixed in your present opinions, modest, sensible men, who do not love disputation, will probably leave you undisturbed in the possession of your error. And by such a manner, you can seldom hope to recommend yourself in *pleasing* your hearers, or to persuade those whose concurrence you desire. Pope says, judiciously:

Men should be taught as if you taught them
   not,
And things unknown propos'd as things
   forgot;

farther recommending to us

To speak, tho' sure, with seeming Diffidence.

And he might have coupled with this line that which he has coupled with another, I think less properly,

For want of Modesty is want of Sense.

If you ask why *less properly?* I must repeat the lines,

Immodest Words admit of *no* Defence;
For Want of Modesty is Want of Sense

Now, is not *want of sense* (where a man is so unfortunate as to want it) some apology for his *want of modesty?* and would not the lines stand more justly thus?

Immodest Words admit *but this* Defence,
That Want of Modesty is Want of Sense.

This, however, I should submit to better judgments.

My brother had, in 1720 or 21, begun to print a newspaper. It was the second that appeared in America, and was called the *New England Courant*. The only one before it was the *Boston News-Letter*. I remember his being dissuaded by some of his friends from the undertaking, as not likely to succeed, one newspaper being, in their judgment, enough for America. At this time (1771) there are not less than five-and-twenty. He went on, however, with the undertaking, and after having worked in composing the types and printing off the sheets, I was employed to carry the papers through the streets to the customers.

He had some ingenious men among his friends, who amused themselves by writing little pieces for his paper, which gained it credit and made it more in demand, and these gentlemen often visited us. Hearing their conversations, and their accounts of the approbation their papers were received with, I was excited to try my hand among them; but, being still a boy, and suspecting that my brother would object to printing anything of mine in his paper if he knew it to be mine, I contrived to disguise my hand and, writing an anonymous paper, I put in at night under the door of the printing-house. It was found in the morning and communicated to his writing friends when they called in as usual. They read it, commented on it in my hearing, and I had the exquisite pleasure of finding it met with their approbation, and that, in their different guesses at the author, none were named but men of some character among us for learning and ingenuity. I suppose now that I was rather lucky in my judges, and that perhaps they were not really so very good ones as I then esteemed them.

Encouraged, however, by this, I wrote and conveyed in the same way to the press several more papers which were equally approved; and I kept my secret till my small fund of sense for such performances was pretty well exhausted, and then I discovered it, when I began to be considered a little more by my brother's acquaintance, and in a manner that did not quite please him, as he thought, probably with reason, that it tended to make me too vain. And perhaps this might be one occasion of the differences that we began to have about this time. Though a brother, he considered himself as my master, and me as his apprentice, and accordingly expected the same services from me as he would from another, while I thought he demeaned me too much in some he required of me, who from a brother expected more indulgence. Our disputes were often brought before our father, and I fancy I was either generally in the right, or else a better pleader, because the judgment was generally in my favor. But my brother was passionate, and had often beaten me, which I took extremely amiss; and, thinking my apprenticeship very tedious, I was continually wishing for some opportunity of shortening it, which at length offered in a manner unexpected.[1]

One of the pieces in our newspaper on some political point, which I have now forgotten, gave offense to the Assembly. He was taken up, censured, and imprisoned for a month, by the speaker's warrant, I suppose because he would not discover his author. I too was taken up and examined before the council; but, though I did not give them any satisfaction, they contented themselves with admonishing me, and dismissed me, considering me, perhaps, as an apprentice

[1] I fancy his harsh and tyrannical treatment of me might be a means of impressing me with that aversion to arbitrary power that has stuck to me through my whole life.

who was bound to keep his master's secrets.

During my brother's confinement, which I resented a good deal, notwithstanding our private differences, I had the management of the paper; and I made bold to give our rulers some rubs in it, which my brother took very kindly, while others began to consider me in an unfavorable light, as a young genius that had a turn for libeling and satire. My brother's discharge was accompanied with an order of the House (a very odd one), that "James Franklin should no longer print the paper called the *New England Courant.*"

There was a consultation held in our printing-house among his friends what he should do in this case. Some proposed to evade the order by changing the name of the paper; but my brother seeing inconveniences in that, it was finally concluded on as a better way to let it be printed for the future under the name of *Benjamin Franklin;* and to avoid the censure of the Assembly, that might fall on him as still printing it by his apprentice, the contrivance was that my old indenture should be returned to me, with a full discharge on the back of it, to be shown on occasion; but to secure to him the benefit of my service, I was to sign new indentures for the remainder of the term, which were to be kept private. A very flimsy scheme it was; however, it was immediately executed, and the paper went on accordingly under my name for several months.

At length, a fresh difference arising between my brother and me, I took upon me to assert my freedom, presuming that he would not venture to produce the new indentures. It was not fair in me to take this advantage, and this I therefore reckon one of the first errata of my life; but the unfairness of it weighed little with me when under the impressions of resentment for the blows his passion too often urged him to bestow upon me,

though he was otherwise not an ill-natured man; perhaps I was too saucy and provoking.

When he found I would leave him, he took care to prevent my getting employment in any other printing-house of the town, by going round and speaking to every master, who accordingly refused to give me work. I then thought of going to New York, as the nearest place where there was a printer; and I was the rather inclined to leave Boston when I reflected that I had already made myself a little obnoxious to the governing party, and, from the arbitrary proceedings of the Assembly in my brother's case, it was likely I might, if I stayed, soon bring myself into scrapes; and farther, that my indiscreet disputations about religion began to make me pointed at with horror by good people as an infidel or atheist. I determined on the point, but my father now siding with my brother, I was sensible that, if I attempted to go openly, means would be used to prevent me. My friend Collins, therefore, undertook to manage a little for me. He agreed with the captain of a New York sloop for my passage, under the notion of my being a young acquaintance of his, that had got a naughty girl with child, whose friends would compel me to marry her, and therefore I could not appear or come away publicly. So I sold some of my books to raise a little money, was taken on board privately, and as we had a fair wind, in three days I found myself in New York, near three hundred miles from home, a boy of about seventeen, without the least recommendation to, or knowledge of, any person in the place, and with very little money in my pocket.

My inclinations for the sea were by this time worn out, or I might now have gratified them. But, having a trade, and supposing myself a pretty good workman, I offered my service to the printer in the place, old Mr. William Bradford, who had been the first printer in Pennsylvania, but removed from thence upon the quarrel of George Keith. He could give me no employment, having little to do and help enough already; but, says he, "My son at Philadelphia has lately lost his principal hand, Aquila Rose, by death; if you go thither, I believe he may employ you." Philadelphia was one hundred miles further; I set out, however, in a boat for Amboy, leaving my chest and things to follow me round by sea.

In crossing the bay, we met with a squall that tore our rotten sails to pieces, prevented our getting into the Kill, and drove us upon Long Island. In our way, a drunken Dutchman, who was a passenger too, fell overboard; when he was sinking, I reached through the water to his shock pate, and drew him up, so that we got him in again. His ducking sobered him a little, and he went to sleep, taking first out of his pocket a book, which he desired I would dry for him. It proved to be my old favorite author, Bunyan's *Pilgrim's Progress*, in Dutch, finely printed on good paper, with copper cuts, a dress better than I had ever seen it wear in its own language. I have since found that it has been translated into most of the languages of Europe, and suppose it has been more generally read than any other book, except perhaps the Bible. Honest John was the first that I know of who mixed narration and dialogue, a method of writing very engaging to the reader, who in the most interesting parts finds himself, as it were, brought into the company and present at the discourse. Defoe in his *Crusoe*, his *Moll Flanders*, *Religious Courtship*, *Family Instructor*, and other pieces, has imitated it with success; and Richardson has done the same in his *Pamela*, etc.

When we drew near the island, we found it was at a place where there could be no landing, there being a great surf on the stony beach. So we dropped anchor, and swung round towards the shore. Some people came down to the water edge and hallowed us, as we did to them; but the wind was so high, and the surf so loud, that we could not hear so as to understand each other. There were canoes on the shore, and we made signs, and hallowed that they should fetch us; but they either did not understand us, or thought it impracticable, so they went away, and night coming on, we had no remedy but to wait till the wind should abate; and in the mean time the boatman and I concluded to sleep if we could; and so crowded into the scuttle, with the Dutchman, who was still wet, and the spray, beating over the head of our boat, leaked through to us, so that we were soon almost as wet as he. In this manner we lay all night, with very little rest; but, the wind abating the next day, we made a shift to reach Amboy before night, having been thirty hours on the water, without victuals or any drink but a bottle of filthy rum, the water we sailed on being salt.

In the evening I found myself very feverish, and went into bed; but having read somewhere that cold water drank plentifully was good for a fever I followed the prescription, sweat plentifully most of the night; my fever left me, and in the morning, crossing the ferry, I proceeded on my journey on foot, having fifty miles to Burlington, where I was told I should find boats that would carry me the rest of the way to Philadelphia.

It rained very hard all the day; I was thoroughly soaked, and by noon a good deal tired; so I stopped at a poor inn, where I stayed all night, beginning now to wish I had never left home. I cut so miserable a figure, too, that I found, by the questions asked me, I was suspected to be some runaway servant, and in danger of being taken up on that suspicion. However, I proceeded the next day, and got in the evening to an inn, within eight or ten miles of Burlington, kept by one Dr. Brown. He entered into conversation with me while I took some refreshment, and, finding I had read a little, became very sociable and friendly. Our acquaintance continued as long as he lived. He had been, I imagine, an itinerant doctor, for there was no town in England or country in Europe of which he could not give a very particular account. He had some letters, and was ingenious, but much of an unbeliever, and wickedly undertook some years after to travesty the Bible in doggerel verse, as Cotton had done Virgil. By this means he set many of the facts in a very ridiculous light, and might have hurt weak minds if his work had been published; but it never was.

At his house I lay that night, and the next morning reached Burlington, but had the mortification to find that the regular boats were gone a little before my coming, and no other expected to go till Tuesday, this being Saturday; wherefore I returned to an old woman in the town, of whom I had bought gingerbread to eat on the water, and asked her advice. She invited me to lodge at her house till a passage by water should offer; and, being tired with my foot traveling, I accepted the invitation. She, understanding I was a printer, would have had me stay at that town and follow my business, being ignorant of the stock necessary to begin with. She was very hospitable, gave me a dinner of ox-cheek with great good will, accepting only of a pot of ale in return; and I thought myself fixed till Tuesday should come. However, walking in the evening by the side of the river, a boat came by, which I found was going towards Philadelphia, with several people in her. They took me in, and, as there was no wind, we rowed all the way; and about midnight, not having yet seen the city, some of the company were confident we must have passed it, and would row no farther; the others knew

not where we were; so we put towards the shore, got into a creek, landed near an old fence, with the rails of which we made a fire, the night being cold (in October), and there we remained till daylight. Then one of the company knew the place to be Cooper's Creek, a little above Philadelphia, which we saw as soon as we got out of the creek, and arrived there about eight or nine o'clock on the Sunday morning, and landed at the Market Street wharf.

I have been the more particular in this description of my journey, and shall be so of my first entry into that city, that you may in your mind compare such unlikely beginnings with the figure I have since made there. I was in my working dress, my best clothes being to come round by sea. I was dirty from my journey; my pockets were stuffed out with shirts and stockings; I knew no soul nor where to look for lodging. I was fatigued with traveling, rowing, and want of rest; I was very hungry; and my whole stock of cash consisted of a Dutch dollar and about a shilling in copper. The latter I gave the people of the boat for my passage, who at first refused it, on account of my rowing; but I insisted on their taking it, a man being sometimes more generous when he has but a little money than when he has plenty, perhaps through fear of being thought to have but little.

Then I walked up the street, gazing about, till near the market-house I met a boy with bread. I had made many a meal on bread, and, inquiring where he got it, I went immediately to the baker's he directed me to, in Second Street, and asked for biscuit, intending such as we had in Boston; but they, it seems, were not made in Philadelphia. Then I asked for a three-penny loaf, and was told they had none such. So, not considering or knowing the difference of money, and the greater cheapness nor the names of his bread, I bade him give me three-penny-worth of any sort. He gave me, accordingly, three great puffy rolls. I was surprised at the quantity, but took it, and, having no room in my pockets, walked off with a roll under each arm, and eating the other. Thus I went up Market Street as far as Fourth Street, passing by the door of Mr. Read, my future wife's father; when she, standing at the door, saw me, and thought I made, as I certainly did, a most awkward, ridiculous appearance. Then I turned and went down Chestnut Street and part of Walnut Street, eating my roll all the way, and, coming round, found myself again at Market Street wharf, near the boat I came in, to which I went for a draught of the river water; and, being filled with one of my rolls, gave the other two to a woman and her child that came down the river in the boat with us, and were waiting to go farther.

Thus refreshed, I walked again up the street, which by this time had many clean-dressed people in it, who were all walking the same way. I joined them, and thereby was led into the great meeting-house of the Quakers near the market. I sat down among them, and, after looking round awhile and hearing nothing said, being very drowsy through labor and want of rest the preceding night, I fell fast asleep, and continued so till the meeting broke up, when one was kind enough to rouse me. This was, therefore, the first house I was in, or slept in, in Philadelphia.

Walking down again toward the river and looking in the faces of people, I met a young Quaker man, whose countenance I liked and accosting him, requested he would tell me where a stranger could get lodging. We were then near the sign of the Three Mariners. "Here," says he, "is one place that entertains strangers, but it is not a reputable house; if thee wilt walk with me, I'll show thee a better." He brought me to the Crooked Billet in Water Street. Here I got a dinner; and while I was eating it several sly questions were asked me,

as it seemed to be suspected from my youth and appearance that I might be some runaway.

After dinner my sleepiness returned, and, being shown to a bed, I lay down without undressing, and slept till six in the evening, was called to supper, went to bed again very early, and slept soundly till next morning. Then I made myself as tidy as I could and went to Andrew Bradford the printer's. I found in the shop the old man his father, whom I had seen at New York, and who, traveling on horseback, had got to Philadelphia before me. He introduced me to his son, who received me civilly, gave me a breakfast, but told me he did not at present want a hand, being lately supplied with one; but there was another printer in town, lately set up, one Keimer, who perhaps might employ me; if not, I should be welcome to lodge at his house, and he would give me a little work to do now and then till fuller business should offer.

The old gentleman said he would go with me to the new printer; and when we found him, "Neighbor," says Bradford, "I have brought to see you a young man of your business; perhaps you may want such a one." He asked me a few questions, put a composing stick in my hand to see how I worked, and then said he would employ me soon, though he had just then nothing for me to do; and, taking old Bradford, whom he had never seen before, to be one of the town's people that had a good will for him, entered into a conversation on his present undertaking and prospects; while Bradford, not discovering that he was the other printer's father, on Keimer's saying he expected soon to get the greatest part of the business into his own hands, drew him on by artful questions, and starting little doubts, to explain all his views, what interest he relied on, and in what manner he intended to proceed. I, who stood by and heard all, saw immediately that one of them was a crafty old sophister, and the other a mere novice. Bradford left me with Keimer, who was greatly surprised when I told him who the old man was.

Keimer's printing-house, I found, consisted of an old shattered press, and one small, worn-out font of English, which he was then using himself, composing an elegy on Aquila Rose, before mentioned, an ingenious young man, of excellent character, much respected in the town, clerk of the Assembly, and a pretty poet. Keimer made verses too, but very indifferently. He could not be said to write them, for his manner was to compose them in the types directly out of his head. So there being no copy, but one pair of cases, and the elegy likely to require all the letter, no one could help him. I endeavored to put his press (which he had not yet used, and of which he understood nothing) into order fit to be worked with; and, promising to come and print off his elegy as soon as he should have got it ready, I returned to Bradford's, who gave me a little job to do for the present, and there I lodged and dieted. A few days after, Keimer sent for me to print off the elegy. And now he had got another pair of cases, and a pamphlet to reprint, on which he set me to work.

These two printers I found poorly qualified for their business. Bradford had not been bred to it, and was very illiterate; and Keimer, though something of a scholar, was a mere compositor, knowing nothing of presswork. He had been one of the French prophets, and could act their enthusiastic agitations. At this time he did not profess any particular religion, but something of all on occasion; was very ignorant of the world, and had, as I afterward found, a good deal of the knave in his composition. He did not like my lodging at Bradford's while I worked with him. He had a house, indeed, but without furniture, so he could not lodge me; but he got me a lodging at Mr. Read's, before mentioned, who was the owner of his house; and, my chest and clothes being come by this time, I made rather a more respectable appearance in the eyes of Miss Read than I had done when she first happened to see me eating my roll in the street.

Mark Twain

✳ 1835-1910

Few writers have used words more simply to better effect than Samuel Langhorne Clemens, who wrote and spoke as Mark Twain, delighting audiences and readers with his laconic and apparently artless colloquialism. The essay on James Fenimore Cooper appeared first in the NORTH AMERICAN REVIEW *in July, 1895, but has been reprinted often and read with delight ever since; an extension of these remarks, found among Clemens's unpublished manuscripts, was printed in the* NEW ENGLAND QUARTERLY *in September, 1946. It is natural that Mark Twain, whose own style was built on the directness and rhythmic patterns of Western speech, should resent the wooden bookishness and pretension of the earlier novelist. Cooper was a sitting duck, and Mark Twain peppered him effectively. What he failed to see was that Cooper sometimes wrote effectively, though in a manner different from Mark Twain's.*

Fenimore Cooper's Literary Offenses

The Pathfinder and The Deerslayer stand at the head of Cooper's novels as artistic creations. There are others of his works which contain parts as perfect as are to be found in these, and scenes even more thrilling. Not one can be compared with either of them as a finished whole.

The defects in both of these tales are comparatively slight. They were pure works of art.

PROF. LOUNSBURY.

The five tales reveal an extraordinary fulness of invention.

. . . One of the very greatest characters in fiction, Natty Bumppo . . .

The craft of the woodsman, the tricks of the trapper, all the delicate art of the forest, were familiar to Cooper from his youth up.

PROF. BRANDER MATTHEWS.

Cooper is the greatest artist in the domain of romantic fiction yet produced by America.

WILKIE COLLINS.

It seems to me that it was far from right for the Professor of English Literature in Yale, the Professor of English Literature in Columbia, and Wilkie Collins to deliver opinions on Cooper's literature without having read some of it. It would have been much more decorous to keep silent and let persons talk who have read Cooper.

Cooper's art has some defects. In one place in *Deerslayer*, and in the restricted space of two-thirds of a page, Cooper has scored 114 offences against literary art out of a possible 115. It breaks the record.

There are nineteen rules governing literary art in the domain of romantic fiction—some say twenty-two. In *Deerslayer* Cooper violated eighteen of them. These eighteen require:

1. That a tale shall accomplish something and arrive somewhere. But the *Deerslayer* tale accomplishes nothing and arrives in the air.

2. They require that the episodes of a tale shall be necessary part of the tale, and shall help to develop it. But as the *Deerslayer* tale is not a tale, and accomplishes nothing and arrives nowhere, the episodes have no rightful place in the work, since there was nothing for them to develop.

3. They require that the personages in a tale shall be alive, except in the case of corpses, and that always the reader shall be able to tell the corpses from the others. But this detail has often been overlooked in the *Deerslayer* tale.

4. They require that the personages in a tale, both dead and alive, shall exhibit a sufficient excuse for being there. But this detail also has been overlooked in the *Deerslayer* tale.

5. They require that when the personages of a tale deal in conversation, the talk shall sound like human talk, and be talk such as human beings would be likely to talk in the given circumstances, and have a discoverable meaning, also a discoverable purpose, and a show of relevancy, and remain in the neighborhood of the subject in hand, and be interesting to the reader, and help out the tale, and stop when the people cannot think of anything more to say. But this requirement has been ignored from the beginning of the *Deerslayer* tale to the end of it.

6. They require that when the author describes the character of a personage in his tale, the conduct and conversation of that personage shall justify said description. But this law gets little or no attention in the *Deerslayer* tale, as Natty Bumppo's case will amply prove.

7. They require that when a personage talks like an illustrated, gilt-edged, tree-calf, hand-tooled, seven-dollar Friendship's Offering in the beginning of a paragraph, he shall not talk like a Negro minstrel in the end of it. But this rule is flung down and danced upon in the *Deerslayer* tale.

8. They require that crass stupidities shall not be played upon the reader as "the craft of the woodsman, the delicate

art of the forest," by either the author or the people in the tale. But this rule is persistently violated in the *Deerslayer* tale.

9. They require that the personages of a tale shall confine themselves to possibilities and let miracles alone; or, if they venture a miracle, the author must so plausibly set it forth as to make it look possible and reasonable. But these rules are not respected in the *Deerslayer* tale.

10. They require that the author shall make the reader feel a deep interest in the personages of his tale and in their fate, and that he shall make the reader love the good people in the tale and hate the bad ones. But the reader of the *Deerslayer* tale dislikes the good people in it, is indifferent to the others, and wishes they would all get drowned together.

11. They require that the characters in a tale shall be so clearly defined that the reader can tell beforehand what each will do in a given emergency. But in the *Deerslayer* tale this rule is vacated.

In addition to these large rules there are some little ones. These require that the author shall

12. *Say* what he is proposing to say, not merely come near it.

13. Use the right word, not its second cousin.

14. Eschew surplusage.

15. Not omit necessary details.

16. Avoid slovenliness of form.

17. Use good grammar.

18. Employ a simple and straightforward style.

Even these seven are coldly and persistently violated in the *Deerslayer* tale.

Cooper's gift in the way of invention was not a rich endowment; but such as it was he liked to work it, he was pleased with the effects, and indeed he did some quite sweet things with it. In his little box of stage properties he kept six or eight cunning devices, tricks, artifices for his savages and woodsmen to deceive and circumvent each other with, and he was never so happy as when he was working these innocent things and seeing them go. A favorite one was to make a moccasined person tread in the tracks of the moccasined enemy, and thus hide his own trail. Cooper wore out barrels and barrels of moccasins in working that trick. Another stage-property that he pulled out of his box pretty frequently was his broken twig. He prized his broken twig above all the rest of his effects, and worked it the hardest. It is a restful chapter in any book of his when somebody doesn't step on a dry twig and alarm all the reds and whites for two hundred yards around. Every time a Cooper person is in peril, and absolute silence is worth four dollars a minute, he is sure to step on a dry twig. There may be a hundred handier things to step on, but that wouldn't satisfy Cooper. Cooper requires him to turn out and find a dry twig; and if he can't do it, go and borrow one. In fact, the Leather Stocking Series ought to have been called the Broken Twig Series.

I am sorry there is not room to put in a few dozen instances of the delicate art of the forest, as practised by Natty Bumppo and some of the other Cooperian experts. Perhaps we may venture two or three samples. Cooper was a sailor—a naval officer; yet he gravely tells us how a vessel, driving towards a lee shore in a gale, is steered for a particular spot by her skipper because he knows of an *undertow* there which will hold her back against the gale and save her. For just pure woodcraft, or sailorcraft, or whatever it is, isn't that neat? For several years Cooper was daily in the society of artillery, and he ought to have noticed that when a cannon-ball strikes the ground it either buries itself or skips a hundred feet or so; skips again a hundred feet or so—and so on, till finally it gets tired and rolls. Now in one place he loses some "females"—as he always calls women—in the edge of a wood near a plain at night in a fog, on purpose to give Bumppo a chance to show off the delicate art of the forest before the reader. These mislaid people are hunting for a fort. They hear a cannon-blast, and a cannon-ball presently comes rolling into the wood and stops at their feet. To the females this suggests nothing. The case is very different with the admirable Bumppo. I wish I may never know peace again if he doesn't strike out promptly and *follow the track* of that cannon-ball across the plain through the dense fog and find the fort. Isn't it a daisy? If Cooper had any real knowledge of Nature's ways of doing things, he had a most delicate art in concealing the fact. For instance: one of his acute Indian experts, Chingachgook (pronounced Chicago, I think), has lost the trail of a person he is tracking through the forest. Apparently that trail is hopelessly lost. Neither you nor I could ever have guessed out the way to find it. It was very different with Chicago. Chicago was not stumped for long. He turned a running stream out of its course and there, in the slush in its old bed, were that person's moccasin tracks. The current did not wash them away, as it would have done in all other like cases —no, even the eternal laws of Nature have to vacate when Cooper wants to put up a delicate job of woodcraft on the reader.

We must be a little wary when Brander Matthews tells us that Cooper's books "reveal an extraordinary fulness of invention." As a rule, I am quite willing to accept Brander Matthews's literary judgments and applaud his lucid and graceful phrasing of them, but that particular statement needs to be taken with a few tons of salt. Bless your heart, Cooper hadn't any more invention than a horse, and I don't mean a high-class horse, either, I mean a clothes-horse. It would be very difficult to find a really clever "situation" in Cooper's books, and still more difficult to find one of any kind which he has failed to render absurd by his handling of it. Look at the episodes of "the caves"; and at the celebrated scuffle between Maqua and those others on the table-land a few days later; and at Hurry Harry's queer water-transit from the castle to the ark; and at Deerslayer's half-hour with his first corpse; and at the quarrel between Hurry Harry and Deerslayer later; and at—but choose for yourself; you can't go amiss.

If Cooper had been an observer his inventive faculty would have worked better; not more interestingly, but more rationally, more plausibly. Cooper's proudest creations in the way of "situations" suffer noticeably from the absence of the observer's protecting gift. Cooper's eye was splendidly inaccurate. Cooper seldom saw anything correctly. He saw nearly all things as through a glass eye, darkly. Of course a man who cannot see the commonest little every-day matters accurately is working at a disadvantage when he is constructing a "situation." In the *Deerslayer* tale Cooper has a stream which is fifty feet wide where it flows out of a lake; it presently narrows to twenty as it meanders along for no given reason, and yet when a stream acts like that it ought to be required to explain itself. Fourteen pages later the width of the brook's outlet from the lake has suddenly shrunk thirty feet, and become "the narrowest part of the stream." This shrinkage is not accounted for. The stream has bends in it, a sure indication that it has alluvial banks and cuts them; yet these bends are only thirty and fifty feet long. If Cooper had been a nice and punctilious observer he would have noticed that the bends were oftener nine hundred feet long than short of it.

Cooper made the exit of that stream fifty feet wide, in the first place, for no particular reason; in the second place, he narrowed it to less than twenty to accommodate some Indians. He bends a "sapling" to the form of an arch over this narrow passage, and conceals six Indians in its foliage. They are "laying" for a settler's scow or ark which is coming up the stream on its way to the lake; it is being hauled against the stiff current by a rope whose stationary end is anchored in the lake; its rate of progress cannot be more than a mile an hour. Cooper describes the ark, but pretty obscurely. In the matter of dimensions "it was little more than a modern canal-boat." Let us guess, then, that it was about one hundred and forty feet long. It was of "greater breadth than common." Let us guess, then, that it was about sixteen feet wide. This leviathan had been prowling down bends which were but a third as long as itself, and scraping between banks where it had only two feet of space to spare on each side. We cannot too much admire this miracle. A low-roofed log dwelling occupies "two-thirds of the ark's length" —a dwelling ninety feet long and sixteen feet wide, let us say, a kind of vestibule train. The dwelling has two rooms, each forty-five feet long and sixteen feet wide, let us guess. One of them is the bedroom of the Hutter girls, Judith and Hetty; the other is the parlor in the daytime, at night it is papa's bed-chamber. The ark is arriving at the stream's exit now, whose width has been reduced to less than twenty feet to accommodate the Indians—say to eighteen. There is a foot to spare on each side of the boat. Did the Indians notice that there was going to be a tight squeeze there? Did they notice that they could make money by climbing down out of that arched sapling and just stepping aboard when the ark scraped by? No, other Indians would have noticed these things but Cooper's Indians never notice anything. Cooper thinks they are marvelous crea-

tures for noticing but he was almost always in error about his Indians. There was seldom a sane one among them.

The ark is one hundred and forty feet long; the dwelling is ninety feet long. The idea of the Indians is to drop softly and secretly from the arched sapling to the dwelling as the ark creeps along under it at the rate of a mile an hour, and butcher the family. It will take the ark a minute and a half to pass under. It will take the ninety-foot dwelling a minute to pass under. Now, then, what did the six Indians do? It would take you thirty years to guess and even then you would have to give up, I believe. Therefore, I will tell you what the Indians did. Their chief, a person of quite extraordinary intellect for a Cooper Indian, warily watched the canal-boat as it squeezed along under him and when he had got his calculations fined down to exactly the right shade, as he judged, he let go and dropped. And *missed the house!* That is actually what he did. He missed the house and landed in the stern of the scow. It was not much of a fall, yet it knocked him silly. He lay there unconscious. If the house had been ninety-seven feet long he would have made the trip. The fault was Cooper's, not his. The error lay in the construction of the house. Cooper was no architect.

There still remained in the roost five Indians. The boat has passed under and is now out of their reach. Let me explain what the five did—you would not be able to reason it out for yourself. No. 1 jumped for the boat but fell in the water astern of it. Then No. 2 jumped for the boat but fell in the water still farther astern of it. Then No. 3 jumped for the boat and fell a good way astern of it. Then No. 4 jumped for the boat and fell in the water *away* astern. Then even No. 5 made a jump for the boat— for he was a Cooper Indian. In the matter of intellect, the difference between a Cooper Indian and the Indian that stands in front of the cigar-shop is not spacious. The scow episode is really a sublime burst of invention but it does not thrill, because the inaccuracy of the details throws a sort of air of fictitiousness and general improbability over it. This comes of Cooper's inadequacy as an observer.

The reader will find some examples of Cooper's high talent for inaccurate observation in the account of the shooting-match in *The Pathfinder.*

A common wrought nail was driven lightly into the target, its head having been first touched with paint.

The color of the paint is not stated— an important omission, but Cooper deals freely in important omissions. No, after all, it was not an important omission, for this nail-head is *a hundred yards from* the marksmen and could not be seen by them at that distance, no matter what its color might be. How far can the best eyes see a common house-fly? A hundred yards? It is quite impossible. Very well, eyes that cannot see a house-fly that is a hundred yards away cannot see an ordinary nailhead at that distance, for the size of the two objects is the same. It takes a keen eye to see a fly or a nail-head at fifty yards—one hundred and fifty feet. Can the reader do it?

The nail was lightly driven, its head painted, and game called. Then the Cooper miracles began. The bullet of the first marksman chipped an edge of the nail-head; the next man's bullet drove the nail a little way into the target —and removed all the paint. Haven't the miracles gone far enough now? Not to suit Cooper; for the purpose of this whole scheme is to show off his prodigy, Deerslayer-Hawkeye-Long-Rifle-Leather-Stocking-Pathfinder-Bumppo before the ladies.

"Be all ready to clench it, boys!" cried out Pathfinder, stepping into his friend's tracks the instant they were vacant. "Never mind a new nail; I can see that, though the paint is gone, and what I can see I can hit at a hundred yards, though it were only a mosquito's eye. Be ready to clench!"

The rifle cracked, the bullet sped its way, and the head of the nail was buried in the wood, covered by the piece of flattened lead.

There, you see, is a man who could hunt flies with a rifle, and command a ducal salary in a Wild West show to-day if we had him back with us.

The recorded feat is certainly surprising just as it stands; but it is not surprising enough for Cooper. Cooper adds a touch. He has made Pathfinder do this miracle with another man's rifle; and not only that, but Pathfinder did not have even the advantage of loading it himself. He had everything against him, and yet he made that impossible shot; and not only made it, but did it with absolute confidence, saying, "Be ready to clench." Now a person like that would have undertaken that same feat with a brickbat, and with Cooper to help he would have achieved it, too.

Pathfinder showed off handsomely that day before the ladies. His very first feat was a thing which no Wild West show can touch. He was standing with the group of marksmen, observing—a hundred yards from the target, mind; one Jasper raised his rifle and drove the centre of the bull's-eye. Then the Quartermaster fired. The target exhibited no result this time. There was a laugh. "It's a dead miss," said Major Lundie. Pathfinder waited an impressive moment or two; then said, in that calm, indifferent, know-it-all way of his, "No, Major, he has covered Jasper's bullet, as will be seen if any one will take the trouble to examine the target."

Wasn't it remarkable! How *could* he see that little pellet fly through the air and enter that distant bullet-hole? Yet that is what he did; for nothing is impossible to a Cooper person. Did any of those people have any deep-seated doubts about this thing? No; for that would imply sanity, and these were all Cooper people.

The respect for Pathfinder's skill and for his *quickness and accuracy of sight* (the italics are mine) was so profound and general, that the instant he made this declaration the spectators began to distrust their own opinions, and a dozen rushed to the target in order to ascertain the fact. There, sure enough, it was found that the Quartermaster's bullet had gone through the hole made by Jasper's, and that, too, so accurately as to require a minute examination to be certain of the circumstance, which, however, was soon clearly established by discovering one bullet over the other in the stump against which the target was placed.

They made a "minute" examination; but never mind, how could they know that there were two bullets in that hole without digging the latest one out? for neither probe nor eyesight could prove the presence of any more than one bullet. Did they dig? No; as we shall see. It is the Pathfinder's turn now; he steps out before the ladies, takes aim, and fires.

But, alas! here is a disappointment; an incredible, an unimaginable disappointment—for the target's aspect is unchanged; there is nothing there but that same old bullet-hole!

"If one dared to hint at such a thing," cried Major Duncan, "I should say that the Pathfinder has also missed the target!"

As nobody had missed it yet, the "also" was not necessary; but never mind about that, for the Pathfinder is going to speak.

"No, no, Major," said he, confidently, "that *would* be a risky declaration. I didn't load the piece, and can't say what was in it; but if it was lead, you will find the bullet driving down those of the Quartermaster and Jasper, else is not my name Pathfinder."

A shout from the target announced the truth of this assertion.

Is the miracle sufficient as it stands? Not for Cooper. The Pathfinder speaks again, as he "now slowly advances toward the stage occupied by the females":

"That's not all, boys, that's not all; if you find the target touched at all, I'll own to a miss. The Quartermaster cut the wood, but you'll find no wood cut by that last messenger."

The miracle is at last complete. He knew—doubtless *saw*—at the distance of a hundred yards—that his bullet had passed into the hole *without fraying the edges.* There were now three bullets in that one hole, three bullets embedded processionally in the body of the stump back of the target. Everybody knew this, somehow or other, and yet nobody had dug any of them out to make sure. Cooper is not a close observer but he is interesting. He is certainly always that, no matter what happens. And he is more interesting when he is not noticing what he is about than when he is. This is a considerable merit.

The conversations in the Cooper books have a curious sound in our modern ears. To believe that such talk really ever came out of people's mouths would be to believe that there was a time when time was of no value to a person who thought he had something to say, when it was the custom to spread a two-minute remark out to ten, when a man's mouth was a rolling-mill and busied itself all day long in turning four-foot pigs of thought into thirty-foot bars of conversational railroad iron by attenuation, when subjects were seldom faithfully stuck to but the talk wandered all around and arrived nowhere, when conversations consisted mainly of irrelevancies with here and there a relevancy, a relevancy with an embarrassed look, as not being able to explain how it got there.

Cooper was certainly not a master in the construction of dialogue. Inaccurate observation defeated him here as it defeated him in so many other enterprises of his. He even failed to notice that the man who talks corrupt English six days in the week must and will talk it on the seventh, and can't help himself. In the *Deerslayer* story he lets Deerslayer talk the showiest kind of book-talk sometimes, and at other times the basest of base dialects. For instance, when some one asks him if he has a sweetheart, and if so where she abides, this is his majestic answer:

"She's in the forest—hanging from the boughs of the trees, in a soft rain—in the dew on the open grass—the clouds that float about in the blue heavens—the birds that sing in the woods—the sweet springs where I slake my thirst—and in all the other glorious gifts that come from God's Providence!"

And he preceded that, a little before, with this:

"It consarns me as all things that touches a fri'nd consarns a fri'nd."

And this is another of his remarks:

"If I was Injin born, now, I might tell of this, or carry in the scalp and boast of the expl'ite afore the whole tribe; or if my inimy had only been a bear"—and so on.

We cannot imagine such a thing as a veteran Scotch Commander-in-Chief comporting himself in the field like a windy melodramatic actor, but Cooper could. On one occasion Alice and Cora were being chased by the French through a fog in the neighborhood of their father's fort:

"*Point de quartier aux coquins!*" cried an eager pursuer, who seemed to direct the operations of the enemy.

"Stand firm and be ready, my gallant 60ths!" suddenly exclaimed a voice above them; "wait to see the enemy; fire low, and sweep the glacis."

"Father! father!" exclaimed a piercing cry from out the mist; "it is I! Alice! thy own Elsie! spare, O! save your daughters!"

"Hold!" shouted the former speaker, in the awful tones of parental agony, the sound reaching even to the woods, and rolling back in solemn echo. "'Tis she! God has restored me my children! Throw open the sally-port; to the field, 60ths, to the field! pull not a trigger, lest ye kill my lambs! Drive off these dogs of France with your steel!"

Cooper's word-sense was singularly dull. When a person has a poor ear for music he will flat and sharp right along without knowing it. He keeps near the tune, but it is *not* the tune. When a person has a poor ear for words, the result is a literary flatting and sharping; you perceive what he is intending to say, but you also perceive that he doesn't *say* it. This is Cooper. He was not a word-musician. His ear was satisfied with the *approximate* word. I will furnish some circumstantial evidence in support of this charge. My instances are gathered from half a dozen pages of the tale called *Deerslayer*. He uses "verbal" for "oral"; "precision" for "facility"; "phenomena" for "marvels"; "necessary" for "predetermined"; "unsophisticated" for "primitive"; "preparation" for "expectancy"; "rebuked" for "subdued"; "dependent on" for "resulting from"; "fact" for "condition"; "fact" for "conjecture"; "precaution" for "caution"; "explain" for "determine"; "mortified" for "disappointed"; "meretricious" for "factitious"; "materially" for "considerably"; "decreasing" for "deepening"; "increasing" for "disappearing"; "embedded" for "inclosed"; "treacherous" for "hostile"; "stood" for "stooped"; "softened" for "replaced"; "rejoined" for "remarked"; "situation" for "condition"; "different" for "differing"; "insensible" for "unsentient"; "brevity" for "celerity"; "distrusted" for "suspicious"; "mental imbecility" for "imbecility"; "eyes" for "sight"; "counteracting" for "opposing"; "funeral obsequies" for "obsequies."

There have been some daring people in the world who claimed that Cooper could write English, but they are all dead now—all dead but Lounsbury. I don't remember that Lounsbury makes the claim in so many words, still he makes it, for he says that *Deerslayer* is a "pure work of art." Pure, in that connection, means faultless—faultless in all details—and language is a detail. If Mr. Lounsbury had only compared Cooper's English with the English which he writes himself—but it is plain that he didn't; and so it is likely that he imagines until this day that Cooper's is as clean and compact as his own. Now I feel sure, deep down in my heart, that Cooper wrote about the poorest English that exists in our language, and that the English of *Deerslayer* is the very worst that even Cooper ever wrote.

I may be mistaken, but it does seem to me that *Deerslayer* is not a work of art in any sense; it does seem to me that it is destitute of every detail that goes to the making of a work of art; in truth, it seems to me that *Deerslayer* is just simply a literary *delirium tremens*.

A work of art? It has no invention; it has no order, system, sequence, or result; it has no life-likeness, no thrill, no stir, no seeming of reality; its characters are confusedly drawn, and by their acts and words they prove that they are not the sort of people the author claims that they are; its humor is pathetic; its pathos is funny; its conversations are—oh! indescribable; its love-scenes odious; its English a crime against the language.

Counting these out, what is left is Art. I think we must all admit that.

Walt Whitman

✳ 1819-1892

Not many among his literary fellows understood or sympathized with Edgar Allan Poe as completely and generously as Walt Whitman. His own poetry was very different, and so was his attitude toward the responsibilities of the poet, but he recognized Poe's thwarted genius at the same time that he knew his weaknesses: a quarter of a century after the older poet's death, Whitman was the only one of the principal writers of the nineteenth century who attended, though it seems almost inadvertantly, the memorial services in Baltimore at which in 1875 Poe's tombstone was unveiled. The dream of a vessel adrift in a storm which he recounted then is often remembered among the most perceptive brief characterizations of one poet by another.

Edgar Poe's Significance

In diagnosing this disease called humanity—to assume for the nonce what seems a chief mood of the personality and writings of my subject—I have thought that poets, somewhere or other on the list, present the most mark'd indications. Comprehending artists in a mass, musicians, painters, actors, and so on, and considering each and all of them as radiations or flanges of that furious whirling wheel, poetry, the centre and axis of the whole, where else indeed may we so well investigate the causes, growths, tally-marks of the time—the age's matter and malady?

By common consent there is nothing better for man or woman than a perfect and noble life, morally without flaw, happily balanced in activity, physically sound and pure, giving its due proportion, and no more, to the sympathetic, the human emotional element—a life, in all these, unhasting, unresting, untiring to the end. And yet there is another shape of personality dearer far to the artist-sense, (which likes the play of strongest lights and shades) where the perfect character, the good, the heroic, although never attain'd, is never lost sight of, but through failures, sorrows, temporary downfalls, is return'd to again and again, and while often violated, is passionately adhered to as long as mind, muscles, voice, obey the power we call volition. This sort of personality we see more or less in Burns, Byron, Schiller, and George Sand. But we do not see it in Edgar Poe. (All this is the result of reading at intervals the last three days a new volume of his poems—I took it on my rambles down by the pond, and by degrees read it all through there.) While to the character first outlined the service Poe renders is certainly that entire contrast and contradiction which is next best to fully exemplifying it.

Almost without the first sign of moral principle, or of the concrete or its heroisms, or the simpler affections of the heart, Poe's verses illustrate an intense faculty for technical and abstract beauty, with the rhyming art to excess, an incorrigible propensity toward nocturnal themes, a demoniac undertone behind every page—and, by final judgment, probably belong among the electric lights of imaginative literature, brilliant and dazzling, but with no heat. There is an indescribable magnetism about the poet's life and reminiscences, as well as the poems. To one who could work out their subtle retracing and restrospect, the latter would make a close tally no doubt between the author's birth and antecedents, his childhood and youth, his physique, his so-call'd education, his studies and associates, the literary and social Baltimore, Richmond, Philadelphia and New York, of those times—not only the places and circumstances in themselves, but often, very often, in a strange spurning of, and reaction from them all.

The following from a report in the Washington *Star* of November 16, 1875, may afford those who care for it something further of my point of view toward this interesting figure and influence of our era. There occurr'd about that date in Baltimore a public reburial of Poe's remains, and dedication of a monument over the grave:

Being in Washington on a visit at the time, "the old gray" went over to Baltimore, and though ill from paralysis, consented to hobble up and silently take a seat on the platform, but refused to make any speech, saying, "I have felt a strong impulse to come over and be here today myself in memory of Poe, which I have obey'd, but not the slightest impulse to make a speech, which, my dear friends, must also be obeyed." In an informal circle, however, in conversation after the ceremonies, Whitman said: "For a long while, and until lately, I had a distaste for Poe's writings. I wanted and still want for poetry, the clear sun shining, and fresh air blowing—the strength and power of health, not of delerium, even amid the stormiest passions—with always the background of the eternal moralities. Non-complying with these requirements, Poe's genius has yet conquer'd a special recognition for itself, and I too have come to fully admit it, and appreciate it and him.

"In a dream I once had, I saw a vessel on the sea, at midnight, in a storm. It was no great full rigg'd ship, nor majestic steamer, steering firmly through the gale, but seem'd one of those superb little schooner yachts I had often seen lying anchor'd, rocking so jauntily, in the waters around New York, or up Long Island sound—now flying uncontroll'd with torn sails and broken spars through the wild sleet and winds and waves of the night. On the deck was a slender, slight, beautiful figure, a dim man, apparently enjoying all the terror, the murk, and the dislocation of which he was the center and the victim. That figure of my lurid dream might stand for Edgar Poe, his spirit, his fortunes, and his poems—themselves all lurid dreams."

Much more may be said, but I most desired to exploit the idea put at the beginning. By its popular poets the calibers of an age, the weak spots of its embankments, its subcurrents (often more significant than the biggest surface ones), are unerringly indicated. The lush and the weird that have taken such extraordinary possession of nineteenth century verse-lovers—what mean they? The inevitable tendency of poetic culture to morbidity, abnormal beauty—the sickliness of all technical thought or refinement in itself—the abnegation of the perennial and democratic concretes at first hand, the body, the earth and sea, sex and the like—and the substitution of something for them at second or third hand—what bearings have they on current pathological study?

Herman Melville
✳ 1819-1891

This essay, which appeared in the New York LITERARY WORLD *in August, 1850, gave first public notice of the discovery of Nathaniel Hawthorne by Herman Melville. The subsequent friendship between the two has become one of the most pleasantly remembered incidents of our literary history, and a weighing of the influence of one upon the other a favorite topic for literary essayists. Melville was later to amend his opinion that the* MOSSES FROM AN OLD MANSE *was superlatively among Hawthorne's best, and after very few years the two men drifted apart, but Melville's early recognition of the blackness as well as the light in Hawthorne places him at the head of a long procession of critics who have discovered similar ambiguities in Melville's writing as well.*

Hawthorne and His Mosses

. . . Stretched on that new-mown clover, the hillside breeze blowing over me through the wide barn door, and soothed by the hum of the bees in the meadows around, how magnificently stole over me this Mossy Man! and how amply, how bountifully, did he redeem that delicious promise to his guests in the Old Manse, of whom it is written: "Others could give them pleasure, or amusement, or instruction—these could be picked up anywhere; but it was for me to give them rest—rest, in a life of trouble! What better could be done for those weary and world-worn spirits? . . . what better could be done for anybody who came within our magic circle than to throw the spell of a tranquil spirit over him?" So all that day, half buried in new clover, I watched this Hawthorne's "Assyrian dawn, and Paphian sunset and moonrise from the summit of our eastern hill."

The soft ravishments of the man spun me round about in a web of dreams, and when the book was closed, when the spell was over, this wizard "dismissed me with but misty reminiscences, as if I had been dreaming of him."

What a wild moonlight of contemplative humor bathes that Old Manse!— the rich and rare distilment of a spicy and slowly-oozing heart. No rollicking rudeness, no gross fun fed on fat dinners, and bred in the lees of wine,—but a humor so spiritually gentle, so high, so deep, and yet so richly relishable, that it were hardly inappropriate in an angel. It is the very religion of mirth; for nothing so human but it may be advanced to that. The orchard of the Old Manse seems the visible type of the fine mind that has described it—those twisted and contorted old trees, "they stretch out their crooked branches, and take such hold of the imagination that we remember them as humorists and odd-fellows." And then, as surrounded by these grotesque forms, and hushed in the noonday repose of this Hawthorne's spell, how aptly might the still fall of his ruddy thoughts into your soul be symbolized by: "In the stillest afternoon, if I listened, the thump of a great apple was audible, falling without a breath of wind, from the mere necessity of perfect ripeness." For no less ripe than ruddy are the apples of the thoughts and fancies in this sweet Man of Mosses. . . .

But he has still other apples, not quite so ruddy, though full as ripe: apples that have been left to wither on the tree, after the pleasant autumn gathering is past. . . . And we see that suffering, sometime or other, in some shape or other— this only can enable any man to depict it in others. All over him, Hawthorne's melancholy rests like an Indian summer, which, though bathing a whole country in one softness, still reveals the distinctive hue of every towering hill and far-winding vale.

But it is the least part of genius that attracts admiration. Where Hawthorne is known, he seems to be deemed a pleasant writer, with a pleasant style,—a sequestered, harmless man, from whom any deep and weighty thing would hardly be anticipated—a man who means no meanings. But there is no man in whom humor and love, like mountain peaks, soar to such a rapt height as to receive the irradiations of the upper skies; there is no man in whom humor and love are developed in that high form called genius; no such man can exist without also possessing, as the indispensable complement of these, a great, deep intellect, which drops down into the universe like a plummet. Or, love and humor are only the eyes through which such an intellect views this world. The great beauty in such a mind is but the product of its strength. . . .

For spite of all the Indian-summer sunlight on the hither side of Hawthorne's soul, the other side—like the dark half of the physical sphere—is shrouded in a blackness ten times black. But this darkness but gives more effect to the ever-moving dawn, that forever advances through it, and circumnavigates his world. Whether Hawthorne has simply availed himself of this mystical blackness as a means to the wondrous effects he makes it to produce in his lights and shades; or whether there really lurks in him, perhaps unknown to himself, a touch of Puritanic gloom,— this I cannot altogether tell. Certain it is, however, that this great power of blackness in him derives its force from its appeals to that Calvinistic sense of Innate Depravity and Original Sin, from whose visitations, in some shape or other, no deeply thinking mind is always and wholly free. For, in certain moods, no man can weigh this world without throwing in something, something like Original Sin, to strike the uneven balance. At all events, perhaps no writer has ever wielded this terrific thought with greater terror than this same harmless Hawthorne. Still more: this black conceit pervades him through and through. You may be witched by his sunlight—transported by the bright gildings in the skies he builds over you; but there is the blackness of darkness beyond; and even his bright gildings but fringe and play upon the edges of thunder-clouds. In one word, the world is mistaken in this Nathaniel Hawthorne. He himself must often have smiled at its absurd misconception of him. He is immeasurably deeper than the plummet of the mere critic. For it is not the brain that can test such a man; it is only the heart. You cannot come to know greatness by inspecting it; there is no glimpse to be caught of it, except by intuition; you need not ring it, you but touch it, and you find it is gold.

Now it is that blackness in Hawthorne, of which I have spoken, that so fixes and fascinates me. It may be, nevertheless, that it is too largely developed in him. Perhaps he does not give us a ray of light for every shade of his dark.

But however this may be, this blackness it is that furnishes the infinite obscure of his background—that background against which Shakespeare plays his grandest conceits, the things that have made for Shakespeare his loftiest but most circumscribed renown, as the profoundest of thinkers. For by philosophers Shakespeare is not adored, as the great man of tragedy and comedy. . . . But it is those deep, far-away things in him; those occasional flashings-forth of the intuitive Truth in him; those short, quick probings at the very axis of reality— these are the things that make Shakespeare, Shakespeare. Through the mouths of the dark characters of Hamlet, Timon, Lear, and Iago, he craftily says, or sometimes insinuates the things which we feel so terrifically true that it were well all but madness for any good man, in his proper character, to utter, or even hint of them. Tormented into desperation, Lear, the frantic king, tears off his mask, and speaks the same madness of vital truth. But, as I before said, it is the least part of genius that attracts admiration. And so, much of the blind, unbridled admiration that has been heaped upon Shakespeare has been lavished upon the least part of him. And few of his endless commentators and critics seem to have remembered, or even perceived, that the immediate products of a great mind are not so great as that undeveloped and sometimes undevelopable yet dimly discernible greatness to which these immediate products are but the infallible indices. In Shakespeare's tomb lied infinitely more than Shakespeare ever wrote. And if I magnify Shakespeare, it is not so much for what he did do as for what he did not do, or refrained from doing. For in this world of lies, Truth is forced to fly like a sacred white doe in the woodlands; and only by cunning glimpses will she reveal herself, as in Shakespeare and other masters of the great Art of Telling the Truth, even though it be covertly and by snatches.

But if this view of the all-popular Shakespeare be seldom taken by his readers, and if very few who extol him have ever read him deeply, or, perhaps, only have seen him on the tricky stage (which alone made, and is still making him, his mere mob renown)—if few men have time, or patience, or palate, for the spiritual truth as it is in that great genius —it is then no matter of surprise that in a contemporaneous age Nathaniel Hawthorne is a man as yet utterly mistaken among men. Here and there, in some quiet armchair in the noisy town, or some deep nook among the noiseless mountains, he may be appreciated for something of what he is. But unlike Shakespeare, who was forced to the contrary course by circumstances, Hawthorne (either from simple disinclination, or else from inaptitude) refrains from all popularizing noise and show of broad farce and blood-besmeared tragedy; content with the still, rich utterance of a great intellect in repose, and which sends few thoughts into circulation, except they be arterialized at his large warm lungs, and expanded by his honest heart. . . .

Gainsay it who will, as I now write, I am Posterity speaking by proxy—and after-times will make it more than good, when I declare that the American who up to the present day has evinced, in literature, the largest brain with the largest heart, that man is Nathaniel Hawthorne.

John Jay Chapman
✳ 1862-1933

John Jay Chapman was at the beginning of his career as literary critic and courageous political reformer when he published his estimate of Emerson in the AT-

LANTIC MONTHLY *in 1897, and included it a year later as the title essay of* EMERSON AND OTHER ESSAYS. *Much of Chapman's subsequent life was dedicated to liberal causes and to what seemed to him the lost cause of renewing passionate involvement among his countrymen: "The American," was his complaint, "is incapable of taking a real interest in anything." In William Lloyd Garrison, on whom he published what is perhaps his best book in 1913, and in Emerson, Chapman found two men who, whatever their shortcomings otherwise, did care, and who called on other men to apply themselves toward becoming or doing the best their capacities would allow —and not in superficial ways, like making lots of money. All around him Chapman saw stupid men becoming wealthy, while intellect and capacity for passion withered. If he read Emerson partially, he did recognize as well as any commentator except Thomas Carlyle that in speaking of the sufficiency of the individual Emerson was not speaking in ordinary terms of democracy.*

Emerson

"Leave this hypocritical prating about the masses. Masses are rude, lame, unmade, pernicious in their demands and influence, and need not to be flattered, but to be schooled. I wish not to concede anything to them, but to tame, drill, divide, and break them up, and draw individuals out of them. The worst of charity is that the lives you are asked to preserve are not worth preserving. Masses! The calamity is the masses. I do not wish any mass at all, but honest men only, lovely, sweet, accomplished women only, and no shovel-handed, narrow-brained, gin-drinking million stockingers or lazzoroni at all. If government knew how, I should like to see it check, not multiply the population. When it

reaches its true law of action, every man that is born will be hailed as essential. Away with this hurrah of masses, and let us have the considerate vote of single men spoken on their honor and their conscience."

This extract from *The Conduct of Life* gives fairly enough the leading thought of Emerson's life. The unending warfare between the individual and society shows us in each generation a poet or two, a dramatist or a musician who exalts and deifies the individual, and leads us back again to the only object which is really worthy of enthusiasm or which can permanently excite it,—the character of a man. It is surprising to find this identity of content in all great deliverances. The only thing we really admire is personal liberty. Those who fought for it and those who enjoyed it are our heroes.

But the hero may enslave his race by bringing in a system of tyranny; the battle-cry of freedom may become a dogma which crushes the soul; one good custom may corrupt the world. And so the inspiration of one age becomes the damnation of the next. This crystallizing of life into death has occurred so often that it may almost be regarded as one of the laws of progress.

Emerson represents a protest against the tyranny of democracy. He is the most recent example of elemental hero-worship. His opinions are absolutely unqualified except by his temperament. He expresses a form of belief in the importance of the individual which is independent of any personal relations he has with the world. It is as if a man had been withdrawn from the earth and dedicated to condensing and embodying this eternal idea—the value of the individual soul—so vividly, so vitally, that his words could not die, yet in such illusive and abstract forms that by no chance and by no power could his creed be used for purposes of tyranny. Dogma cannot be extracted from it. Schools cannot be built on it. It either lives as the spirit lives, or else it evaporates and leaves nothing. Emerson was so afraid of the letter that killeth that he would hardly trust his words to print. He was assured there was no such thing as literal truth, but only literal falsehood. He therefore resorted to metaphors which could by no chance be taken literally. And he has probably succeeded in leaving a body of work which cannot be made to operate to any other end than that for which he designed it. If this be true, he has accomplished the inconceivable feat of eluding misconception. If it be true, he stands alone in the history of teachers; he has circumvented fate, he has left an unmixed blessing behind him. . . .

His works are all one single attack on the vice of the age, moral cowardice. He assails it not by railings and scorn, but by positive and stimulating suggestion. The imagination of the reader is touched by every device which can awake the admiration for heroism, the consciousness of moral courage. Wit, quotation, anecdote, eloquence, exhortation, rhetoric, sarcasm, and very rarely denunciation, are launched at the reader, till he feels little lambent flames beginning to kindle in him. He is perhaps unable to see the exact logical connection between two paragraphs of an essay, yet he feels they are germane. He takes up Emerson tired and apathetic, but presently he feels himself growing heady and truculent, strengthened in his most inward vitality, surprised to find himself again master in his own house.

The difference between Emerson and the other moralists is that all these stimulating pictures and suggestions are not given by him in illustration of a general proposition. They have never been through the mill of generalization in his own mind. He himself could not have told you their logical bearing on one

another. They have all the vividness of disconnected fragments of life, and yet they all throw light on one another, like the facets of a jewel. But whatever cause it was that led him to adopt his method of writing, it is certain that he succeeded in delivering himself of his thought with an initial velocity and carrying power such as few men ever attained. He has the force at his command of the thrower of the discus.

His style is American, and beats with the pulse of the climate. He is the only writer we have had who writes as he speaks, who makes no literary parade, has no pretensions of any sort. He is the only writer we have had who has wholly subdued his vehicle to his temperament. It is impossible to name his style without naming his character: they are one thing.

Both in language and in elocution Emerson was a practised and consummate artist, who knew how both to command his effects and to conceal his means. The casual, practical, disarming directness with which he writes puts any honest man at his mercy. What difference does it make whether a man who can talk like this is following an argument or not? You cannot always see Emerson clearly; he is hidden by a high wall; but you always know exactly on what spot he is standing. You judge it by the flight of the objects he throws over the wall,—a bootjack, an apple, a crown, a razor, a volume of verse. With one or other of these missiles, all delivered with a very tolerable aim, he is pretty sure to hit you. These catchwords stick in the mind. People are not in general influenced by long books or discourses, but by odd fragments of observation which they overhear, sentences or head-lines which they read while turning over a book at random or while waiting for dinner to be announced. These are the oracles and orphic words that get lodged in the mind and bend a man's most stubborn will. Emerson called them the Police of the Universe. His works are a treasury of such things. They sparkle in the mine, or you may carry them off in your pocket. They get driven into your mind like nails, and on them catch and hang your own experiences, till what was once his thought has become your character. . . .

Much of what Emerson wrote about the United States in 1850 is true of the United States to-day. It would be hard to find a civilized people who are more timid, more cowed in spirit, more illiberal, than we. It is easy to-day for the educated man who has read Bryce and Tocqueville to account for the mediocrity of American literature. The merit of Emerson was that he felt the atmospheric pressure without knowing its reason. He felt he was a cabined, cribbed, confined creature, although every man about him was celebrating Liberty and Democracy, and every day was Fourth of July. He taxes language to its limits in order to express his revolt. He says that no man should write except what he has discovered in the process of satisfying his own curiosity, and that every man will write well in proportion as he has contempt for the public.

Emerson seems really to have believed that if any man would only resolutely be himself, he would turn out to be as great as Shakespeare. He will not have it that anything of value can be monopolized. His review of the world, whether under the title of Manners, Self-Reliance, Fate, Experience, or what-not, leads him to the same thought. His conclusion is always the finding of eloquence, courage, art, intellect, in the breast of the humblest reader. He knows that we are full of genius and surrounded by genius, and that we have only to throw something off, not to acquire any new thing, in order to be bards, prophets, Napoleons, and Goethes. This belief is the secret of his stimulating power. It is this which

gives his writings a radiance like that which shone from his personality.

The deep truth shadowed forth by Emerson when he said that "all the American geniuses lacked nerve and dagger" was illustrated by our best scholar. Lowell had the soul of the Yankee, but in his habits of writing he continued English tradition. His literary essays are full of charm. The Commemoration Ode is the high-water mark of the attempt to do the impossible. It is a fine thing, but it is imitative and secondary. It has paid the inheritance tax. Twice, however, at a crisis of pressure, Lowell assumed his real self under the guise of a pseudonym; and with his own hand he rescued a language, a type, a whole era of civilization from oblivion. Here gleams the dagger and here is Lowell revealed. His limitations as a poet, his too much wit, his too much morality, his mixture of shrewdness and religion, are seen to be the very elements of power. The novelty of the Biglow Papers is as wonderful as their world-old naturalness. They take rank with greatness, and they were the strongest political tracts of their time. They imitate nothing; they are real.

Emerson himself was the only man of his times who consistently and utterly expressed himself, never measuring himself for a moment with the ideals of others, never troubling himself for a moment with what literature was or how literature should be created. The other men of his epoch, and among whom he lived, believed that literature was a very desirable article, a thing you could create if you were only smart enough. But Emerson had no literary ambition. He cared nothing for belles-lettres. The consequence is that he stands above his age like a colossus. While he lived his figure could be seen from Europe towering like Atlas over the culture of the United States.

Great men are not always like wax

which their age imprints. They are often the mere negation and opposite of their age. They give it the lie. They become by revolt the very essence of all the age is not, and that part of the spirit which is suppressed in ten thousand breasts gets lodged, isolated, and breaks into utterance in one. Through Emerson spoke the fractional spirits of a multitude. He had not time, he had not energy left over to understand himself; he was a mouthpiece.

If a soul be taken and crushed by democracy till it utter a cry, that cry will be Emerson. The region of thought he lived in, the figures of speech he uses, are of an intellectual plane so high that the circumstances which produced them may be forgotten; they are indifferent. The Constitution, Slavery, the War itself, are seen as mere circumstances. They did not confuse him while he lived; they are not necessary to support his work now that it is finished. Hence comes it that Emerson is one of the world's voices. He was heard afar off. His foreign influence might deserve a chapter by itself. Conservatism is not confined to this country. It is the very basis of all government. The bolts Emerson forged, his thought, his wit, his perception, are not provincial. They were found to carry inspiration to England and Germany. Many of the important men of the last half century owe him a debt. It is not yet possible to give any account of his influence abroad, because the memoirs which will show it are only beginning to be published. We shall have them in due time; for Emerson was an outcome of the world's progress. His appearance marks the turning-point in the history of that enthusiasm for pure democracy which has tinged the political thought of the world for the past one hundred and fifty years. The youths of England and Germany may have been surprised at hearing from America a piercing voice of protest against the very

influences which were crushing them at home. They could not realize that the chief difference between Europe and America is a difference in the rate of speed with which revolutions in thought are worked out.

While the radicals of Europe were revolting in 1848 against the abuses of a tyranny whose roots were in feudalism, Emerson, the great radical of America, the arch-radical of the world, was revolting against the evils whose roots were in universal suffrage. By showing the identity in essence of all tyranny, and by bringing back the attention of political thinkers to its starting-point, the value of human character, he has advanced the political thought of the world by one step. He has pointed out for us in this country to what end our efforts must be bent.

James Russell Lowell
✳ 1819-1891

It is probable that James Russell Lowell understood as little of the essence of Thoreau as did most men who had only heard about the strange little man from Concord who lived alone and liked it, but he was able to run his pen with such verve over the surface qualities of the man that his essay, which appeared in the ATLANTIC MONTHLY *in 1865 as a review of Emerson's edition of Thoreau's* LETTERS TO VARIOUS PERSONS, *has remained a favorite even among people who find it neither fair nor greatly informative of anything except Lowell's genteel pose. Lowell did and said almost everything with easy grace, but after brief involvement with the abolition movement during his young manhood, seems seldom to have cared enough about anything to be*

*more than casually provocative. The fact
that there is almost nothing wrong with
his writing except that it does not remain alive is perhaps the severest indictment against him.*

Thoreau

. . . Among the pistillate plants kindled
to fruitage by the Emersonian pollen,
Thoreau is thus far the most remarkable;
and it is something eminently fitting that
his posthumous works should be offered
us by Emerson, for they are strawberries
from his own garden. A singular mixture
of varieties, indeed, there is;—alpine,
some of them, with the flavor of rare
mountain air; others wood, tasting of
sunny roadside banks or shy openings in
the forest; and not a few seedlings
swollen hugely by culture, but lacking
the fine natural aroma of the more
modest kinds. Strange books these are of
his, and interesting in many ways,—instructive chiefly as showing how considerable a crop may be raised on a comparatively narrow close of mind, and
how much a man may make of his life
if he will assiduously follow it, though
perhaps never truly finding it at last.

We have just been renewing our recollection of Mr. Thoreau's writings, and
have read through his six volumes in the
order of their production. We shall try
to give an adequate report of their impression upon us both as critic and as
mere reader. He seems to us to have
been a man with so high a conceit of
himself that he accepted without questioning, and insisted on our accepting,
his defects and weaknesses of character
as virtues and powers peculiar to himself. Was he indolent, he finds none of
the activities which attract or employ
the rest of mankind worthy of him. Was
he wanting in the qualities that make
success, it is success that is contemptible,

and not himself that lacks persistency
and purpose. Was he poor, money was
an unmixed evil. Did his life seem a
selfish one, he condemns doing good as
one of the weakest of superstitions. To
be of use was with him the most killing
bait of the wily tempter Usefulness. He
had no faculty of generalization from
the outside of himself, or at least no experience which would supply the material of such, and he makes his own
whim the law, his own range the horizon
of the universe. He condemns a world,
the hollowness of whose satisfactions he
had never had the means of testing, and
we recognize Apemantus behind the
mask of Timon. He had little active
imagination; of the receptive he had
much. His appreciation is of the highest
quality; his critical power, from want of
continuity of mind, very limited and inadequate. He somewhere cites a simile
from Ossian, as an example of the superiority of the old poetry to the new,
though, even were the historic evidence
less convincing, the sentimental melancholy of those poems should be con-
clusive of their modernness. He had not
artistic power such as controls a great
work to the serene balance of completeness, but exquisite mechanical skill in
the shaping of sentences and paragraphs,
or (more rarely) short bits of verses for
the expression of a detached thought,
sentiment, or image. His works give one
the feeling of a sky full of stars,—something impressive and exhilarating certainly, something high overhead and
freckled thickly with spots of isolated
brightness; but whether these have any
natural relation with each other, or have
any concern with our mundane matters,
is for the most part matter of conjecture,
—astrology as yet, and not astronomy.

It is curious, considering what Thoreau afterwards became, that he was not
by nature an observer. He only saw the
things he looked for, and was less poet
than naturalist. Till he built his Walden

shanty, he did not know that hickory grew in Concord. Till he went to Maine, he had never seen phosphorescent wood, a phenomenon early familiar to most country boys. At forty he speaks of the seeding of the pine as a new discovery, though one should have thought that its gold-dust of blowing pollen might have earlier drawn his eye. Neither his attention nor his genius was of the spontaneous kind. He discovered nothing. He thought everything a discovery of his own, from moonlight to the planting of acorns and nuts by squirrels. This is a defect in his character, but one of his chief charms as a writer. Everything grows fresh under his hand. He delved in his mind and nature; he planted them with all manner of native and foreign seeds, and reaped assiduously. He was not merely solitary, he would be isolated, and succeeded at last in almost persuading himself that he was autochthonous. He valued everything in proportion as he fancied it to be exclusively his own. He complains in *Walden* that there is no one in Concord with whom he could talk of Oriental literature, though the man was living within two miles of his hut who had introduced him to it. This intellectual selfishness becomes sometimes almost painful in reading him. He lacked that generosity of "communication" which Johnson admired in Burke. De Quincey tells us that Wordsworth was impatient when any one else spoke of mountains, as if he had a peculiar property in them. And we can readily understand why it should be so: no one is satisfied with another's appreciation of his mistress. But Thoreau seems to have prized a lofty way of thinking (often we should be inclined to call it a remote one) not so much because it was good in itself as because he wished few to share it with him. It seems now and then as if he did not seek to lure others up "above our lower region of turmoil," but to leave his own name cut on the moun-

tain peak as the first climber. This itch of originality infects his thought and style. To be misty is not to be mystic. He turns commonplaces end for end, and fancies it makes something new of them. As we walk down Park Street, our eye is caught by Dr. Windship's dumbbells, one of which bears an inscription testifying that it is the heaviest ever put at arm's length by an athlete; and in reading Mr. Thoreau's books we cannot help feeling as if he sometimes invited our attention to a particular sophism or paradox as the biggest yet maintained by any single writer. He seeks, at all risks, for perversity of thought, and revives the age of *concetti* while he fancies himself going back to preclassical nature. "A day," he says, "passed in the society of those Greek sages, such as described in the Banquet of Xenophon, would not be comparable with the dry wit of decayed cranberry-vines and the fresh Attic salt of the moss-beds." It is not so much the True that he loves as the Out-of-the-Way. As the Brazen Age shows itself in other men by exaggeration of phrase, so in him by extravagance of statement. He wishes always to trump your suit and to *ruff* when you least expect it. Do you love Nature because she is beautiful? He will find a better argument in her ugliness. Are you tired of the artificial man? He instantly dresses you up an ideal in a Penobscot Indian, and attributes to this creature of his otherwise-mindedness as peculiarities things that are common to all woodsmen, white or red, and this simply because he has not studied the pale-faced variety.

The notion of an absolute originality, as if one could have a patent-right in it, is an absurdity. A man cannot escape in thought, any more than he can in language, from the past and the present. As no one ever invents a word, and yet language somehow grows by general contribution and necessity, so it is with thought. Mr. Thoreau seems to us to insist in public on going back to flint and steel, when there is a match-box in his pocket which he knows very well how to use at a pinch. Originality consists in power of digesting and assimilating thoughts, so that they become part of our life and substance. Montaigne, for example, is one of the most original of authors, though he helped himself to ideas in every direction. But they turn to blood and coloring in his style, and give a freshness of complexion that is forever charming. In Thoreau much seems yet to be foreign and unassimilated showing itself in symptoms of indigestion. A preacher up of Nature, we now and then detect under the surly and stoic garb something of the sophist and sentimentalizer. We are far from implying that this was conscious on his part. But it is much easier for a man to impose on himself when he measures only with himself. A greater familiarity with ordinary men would have done Thoreau good, by showing him how many fine qualities are common to the race. The radical vice of his theory of life was, that he confounded physical with spiritual remoteness from men. One is far enough withdrawn from his fellows if he keeps himself clear of their weaknesses. He is not so truly withdrawn as exiled, if he refuse to share in their strength. It is a morbid self-consciousness that pronounces the world of men empty and worthless before trying it, the instinctive evasion of one who is sensible of some innate weakness, and retorts the accusation of it before any has made it but himself. To a healthy mind, the world is a constant challenge of opportunity. Mr. Thoreau had not a healthy mind, or he would not have been so fond of prescribing. His whole life was a search for a doctor. The old mystics had a wiser sense of what the world was worth. They ordained a severe apprenticeship to law and even ceremonial, in order to the gaining of freedom and mastery over

these. Seven years of service for Rachel were to be rewarded at last with Leah. Seven other years of faithfulness with her were to win them at last the true bride of their souls. Active Life was with them the only path to the Contemplative.

Thoreau had no humor, and this implies that he was a sorry logician. Himself an artist in rhetoric, he confounds thought with style when he undertakes to speak of the latter. He was forever talking of getting away from the world, but he must be always near enough to it, nay, to the Concord corner of it, to feel the impression that he makes. He verifies the shrewd remark of Sainte-Beuve, "On touche encore à son temps et très-fort, même quand on le repousse." This egotism of his is a Stylites pillar after all, a seclusion which keeps him in the public eye. The dignity of man is an excellent thing, but therefore to hold one's self too sacred and precious is the reverse of excellent. There is something delightfully absurd in six volumes addressed to a world of such "vulgar fellows" as Thoreau affirmed his fellow-men to be. We once had a glimpse of a genuine solitary who spent his winters one hundred and fifty miles beyond all human communication, and there dwelt with his rifle as his only confidant. Compared with this, the shanty on Walden Pond has something the air, it must be confessed, of the Hermitage of La Chevrette. We do not believe that the way to a true cosmopolitanism carries one into the woods or the society of musquashes. Perhaps the narrowist provincialism is that of Self; that of Kleinwinkel is nothing to it. The natural man, like the singing birds, comes out of the forest as inevitably as the natural bear and the wildcat stick there. To seek to be natural implies a consciousness that forbids all naturalness forever. It is as easy—and no easier—to be natural in a *salon* as in a swamp, if one do not aim at it, for what we call unnaturalness always has its spring in a man's thinking too much about himself. "It is impossible," said Turgot, "for a vulgar man to be simple."

We look upon a great deal of modern sentimentalism about Nature as a mark of disease. It is one more symptom of the general liver-complaint. In a man of wholesome constitution the wilderness is well enough for a mood or a vacation, but not for a habit of life. Those who have most loudly advertised their passion for seclusion and their intimacy with nature, from Petrarch down, have been mostly sentimentalists, unreal men, misanthropes on the spindle side, solacing an uneasy suspicion of themselves by professing contempt for their kind. They make demands on the world in advance proportioned to their inward measure of their own merit, and are angry that the world pays only by the visible measure of performance. It is true of Rousseau, the modern founder of the sect, true of St. Pierre, his intellectual child, and of Chateaubriand, his grandchild, the inventor of what we may call the primitive forest cure, and who first was touched by the solemn falling of a tree from natural decay in the windless silence of the woods. It is a very shallow view that affirms trees and rocks to be healthy, and cannot see that men in communities are just as true to the laws of their organization and destiny; that can tolerate the puffin and the fox, but not the fool and the knave; that would shun politics because of its demagogues, and snuff up the stench of the obscene fungus. The divine life of Nature is more wonderful, more various, more sublime in man than in any other of her works, and the wisdom that is gained by commerce with men, as Montaigne and Shakespeare gained it, or with one's own soul among men, as Dante, is the most delightful, as it is the most precious, of all. In outward nature it is still man that interests us, and we care less for the things seen

than the way in which poetic eyes like Wordsworth's or Thoreau's see them, and the reflections they cast there. To hear the to-do that is often made over the simple fact that man sees the image of himself in the outside world, one is reminded of a savage when he for the first time catches a glimpse of himself in a looking-glass. "Venerable child of Nature," we are tempted to say, "to whose science in the invention of the tobacco-pipe, to whose art in tatooing of thine undegenerate hide not yet enslaved by tailors, we are slowly striving to climb back, the miracle thou beholdest is sold in my unhappy country for a shilling!" If matters go on as they have done, and everybody must needs blab of all the favors that have been done him by roadside and river-brink and woodland walk, as if to kiss and tell were no longer treachery, it would be a positive refreshment to meet a man who is as superbly indifferent to Nature as she is to him. By and by we shall have John Smith, of No. 12, 12th Street, advertising that he is not the J. S. who saw a cowlily on Thursday last, as he never saw one in his life, would not see one if he could, and is prepared to prove an alibi on the day in question.

Solitary communion with Nature does not seem to have been sanitary or sweetening in its influence on Thoreau's character. On the contrary, his letters show him more cynical as he grew older. While he studied with respectful attention the minks and woodchucks, his neighbors, he looked with utter contempt on the august drama of destiny of which his country was the scene, and on which the curtain had already risen. He was converting us back to a state of nature "so eloquently," as Voltaire said of Rousseau, "that he almost persuaded us to go on all fours," while the wiser fates were making it possible for us to walk erect for the first time. Had he conversed more with his fellows, his sympathies would have widened with the assurance that his peculiar genius had more appreciation, and his writings a larger circle of readers, or at least a warmer one, than he dreamed of. We have the highest testimony to the natural sweetness, sincerity, and nobleness of his temper and in his books an equally irrefragable one to the quality of his mind. He was not a strong thinker, but a sensitive feeler. Yet his mind strikes us as cold and wintry in its purity. A light snow has fallen everywhere where he seems to come on the track of the shier sensations that would elsewhere leave no trace. We think greater compression would have done more for his fame. A feeling of sameness comes over us as we read so much. Trifles are recorded with an over-minute punctuality and conscientiousness of detail. We cannot help thinking sometimes of the man who

watches, starves, freezes, and sweats
To learn but catechisms and alphabets
Of unconcerning things, matter of fact.

and sometimes of the saying of the Persian poet, that "when the owl would boast, he boasts of catching mice at the edge of a hole." We could readily part with some of his affectations. It was well enough for Pythagoras to say, once and for all, "When I was Euphorbus at the siege of Troy"; not so well for Thoreau to travesty it into "When I was a shepherd on the plains of Assyria." A naive thing said over again is anything but naive. But with every exception, there is no writing comparable with Thoreau's in kind, that is comparable with it in degree where it is best; where it disengages itself, that is, from the tangled roots and dead leaves of a second-hand Orientalism, and runs limpid and smooth and broadening as it runs, a mirror for whatever is grand and lovely in both worlds.

George Sand says neatly, that "Art is not a study of positive reality," (ac-

tuality were the fitter word,) "but a seeking after ideal truth." It would be doing very inadequate justice to Thoreau if we left it to be inferred that this ideal element did not exist in him, and that too in larger proportion, if less obtrusive, than his nature-worship. He took nature as the mountain-path to an ideal world. If the path wind a good deal, if he record too faithfully every trip over a root, if he botanize somewhat wearisomely, he gives us now and then superb outlooks from some jutting crag, and brings us out at last into an illimitable ether, where the breathing is not difficult for those who have any true touch of the climbing spirit. His shanty-life was a mere impossibility, so far as his own conception of it goes, as an entire independency of mankind. The tub of Diogenes had a sounder bottom. Thoreau's experiment actually presupposed all that complicated civilization which it theoretically abjured. He squatted on another man's land; he borrows an axe; his board, his nails, his bricks, his mortar, his books, his lamp, his fish-hooks, his plow, his hoe, all turn state's evidence against him as an accomplice in the sin of that artificial civilization which rendered it possible that such a person as Henry D. Thoreau should exist at all. *Magnis tamen excidit ausis.* His aim was a noble and a useful one, in the direction of "plain living and high thinking." It was a practical sermon on Emerson's text that "things are in the saddle and ride mankind," an attempt to solve Carlyle's problem of "lessening your denominator." His whole life was a rebuke of the waste and aimlessness of our American luxury, which is an abject enslavement to tawdry upholstery. He had "fine translunary things" in him. His better style as a writer is in keeping with the simplicity and purity of his life. We have said that his range was narrow, but to be a master is to be a master. He had caught his English at its living source, among the poets and prose-writers of its best days; his literature was extensive and recondite; his quotations are always nuggets of the purest ore; there are sentences of his as perfect as anything in the language, and thoughts as clearly crystallized; his metaphors and images are always fresh from the soil; he had watched Nature like a detective who is to go upon the stand; as we read him, it seems as if all out-of-doors had kept a diary and become its own Montaigne; we look at the landscape in a Claude Lorraine glass; compared with his, all other books of similar aim, even White's Selborne, seem dry as a country clergyman's meteorological journal in an old almanac. He belongs with Donne and Browne and Novalis; if not with the originally creative men, with a scarcely smaller class who are peculiar, and whose leaves shed their invisible thought-seed like ferns.

R. P. Blackmur
❋ 1904-

Richard Palmer Blackmur is a poet and critic who teaches at Princeton University. Among his volumes of essays are THE DOUBLE AGENT (*1935*), THE EXPENSE OF GREATNESS (*1940*), LANGUAGE AS GESTURE (*1952*), THE LION AND THE HONEYCOMB (*1955*), *and* FORM AND VALUE IN MODERN POETRY (*1957*). *He is the editor of* HENRY JAMES, THE ART OF THE NOVEL: CRITICAL PREFACES (*1934*) *and* AMERICAN SHORT NOVELS (*1960*).

The Craft of Herman Melville

This essay proposes to approach Herman Melville altogether gingerly and from behind the safe bulwark of his assured position—whatever that is—in American literature,—whatever *that* may be. The tacit assumption will be all along that Melville is a sufficiently great writer in a sufficiently interesting literature to make the sidelong look, the biased comment, and even a little boring-from-within, each valuable in itself, if perhaps only as characterising an inadequate response on the part of one reader. We need, of course, a preliminary assertion to get us under way; and the last thing we want is anything in the direction of reducing Melville's greatness to sub-human terms. What we want is an assertion that, pursued, will elucidate one aspect of the work actually performed, irrespective of its greatness.

If we assert that Melville was an imaginative artist in the realm of fiction, then it is legitimate to think of him as he was concerned with the craft of fiction in his two most interesting works, *Moby Dick* and *Pierre*. As a further limitation, let us think of the craft principally under two heads: dramatic form with its inspiriting conventions, and the treatment of language itself as a medium. Other matters may come in by the way, and further matters may suggest themselves in conclusion; but the mode of discovery will be everywhere at bottom in the consideration of the tools by which Melville himself secured his effects: the tools of craft.

It is of preliminary interest that Melville never influenced the direction of the art of fiction, though in *Pierre* he evidenced the direction, and it is astonishing, when you consider the magnitude of his sensibility, that he never affected the modes of apprehension, the sensibilities, of even the ablest of his admirers. He added nothing to the novel as a form, and his work nowhere showed conspicuous mastery of the formal devices of fiction which he used. Unlike most great writers of fiction, he left nothing to those who followed him except the general stimulus of high and devoted purpose and the occasional particular spur of an image or a rhythm. It is not that he is inimitable but that there was nothing formally organised enough in his work to imitate or modify or perfect. It is easy enough to say on this score that Melville was a sport, and unique, and perhaps that is the right thing to say; but it would be more useful if we were able to say that Melville's lack of influence at least partly arose from a series of technical defects in persuasive craft—from an inefficient relation between the writer and the formal elements of his medium. None of us would want to recommend his wares along the lines of Melville's strategy. To adumbrate such a statement is a part of this essay's purpose.

Of secondary, but deeply contributory interest is the fact that though a young man still as writers go, Melville wrote nothing of major significance in the forty years he lived after writing *Pierre*. (I mean that only a lesser case could be made out for *The Confidence Man* and *Billy Budd* than for *Pierre*, not that the later books were uninteresting; they could not fail of interest as forced through Melville's sensibility.) It was not that his mind rotted or that insight faltered. It was not, I think, that the poor reception of *Pierre*, nor the long aggravation of his private life, dried his desire as a novelist. It was, I think, partly bad luck—the luck of the age, if you like—though it was no worse than Dante's luck and not so bad as Villon's, as Melville himself knew; and it was partly that his work discovered for itself, if we may say so, and in the very process of writing, that it was not meant to be fiction. Melville was only a story teller betimes, for illustrative or apologetic or evangelical purposes, and when the *writing* of *Pierre* proved that the material of illustration had been exhausted in *Moby Dick*—which is one way of noting the breakdown of *Pierre* as a story—there was no

longer any need to tell a story. His means determined, as they always do, not the ends in view, but the ends achieved; and Melville had never predominantly relied upon the means of the novelist, had never attempted to use more than the overt form of the novel, until he attempted to compose *Pierre*.

What is really interesting, and what this essay intends to make most use of in this corner, is the light that *Pierre*, technically considered as a novel, casts upon the means, quite different from the means of fiction, which Melville actually employed both in *Moby Dick* and *Pierre* itself. For these books with their great effects, if they were not written out of the means of the novelist, were written out of great means of some other mode or modes of the imagination. It will most likely appear that there is an operative connection between Melville's lack of influence upon following writers and his forty years of comparative silence; and it is, again, a connection, as moral as may be, that can best be seen as a technical consideration. Similarly, the problem of the inarticulateness of *Hamlet* is better accounted for technically than philosophically. We shall see, or try to see, what modes determined what ends—but always provisionally within the modes of the rational imagination.

There is, again on this train, a dubious kind of consideration which in the very doubtfulness of its nature exerts its great attraction. In our literature we are accustomed to the question precisely because it gets itself asked at every turn. It is a coroner's question: what devilish thing did his age do to Melville? What malevolence was there in the current of American life that struck from the heights of possibility writer after writer, even those most satisfied with the American scene?—for the Longfellows, the Whittiers, the Holmeses were as fatally struck as Hawthorne and Melville and Mark Twain. But does an age act? Is not an age itself a long action, an unfolding, a display, a history, with limits set by the discernment and capacity of the observer, never by Clio herself? And is not every age an enemy of every artist it cannot directly use, an enemy not out of antipathy but of inner necessity? An age moves; it is momentum felt. An artist expresses an arrested version of movement, expresses it at the level of actuality. But this is pushing consequence intolerably. We are all enemies of our age the moment we begin to tamper with it, whether we arrest it to take its picture, hasten it towards its end in the guise of leadership, or just consciously live in it our own lives. Consciousness is the agent, not the age.

It is the whole consciousness, not its mere miniscule conscience, that makes us cowards. Hence in all large doings we are adept at removing compassion from our experience by at once inserting it in the formula of a dead convention; and so are often enabled to skip consciousness, along with conscience, altogether. How otherwise could we attend the Christian service of Holy Communion, quite aside from the matter of faith and for the "poetry" in it merely, without terror and dismay and the conviction of inadequacy? How could we attend *King Lear* on the stage if we did not commonly channelise our attention upon the obscuring details of the performance, letting the actual play work in us, if at all, unawares? This is precisely what the artist cannot substantially do if his work is to live; and this is precisely what society compels him to seem to do if his work is to succeed in the open,—that is, be widely persuasive upon the consciousness of the great audience most artists aim at. Upon his skill and luck in performing this equivocal act depends all that part of an artist's achievement which rests on a firm relation with his age.

Here we have a crux in the deliberately maintained, wilfully heightened consciousness of the artist. It is the crux in which we see that the conceptual faculty of consciousness is honesty if we can manage it, but that the executive faculty of consciousness must be hypocrisy. I do not wish to strain or seem far-fetched, but I believe this to be a technical matter in so far as we think of the arts—whatever it may be in religion or politics, which are not always condemned to actuality but can often play free havoc with the ideal. What it comes to in practice is that the artist must dramatise his theme, his vision, his observation, his "mere" story, in terms of existing conventions however adverse those conventions may seem to his intentions, or however hollow or vain they ring when struck. The deadest convention was meant for life—to take its place, and if by putting life into it the artist does not always change it for the better, he at least shows it for what it is. Instinctive artists commonly resort to the nearest conventions susceptible of dramas. Consider the negro spirituals or the anonymous architecture of the twelfth century. Highly individualised artists have done the same. There is Dante who mastered the conventions of Thomistic Christianity to respect the actuality—far from Thomistic—of fourteenth century Italy; and there is Henry James who resorted to the "social" conventions so well that many people for long believed he was taken in by them, when his predominant concern was to dramatise the actual good and evil of his time in terms of the conventions through which he most saw good and evil operating.

The point here is, for us, that Melville either refused or was unable to resort to the available conventions of his time as if they were real; he either preferred or was compelled to resort to most of the conventions he used for dramatic purposes not only as if they were unreal but also as if they were artificial.

Artificial they surely were to the kind of philosopher Melville was—though they would not have seemed unreal to Montaigne or Plato; but to the dramatist of any description they would have glowed with the possibility of every reality. As for Melville's case we have his own words, put in extremity, for his attitude towards all conventions of the mind.

For the more and the more that he wrote, and the deeper and deeper that he dived, Pierre saw the everlasting elusiveness of Truth; the universal lurking insincerity of even the greatest and purest written thoughts. Like knavish cards, the leaves of all great books were covertly packed. He was but packing one set the more; and that a very poor and jaded set and pack indeed.

Here we see the ineptitude, for the artist, of moral pre-occupation with what ought to be as compared with the equally moral obsession with what is. As thought, we can leave Melville's text alone, and insist merely that as an artist Melville misunderstood the import of his own words. The "universal lurking insincerity" he spoke of, is just the most fascinating aspect of the face of dramatic truth; and the conviction of it should liberate the artist's honesty among his material generally, as the preposterous fables of *Lear*, *Othello*, and the *Merchant of Venice* particularly liberated the profound honesty of Shakespeare, or as the *smallness* of life in Emma Bovary's town liberated Flaubert's honesty. Melville apparently felt that his insight condemned him to a species of dishonesty. Feeling the necessity—feeling the condemned state as unreprievable—he proceeded to employ conventions of character and form in which he obviously and almost avowedly did not believe. Had he been a convicted and not a condemned novelist he would have felt his insight of insincerity on the same level that he felt the convention

in the following lines, in which he never detected the insincerity at all.

It is a thing most sorrowful, nay shocking, to expose the fall of valor in the soul. Men may seem detestable as joint stock-companies and nations; knaves, fools, and murderers there may be; men may have mean and meagre faces; but man, in the ideal, is so noble and so sparkling, such a grand and glowing creature, that over any ignominious blemish in him all his fellows should run to throw their costliest robes. That immaculate manliness we feel within ourselves, so far within us, that it remains intact though all the outer character seem gone; bleeds with the keenest anguish at the undraped spectacle of a valor-ruined man. Nor can piety itself, at such a shameful sight, completely stifle her upbraidings against the permitting stars.

At his best—his best as a novelist of character and aspiration—this sentiment controlled Melville's perception of dramatic fate. Had he felt the immaculate manliness as Henry James, say, felt his perception of the Sacred Fount, as a germinal, copulative, and plastic principle in every human relation, and also as the very prod and forward stress towards form, then his sentiment would not only have opened up inexhaustible subject-matter, but would also have required of him that in his execution every resource, every trick, every mediate insincerity, either of craft or of social pattern, be used for the utmost there was in them. That would have been to work on the representative, the dramatic level. What he did, as we shall see more particularly below, was to work on the putative level. His work constantly *said* what it was doing or going to do, and then, as a rule, stopped short.

As it happens, Melville's is not a putative smallness but a putative immensity, and he puts it with such eloquence that the mere statement produces a lasting tone in the general atmosphere. He was without knowing it in the habit of succumbing to the greatest insincerity of all, the intoxicating insincerity of cadence and rhythm and apt image, or, to put it on another plane, the insincerity of surrendering to the force of a single insight, which sometimes amounts to a kind of self-violation. Who can measure for example the effect of the preparatory statements about Ahab upon our actual reception of him when he appears? For instance, in chapter XVI there is a paragraph about the greatness of some whaling men rising from a combination of Quaker blood and the perils of the sea. "Nor will it at all detract from him, dramatically regarded, if either by birth or other circumstances, he have what seems a half wilful, over-ruling morbidness at the bottom of his nature. For all men tragically great are made so through a certain morbidness. Be sure of this, O young ambition, all mortal greatness is but disease." . . . This is but one of the many preparatory, almost minatory statements that Melville made about Ahab. Many directly named him; many more, like this one, were purely indirect and putative in character. Ahab is not mentioned, but the reader who remembers the passage will know that it was he who was meant all the same; and if the reader does remember it may well occur to him that Melville meant his sentences about greatness and disease to spread throughout the novel. They were planted of a purpose, whether by instinct or intention, to prefigure in the general atmosphere the specific nature of the burden Ahab wore.

The interesting thing is that Melville preferred to make his statement, in which one version of the whole theme of the book is expressed, not only baldly in isolation, but out of place and rootlessly; which is how the reader will ultimately remember it. It worked, indeed; but it worked outside the story. A dramatist would have been compelled to

find the sentiment of these sentences in a situation, an action, and they could have been used only as the situation called for them and the action carried them along; and a novelist when he can should follow the example of the dramatist. Melville, as we have said, preferred the non-dramatic mode. To put it sharply, he did not write of characters in action; he employed the shells of stock characters, heightened or resounding only by the eloquence of the author's voice, to witness, illustrate, decorate, and often as it happened to impede and stultify an idea in motion. This is, if you like, the mode of allegory—the highest form of the putative imagination, in which things are *said* but need not be *shown* to be other than they seem, and thus hardly require to *be* much of anything. But successful allegory—*La Vita Nuova* and *Pilgrim's Progress*—requires the preliminary possession of a complete and stable body of belief appropriate to the theme in hand. Melville was not so equipped; neither was Hawthorne; neither was anyone in nineteenth-century America or since. That is why Melville's allegorical devices and patterns had to act *as if* they were agents in a novel; and that is why we are compelled to judge Melville at his most allegorical yet formally as a novelist.

Perhaps the point needs labouring. Many critics—many students of Melville—have done a good deal to make an allegorical interpretation of *Moby Dick,* and I am sure they are right and accurate in the form of what they say. Melville certainly had allegorical intentions. My argument—again it is technical—is that the elaboration of these intentions was among the causes that prevented him from the achievement of enacting composition and the creation of viable characters. He mistook allegory in *Moby Dick* as a sufficient enlivening agent for the form of the novel. Actually it was a chief defective element which, due to the peculiarly confused, inconsistent and incomplete state of belief he was in, he could not possibly have used to good advantage. In the craft of writing, in any form of expression, artificial allegory, like willed mysticism (of which Melville showed a trace), is a direct and easy mode only in that it puts so much in by intention as to leave nearly everything out in execution. Bad allegory, even to the allegorist, comes very soon to seem not worth doing; which is why charades and political parties break down. Melville's allegory in *Moby Dick* broke down again and again and with each resumption got more and more verbal, and more and more at the mercy of the encroaching event it was meant to transcend. It was an element in the putative mode in which, lofty as it was, Melville himself could not long deeply believe.

We have so far been concerned mostly with what Melville did not do as a practitioner in the novel and with certain possible causes which, technically, prevented him from doing what he wanted to do. Let us now examine particular instances of what he did do under the two heads first mentioned: dramatic form with its inspiriting conventions, and the treatment of language itself as medium. If anything so far said has made its point it will be in the degree that it certifies and illuminates what follows—in the degree, that is, that it makes it seem natural and just and necessary to find so much fault in a genius so great.

The dramatic form of a novel is what holds it together, makes it move, gives it a centre and establishes a direction; and it includes the agency of perception, the consciousness set up in the book upon which, or through which, the story is registered. Dramatic form cannot in practice be wholly isolated from other formal elements; form is the way things go together in their medium—and the medium itself, here language, may prop-erly be considered the major element of form; but we may think of different ways in which things go together in a given work, and strangely, the labour of abstraction and violation will seem to deepen our intimacy with the substance of the work and, more valuable, to heighten our sense of how that substance is controlled. The sense of control is perhaps the highest form of apprehension; it is understanding without immersion.

The question we have here to ask then is how did Melville go about controlling his two novels, *Moby Dick* and *Pierre?* The general, strictly true, and mainly irrelevant answer would be: haphazardly —that is, through an attitude which varied from the arrogance of extreme carelessness to the humility of complete attention. It is not that he attended only to what seriously interested him, for he was as careless of what he thought important as of what he thought trivial, but that apparently he had no sure rule as to what required management and what would take care of itself. His rule was vagary, where consequential necessities did not determine otherwise. And even there, Melville's eye was not good; he did not always see that if you took one series of steps your choice of further directions was narrowed, and that you could not step in two directions at once without risk of crippling yourself. It is perhaps his intellectual consistency, which he felt putatively omniform, that made him incorrigibly inconsistent in the technical quarter. For example, in *Moby Dick*, after setting up a single consciousness to get inside of, he shifted from that consciousness at will without sense of inconsistency, and therefore, which is the important thing, without making any effort to warrant the shifts and make them credible. Ignorance could not have excused him, because he had the example of Hawthorne, who was adept at shifting his compositional centres without disturbing his gravity, plumb in front of him. Not ignorance, but ineptitude and failure to discriminate. For the contrary example, I can think of only three occasions of importance in *Pierre*, if we except the digressions of the author himself in his own voice, where the consciousness of the hero is not left the presumed sole register of the story. Of these occasions, two are unnecessary to the story, and the third, where in the very end the perceiving centre is turned over to the turnkey in the prison, funks its job. Yet in *Pierre* the theme cried out, one would think, for as many and as well chosen centres of consciousness as possible, all to be focussed on Pierre himself, the distraught and ambiguous, otherwise not measurable: the principle being that the abnormal can only be seen as viable, as really moving in response to the normal world, if seen through normal eyes.

Meanwhile we have approached a little nearer the composition of the two novels. Melville was right, granting the theme of *Moby Dick,* in choosing Ishmael the novice, to represent a story in which he had only a presumed and minor but omnipresent part; he was only wrong where he breached his choice without covering up. Ishmael, not otherwise ever named, is as mysterious as Ahab, but he is credible because he tells us not what he is but what he sees and what he sees other people see. The mere interposition of a participating consciousness between the story and its readers, once it has been made logical by trying the consciousness to the story, is a prime device of composition: it limits, compacts, and therefore controls what can be told and how. The only error Melville made is that he failed to distinguish between what Ishmael saw and what the author saw on his own account. If an author is to use digressions, which are confusing but legitimate by tradition, he ought to follow Fielding and put them in

interchapters, and especially where the narrative is technically in the first person. Otherwise, as with Ishmael, the narrator will seem to know too much at a given time for the story's good; it will tend to tell itself all at once, and the necessary modicum of stupidity in the operative consciousness will be blighted by excess intelligence. As Ahab said to the carpenter who handed him a lantern: "Thrusted light is worse than presented pistols." Ishmael of course is Melville's alter ego, which explains why so much is imputed to him, but does not condone the excess.

On the whole the mode of Ishmael is a success exactly where the mode of *Pierre* (another alter ego of Melville) is wrong. Ishmael is looking on, and able to see; Pierre is in the centre of his predicament, and lost in the action. Ishmael represents speech; Pierre represents rhetoric. Ishmael reports the abnormal, driven and demonic Ahab, either through his own normal sensibility or through the reported sensibilities of the mates and the crew. Pierre is seen principally without the intervening glass and focus of any sensibility whatever— so that he falls apart into a mere voice whenever he speaks, whereas the voice of Ahab, equally eloquent and rhetorical past belief, rings true in ears that have actually heard it.

It should be noted, curiously, that Ishmael is the only character in the book not "characterised" by Melville; he is merely situated in the centre, explained a little, and let speak his part of recording angel. The curiosity is that all the other characters except Ahab and Queequeg near the beginning (the night at the inn), although given set characterisations as they appear, are far less viable and are far less *present* in the book than Ishmael. The reason may be that the other characters are only pulled out at intervals and are usually given stock jobs to do, set speeches to make, whereas

Ishmael, sacking his creative memory, is occupied all the time. Which suggests two or three things: that character requires the sense of continuous action to show continuously, that the mates and crew were not *in* the book substantially but that their real use was to divide up the representation of the image of Ahab. There is nothing illegitimate about such characters, but to be successful and maintain interest they must be given enough to do to seem everywhere natural, and never obviously used, as here, *only* to make the wheels go round. One suspects, therefore, that Ahab comes out a great figure more because of the eloquence of the author's putative conception of him, and Ishmael's feeling for him, than from any representational aids on the part of the crew. The result is a great figure, not a great character. Ahab is as solitary in the book as he was in his cabin.

Pierre was in his way as compositionally isolated as Ahab; he was so situated, and so equipped as a consciousness, that he recorded his own isolation to the point of solipsism. If Pierre was real, as he was asserted to be, then nothing else properly in the novel was real except in terms of his perception or through the direct and unwarrantable intervention of the author. That is the risk attached to making the protagonist record the action in which he participates to the exclusion of other agents and while the action is going on. Melville instinctively tried to get round the difficulty by resorting to a series of dramatic scenes in which Pierre was chief interlocutor. The device was the right one—or one of the right ones—but it failed to work for a number of reasons, of which the chief was that Melville had no talent for making his dramatic scenes objective except by aid of external and unrelated force—as in *Moby Dick* he was able to resort to the ordinary exigencies of life on a whaling ship. In *Pierre* the White Whale was entirely in the protagonist's own in-

adequate perception of it and the real weight of the book—what it was really about: tragedy by unconsidered virtue—was left for the author's digressions and soliloquies to carry as it could; which is to say that the book had no compositional centre at all.

Something of the same sort may also be true of *Moby Dick*. Is it not possible to say that Ishmael, the narrator, provides only a false centre? Is it not true that a great part of the story's theme escapes him, is not recorded through his sensibility, either alone or in connection with others? Then the real centre would lie where? It would lie variously, I think, in the suspense attached to the character of Ahab and the half imputed, half demonstrated peril of the White Whale—the cold, live evil that is momently present. If we think of the book in that way, we may say that its compositional form is a long, constantly interrupted but as constantly maintained suspense, using as nexi or transitions the recurring verbal signs of Melville's allegory, Ahab's character, and the business of whaling. The business of whaling, including both the essays on anatomy and those on butchery, takes the most space and provides the most interest. All the reader has to do is to *feel* whaling as interest and he will recognise it as a compositional device mounting to the force of drama. Indeed we speak of the drama of whaling, or of cotton, or of gold without substantial injustice to the language; and I cannot for the life of me see why the drama of whaling should not be as efficient an agent of interest, if well felt, as the drama of who fired the second shot; and with Melville there is the additional advantage that the business of whaling points to the everlasting assassin instead of the casual and no doubt remorseful murderer. Interest is the thing of prime importance as any artist and any audience will tell you. If it takes up time and prepares for life, it does not matter how it is secured and does not fatally matter if it is overdone or vulgar in its appeal as it is in *Moby Dick*.

But is the real interest in the whaling or in the firing of the shot? Is it not always partly in the presentation, the feeling of detail and design, and partly in the image towards which the design points? Melville was lucky in *Omoo* and *Typee*, to a less degree in *Mardi* and *White Jacket*, and most of all in *Moby Dick*; he was lucky or it was his genius that he had material in perfect factual control with which to take up time and point towards an image—in *Moby Dick* a profound and obsessive image of life. As it happened, it was in each case the material of a special and vanishing experience, dramatic enough in its own right to require very little fictionising— very little actualising—to exert the invaluable hold of natural interest over the average reader. If to interest, you add eloquence, you have all the essentials of the great novel below the first order. Many readers will be deceived and think the provision greater than it is. I have discovered a number of readers who on being asked reported enjoyment of a great story in a book of which Henry James would have said that it told no story to speak of; which indeed it does not.

In *Pierre* we are in a different box; a box quite empty of special material of objective interest to do for compositional strength otherwise lacking. There is no sea, or ship, or whale, or unique tradition of behaviour, no unusual daily life— most precious of all—to give atmosphere, and weight and movement to carry the book towards the image of its chosen end. Melville was required to depend more than ever before upon the actual technique of the craft, and nothing much else, to make the book hang together. What is most illuminating is most pitiful. The glaring weaknesses of *Pierre* show up the hidden weaknesses of *Moby Dick*, and each set of weaknesses shows the other as essential—at least in the critical context in which we here provisionally place both books.

That one novel may criticise another is a commonplace when we think of different authors, as when we say that the novels of Henry James form a criticism of the novels of Flaubert and Turgenev, or that, in a way, the *Comédie Humaine* is a critique of the Waverly Novels. I think it is equally true that a consideration of the failures of a single author will often form the severest criticism of his successes, and a consideration of his successes may relatively improve our estimation of his failures. A great author is of one substance and often of one theme, and the relation between his various creations is bound to be reciprocal, even mutual; each is the other in a different form. So with *Pierre* and *Moby Dick*. If we wish to take up thinking of the two novels together in this way—which is the purpose of this essay—the alert consciousness will be struck with the repetition of the vices of *Pierre* in *Moby Dick*, or struck the other way round with the fact that the tragedy of *Pierre* fails to come off as well as *Moby Dick* only because the later book lacked the demonstrable extraneous interest of whaling. The efforts at plot in the two books are as lame; narrative runs as often offside. Dramatic motive on the subordinate level is as weakly put; Starbuck's tentative rebellion against Ahab and the threatened revenge of Glendinning Stanly and Frederick Tartan upon Pierre are equally unconvincing. The dialogue is as by turns limp and stiff and flowery in one book as the other. The delineations of character are almost interchangeable examples of wooden caricature. And so on. More important, the force and nobility of conception, the profundity of theme, were as great in either book—not from the dramatic execution but in spite of it, in the simple strength of the putative statement, and in the digressions Melville made from the drama in front of him, which he could not manage, into apologues or sermons, which he superbly could.

The strength of the putative statement is only simple when thought of abstractly and as appealing to the intellect—to the putative element in appreciation: as if we read lyric poetry solely for the schematic paraphrase we make of it in popular discussion, or as if, in contemplating war, we thought only of political causes or in terms of the quartermaster's technique alone. What we want is to see what is the source of putative strength and how deeply its appeal is asserted; and in that pursuit we shall find ourselves instantly, I think, in the realm of language itself. Words, and their intimate arrangements, must be the ultimate as well as the immediate source of every effect in the written or spoken arts. Words bring meaning to birth and themselves contained the meaning as an imminent possibility before the pangs of junction. To the individual artist the use of words is an adventure in discovery; the imagination is heuristic among the words it manipulates. The reality you labour desperately or luckily to put into your words—and you may put it in consciously like Coleridge or by instinct as in the great ballads or from piety and passion like the translators of the Bible— you will actually have found there, deeply ready and innately formed to give objective being and specific idiom to what you knew and did not know that you knew. The excitement is past belief; as we know from the many myths of heavenly inspiration. And the routine of discovery is past teaching and past prediction; as we know from the vast reaches of writing, precious and viable to their authors, wholly without the conviction of being. Yet the adventure into the reality of words has a technique

after the fact in the sense that we can distinguish its successful versions from those that failed, can measure provisionally the kinds and intensities of reality secured and attempted, and can even roughly guess at the conditions of convention and belief necessary for its emergence.

Melville is an excellent example for such an essay. We have only to relate the conception of the reality of language just adumbrated to the notion of the putative statement to see whence the strength of the latter comes; and we have only to relate the conception of language to its modifying context of conventions in order to understand the successes and at least excuse the many short-comings and over-leapings of Melville's attempts at the paramount and indefeasible reality that great words show. For Melville habitually used words greatly.

Let us take first an example not at all putative and with as little supporting context of convention as possible: an example of words composed entirely of feelings and the statement of sensuous facts, plus of course the usual situating and correlative elements which are the real syntax of imaginative language.

To a landsman, no whale, nor any sign of a herring, would have been visible at that moment; nothing but a troubled bit of greenish white water, and thin scattered puffs of vapor hovering over it, and suffusingly blowing off to leeward, like the confused scud from white rolling billows. The air around suddenly vibrated and tingled, as it were, like the air over intensely heated plates of iron. Beneath this atmospheric waving and curling, and partially beneath a thin layer of water, also, the whales were swimming. Seen in advance of all the other indications, the puffs of vapor they spouted, seemed their forerunning couriers and detached flying outriders.

This is the bottom level of good writing, whether in prose or verse; and a style which was able to maintain the qualities of accurate objective feeling which it exemplifies at other levels and for other purposes could not help being a great style. The words have feelers of their own, and the author contributes nothing to the emotion they call forth except the final phrasing, which adds nothing but finish to the paragraph. It is an example of words doing their own work; and let no one think it is not imaginative work, or does not come to an emotion, because the mode is that of close description, and neither directly expressive nor enacting. Let us compare it, with achieved emotion in mind, with a deliberately "emotional" description taken from the chapter called Enceladus in *Pierre*.

Cunningly masked hitherto, by the green tapestry of the interlacing leaves, a terrific towering palisade of dark mossy massiness confronted you; and, trickling with unevaporable moisture, distilled upon you from its beetling brow slow thunder-showers of water-drops, chill as the last dews of death. . . . All round and round, the grim scarred rocks rallied and re-rallied themselves; shot up, protuded, stretched, swelled, and eagerly reached forth; on every side bristlingly radiated with hideous repellingness. . . . 'Mid this spectacle of wide and wanton spoil, insular noises of falling rocks would boomingly explode upon the silence and fright all the echoes, which ran shrieking in and out among the caves, as wailing women and children in some assaulted town.

This is, if I may insist on the term, putative description. It asserts itself to be description and passes for description until it is looked into, when you see that it is primarily the *assertion* of an emotional relation to landscape, and through effects of which landscape is incapable. Its force depends on the looseness, vagueness, and tumultuousness of the motion of the words. As a matter of fact the words are so chosen and arranged that they cannot contribute any material

of emotion beyond that which may be contained in a stock exclamation. The primary point of our comparison is that the second passage dilutes and wastes an emotion assumed to have existed prior to its expression, whereas the first passage built up and united the elements of an emotion which exists only and actually in the words employed. The first passage discovers its meaning in words, the second never reached the condition of meaning. The first passage reminds you of Gerard Hopkins, the second of Ann Radcliffe; a contrast which brings up the secondary point of our comparison.

The spirit of the gothic novel ran frothily through the popular literature of America in the first half of the nineteenth century, ending possibly with its own travesty in *The Black Crook*. Melville, faced with the bad necessity, as it must have seemed to him, of popularising the material of *Pierre* and *Moby Dick*, adopted outright the gothic convention of language with all its archaisms and rhetorical inflations. The effect in the two books was similar in fact though not quite the same in effect. Some of the soliloquies in *Moby Dick* seem more like tantrums than poetry, but they were the tantrums of a great imagination fed with mastered material. In *Pierre*, without any fund of nourishing material, the dialogues, soliloquies, and meditations get lost in the flatulence of words.

Now, the gothic convention is not insusceptible of reality in itself, as we see in Beckford and Peacock and Brontë—perhaps in Poe and occasionally in Hawthorne—but it requires on the part of the author unconditional assent to it as a convention. This assent Melville could not give; he used it, so far as I can see, as a solemn fraud and hoped for the best. In *Moby Dick* the fraud passed preliminary muster because the lofty "unreal" terror that rode the *Pequod* made it seem at least plausible, even in its greatest extravagance, as a vehicle of response. And there is the further defence, often made, that the worst excesses of language and sentiment are excusable because of the poetry they are supposed to hold. To which the answer is that the poetry would have been better without the excess; when Melville dropped the mode and wrote in language comparable to the passage first quoted above, as in Ahab's last soliloquy, better poetry was actually produced. But no one, so far as I know, unless it be Foster Damon who writes *con amore* of anything both American and gothic, has defended the excesses of *Pierre*, of which the passage quoted above is a tame example.

It may be said in passing that what is often called the Elizabethan influence in Melville's prose might more accurately be called the gothic influence heightened by the greatness of Melville's intentions. If I may have the notation for what it is worth, I suspect that in "the three boats swung over the sea like three samphire baskets over high cliffs," while the samphire baskets undoubtedly came from *King Lear*, still they had got well spattered with gothic mire on the long journey. Again, the sister-brother crux in *Pierre*, while it may be found in John Ford has a very different reality of expression from that in Ford's verse.

The menacings in thy eyes are dear delights to me; I grow up with thy own glorious stature; and in thee, my brother, I see God's indignant ambassador to me, saying —Up, up, Isabel, and take no terms from the common world, but do thou make terms to it, and grind thy fierce rights out of it! Thy catching nobleness unsexes me, my brother; and now I know that in her most exalted moment, then woman no more feels the twin-born softness of her breasts, but feels chain-armour palpitating there!

These lines, spoken by Isabel in response to similar declarations on the part of Pierre on the occasion of their second conversation, could not have been matched in Ford, but they could be matched a hundred times in the popular gothics. As for the minor effects of Elizabethan influence, where it has been said, by Mumford among others, that Melville's prose is Websterian—and perhaps it sometimes is—yet it far more often supplies us with Marlovian tropes. For every phrase such as "the cheeks of his soul collapsed in him," there are a dozen on the tone of the following: "With a frigate's anchors for my bridle-bits and fasces of harpoons for spurs, would I could mount that whale and leap the topmast skies . . . !" This is the Marlowe of Tamerlane, and the unregenerate Marlowe letting himself go, not the Marlowe remodelled and compacted of *Faustus* and *The Jew*. Occasionally there is such a triumphant meeting of rhetoric and insight as the passage which contains the famous phrases: "To trail the genealogies of these high mortal miseries, carries us at last among the sourceless primogenitures of the gods,"—a passage more mindful of the *Urn Burial* than of anything in *The Duchess of Malfi*, but which is mindful most of Melville himself.

If it was the gothic excess that gave occasional opportunity for magnificent flashes, we should be grateful to it that much: it is at least a delight by the way; but it far more often produced passages like the speech of Isabel, which are perhaps collector's items, but not delights. Besides, what is most and finally illuminating, when Melville really had something to say, and was not making a novel, he resorted to another mode, which was perhaps the major expressive mode of his day, the mode of the liberal Emersonian sermon, the moral apologue on the broad Christian basis. There Melville's natural aptitude lay; when he preaches he is released, and only then, of all weak specifications. That the sermon was to say the best of it an artificial mode in fiction mattered nothing, and emphasises the fact that Melville was only a novelist betimes. He made only the loosest efforts to tie his sermons into his novels, and was quite content if he could see that his novels illustrated his sermons and reasonably content if they did not; or so the books would show. He preached without scruple, and with full authority, because he felt in full command of the mode he used: he believed in its convention of structure and its deeper convention of its relation to society with all his heart. Father Mapple's sermon on Jonah and Plotinus Plinlimmon's lecture—it is really a sermon—on Chronometricals and Horologicals are the two sustained examples of self-complete form in his work. The doctrine might not have appealed to Channing or Parker, but the form, the execution, the litheness and vigour and verve, the homely aptnesses, the startling comparisons, the lucidity of presentation of hard insights, the dramatic and pictorial quality of the illustrations, and above all the richness of impact and the weighted speed of the words, would have appealed as near perfection.

The curiosity—and Melville looked at is all curiosity—that needs emphasis here is that the vices of his style either disappeared or transpired only as virtues when he shifted his mode to the sermon, and this without any addition of insight or eloquence, but simply, I believe, because he had found a mode which suited the bent of his themes, which allowed the putative statement to reach its full glory without further backing, which made room for rhetoric and demanded digression, and which did not trouble him, so great was his faith in it, with its universal lurking insincerity. Consider the following lines, which form the counter sermon to Plinlimmon's lecture in *Pierre*.

All profound things, and emotions of things are preceded and attended by Silence. What a silence is that with which the pale bride precedes the responsive *I will*, to the priest's solemn question, *Wilt thou have this man for thy husband?* In silence, too, the wedded hands are clasped. Yea, in silence the child Christ was born into the world. Silence is the general consecration of the universe. Silence is the invisable laying on of the Divine Pontiff's hands upon the world. Silence is at once the most harmless and the most awful thing in all nature. It speaks of the Reserved Forces of Fate. Silence is the only Voice of our God.

Nor is this so august Silence confined to things simply touching or grand. Like the air, Silence permeates all things, and produces its magical power, as well during that peculiar mood which prevails at a solitary traveller's first setting forth on a journey, as at the unimaginable time when before the world was, Silence brooded on the face of the waters.

The author of these paragraphs was at home in his words and completely mastered by them; and he had reached in that language, what Pierre never reached, the "sense of uncapitulatable security, which is only the possession of the furthest advanced and profoundest souls."

In our present context there seems little more to say. The consideration of Melville as a novelist should have shown, at least in the superficial aspects which this brief essay has been able to touch, that it was precisely the practice of that craft that put his books, and himself, at a loss, and left him silent, stultified, and, before the great face of possibility, impotent for forty years of mature life. I trust that it will have been shown as at least plausible that Melville suffered the exorbitant penalty of his great failure, not as a result of the injuries inflicted upon him by his age, but because of his radical inability to master a technique—that of the novel—radically foreign to his sensibility. The accidents of his career, the worse accidents of his needs, brought him to a wrong choice. Yet had he made a right choice, the accident of his state of beliefs might well have silenced him altogether. Judging by the reception of his two serious books, he would have been anathema as a preacher and unpublishable as an essayist. We should be grateful for his ill luck in only a lesser sense than we are for Dante's, or we should have lost the only great imagination in the middle period of the American nineteenth century: a putative statement to which all readers must assent.

Henry David Thoreau
✳ 1817-1862

Thoreau was of two minds about Whitman. When he first read LEAVES OF GRASS *he was attracted but he was also repelled: it was, he thought, "as if the beasts spoke." But the longer he read, the more he admired. The following estimate was written in a letter to a friend on December 7, 1856, after a visit to Whitman in Brooklyn.*

Walt Whitman

Walt Whitman . . . is the most interesting fact to me at present. I have read his second edition (which he gave me), and it has done me more good than any reading for a long time. Perhaps I remember best the poem of Walt Whitman, an American, and the Sun Down Poem. There are two or three pieces in the book which are disagreeable, to say the least, simply sensual. He does not celebrate love at all. It is as if the beasts spoke. I think that men have not been ashamed of themselves without reason. No doubt there have always been dens where such deeds were unblushingly re-

cited, and it is no merit to compete with their inhabitants. But even on this side he has spoken more truth than any American or modern that I know. I have found his poem exhilarating, encouraging. As for its sensuality—and it may turn out to be less sensual than it appears—I do not so much wish that those parts were not written, as that men and women were so pure that they could read them without harm, that is, without understanding them. One woman told me that no woman could read it—as if a man could read what a woman could not. Of course Walt Whitman can communicate to us no experience, and if we are shocked, whose experience is it that we are reminded of?

On the whole, it sounds to me very brave and American, after whatever deductions. I do not believe that all the sermons, so called, that have been preached in this land put together are equal to it for preaching.

We ought to rejoice greatly in him. He occasionally suggests something a little more than human. You can't confound him with the other inhabitants of Brooklyn or New York. How they must shudder when they read him! He is awfully good.

To be sure I sometimes feel a little imposed on. By his heartiness and broad generalities he puts me in a liberal frame of mind prepared to see wonders—as it were, sets me upon a hill or in the midst of a plain—stirs me well up, and then—throws in a thousand of brick. Though rude and sometimes ineffectual, it is a great primitive poem,—an alarum or trumpet-note ringing through the American camp. Wonderfully like the Orientals, too, considering that when I asked him if he had read them, he answered, "No: tell me about them."

I did not get far in conversation with him—two more being present—and among the few things which I chanced to say, I remember that one was, in answer to him as representing America, that I did not think that much of America or of politics, and so on, which may have been somewhat of a damper to him.

Since I have seen him, I find that I am not disturbed by any brag or egoism in his book. He may turn out the least braggart of all, having a better right to be confident.

He is a great fellow.

Sidney Lanier

❋ 1842-1881

The attitude of Sidney Lanier toward Whitman was as mixed as that of Thoreau. In his own more consciously musical verse, the Southern poet lamented the loss of grace and discrimination among his countrymen, so that public remarks which the aging Whitman was increasingly fond of making about the Poetry of the Future seemed particularly distasteful to him. Though he spoke often elsewhere in admiration of Whitman, Lanier seems unable to have resisted the temptation to insert the following rhetorical flight into one of the lectures on the English novel which he delivered in 1881 at the Johns Hopkins University.

Walt Whitman: The Dandy-Upside-Down

. . . If we are presented with a poetry which claims to be democratic because it—the poetry—is measurelessly vicious, purposely eructant, striving after ruggedness, despising grace, like the democracy described by Whitman; then we reply that as a matter of fact there never was any such American democracy and that the poetry which represents it has no constituency. And herein seems a most abundant solution of the fact . . . that the actually existing democracy have never accepted Whitman's poetry. But here we are met with the cry of strength and manliness. Everywhere throughout Whitman's poetry the "rude muscle," the brawn, the physical bigness of the American prairie, the sinew of the Western backwoodsman, are apotheosized, and all these, as Whitman claims, are fitly chanted in his "savage song."

Here, then, is a great stalwart man, in perfect health, all brawn and muscle, set up before us as the ideal of strength. Let us examine this strength a little. For one, I declare that I do not find it impressive. Yonder, in a counting-room of Baltimore —alas, in how many counting-rooms!— a young man with weak eyes bends over a ledger, and painfully casts up the figures day by day, on pitiful wages, to support his mother, or send his younger brother to school, or some such matter. If we watch this young man when he takes down his hat, lays off his ink-splotched office-coat, and starts home for dinner, we perceive that he is in every respect the opposite of the stalwart Whitman ideal; his chest is not huge, his legs are inclined to be pipe-stems, and his dress is like that of any other bookkeeper. Yet the weak-eyed, pipe-stem-legged young man impresses me as more of a man, more of a democratic man than the tallest of Whitman's roughs; to the eye of my spirit there is more strength in this young man's daily endurance of petty care and small weariness, for love, more of the sort of stuff which makes a real democracy and a sound republic, than in an army of Whitman's unshaven loafers. . . .

In the name of all really manful democracy, in the name of the true strength that only can make our republic reputable among the nations, let us repudiate the strength that is no stronger than the human biceps, let us repudiate the manfulness that averages no more than six feet high. My democrat, the democrat whom I contemplate with pleasure, the democrat who is to write or read the poetry of the future, may have a mere thread for his biceps, yet he shall be strong enough to handle hell; he shall play ball with the earth; and albeit his stature may be no more than a boy's, he shall still be taller than great redwoods of California; his height shall be the height of great resolution and love and faith and beauty and knowledge and subtle meditation; his head shall be forever among the stars. . . . (I complain of Whitman's democracy that it has no provision for the sick, or small, or puny, or plain-featured, or hump-backed, or any deformed people, and that his democracy is really the worst kind of aristocracy, being an aristocracy of nature's favorites in the matter of muscle.) . . .

And lastly, the Poetry of the Future holds that all modern poetry, Tennyson particularly, is dainty and over-perfumed, and Whitman speaks of it with that contempt which he everywhere affects for the dandy. But surely—I do not mean this disrespectfully—what age of time has ever yielded such a dandy as the founder of this school, Whitman himself? The simpering beau who is the product of the tailor's art is certainly absurd enough; but what difference is there between that and the other dandyupside-down who from equal motives of affectation throws away coat and vest, dons a slouch hat, opens his shirt so as to expose his breast, and industriously circulates his portrait, thus taken, in his own books? And this dandyism—the dandyism of the roustabout—I find in Whitman's poetry from beginning to end. Everywhere it is conscious of itself, everywhere it is posing to see if it cannot assume a naïve and striking attitude,

everywhere it is screwing up its eye, not into an eyeglass like the conventional dandy, but into an expression supposed to be fearsomely rough and barbaric and frightful to the terror-stricken reader, and it is almost safe to say that one half of Whitman's poetic work has consisted of a detailed description of the song he is going to sing. It is the extreme of sophistication in writing.

Allen Tate

✳ 1899-

A poet himself, Allen Tate writes best in prose when his subject is poetry. Prominent among the Southern literary group known as the Nashville Fugitives, he has been an editor of the HOUND AND HORN *and the* SEWANEE REVIEW, *consultant in poetry at the Library of Congress, resident fellow in writing at Princeton University, senior fellow of the Kenyon School of Letters, and has taught at several institutions, most recently at the University of Minnesota. His miscellaneous writings in prose have been gathered to such volumes as* REACTIONARY ESSAYS ON POETRY AND IDEAS (1936), ON THE LIMITS OF POETRY (1945), THE FORLORN DEMON (1953), *and* THE MAN OF LETTERS IN THE MODERN WORLD (1955). *This essay on Emily Dickinson appeared in* REACTIONARY ESSAYS.

Emily Dickinson

Great poetry needs no special features of difficulty to make it mysterious. When it has them, the reputation of the poet is likely to remain uncertain. This is still true of Donne, and it is true of Emily

Dickinson, whose verse appeared in an age unfavorable to the use of intelligence in poetry. Her poetry is not like any other poetry of her time; it is not like any of the innumerable kinds of verse written today. In still another respect it is far removed from us. It is a poetry of ideas, and it demands of the reader a point of view—not an opinion of the New Deal or of the League of Nations, but an ingrained philosophy that is fundamental, a settled attitude that is almost extinct in this eclectic age. Yet it is not the sort of poetry of ideas which, like Pope's, requires a point of view only. It requires also, for the deepest understanding, which must go beneath the verbal excitement of the style, a highly developed sense of the specific quality of poetry—a quality that most persons accept as the accidental feature of something else that the poet thinks he has to say. This is one reason why Miss Dickinson's poetry has not been widely read.

There is another reason, and it is a part of the problem peculiar to a poetry that comes out of fundamental ideas. We lack a tradition of criticism. There were no points of critical reference passed on to us from a preceding generation. I am not upholding here the so-called dead hand of tradition, but rather a rational insight into the meaning of the present in terms of some imaginable past implicit in our own lives: we need a body of ideas that can bear upon the course of the spirit and yet remain coherent as a rational instrument. We ignore the present, which is momentarily translated into the past, and derive our standards from imaginative constructions of the future. The hard contingency of fact invariably breaks these standards down, leaving us the intellectual chaos which is the sore distress of American criticism. Marxian criticism has become the latest disguise of this heresy.

Still another difficulty stands between us and Miss Dickinson. It is the failure of the scholars to feel more than biographical curiosity about her. We have scholarship, but that is no substitute for a critical tradition. Miss Dickinson's value to the research scholar, who likes historical difficulty for its own sake, is slight; she is too near to possess the remoteness of literature. Perhaps her appropriate setting would be the age of Cowley or of Donne. Yet in her own historical setting she is, nevertheless, remarkable and special.

Although the intellectual climate into which she was born, in 1830, had, as all times have, the features of a transition, the period was also a major crisis culminating in the war between the States. After that war, in New England as well as in the South, spiritual crises were definitely minor until the First World War.

Yet, a generation before the war of 1861–65, the transformation of New England had begun. When Samuel Slater in 1790 thwarted the British embargo on mill machinery by committing to memory the whole design of a cotton spinner and bringing it to Massachusetts, he planted the seed of the "Western spirit." By 1825 its growth in the East was rank enough to begin choking out the ideas and habits of living that New England along with Virginia had kept in unconscious allegiance to Europe. To the casual observer, perhaps, the New England character of 1830 was largely an eighteenth-century character. But theocracy was on the decline, and industrialism was rising—as Emerson, in an unusually lucid moment, put it, "Things are in the saddle." The energy that had built the meeting-house ran the factory.

Now the idea that moved the theocratic state is the most interesting historically of all American ideas. It was, of course, powerful in seventeenth-century England, but in America, where the long arm of Laud could not reach, it acquired an unchecked social and political influence. The important thing to re-member about the puritan theocracy is that it permeated, as it could never have done in England, a whole society. It gave final, definite meaning to life, the life of pious and impious, of learned and vulgar alike. It gave—and this is its significance for Emily Dickinson, and in only slightly lesser degree for Melville and Hawthorne—it gave an heroic pro-portion and a tragic mode to the experi-ence of the individual. The history of the New England theocracy, from Apostle Eliot to Cotton Mather, is rich in gigantic intellects that broke down—or so it must appear to an outsider—in a kind of moral decadence and depravity. Socially we may not like the New England idea. Yet it had an immense, incalculable value for literature: it dramatized the human soul.

But by 1850 the great fortunes had been made (in the rum, slave, and mill-ing industries), and New England be-came a museum. The whatnots groaned under the load of knickknacks, the fine china dogs and cats, the pieces of Orien-tal jade, the chips off the leaning tower of Pisa. There were the rare books and the cosmopolitan learning. It was all equally displayed as the evidence of a superior culture. The Gilded Age had already begun. But culture, in the true sense, was disappearing. Where the old order, formidable as it was, had held all this personal experience, this eclectic ex-citement, in a comprehensible whole, the new order tended to flatten it out in a common experience that was not quite in common; it exalted more and more the personal and the unique in the interior sense. Where the old-fashioned puritans got together on a rigid doctrine, and could thus be individualists in manners, the nineteenth-century New Englander, lacking a genuine religious center, began to be a social conformist. The common idea of the Redemption, for example, was replaced by the conformist idea of

respectability among neighbors whose spiritual disorder, not very evident at the surface, was becoming acute. A great idea was breaking up, and society was moving towards external uniformity, which is usually the measure of the spiritual sterility inside.

At this juncture Emerson came upon the scene: the Lucifer of Concord, he had better be called hereafter, for he was the light-bearer who could see noth-ing but light, and was fearfully blind. He looked around and saw the uniformity of life, and called it the routine of tradition, the tyranny of the theological idea. The death of Priam put an end to the hope of Troy, but it was a slight feat of arms for the doughty Pyrrhus; Priam was an old gentleman and almost dead. So was theocracy; and Emerson killed it. In this way he accelerated a tendency that he disliked. It was a great intellectual mis-take. By it Emerson unwittingly became the prophet of a piratical industrialism, a consequence of his own transcendental individualism that he could not foresee. He was hoist with his own petard.

He discredited more than any other man the puritan drama of the soul. The age that followed, from 1865 on, expired in a genteel secularism, a mildly didactic order of feeling whose ornaments were Lowell, Longfellow, and Holmes. "After Emerson had done his work," says Mr. Robert Penn Warren, "any tragic pos-sibilities in that culture were dissipated." Hawthorne alone in his time kept pure, in the primitive terms, the primitive vision; he brings the puritan tragedy to its climax. Man, measured by a great idea outside himself, is found wanting. But for Emerson man is greater than any idea and, being himself the Over-Soul, is innately perfect; there is no struggle be-cause—I state the Emersonian doctrine, which is very slippery, in its extreme terms—because there is no possibility of error. There is no drama in human char-acter because there is no tragic fault. It is not surprising, then, that after Emerson New England literature tastes like a sip of cambric tea. Its center of vision has disappeared. There is Hawthorne looking back, there is Emerson looking not too clearly at anything ahead: Emily Dickinson, who has in her something of both, comes in somewhere between.

With the exception of Poe there is no other American poet whose work so steadily emerges, under pressure of certain disintegrating obsessions, from the framework of moral character. There is none of whom it is truer to say that the poet *is* the poetry. Perhaps this explains the zeal of her admirers for her biography; it explains, in part at least, the gratuitous mystery that Mrs. Bianchi, a niece of the poet and her official biographer, has made of her life. The devoted controversy that Miss Josephine Pollitt and Miss Genevieve Taggard started a few years ago with their excellent books shows the extent to which the critics feel the intimate connection of her life and work. Admiration and affection are pleased to linger over the tokens of a great life; but the solution to the Dickinson enigma is peculiarly superior to fact.

The meaning of the identity—which we merely feel—of character and poetry would be exceedingly obscure, even if we could draw up a kind of Binet correlation between the two sets of "facts." Miss Dickinson was a recluse; but her poetry is rich with a profound and varied experience. Where did she get it? Now some of the biographers, nervous in the presence of this discrepancy, are eager to find her a love affair, and I think this search is due to a modern prejudice: we believe that no virgin can know enough to write poetry. We shall never learn where she got the rich quality of her mind. The moral image that we have of Miss Dickinson stands out in every poem; it is that of a dominating spinster whose very sweetness must have been

formidable. Yet her poetry constantly moves within an absolute order of truths that overwhelmed her simply because to her they were unalterably fixed. It is dangerous to assume that her "life," which to the biographers means the thwarted love affair she is supposed to have had, gave to her poetry a decisive direction. It is even more dangerous to suppose that it made her a poet.

Poets are mysterious, but a poet, when all is said, is not much more mysterious than a banker. The critics remain spellbound by the technical license of her verse and by the puzzle of her personal life. Personality is a legitimate interest because it is an incurable interest, but legitimate as a personal interest only; it will never give up the key to anyone's verse. Used to that end, the interest is false. "It is apparent," writes Mr. Conrad Aiken, "that Miss Dickinson became a hermit by deliberate and conscious choice"—a sensible remark that we cannot repeat too often. If it were necessary to explain her seclusion with disappointment in love, there would remain the discrepancy between what the seclusion produced and the seclusion looked at as a cause. The effect, which is her poetry, would imply the whole complex of anterior fact, which was the social and religious structure of New England.

The problem to be kept in mind is thus the meaning of her "deliberate and conscious" decision to withdraw from life to her upstairs room. This simple fact is not very important. But that it must have been her sole way of acting out her part in the history of her culture, which made, with the variations of circumstance, a single demand upon all its representatives—this is of the greatest consequence. All pity for Miss Dickinson's "starved life" is misdirected. Her life was one of the richest and deepest ever lived on this continent.

When she went upstairs and closed the door, she mastered life by rejecting it. Others in their way had done it before; still others did it later. If we suppose —which is to suppose the improbable— that the love affair precipitated the seclusion, it was only a pretext; she would have found another. Mastery of the world by rejecting the world was the doctrine, even if it was not always the practice, of Jonathan Edwards and Cotton Mather. It is the meaning of fate in Hawthorne: his people are fated to withdraw from the world and to be destroyed. And it is one of the great themes of Henry James.

There is a moral emphasis that connects Hawthorne, James, and Miss Dickinson, and I think it is instructive. Between Hawthorne and James lies an epoch. The temptation to sin, in Hawthorne, is, in James, transformed into the temptation not to do the "decent thing." A whole world-scheme, a complete cosmic background, has shrunk to the dimensions of the individual conscience. This epoch between Hawthorne and James lies in Emerson. James found himself in the post-Emersonian world, and he could not, without violating the detachment proper to an artist, undo Emerson's work; he had that kind of intelligence which refuses to break its head against history. There was left to him only the value, the historic role, of rejection. He could merely escape from the physical presence of that world which, for convenience, we may call Emerson's world: he could only take his Americans to Europe upon the vain quest of something that they had lost at home. His characters, fleeing the wreckage of the puritan culture, preserved only their honor. Honor became a sort of forlorn hope struggling against the forces of "pure fact" that had got loose in the middle of the century. Honor alone is a poor weapon against nature, being too personal, finical, and proud, and James achieved a victory by refusing to engage the whole force of the enemy.

In Emily Dickinson the conflict takes place on a vaster field. The enemy to all those New Englanders was Nature, and Miss Dickinson saw into the character of this enemy more deeply than any of the others. The general symbol of Nature, for her, is Death, and her weapon against Death is the entire powerful dumb-show of the puritan theology led by Redemption and Immortality. Morally speaking, the problem for James and Miss Dickinson is similar. But her advantages were greater than his. The advantages lay in the availability to her of the puritan ideas on the theological plane.

These ideas, in her poetry, are momently assailed by the disintegrating force of Nature (appearing as Death) which, while constantly breaking them down, constantly redefines and strengthens them. The values are purified by the triumphant withdrawal from Nature, by their power to recover from Nature. The poet attains to a mastery over experience by facing its utmost implications. There is the clash of powerful opposites, and in all great poetry—for Emily Dickinson is a great poet—it issues in a tension between abstraction and sensation in which the two elements may be, of course, distinguished logically, but not really. We are shown our roots in Nature by examining our differences with Nature; we are renewed by Nature without being delivered into her hands. When it is possible for a poet to do this for us with the greatest imaginative comprehension, a possibility that the poet cannot himself create, we have the perfect literary situation. Only a few times in the history of English poetry has this situation come about: notably, the period between about 1580 and the Restoration. There was a similar age in New England from which emerged two talents of the first order—Hawthorne and Emily Dickinson.

There is an epoch between James and Miss Dickinson. But between her and Hawthorne there exists a difference of intellectual quality. She lacks almost radically the power to seize upon and understand abstractions for their own sake; she does not separate them from the sensuous illuminations that she is so marvelously adept at; like Donne, she *perceives abstraction* and *thinks sensation*. But Hawthorne was a master of ideas, within a limited range; this narrowness confined him to his own kind of life, his own society, and out of it grew his typical forms of experience, his steady, almost obsessed vision of man; it explains his depth and intensity. Yet he is always conscious of the abstract, doctrinal aspect of his mind, and when his vision of action and emotion is weak, his work becomes didactic. Now Miss Dickinson's poetry often runs into quasi-homiletic forms, but it is never didactic. Her very ignorance, her lack of formal intellectual training, preserved her from the risk that imperiled Hawthorne. She cannot reason at all. She can only *see*. It is impossible to imagine what she might have done with drama or fiction; for, not approaching the puritan temper and through it the puritan myth, through human action, she is able to grasp the terms of the myth directly and by a feat that amounts almost to anthropomorphism, to give them a luminous tension, a kind of drama, among themselves.

One of the perfect poems in English is "The Chariot," and it illustrates better than anything else she wrote the special quality of her mind. I think it will illuminate the tendency of this discussion:

Because I could not stop for death,
He kindly stopped for me;
The carriage held but just ourselves
And immortality.

We slowly drove, he knew no haste,
And I had put away
My labor, and my leisure too,
For his civility.

We passed the school where children played,
Their lessons scarcely done;
We passed the fields of gazing grain,
We passed the setting sun.

We paused before a house that seemed
A swelling of the ground;
The roof was scarcely visible,
The cornice but a mound.

Since then 'tis centuries; but each
Feels shorter than the day
I first surmised the horses' heads
Were toward eternity.

If the word "great" means anything in poetry, this poem is one of the greatest in the English language. The rhythm charges with movement the pattern of suspended action back of the poem. Every image is precise and, moreover, not merely beautiful, but fused with the central idea. Every image extends and intensifies every other. The third stanza especially shows Miss Dickinson's power to fuse, into a single order of preception, a heterogeneous series: the children, the grain, and the setting sun (time) have the same degree of credibility; the first subtly preparing for the last. The sharp *gazing* before *grain* instills into nature a cold vitality of which the qualitative richness has infinite depth. The content of death in the poem eludes explicit definition. He is a gentleman taking a lady out for a drive. But note the restraint that keeps the poet from carrying this so far that it becomes ludicrous and incredible; and note the subtly interfused erotic motive, which the idea of death has presented to most romantic poets, love being a symbol interchangeable with death. The terror of death is objectified through this figure of the genteel driver, who is made ironically to serve the end of Immortality. This is the heart of the poem: she has presented a typical Christian theme in its final irresolution, without making any final statements about it. There is no solution to the problem; there can be only a presentation of it in the full context of intellect and feeling. A construction of the human will, elaborated with all the abstracting powers of the mind, is put to the concrete test of experience: the idea of immortality is confronted with the fact of physical disintegration. We are not told what to think; we are told to look at the situation.

The framework of the poem is, in fact, the two abstractions, mortality and eternity, which are made to associate in equality with the images: she sees the ideas, and thinks the perceptions. She did, of course, nothing of the sort; but we must use the logical distinctions, even to the extent of paradox, if we are to form any notion of this rare quality of mind. She could not in the proper sense think at all, and unless we prefer the feeble poetry of moral ideas that flourished in New England in the eighties, we must conclude that her intellectual deficiency contributed at least negatively to her great distinction. Miss Dickinson is probably the only Anglo-American poet of her century whose work exhibits the perfect literary situation—in which is possible the fusion of sensibility and thought. Unlike her contemporaries, she never succumbed to her ideas, to easy solutions, to her private desires.

Philosophers must deal with ideas, but the trouble with most nineteenth-century poets is too much philosophy; they are nearer to being philosophers than poets, without being in the true sense either. Tennyson is a good example of this; so is Arnold in his weak moments. There have been poets like Milton and Donne, who were not spoiled for their true business by leaning on a rational system of ideas, who understood the poetic use of ideas. Tennyson tried to mix a little Huxley and a little Broad Church, without understanding either Broad Church or Huxley; the result was fatal, and what is worse, it was shallow. Miss Dickinson's ideas were deeply imbedded in her character, not taken from the latest tract. A conscious cultivation of ideas in poetry is always dangerous, and even Milton escaped ruin only by having an instinct for what in the deepest sense he understood. Even at that there

is a remote quality in Milton's approach to his material, in his treatment of it; in the nineteenth century, in an imperfect literary situation where literature was confused with documentation, he might have been a pseudo-philosopher-poet. It is difficult to conceive Emily Dickinson and John Donne succumbing to rumination about "problems"; they would not have written at all.

Neither the feeling nor the style of Miss Dickinson belongs to the seventeenth century; yet between her and Donne there are remarkable ties. Their religious ideas, their abstractions, are momently toppling from the rational plane to the level of perception. The ideas, in fact, are no longer the impersonal religious symbols created anew in the heat of emotion, that we find in poets like Herbert and Vaughan. They have become, for Donne, the terms of personality; they are mingled with the miscellany of sensation. In Miss Dickinson, as in Donne, we may detect a singularly morbid concern, not for religious truth, but for personal revelation. The modern word is self-exploitation. It is egoism grown irresponsible in religion and decadent in morals. In religion it is blasphemy; in society it means usually that culture is not self-contained and sufficient, that the spiritual community is breaking up. This is, along with some other features that do not concern us here, the perfect literary situation.

2

Personal revelation of the kind that Donne and Miss Dickinson strove for, in the effort to understand their relation to the world, is a feature of all great poetry; it is probably the hidden motive for writing. It is the effort of the individual to live apart from a cultural tradition that no longer sustains him. But this culture, which I now wish to discuss a little, is indispensable: there is a great deal of shallow nonsense in modern criticism which holds that poetry—and this is a half-truth that is worse than false—is essentially revolutionary. It is only indirectly revolutionary: the intellectual and religious background of an age no longer contains the whole spirit, and the poet proceeds to examine that background in terms of immediate experience. But the background is necessary; otherwise all the arts (not only poetry) would have to rise in a vacuum. Poetry does not dispense with tradition; it probes the deficiencies of a tradition. But it must have a tradition to probe. It is too bad that Arnold did not explain his doctrine, that poetry is a criticism of life, from the viewpoint of its background: we should have been spared an era of academic misconception, in which criticism of life meant a diluted pragmatism, the criterion of which was respectability. The poet in the true sense "criticizes" his tradition, either as such, or indirectly by comparing it with something that is about to replace it; he does what the root-meaning of the verb implies—he *discerns* its real elements and thus establishes its value, by putting it to the test of experience.

What is the nature of a poet's culture? Or, to put the question properly, what is the meaning of culture for poetry? All the great poets become the material of what we popularly call culture; we study them to acquire it. It is clear that Addison was more cultivated than Shakespeare; nevertheless Shakespeare is a finer source of culture than Addison. What is the meaning of this? Plainly it is that learning has never had anything to do with culture except instrumentally: the poet must be exactly literate enough to write down fully and precisely what he has to say, but no more. The source of a poet's true culture lies back of the paraphernalia of culture, and not all the historical activity of an enlightened age can create it.

A culture cannot be consciously created. It is an available source of ideas that are imbedded in a complete and homogeneous society. The poet finds himself balanced upon the moment when such a world is about to fall, when it threatens to run out into looser and less self-sufficient impulses. This world order is assimilated, in Miss Dickinson, as medievalism was in Shakespeare, to the poetic vision; it is brought down from abstraction to personal sensibility.

In this connection it may be said that the prior conditions for great poetry, given a great talent, may be reduced to two: the thoroughness of the poet's discipline in an objective system of truth, and his lack of consciousness of such a discipline. For this discipline is a number of fundamental ideas the origin of which the poet does not know; they give form and stability to his fresh perceptions of the world; and he cannot shake them off. This is his culture, and, like Tennyson's God, it is nearer than hands and feet. With reasonable certainty we unearth the elements of Shakespeare's culture, and yet it is equally certain—so innocent was he of his own resources—that he would not know what our discussion is about. He appeared at the collapse of the medieval system as a rigid pattern of life, but that pattern remained in Shakespeare what Shelley called a "fixed point of reference" for his sensibility. Miss Dickinson, as we have seen, was born into the equilibrium of an old and a new order. Puritanism could not be to her what it had been to the generation of Cotton Mather—a body of absolute truths; it was an unconscious discipline timed to the pulse of her life.

The perfect literary situation: it produces, because it is rare, a special and perhaps the most distinguished kind of poet. I am not trying to invent a new critical category. Such poets are never very much alike on the surface; they show us all the varieties of poetic feeling; and, like other poets, they resist all classification but that of temporary convenience. But, I believe, Miss Dickinson and John Donne would have this in common: their sense of the natural world is not blunted by a too-rigid system of ideas; yet the ideas, the abstractions, their education or their intellectual heritage, are not so weak as to let their immersion in nature, or their purely personal quality, get out of control. The two poles of the mind are not separately visible; we infer them from the lucid tension that may be most readily illustrated by polar activity. There is no thought as such at all; nor is there feeling; there is that unique focus of experience which is at once neither and both.

Like Miss Dickinson, Shakespeare is without opinions; his peculiar merit is also deeply involved in his failure to think about anything; his meaning is not in the content of his expression; it is in the tension of the dramatic relations of his characters. This kind of poetry is at the opposite of intellectualism. (Miss Dickinson is obscure and difficult, but that is not intellectualism.) To T. W. Higginson, the editor of *The Atlantic Monthly*, who tried to advise her, she wrote that she had no education. In any sense that Higginson could understand, it was quite true. His kind of education was the conscious cultivation of abstractions. She did not reason about the world she saw; she merely saw it. The "ideas" implicit in the world within her rose up, concentrated in her immediate perception.

That kind of world at present has for us something of the fascination of a buried city. There is none like it. When such worlds exist, when such cultures flourish, they support not only the poet but all members of society. For, from these, the poet differs only in his gift for exhibiting the structure, the internal lineaments, of his culture by threatening to tear them apart: a process that concentrates the symbolic emotions of so-

ciety while it seems to attack them. The poet may hate his age; he may be an outcast like Villon; but this world is always there as the background to what he has to say. It is the lens through which he brings nature to focus and control—the clarifying medium that concentrates his personal feeling. It is ready-made; he cannot make it; with it, his poetry has a spontaneity and a certainty of direction that, without it, it would lack. No poet could have invented the ideas of "The Chariot"; only a great poet could have found their imaginative equivalents. Miss Dickinson was a deep mind writing from a deep culture, and when she came to poetry, she came infallibly.

Infallibly, at her best; for no poet has ever been perfect, nor is Emily Dickinson. Her precision of statement is due to the directness with which the abstract framework of her thought acts upon its unorganized material. The two elements of her style, considered as point of view, are immortality, or the idea of permanence and the physical process of death or decay. Her diction has two corresponding features: words of Latin or Greek origin and, sharply opposed to these, the concrete Saxon element. It is this verbal conflict that gives her verse its high tension; it is not a device deliberately seized upon, but a feeling for language that senses out the two fundamental components of English and their metaphysical relation: the Latin for ideas and the Saxon for perceptions—the peculiar virtue of English as a poetic language.

Like most poets Miss Dickinson often writes out of habit; the style that emerged from some deep exploration of an idea she carried on as verbal habit when she has nothing to say. She indulges herself:

There's something quieter than sleep
Within this inner room!
It wears a sprig upon its breast,
And will not tell its name.

Some touch it and some kiss it,
Some chafe its idle hand;
It has a simple gravity
I do not understand!

While simple hearted neighbors
Chat of the "early dead,"
We, prone to periphrasis,
Remark that birds have fled!

It is only a pert remark; at best a superior kind of punning—one of the worst specimens of her occasional interest in herself. But she never had the slightest interest in the public. Were four poems or five published in her lifetime? She never felt the temptation to round off a poem for public exhibition. Higginson's kindly offer to make her verse "correct" was an invitation to throw her work into the public ring—the ring of Lowell and Longfellow. He could not see that he was tampering with one of the rarest literary integrities of all time. Here was a poet who had no use for the supports of authorship—flattery and fame; she never needed money.

She had all the elements of a culture that has broken up, a culture that on the religious side takes its place in the museum of spiritual antiquities. Puritanism, as a unified version of the world, is dead; only a remnant of it in trade may be said to survive. In the history of puritanism she comes between Hawthorne and Emerson. She has Hawthorne's matter, which a too irresponsible personality tends to dilute into a form like Emerson's; she is often betrayed by words. But she is not the poet of personal sentiment; she has more to say than she can put down in any one poem. Like Hardy and Whitman, she must be read entire; like Shakespeare, she never gives up her meaning in a single line.

She is therefore a perfect subject for the kind of criticism which is chiefly concerned with general ideas. She exhibits one of the permanent relations between personality and objective truth, and she deserves the special attention of our time, which lacks that kind of truth.

She has Hawthorne's intellectual toughness, a hard, definite sense of the physical world. The highest flights to God, the most extravagant metaphors of the strange and the remote, come back to a point of casuistry, to a moral dilemma of the experienced world. There is, in spite of the homiletic vein of utterance, no abstract speculation, nor is there a message to society; she speaks wholly to the individual experience. She offers to the unimaginative no riot of vicarious sensation; she has no useful maxims for men of action. Up to this point her resemblance to Emerson is slight: poetry is a sufficient form of utterance, and her devotion to it is pure. But in Emily Dickinson the puritan world is no longer self-contained; it is no longer complete; her sensibility exceeds its dimensions. She has trimmed down its supernatural proportions; it has become a morality; instead of the tragedy of the spirit there is a commentary upon it. Her poetry is a magnificent personal confession, blasphemous and, in its self-revelation, its honesty, almost obscene. It comes out of an intellectual life towards which it feels no moral responsibility. Cotton Mather would have burnt her for a witch.

Henry David Thoreau
❈ 1817-1862

The lifelong quest of Henry David Thoreau was to discover a method of weaving words into a net delicate enough to catch and strong enough to hold all meaning. The enterprise was beyond his or any man's capacity, but in pursuing it he did learn to use language as few Americans had done before. His continu-

ing advice to other men and to himself was to wake up, to keep eyes open and senses alert for discovery of whatever life had to offer: his achievement, it has been said, is that he slept only at night in bed. WALDEN, *published in 1854, is not so much a plea to strip life bare by throwing off inessentials as it is an argument for filling life full with important occupation. "Where I Lived, and What I Lived For," the second chapter of that book, like most of Thoreau's writing, says something more than just what its title seems to indicate.*

Where I Lived, and What I Lived For

At a certain season of our life we are accustomed to consider every spot as the possible site of a house. I have thus surveyed the country on every side within a dozen miles of where I live. In imagination I have bought all the farms in succession, for all were to be bought and I knew their price. I walked over each farmer's premises, tasted his wild apples, discoursed on husbandry with him, took his farm at his price, at any price, mortgaging it to him in my mind; even put a higher price on it—took everything but a deed of it—took his word for his deed, for I dearly love to talk—cultivated it, and him too to some extent, I trust, and withdrew when I had enjoyed it long enough, leaving him to carry it on. This experience entitled me to be regarded as a sort of real-estate broker by my friends. Wherever I sat, there I might live, and the landscape radiated from me accordingly. What is a house but a *sedes,* a seat?—better if a country seat. I discovered many a site for a house not likely to be soon improved, which some might have thought too far from the village but to my eyes the vil-

lage was too far from it. Well, there I might live, I said; and there I did live, for an hour, a summer and a winter life; saw how I could let the years run off, buffet the winter through, and see the spring come in. The future inhabitants of this region, wherever they may place their houses, may be sure that they have been anticipated. An afternoon sufficed to lay out the land into orchard, wood lot, and pasture, and to decide what fine oaks or pines should be left to stand before the door, and whence each blasted tree could be seen to the best advantage; and then I let it lie, fallow perchance, for a man is rich in proportion to the number of things which he can afford to let alone.

My imagination carried me so far that I even had the refusal of several farms—the refusal was all I wanted—but I never got my fingers burned by actual possession. The nearest that I came to actual possession was when I bought the Hollowell place, and had begun to sort my seeds, and collected materials with which to make a wheelbarrow to carry it on or off with; but before the owner gave me a deed of it, his wife—every man has such a wife—changed her mind and wished to keep it, and he offered me ten dollars to release him. Now, to speak the truth, I had but ten cents in the world and it surpassed my arithmetic to tell if I was that man who had ten cents, or who had a farm, or ten dollars, or all together. However, I let him keep the ten dollars and the farm too, for I had carried it far enough; or rather, to be generous, I sold him the farm for just what I gave for it, and as he was not a rich man, made him a present of ten dollars, and still had my ten cents, and seeds, and materials for a wheelbarrow left. I found thus that I had been a rich man without any damage to my poverty. But I retained the landscape, and I have since annually carried off what it yielded without a wheelbarrow. With respect to landscapes—

> I am monarch of all I *survey*,
> My right there is none to dispute.

I have frequently seen a poet withdraw, having enjoyed the most valuable part of a farm, while the crusty farmer supposed that he had got a few wild apples only. Why, the owner does not know it for many years when a poet has put his farm in rime, the most admirable kind of invisible fence, has fairly impounded it, milked it, skimmed it, and got all the cream, and left the farmer only the skimmed milk.

The real attractions of the Hollowell farm to me were: its complete retirement, being about two miles from the village, half a mile from the nearest neighbor, and separated from the highway by a broad field; its bounding on the river, which the owner said protected it by its fogs from frosts in the spring, though that was nothing to me; the gray color and ruinous state of the house and barn; and the dilapidated fences, which put such an interval between me and the last occupant; the hollow and lichen-covered apple trees, gnawed by rabbits, showing what kind of neighbors I should have; but above all, the recollection I had of it from my earliest voyages up the river when the house was concealed behind a dense grove of red maples through which I heard the house dog bark. I was in haste to buy it before the proprietor finished getting out some rocks, cutting down the hollow apple trees, and grubbing up some young birches which had sprung up in the pasture, or in short, had made any more of his improvements. To enjoy these advantages I was ready to carry it on; like Atlas, to take the world on my shoulders —I never heard what compensation he received for that—and do all those things which had no other motive or excuse but that I might pay for it and be unmolested

in my possession of it; for I knew all the while that it would yield the most abundant crop of the kind I wanted if I could only afford to let it alone. But it turned out as I have said.

All that I could say, then, with respect to farming on a large scale—I have always cultivated a garden—was that I had had my seeds ready. Many think that seeds improve with age. I have no doubt that time discriminates between the good and the bad; and when at last I shall plant, I shall be less likely to be disappointed. But I would say to my fellows once for all, as long as possible live free and uncommitted. It makes but little difference whether you are committed to a farm or the county jail.

Old Cato, whose "De Re Rusticâ" is my "Cultivator," says—and the only translation I have seen makes sheer nonsense of the passage—"When you think of getting a farm turn it thus in your mind, not to buy greedily; nor spare your pains to look at it, and do not think it enough to go round it once. The oftener you go there the more it will please you, if it is good." I think I shall not buy greedily, but go round and round it as long as I live and be buried in it first, that it may please me the more at last.

The present was my next experiment of this kind, which I purpose to describe more at length, for convenience putting the experience of two years into one. As I have said, I do not propose to write an ode to dejection, but to brag as lustily as chanticleer in the morning standing on his roost, if only to wake my neighbors up.

When first I took up my abode in the woods, that is, began to spend my nights as well as days there, which by accident was on Independence Day, or the Fourth of July, 1845, my house was not finished for winter but was merely a defense against the rain, without plastering or chimney, the walls being of rough, weather-stained boards, with wide chinks, which made it cool at night. The upright white hewn studs and freshly planed door and window casings gave it a clean and airy look, especially in the morning when its timbers were saturated with dew, so that I fancied that by noon some sweet gum would exude from them. To my imagination it retained throughout the day more or less of this auroral character, reminding me of a certain house on a mountain which I had visited a year before. This was an airy and unplastered cabin fit to enter-tain a traveling god, and where a god-dess might trail her garments. The winds which passed over my dwelling were such as sweep over the ridges of moun-tains, bearing the broken strains, or celestial parts only, of terrestrial music. The morning wind forever blows, the poem of creation is uninterrupted; but few are the ears that hear it. Olympus is but the outside of the earth everywhere.

The only house I had been the owner of before, if I except a boat, was a tent which I used occasionally when making excursions in the summer, and this is still rolled up in my garret; but the boat, after passing from hand to hand, has gone down the stream of time. With this more substantial shelter about me, I had made some progress toward settling in the world. This frame, so slightly clad, was a sort of crystallization around me and reacted on the builder. It was sug-gestive somewhat as a picture in out-lines. I did not need to go outdoors to take the air, for the atmosphere within had lost none of its freshness. It was not so much within doors as behind a door where I sat even in the rainiest weather. The Harivansa says, "An abode without birds is like a meat without seasoning." Such was not my abode, for I found my-self suddenly neighbor to the birds; not by having imprisoned one but having caged myself near them. I was not only nearer to some of those which commonly

frequent the garden and the orchard but to those wilder and more thrilling song-sters of the forest which never, or rarely, serenade a villager—the wood thrush, the veery, the scarlet tanager, the field sparrow, the whippoorwill, and many others.

I was seated by the shore of a small pond about a mile and a half south of the village of Concord and somewhat higher than it, in the midst of an ex-tensive wood between that town and Lincoln and about two miles south of that our only field known to fame, Con-cord Battle Ground; but I was so low in the woods that the opposite shore half a mile off, like the rest, covered with wood, was my most distant horizon. For the first week, whenever I looked out on the pond it impressed me like a tarn high up on the side of a mountain, its bottom far above the surface of other lakes, and as the sun arose, I saw it throwing off its nightly clothing of mist, and here and there, by degrees, its soft ripples or its smooth reflecting surface was revealed, while the mists, like ghosts, were stealthily withdrawing in every direction into the woods, as at the breaking up of some nocturnal con-venticle. The very dew seemed to hang upon the trees later into the day than usual, as on the sides of mountains.

This small lake was of most value as a neighbor in the intervals of a gentle rain-storm in August, when both air and water being perfectly still but the sky overcast, midafternoon had all the seren-ity of evening, and the wood thrush sang around and was heard from shore to shore. A lake like this is never smoother than at such a time; and the clear por-tion of the air above it being shallow and darkened by clouds, the water full of light and reflections becomes a lower heaven itself so much the more im-portant. From a hilltop near by, where the wood had been recently cut off, there was a pleasing vista southward across the pond through a wide indentation in the hills which form the shore there, where their opposite sides sloping toward each other suggested a stream flowing out in that direction through a wooded valley, but stream there was none. That way I looked between and over the near green hills to some distant and higher ones in the horizon tinged with blue. Indeed, by standing on tiptoe I could catch a glimpse of some of the peaks of the still bluer and more distant mountain ranges in the northwest, those true-blue coins from heaven's own mint, and also of some portion of the village. But in other directions, even from this point, I could not see over or beyond the woods which surrounded me. It is well to have some water in your neighborhood, to give buoyancy to and float the earth. One value even of the smallest well is that when you look into it you see that earth is not continent but insular. This is as important as that it keeps butter cool. When I looked across the pond from this peak toward the Sudbury meadows, which in time of flood I distinguished elevated perhaps by a mirage in their seething valley like a coin in a basin, all the earth beyond the pond appeared like a thin crust insulated and floated even by this small sheet of intervening water, and I was reminded that this on which I dwelt was but *dry land.*

Though the view from my door was still more contracted, I did not feel crowded or confined in the least. There was pasture enough for my imagination. The low shrub oak plateau to which the opposite shore arose stretched away toward the prairies of the West and the steppes of Tartary affording ample room for all the roving families of men. "There are none happy in the world but beings who enjoy freely a vast horizon," said Damodara, when his herds required new and larger pastures.

Both place and time were changed, and I dwelt nearer to those parts of the universe and to those eras in history which had most attracted me. Where I lived was as far off as many a region viewed nightly by astronomers. We are wont to imagine rarer and delectable places in some remote and more celestial corner of the system, behind the constellation of Cassiopeia's Chair, far from noise and disturbance. I discovered that my house actually had its site in such a withdrawn but forever new and unprofaned part of the universe. If it were worth the while to settle in those parts near to the Pleiades or the Hyades, to Aldebaran or Altair, then I was really there, or at an equal remoteness from the life which I had left behind, dwindled and twinkling with as fine a ray to my nearest neighbor and to be seen only in moonless nights by him. Such was that part of creation where I had squatted—

There was a shepherd that did live,
  And held his thoughts as high
As were the mounts whereon his flocks
  Did hourly feed him by.

What should we think of the shepherd's life if his flocks always wandered to higher pastures than his thoughts?

Every morning was a cheerful invitation to make my life of equal simplicity, and I may say innocence, with Nature herself. I have been as sincere a worshipper of Aurora as the Greeks. I got up early and bathed in the pond; that was a religious exercise, and one of the best things which I did. They say that characters were engraven on the bathing tub of King Tching-thang to this effect: "Renew thyself completely each day; do it again, and again, and forever again." I can understand that. Morning brings back the heroic ages. I was as much affected by the faint hum of a mosquito making its invisible and unimaginable tour through my apartment at earliest dawn, when I was sitting with door and windows open, as I could be by any trumpet that ever sang of fame. It was Homer's requiem; itself an Iliad and Odyssey in the air, singing its own wrath and wanderings. There was something cosmical about it; a standing advertisement, till forbidden, of the everlasting vigor and fertility of the world. The morning, which is the most memorable season of the day, is the awakening hour. Then there is least somnolence in us; and for an hour, at least, some part of us awakes which slumbers all the rest of the day and night. Little is to be expected of that day, if it can be called a day, to which we are not awakened by our Genius but by the mechanical nudgings of some servitor, are not awakened by our own newly acquired force and aspirations from within, accompanied by the undulations of celestial music instead of factory bells, and a fragrance filling the air—to a higher life than we fell asleep from; and thus the darkness bear its fruit, and prove itself to be good, no less than the light. That man who does not believe that each day contains an earlier, more sacred, and auroral hour than he has yet profaned, has despaired of life and is pursuing a descending and darkening way. After a partial cessation of his sensuous life, the soul of man, or its organs rather, are reinvigorated each day, and his Genius tries again what noble life it can make. All memorable events, I should say, transpire in morning time and in a morning atmosphere. The Vedas say, "All intelligences awake with the morning." Poetry and art, and the fairest and most memorable of the actions of men, date from such an hour. All poets and heroes, like Memnon, are the children of Aurora, and emit their music at sunrise. To him whose elastic and vigorous thought keeps pace with the sun, the day is a perpetual morning. It matters not what the clocks say or the attitudes and labors of men. Morning is when I am awake and there is a dawn in me. Moral reform is the effort to throw off sleep. Why is it that men give so poor an account of their day if they have not been slumbering? They are not such poor calculators. If they had not been overcome with drowsiness, they would have performed something. The millions are awake enough for physical labor; but only one in a million is awake enough for effective intellectual exertion, only one in a hundred millions to a poetic or divine life. To be awake is to be alive. I have never yet met a man who was quite awake. How could I have looked him in the face?

We must learn to reawaken and keep ourselves awake, not by mechanical aids but by an infinite expectation of the dawn, which does not forsake us in our soundest sleep. I know of no more encouraging fact than the unquestionable ability of man to elevate his life by a conscious endeavor. It is something to be able to paint a particular picture, or to carve a statue, and so to make a few objects beautiful; but it is far more glorious to carve and paint the very atmosphere and medium through which we look, which morally we can do. To affect the quality of the day, that is the highest of arts. Every man is tasked to make his life, even in its details, worthy of the contemplation of his most elevated and critical hour. If we refused, or rather used up, such paltry information as we get, the oracles would distinctly inform us how this might be done.

I went to the woods because I wished to live deliberately, to front only the essential facts of life and see if I could not learn what it had to teach, and not, when I came to die, discover that I had not lived. I did not wish to live what was not life, living is so dear; nor did I wish to practise resignation, unless it was quite necessary. I wanted to live deep and suck out all the marrow of life, to live so sturdily and Spartan-like as to put to rout all that was not life, to cut a broad swath and shave close, to drive life into a corner, and reduce it to its lowest terms, and if it proved to be mean, why then to get the whole and genuine meanness of it and publish its meanness to the world; or if it were sublime, to know it by experience and be able to give a true account of it in my next excursion. For most men, it appears to me, are in a strange uncertainty about it, whether it is of the devil or of God, and have *somewhat hastily* concluded that it is the chief end of man here to "glorify God and enjoy him forever."

Still we live meanly, like ants; though the fable tells us that we were long ago changed into men; like pygmies we fight with cranes; it is error upon error, and clout upon clout, and our best virtue has for its occasion a superfluous and evitable wretchedness. Our life is frittered away by detail. An honest man has hardly need to count more than his ten fingers, or in extreme cases he may add his ten toes, and lump the rest. Simplicity, simplicity, simplicity! I say, let your affairs be as two or three, and not a hundred or a thousand; instead of a million count half a dozen, and keep your accounts on your thumbnail. In the midst of this chopping sea of civilized life, such are the clouds and storms and quicksands and thousand-and-one items to be allowed for, that a man has to live, if he would not founder and go to the bottom and not make his port at all, by dead reckoning, and he must be a great calculator indeed who succeeds. Simplify, simplify. Instead of three meals a day, if it be necessary eat but one; instead of a hundred dishes, five; and reduce other things in proportion. Our life is like a German Confederacy, made up of petty states, with its boundary forever fluctuating so that even a German cannot tell you how it is bounded at any moment. The nation itself, with all its so-called internal improvements, which, by the way, are all external and superficial, is just such an unwieldy and overgrown establishment, cluttered with furniture and tripped up by its own traps, ruined by luxury and heedless expense by want of calculation and a worthy aim, as the million households in the land; and the only cure for it, as for them, is in a rigid economy, a stern and more than Spartan simplicity of life and elevation of purpose. It lives too fast. Men think that it is essential that the *Nation* have commerce, and export ice, and talk through a telegraph, and ride thirty miles an hour, without a doubt, whether *they* do or not; but whether we should live like baboons or like men is a little uncertain. If we do not get out sleepers, and forge rails, and devote days and nights to the work, but go to tinkering upon our *lives* to improve *them*, who will build railroads? And if railroads are not built, how shall we get to heaven in season? But if we stay at home and mind our business, who will want railroads? We do not ride on the railroad; it rides upon us. Did you ever think what those sleepers are that underlie the railroad? Each one is a man, an Irishman, or a Yankee man. The rails are laid on them and they are covered with sand, and the cars run smoothly over them. They are sound sleepers, I assure you. And every few years a new lot is laid down and run over; so that if some have the pleasure of riding on a rail, others have the misfortune to be ridden upon. And when they run over a man that is walking in his sleep, a supernumerary sleeper in the wrong position, and wake him up, they suddenly stop the cars and make a hue and cry about it as if this were an exception. I am glad to know that it takes a gang of men for every five miles to keep the sleepers down and level in their beds as it is, for this is a sign that they may sometime get up again.

Why should we live with such hurry and waste of life? We are determined to be starved before we are hungry. Men say that a stitch in time saves nine, and so they take a thousand stitches today to save nine tomorrow. As for *work*, we haven't any of any consequence. We have the Saint Vitus' dance, and cannot possibly keep our heads still. If I should only give a few pulls at the parish bell rope, as for a fire, that is, without setting the bell, there is hardly a man on his farm in the outskirts of Concord, not-withstanding that press of engagements which was his excuse so many times this morning, nor a boy, nor a woman, I might almost say, but would forsake all and follow that sound, not mainly to save property from the flames, but if we will confess the truth, much more to see it burn, since burn it must, and we, be it known, did not set it on fire—or to see it put out and have a hand in it, if that is done as handsomely; yes, even if it were the parish church itself. Hardly a man takes a half-hour's nap after dinner, but when he wakes he holds up his head and asks, "What's the news?" as if the rest of mankind had stood his sentinels. Some give directions to be waked every half-hour, doubtless for no other pur-pose; and then, to pay for it, they tell what they have dreamed. After a night's sleep the news is as indispensable as the breakfast. "Pray tell me anything new that has happened to a man anywhere on this globe"—and he reads it over his coffee and rolls that a man has had his eyes gouged out this morning on the Wachito River; never dreaming the while that he lives in the dark un-fathomed mammoth cave of this world, and has but the rudiment of an eye him-self.

For my part, I could easily do with-out the post office. I think that there are very few important communications made through it. To speak critically, I never received more than one or two let-ters in my life—I wrote this some years ago—that were worth the postage. The penny post is, commonly, an institution through which you seriously offer a man

that penny for his thoughts which is so often safely offered in jest. And I am sure that I never read any memorable news in a newspaper. If we read of one man robbed, or murdered, or killed by accident, or one house burned, or one vessel wrecked, or one steamboat blow up, or one cow run over on the Western Railroad, or one mad dog killed, or one lot of grasshoppers in the winter—we never need read of another. One is enough. If you are acquainted with the principle, what do you care for a myriad instances and applications? To a philoso-pher all *news*, as it is called, is gossip and they who edit and read it are old women over their tea. Yet not a few are greedy after this gossip. There was such a rush, as I hear, the other day at one of the offices to learn the foreign news by the last arrival, that several large squares of plate glass belonging to the establishment were broken by the pres-sure—news which I seriously think a ready wit might write a twelvemonth, or twelve years, beforehand with sufficient accuracy. As for Spain, for instance, if you know how to throw in Don Carlos and the Infanta, and Don Pedro and Se-ville and Granada, from time to time in the right proportions—they may have changed the names a little since I saw the papers—and serve up a bull-fight when other entertainments fail, it will be true to the letter and give us as good an idea of the exact state or ruin of things in Spain as the most succinct and lucid reports under this head in the newspapers: and as for England, almost the last significant scrap of news from that quarter was the revolution of 1649; and if you have learned the history of her crops for an average year, you never need attend to that thing again unless your speculations are of a merely pecu-niary character. If one may judge who rarely looks into the newspapers, nothing new does ever happen in foreign parts, a French revolution not excepted.

What news! how much more important to know what that is which was never old! "Kieou-he-yu (great dignitary of the state of Wei) sent a man to Khoung-tseu to know his news. Khoung-tseu caused the messenger to be seated near him, and questioned him in these terms: What is your master doing? The messenger answered with respect: My master desires to diminish the number of his faults, but he cannot come to the end of them. The messenger being gone, the philosopher remarked: What a worthy messenger! What a worthy messenger!" The preacher, instead of vexing the ears of drowsy farmers on their day of rest at the end of the week—for Sunday is the fit conclusion of an ill-spent week, and not the fresh and brave beginning of a new one—with this one other draggletail of a sermon, should shout with thundering voice, "Pause! Avast! Why so seeming fast, but deadly slow?"

Shams and delusions are esteemed for soundest truths, while reality is fabulous. If men would steadily observe realities only and not allow themselves to be deluded, life, to compare it with such things as we know, would be like a fairy tale and the Arabian Nights' Entertainments. If we respected only what is inevitable and has a right to be, music and poetry would resound along the streets. When we are unhurried and wise, we perceive that only great and worthy things have any permanent and absolute existence, that petty fears and petty pleasures are but the shadow of the reality. This is always exhilarating and sublime. By closing the eyes and slumbering, and consenting to be deceived by shows, men establish and confirm their daily life of routine and habit everywhere, which still is built on purely illusory foundations. Children, who play life, discern its true law and relations more clearly than men, who fail to live it worthily, but who think that they are wiser by experience, that is, by failure.

I have read in a Hindu book, that "there was a king's son, who, being expelled in infancy from his native city, was brought up by a forester, and, growing up to maturity in that state, imagined himself to belong to the barbarous race with which he lived. One of his father's ministers having discovered him, revealed to him what he was, and the misconception of his character was removed, and he knew himself to be a prince. So soul," continues the Hindu philosopher, "from the circumstances in which it is placed, mistakes its own character, until the truth is revealed to it by some holy teacher, and then it knows itself to be *Brahme*." I perceive that we inhabitants of New England live this mean life that we do because our vision does not penetrate the surface of things. We think that that *is* which *appears* to be. If a man should walk through this town and see only the reality, where, think you, would the "Mill-dam" go to? If he should give us an account of the realities he beheld there, we should not recognize the place in his description. Look at a meeting-house, or a courthouse, or a jail, or a shop, or a dwelling house, and say what that thing really is before a true gaze, and they would all go to pieces in your account of them. Men esteem truth remote, in the outskirts of the system, behind the farthest star, before Adam and after the last man. In eternity there is indeed something true and sublime. But all these times and places and occasions are now and here. God himself culminates in the present moment, and will never be more divine in the lapse of all the ages. And we are enabled to apprehend at all what is sublime and noble only by the perpetual instilling and drenching of the reality that surrounds us. The universe constantly and obediently answers to our conceptions; whether we travel fast or slow, the track is laid for us. Let us spend our lives in conceiving then. The poet or the artist never yet had so fair and noble a design but some of his posterity at least could accomplish it.

Let us spend one day as deliberately as Nature, and not be thrown off the track by every nutshell and mosquito's wing that falls on the rails. Let us rise early and fast, or break fast, gently and without perturbation; let company come and let company go, let the bells ring and the children cry—determined to make a day of it. Why should we knock under and go with the stream? Let us not be upset and overwhelmed in that terrible rapid and whirlpool called a dinner, situated in the meridian shallows. Weather this danger and you are safe, for the rest of the way is down hill. With unrelaxed nerves, with morning vigor, sail by it, looking another way, tied to the mast like Ulysses. If the engine whistles, let it whistle till it is hoarse for its pains. If the bell rings, why should we run? We will consider what kind of music they are like. Let us settle ourselves, and work and wedge our feet downward through the mud and slush of opinion, and prejudice, and tradition, and delusion, and appearance, that alluvion which covers the globe, through Paris and London, through New York and Boston and Concord, through church and state, through poetry and philosophy and religion, till we come to a hard bottom and rocks in place, which we can call *reality*, and say, This is, and no mistake; and then begin, having a *point d'appui*, below freshet and frost and fire, a place where you might found a wall or a state, or set a lamp post safely, or perhaps a gauge, not a Nilometer, but a Realometer, that future ages might know how deep a freshet of shams and appearances had gathered from time to time. If you stand right fronting and face to face to a fact, you will see the sun glimmer on both its surfaces, as if it were a cimeter, and feel its sweet edge dividing you through the heart and marrow,

and so you will happily conclude your mortal career. Be it life or death, we crave only reality. If we are really dying, let us hear the rattle in our throats and feel cold in the extremities; if we are alive, let us go about our business.

Time is but the stream I go a-fishing in. I drink at it; but while I drink I see the sandy bottom and detect how shallow it is. Its thin current slides away, but eternity remains. I would drink deeper; fish in the sky, whose bottom is pebbly with stars. I cannot count one. I know not the first letter of the alphabet. I have always been regretting that I was not as wise as the day I was born. The intellect is a cleaver; it discerns and rifts its way into the secret of things. I do not wish to be any more busy with my hands than is necessary. My head is hands and feet. I feel all my best faculties concentrated in it. My instinct tells me that my head is an organ for burrowing, as some creatures use their snout and forepaws, and with it I would mine and burrow my way through these hills. I think that the richest vein is somewhere hereabouts; so by the divining rod and thin rising vapors I judge; and here I will begin to mine.

Ralph Waldo Emerson
✴ 1803-1882

Emerson wrote so often of man as individual that he is sometimes thought of as caring little for man in society. His ESSAYS: FIRST SERIES *in 1841 was almost exclusively about the responsibility of each person to realize himself, a theme which he never abandoned, but in* ESSAYS: SECOND SERIES *three years later he extended his view to examine more of the world in which man moves. "New England Reformers," originally a lecture delivered at Armory Hall in Boston on March 3, 1844, is the concluding essay of that volume.*

New England Reformers

> In the suburb, in the town,
> On the railway, in the square,
> Came a beam of goodness down
> Doubling daylight everywhere:
> Peace now each for malice takes,
> Beauty for his sinful weeds,
> For the angel Hope aye makes
> Him an angel whom she leads.

Whoever has had opportunity of acquaintance with society in New England during the last twenty-five years, with those middle and with those leading sections that may constitute any just representation of the character and aim of the community, will have been struck with the great activity of thought and experimenting. His attention must be commanded by the signs that the Church, or religious party, is falling from the Church nominal, and is appearing in temperance and non-resistance societies; in movements of abolitionists and of socialists; and in very significant assemblies called Sabbath and Bible Conventions; composed of ultraists, of seekers, of all the soul of the soldiery of dissent, and meeting to call in question the authority of the Sabbath, of the priesthood, and of the Church. In these movements nothing was more remarkable than the discontent they begot in the movers. The spirit of protest and of detachment drove the members of these Conventions to bear testimony against the Church, and immediately afterwards to declare their discontent with these Conventions, their independence of their colleagues, and their impatience of the methods whereby they were working. They defied each other, like a congress of kings, each of whom had a realm to rule, and a way of

his own that made concert unprofitable. What a fertility of projects for the salvation of the world! One apostle thought all men should go to farming, and another that no man should buy or sell, that the use of money was the cardinal evil; another that the mischief was in our diet, that we eat and drink damnation. These made unleavened bread, and were foes to the death to fermentation. It was in vain urged by the housewife that God made yeast, as well as dough, and loves fermentation just as dearly as he loves vegetation; that fermentation develops the saccharine element in the grain, and makes it more palatable and more digestible. No; they wish the pure wheat, and will die but it shall not ferment. Stop, dear Nature, these incessant advances of thine; let us scotch these ever-rolling wheels! Others attack the system of agriculture, the use of animal manures in farming, and the tyranny of man over brute nature; these abuses polluted his food. The ox must be taken from the plough and the horse from the cart, the hundred acres of the farm must be spaded, and the man must walk, wherever boats and locomotives will not carry him. Even the insect world was to be defended—that had been too long neglected, and a society for the protection of ground-worms, slugs and mosquitos was to be incorporated without delay. With these appeared the adepts of homœopathy, of hydropathy, of mesmerism, of phrenology, and their wonderful theories of the Christian miracles! Others assailed particular vocations, as that of the lawyer, that of the merchant, of the manufacturer, of the clergyman, of the scholar. Others attacked the institution of marriage as the fountain of social evils. Others devoted themselves to the worrying of churches and meetings for public worship; and the fertile forms of antinomianism among the elder puritans seemed to have their match in the plenty of the new harvest of reform.

With this din of opinion and debate there was a keener scrutiny of institutions and domestic life than any we had known; there was sincere protesting against existing evils, and there were changes of employment dictated by conscience. No doubt there was plentiful vaporing, and cases of backsliding might occur. But in each of these movements emerged a good result, a tendency to the adoption of simpler methods, and an assertion of the sufficiency of the private man. Thus it was directly in the spirit and genius of the age, what happened in one instance when a church censured and threatened to excommunicate one of its members on account of the somewhat hostile part to the church which his conscience led him to take in the anti-slavery business; the threatened individual immediately excommunicated the church, in a public and formal process. This has been several times repeated: it was excellent when it was done the first time, but of course loses all value when it is copied. Every project in the history of reform, no matter how violent and surprising, is good when it is the dictate of a man's genius and constitution, but very dull and suspicious when adopted from another. It is right and beautiful in any man to say, 'I will take this coat, or this book, or this measure of corn of yours'—in whom we see the act to be original, and to flow from the whole spirit and faith of him; for then that taking will have a giving as free and divine; but we are very easily disposed to resist the same generosity of speech when we miss originality and truth to character in it.

There was in all the practical activities of New England for the last quarter of a century, a gradual withdrawal of tender consciences from the social organizations. There is observable throughout, the contest between mechanical and spiritual methods, but with a steady tendency of the thoughtful and virtuous to a deeper belief and reliance on spiritual facts.

In politics, for example, it is easy to see the progress of dissent. The country is full of rebellion; the country is full of kings. Hands off! let there be no control and no interference in the administration of the affairs of this kingdom of me. Hence the growth of the doctrine and of the party of Free Trade, and the willingness to try that experiment, in the face of what appear incontestable facts. I confess, the motto of the Globe newspaper is so attractive to me that I can seldom find much appetite to read what is below it in its columns: "The world is governed too much." So the country is frequently affording solitary examples of resistance to the government, solitary nullifiers, who throw themselves on their reserved rights; nay, who have reserved all their rights, who reply to the assessor and to the clerk of court that they do not know the State, and embarrass the courts of law by non-juring and the commander-in-chief of the militia by non-resistance.

The same disposition to scrutiny and dissent appeared in civil, festive, neighborly, and domestic society. A restless, prying, conscientious criticism broke out in unexpected quarters. Who gave me the money with which I bought my coat? Why should professional labor and that of the counting-house be paid so disproportionately to the labor of the porter and wood-sawyer? This whole business of Trade gives me to pause and think, as it constitutes false relations between men; inasmuch as I am prone to count myself relieved of any responsibility to behave well and nobly to that person whom I pay with money; whereas if I had not that commodity, I should be put on my good behavior in all companies, and man would be a benefactor to man, as being himself his only certificate that he had a right to those aids and services which each asked of the other. Am I not too protected a person? is there not a wide disparity between the lot of me and the lot of thee, my poor brother, my poor sister? Am I not defrauded of my best culture in the loss of those gymnastics which manual labor and the emergencies of poverty constitute? I find nothing healthful or exalting in the smooth conventions of society; I do not like the close air of saloons. I begin to suspect myself to be a prisoner, though treated with all this courtesy and luxury. I pay a destructive tax in my conformity.

The same insatiable criticism may be traced in the efforts for the reform of Education. The popular education has been taxed with a want of truth and nature. It was complained that an education to things was not given. We are students of words: we are shut up in schools, and colleges, and recitation-rooms, for ten or fifteen years, and come out at last with a bag of wind, a memory of words, and do not know a thing. We cannot use our hands, or our legs, or our eyes, or our arms. We do not know an edible root in the woods, we cannot tell our course by the stars, nor the hour of the day by the sun. It is well if we can swim and skate. We are afraid of a horse, of a cow, of a dog, of a snake, of a spider. The Roman rule was to teach a boy nothing that he could not learn standing. The old English rule was, 'All summer in the field, and all winter in the study.' And it seems as if a man should learn to plant, or to fish, or to hunt, that he might secure his subsistence at all events, and not be painful to his friends and fellow-men. The lessons of science should be experimental also. The sight of a planet through a telescope is worth all the course on astronomy; the shock of the electric spark in the elbow, outvalues all the theories, the taste of the nitrous oxide, the firing of an artificial volcano, are better than volumes of chemistry.

One of the traits of the new spirit is

the inquisition it fixed on our scholastic devotion to the dead languages. The ancient languages, with great beauty of structure, contain wonderful remains of genius, which draw, and always will draw, certain like-minded men—Greek men, and Roman men—in all countries, to their study; but by a wonderful drowsiness of usage they had exacted the study of *all* men. Once (say two centuries ago), Latin and Greek had a strict relation to all the science and culture there was in Europe, and the Mathematics had a momentary importance at some era of activity in physical science. These things became stereotyped as *education*, as the manner of men is. But the Good Spirit never cared for the colleges, and though all men and boys were now drilled in Latin, Greek and Mathematics, it had quite left these shells high and dry on the beach, and was now creating and feeding other matters at other ends of the world. But in a hundred high schools and colleges this warfare against common-sense still goes on. Four, or six, or ten years, the pupil is parsing Greek and Latin, and as soon as he leaves the University, as it is ludicrously styled, he shuts those books for the last time. Some thousands of young men are graduated at our colleges in this country every year, and the persons who, at forty years, still read Greek, can all be counted on your hand. I never met with ten. Four or five persons I have seen who read Plato.

But is not this absurd, that the whole liberal talent of this country should be directed in its best years on studies which lead to nothing? What was the consequence? Some intelligent persons said or thought, 'Is that Greek and Latin some spell to conjure with, and not words of reason? If the physician, the lawyer, the divine, never use it to come at their ends, I need never learn it to come at mine. Conjuring is gone out of fashion, and I will omit this conjugating, and go straight to affairs.' So they jumped the Greek and Latin, and read law, medicine, or sermons, without it. To the astonishment of all, the self-made men took even ground at once with the oldest of the regular graduates, and in a few months the most conservative circles of Boston and New York had quite forgotten who of their gownsmen was college-bred, and who was not.

One tendency appears alike in the philosophical speculation and in the rudest democratical movements, through all the petulance and all the puerility, the wish, namely, to cast aside the superfluous and arrive at short methods; urged, as I suppose, by an intuition that the human spirit is equal to all emergencies, alone, and that man is more often injured than helped by the means he uses.

I conceive this gradual casting off of materials aids and the indication of growing trust in the private self-supplied powers of the individual, to be the affirmative principle of the recent philosophy, and that it is feeling its own profound truth and is reaching forward at this very hour to the happiest conclusions. I readily concede that in this, as in every period of intellectual activity, there has been a noise of denial and protest; much was to be resisted, much was to be got rid of by those who were reared in the old, before they could begin to affirm and to construct. Many a reformer perishes in his removal of rubbish; and that makes the offensiveness of the class. They are partial; they are not equal to the work they pretend. They lose their way; in the assault on the kingdom of darkness they expend all their energy on some accidental evil, and lose their sanity and power of benefit. It is of little moment that one or two or twenty errors of our social system be corrected, but of much that the man be in his senses.

The criticism and attack on institutions, which we have witnessed, has made one thing plain, that society gains nothing whilst a man, not himself renovated, attempts to renovate things around him: he has become tediously good in some particular but negligent or narrow in the rest; and hypocrisy and vanity are often the disgusting result.

It is handsomer to remain in the establishment better than the establishment, and conduct that in the best manner, than to make a sally against evil by some single improvement, without supporting it by a total regeneration. Do not be so vain of your one objection. Do you think there is only one? Alas! my good friend, there is no part of society or of life better than any other part. All our things are right and wrong together. The wave of evil washes all our institutions alike. Do you complain of our Marriage? Our marriage is no worse than our education, our diet, our trade, our social customs. Do you complain of the laws of Property? It is a pedantry to give such importance to them. Can we not play the game of life with these counters, as well as with those? in the institution of property, as well as out of it? Let into it the new and renewing principle of love, and property will be universality. No one gives the impression of superiority to the institution, which he must give who will reform it. It makes no difference what you say, you must make me feel that you are aloof from it; by your natural and supernatural advantages do easily see to the end of it—do see how man can do without it. Now all men are on one side. No man deserves to be heard against property. Only Love, only an Idea, is against property as we hold it.

I cannot afford to be irritable and captious, nor to waste all my time in attacks. If I should go out of church whenever I hear a false sentiment I could never stay there five minutes. But why come out? the street is as false as the church, and when I get to my house, or to my manners, or to my speech, I have not got away from the lie. When we see an eager assailant of one of these wrongs, a special reformer, we feel like asking him, What right have you, sir, to your one virtue? Is virtue piecemeal? This is a jewel amidst the rags of a beggar.

In another way the right will be vindicated. In the midst of abuses, in the heart of cities, in the aisles of false churches, alike in one place and in another—wherever, namely, a just and heroic soul finds itself, there it will do what is next at hand, and by the new quality of character it shall put forth it shall abrogate that old condition, law, or school in which it stands, before the law of its own mind.

If partiality was one fault of the movement party, the other defect was their reliance on Association. Doubts such as those I have intimated drove many good persons to agitate the questions of social reform. But the revolt against the spirit of commerce, the spirit of aristocracy, and the inveterate abuses of cities, did not appear possible to individuals; and to do battle against numbers they armed themselves with numbers, and against concert they relied on new concert.

Following or advancing beyond the ideas of St. Simon, of Fourier, and of Owen, three communities have already been formed in Massachusetts on kindred plans, and many more in the country at large. They aim to give every member a share in the manual labor, to give an equal reward to labor and to talent, and to unite a liberal culture with an education to labor. The scheme offers, by the economies of associated labor and expense, to make every member rich, on the same amount of property that, in separate families, would leave every member poor. These new associations are composed of men and women of superior talents and sentiments; yet it may easily be questioned whether such a community will draw, except in its beginnings, the able and the good; whether those who have energy will not prefer their chance of superiority and power in the world, to the humble certainties of the association; whether such a retreat does not promise to become an asylum to those who have tried and failed, rather than a field to the strong; and whether the members will not necessarily be fractions of men, because each finds that he cannot enter it without some compromise. Friendship and association are very fine things, and a grand phalanx of the best of the human race, banded for some catholic object; yes, excellent; but remember that no society can ever be so large as one man. He, in his friendship, in his natural and momentary associations, doubles or multiplies himself; but in the hour in which he mortgages himself to two or ten or twenty, he dwarfs himself below the stature of one.

But the men of less faith could not thus believe, and to such, concert appears the sole specific of strength. I have failed, and you have failed, but perhaps together we shall not fail. Our housekeeping is not satisfactory to us, but perhaps a phalanx, a community, might be. Many of us have differed in opinion, and we could find no man who could make the truth plain, but possibly a college, or an ecclesiastical council, might. I have not been able either to persuade my brother or to prevail on myself to disuse the traffic or the potation of brandy, but perhaps a pledge of total abstinence might effectually restrain us. The candidate my party votes for is not to be trusted with a dollar, but he will be honest in the Senate, for we can bring public opinion to bear on him. Thus concert was the specific in all cases. But concert is neither better nor worse, neither more nor less potent, than individual force. All the men in the world cannot make a statue walk and speak, cannot make a drop of blood, or a blade of grass, any more than one man can. But let there be one man, let there be truth in two men, in ten men, then is concert for the first time possible; because the force which moves the world is a new quality, and can never be furnished by adding whatever quantities of a different kind. What is the use of the concert of the false and the disunited? There can be no concert in two, where there is no concert in one. When the individual is not *individual,* but is dual; when his thoughts look one way and his actions another; when his faith is traversed by his habits; when his will, enlightened by reason, is warped by his sense; when with one hand he rows and with the other backs water, what concert can be?

I do not wonder at the interest these projects inspire. The world is awaking to the idea of union, and these experiments show what it is thinking of. It is and will be magic. Men will live and communicate, and plough, and reap, and govern, as by added ethereal power, when once they are united; as in a celebrated experiment, by expiration and respiration exactly together, four persons lift a heavy man from the ground by the little finger only, and without sense of weight. But this union must be inward, and not one of covenants, and is to be reached by a reverse of the methods they use. The union is only perfect when all the uniters are isolated. It is the union of friends who live in different streets or towns. Each man, if he attempts to join himself to others, is on all sides cramped and diminished of his proportion; and the stricter the union the smaller and the more pitiful he is. But leave him alone, to recognize in every hour and place the secret soul; he will go up and down doing the works of a true member, and, to the astonishment of all, the work will be done with con-

cert, though no man spoke. Government will be adamantine without any governor. The union must be ideal in actual individualism.

I pass to the indication in some particulars of that faith in man, which the heart is preaching to us in these days, and which engages the more regard, from the consideration that the speculations of one generation are the history of the next following.

In alluding just now to our system of education, I spoke of the deadness of its details. But it is open to graver criticism than the palsy of its members: it is a system of despair. The disease with which the human mind now labors is want of faith. Men do not believe in a power of education. We do not think we can speak to divine sentiments in man, and we do not try. We renounce all high aims. We believe that the defects of so many perverse and so many frivolous people who make up society, are organic, and society is a hospital of incurables. A man of good sense but of little faith, whose compassion seemed to lead him to church as often as he went there, said to me that "he liked to have concerts, and fairs, and churches, and other public amusements go on." I am afraid the remark is too honest, and comes from the same origin as the maxim of the tyrant, "If you would rule the world quietly, you must keep it amused." I notice too that the ground on which eminent public servants urge the claims of popular education is fear; 'This country is filling up with thousands and millions of voters, and you must educate them to keep them from our throats.' We do not believe that any education, any system of philosophy, any influence of genius, will ever give depth of insight to a superficial mind. Having settled ourselves into this infidelity, our skill is expended to procure alleviations, diversion, opiates. We adorn the victim with manual skill, his tongue with languages, his body with inoffensive and comely manners. So have we cunningly hid the tragedy of limitation and inner death we cannot avert. Is it strange that society should be devoured by a secret melancholy which breaks through all its smiles and all its gayety and games?

But even one step farther our infidelity has gone. It appears that some doubt is felt by good and wise men whether really the happiness and probity of men is increased by the culture of the mind in those disciplines to which we give the name of education. Unhappily too the doubt comes from scholars, from persons who have tried these methods. In their experience the scholar was not raised by the sacred thoughts amongst which he dwelt, but used them to selfish ends. He was a profane person, and became a showman, turning his gifts to a marketable use, and not to his own sustenance and growth. It was found that the intellect could be independently developed, that is, in separation from the man, as any single organ can be invigorated, and the result was monstrous. A canine appetite for knowledge was generated, which must still be fed but was never satisfied, and this knowledge, not being directed on action, never took the character of substantial, humane truth, blessing those whom it entered. It gave the scholar certain powers of expression, the power of speech, the power of poetry, of literary art, but it did not bring him to peace or to beneficence.

When the literary class betray a destitution of faith, it is not strange that society should be disheartened and sensualized by unbelief. What remedy? Life must be lived on a higher plane. We must go up to a higher platform, to which we are always invited to ascend; there, the whole aspect of things changes. I resist the scepticism of our education and of our educated men. I do not believe that the differences of

opinion and character in men are organic. I do not recognize, beside the class of the good and the wise, a permanent class of sceptics, or a class of conservatives, or of malignants, or of materialists. I do not believe in two classes. You remember the story of the poor woman who importuned King Philip of Macedon to grant her justice, which Philip refused: the woman exclaimed, "I appeal:" the king, astonished, asked to whom she appealed: the woman replied, "From Philip drunk to Philip sober." The text will suit me very well. I believe not in two classes of men, but in man in two moods, in Philip drunk and Philip sober. I think, according to the good-hearted word of Plato, "Unwillingly the soul is deprived of truth." Iron conservative, miser, or thief, no man is but by a supposed necessity which he tolerates by shortness or torpidity of sight. The soul lets no man go without some visitations and holidays of a diviner presence. It would be easy to show, by a narrow scanning of any man's biography, that we are not so wedded to our paltry performances of every kind but that every man has at intervals the grace to scorn his performances, in comparing them with his belief of what he should do; that he puts himself on the side of his enemies, listening gladly to what they say of him, and accusing himself of the same things.

What is it men love in Genius, but its infinite hope, which degrades all it has done? Genius counts all its miracles poor and short. Its own idea is never executed. The Iliad, the Hamlet, the Doric column, the Roman arch, the Gothic minster, the German anthem, when they are ended, the master casts behind him. How sinks the song in the waves of melody which the universe pours over his soul! Before that gracious Infinite out of which he drew these few strokes, how mean they look, though the praises of the world attend them. From the triumphs of his art he turns with desire to this greater defeat. Let those admire who will. With silent joy he sees himself to be capable of a beauty that eclipses all which his hands have done; all which human hands have ever done.

Well, we are all the children of genius, the children of virtue—and feel their inspirations in our happier hours. Is not every man sometimes a radical in politics? Men are conservatives when they are least vigorous, or when they are most luxurious. They are conservatives after dinner, or before taking their rest; when they are sick, or aged. In the morning, or when their intellect or their conscience has been aroused; when they hear music, or when they read poetry, they are radicals. In the circle of the rankest tories that could be collected in England, Old or New, let a powerful and stimulating intellect, a man of great heart and mind act on them, and very quickly these frozen conservators will yield to the friendly influence, these hopeless will begin to hope, these haters will begin to love, these immovable statues will begin to spin and revolve. I cannot help recalling the fine anecdote which Warton relates of Bishop Berkeley, when he was preparing to leave England with his plan of planting the gospel among the American savages. "Lord Bathurst told me that the members of the Scriblerus Club being met at his house at dinner, they agreed to rally Berkeley, who was also his guest, on his scheme at Bermudas. Berkeley, having listened to the many lively things they had to say, begged to be heard in his turn, and displayed his plan with such an astonishing and animating force of eloquence and enthusiasm that they were struck dumb, and, after some pause, rose up all together with earnestness, exclaiming, 'Let us set out with him immediately.'" Men in all ways are better than they seem. They like flattery for the moment, but they know the truth for their

own. It is a foolish cowardice which keeps us from trusting them and speaking to them rude truth. They resent your honesty for an instant, they will thank you for it always. What is it we heartily wish of each other? Is it to be pleased and flattered? No, but to be convicted and exposed, to be shamed out of our nonsense of all kinds, and made men of, instead of ghosts and phantoms. We are weary of gliding ghostlike through the world, which is itself so slight and unreal. We crave a sense of reality, though it comes in strokes of pain. I explain so—by this man-like love of truth—those excesses and errors into which souls of great vigor, but not equal insight, often fall. They feel the poverty at the bottom of all the seeming affluence of the world. They know the speed with which they come straight through the thin masquerade, and conceive a disgust at the indigence of nature: Rousseau, Mirabeau, Charles Fox, Napoleon, Bryon—and I could easily add names nearer home, of raging riders, who drive their steeds so hard, in the violence of living to forget its illusion: they would know the worst, and tread the floors of hell. The heroes of ancient and modern fame, Cimon, Themistocles, Alcibiades, Alexander, Cæsar, have treated life and fortune as a game to be well and skilfully played, but the stake not to be so valued but that any time it could be held as a trifle light as air, and thrown up. Cæsar, just before the battle of Pharsalia, discourses with the Egyptian priest concerning the fountains of the Nile, and offers to quit the army, the empire, and Cleopatra, if he will show him those mysterious sources.

The same magnanimity shows itself in our social relations, in the preference, namely, which each man gives to the society of superiors over that of his equals. All that a man has will he give for right relations with his mates. All that he has will he give for an erect demeanor in every company and on each occasion. He aims at such things as his neighbors prize, and gives his days and nights, his talents and his heart, to strike a good stroke, to acquit himself in all men's sight as a man. The consideration of an eminent citizen, of a noted merchant, of a man of mark in his profession; a naval and military honor, a general's commission, a marshal's baton, a ducal coronet, the laurel of poets, and, anyhow procured, the acknowledgment of eminent merit— have this lustre for each candidate that they enable him to walk erect and unashamed in the presence of some persons before whom he felt himself inferior. Having raised himself to this rank, having established his equality with class after class of those with whom he would live well, he still finds certain others before whom he cannot possess himself, because they have somewhat fairer, somewhat grander, somewhat purer, which extorts homage of him. Is his ambition pure? then will his laurels and his possessions seem worthless: instead of avoiding these men who make his fine gold dim, he will cast all behind him and seek their society only, woo and embrace this his humiliation and mortification, until he shall know why his eye sinks, his voice is husky, and his brilliant talents are paralyzed in this presence. He is sure that the soul which gives the lie to all things will tell none. His constitution will not mislead him. If it cannot carry itself as it ought, high and unmatchable in the presence of any man; if the secret oracles whose whisper makes the sweetness and dignity of his life do here withdraw and accompany him no longer—it is time to undervalue what he has valued, to dispossess himself of what he has acquired, and with Cæsar to take in his hand the army, the empire and Cleopatra, and say, "All these will I relinquish, if you will show me the fountains of the Nile." Dear to us

are those who love us; the swift movements we spend with them are a compensation for a great deal of misery; they enlarge our life; but dearer are those who reject us as unworthy, for they add another life: they build a heaven before us whereof we had not dreamed, and thereby supply to us new powers out of the recesses of the spirit, and urge us to new and unattempted performances.

As every man at heart wishes the best and not inferior society, wishes to be convicted of his error and to come to himself—so he wishes that the same healing should not stop in his thought, but should penetrate his will or active power. The selfish man suffers more from his selfishness than he from whom that selfishness withholds some important benefit. What he most wishes is to be lifted to some higher platform, that he may see beyond his present fear the transalpine good, so that his fear, his coldness, his custom may be broken up like fragments of ice, melted and carried away in the great stream of good will. Do you ask my aid? I also wish to be a benefactor. I wish more to be a benefactor and servant than you wish to be served by me; and surely the greatest good fortune that could befall me is precisely to be so moved by you that I should say, 'Take me and all mine, and use me and mine freely to your ends!' for I could not say it otherwise than because a great enlargement had come to my heart and mind, which made me superior to my fortunes. Here we are paralyzed with fear; we hold on to our little properties, house and land, office and money, for the bread which they have in our experience yielded us, although we confess that our being does not flow through them. We desire to be made great; we desire to be touched with that fire which shall command this ice to stream, and make our existence a benefit. If therefore we start objections to your project, O friend of the slave, or friend of the poor or of the race, understand well that it is because we wish to drive you to drive us into your measures. We wish to hear ourselves confuted. We are haunted with a belief that you have a secret which it would highliest advantage us to learn, and we would force you to impart it to us, though it should bring us to prison or to worse extremity.

Nothing shall warp me from the belief that every man is a lover of truth. There is no pure lie, no pure malignity in nature. The entertainment of the proposition of depravity is the last profligacy and profanation. There is no scepticism, no atheism but that. Could it be received into common belief, suicide would un people the planet. It has had a name to live in some dogmatic theology, but each man's innocence and his real liking of his neighbor have kept it a dead letter. I remember standing at the polls one day when the anger of the political contest gave a certain grimness to the faces of the independent electors, and a good man at my side, looking on the people, remarked, "I am satisfied that the largest part of these men, on either side, mean to vote right." I suppose considerate observers, looking at the masses of men in their blameless and in their equivocal actions, will assent, that in spite of selfishness and frivolity, the general purpose in the great number of persons is fidelity. The reason why any one refuses his assent to your opinion, or his aid to your benevolent design, is in you: he refuses to accept you as a bringer of truth, because though you think you have it, he feels that you have it not. You have not given him the authentic sign.

If it were worth while to run into details this general doctrine of the latent but ever soliciting Spirit, it would be easy to adduce illustration in particulars of a man's equality to the Church, of his equality to the State, and of his equality to every other man. It is yet in all men's memory that, a few years ago, the liberal churches complained that the Calvinistic church denied to them the name of Christian. I think the complaint was confession: a religious church would not complain. A religious man, like Behmen, Fox, or Swedenborg, is not irritated by wanting the sanction of the Church, but the Church feels the accusation of his presence and belief.

It only needs that a just man should walk in our streets to make it appear how pitiful and inartificial a contrivance is our legislation. The man whose part is taken and who does not wait for society in anything, has a power which society cannot choose but feel. The familiar experiment called the hydrostatic paradox, in which a capillary column of water balances the ocean, is a symbol of the relation of one man to the whole family of men. The wise Dandamis, on hearing the lives of Socrates, Pythagoras and Diogenes read, "judged them to be great men every way, excepting that they were too much subjected to the reverence of the laws, which to second and authorize, true virtue must abate very much of its original vigor."

And as a man is equal to the Church and equal to the State, so he is equal to every other man. The disparities of power in men are superficial; and all frank and searching conversation, in which a man lays himself open to his brother, apprises each of their radical unity. When two persons sit and converse in a thoroughly good understanding, the remark is sure to be made, See how we have disputed about words! Let a clear, apprehensive mind, such as every man knows among his friends, converse with the most commanding poetic genius, I think it would appear that there was no inequality such as men fancy, between them; that a perfect understanding, a like receiving, a like perceiving, abolished differences; and the poet would confess that his creative imagination gave him no deep advantage, but only the superficial one that he could express himself and the other could not; that his advantage was a knack, which might impose on indolent men but could not impose on lovers of truth; for they know the tax of talent, or what a price of greatness the power of expression too often pays. I believe it is the conviction of the purest men that the net amount of man and man does not much vary. Each is incomparably superior to his companion in some faculty. His want of skill in other directions has added to his fitness for his own work. Each seems to have some compensation yielded to him by his infirmity, and every hinderance operates as a concentration of his force.

These and the like experiences intimate that man stands in strict connection with a higher fact never yet manifested. There is power over and behind us, and we are the channels of its communications. We seek to say thus and so, and over our head some spirit sits which contradicts what we say. We would persuade our fellow to this or that; another self within our eyes dissuades him. That which we keep back, this reveals. In vain we compose our faces and our words; it holds uncontrollable communication with the enemy, and he answers civilly to us, but believes the spirit. We exclaim, 'There's a traitor in the house!' but at last it appears that he is the true man, and I am the traitor. This open channel to the highest life is the first and last reality, so subtle, so quiet, yet so tenacious, that although I have never expressed the truth, and although I have never heard the expression of it from any other, I know that the whole truth is here for me. What if I cannot answer your questions? I am not pained that I cannot frame a reply to the question, What is the operation we call Providence? There lies the unspoken thing, present, omnipresent. Every time

we converse we seek to translate it into speech, but whether we hit or whether we miss, we have the fact. Every discourse is an approximate answer: but it is of small consequence that we do not get it into verbs and nouns, whilst it abides for contemplation forever.

If the auguries of the prophesying heart shall make themselves good in time, the man who shall be born, whose advent men and events prepare and foreshow, is one who shall enjoy his connection with a higher life, with the man within man; shall destroy distrust by his trust, shall use his native but forgotten methods, shall not take counsel of flesh and blood, but shall rely on the Law alive and beautiful which works over our heads and under our feet. Pitiless, it avails itself of our success when we obey it, and of our ruin when we contravene it. Men are all secret believers in it, else the word justice would have no meaning: they believe that the best is the true; that right is done at last; or chaos would come. It rewards actions after their nature, and not after the design of the agent. 'Work,' it saith to man, 'in every hour, paid or unpaid, see only that thou work, and thou canst not escape the reward: whether thy work be fine or coarse, planting corn or writing epics, so only it be honest work, done to thine own approbation, it shall earn a reward to the senses as well as to the thought: no matter how often defeated, you are born to victory. The reward of a thing well done, is to have done it.'

As soon as a man is wonted to look beyond surfaces, and to see how this high will prevails without an exception or an interval, he settles himself into serenity. He can already rely on the laws of gravity, that every stone will fall where it is due; the good globe is faithful, and carries us securely through the celestial spaces, anxious or resigned, we need not interfere to help it on: and he will learn one day the mild lesson they teach, that our own orbit is all our task, and we need not assist the administration of the universe. Do not be so impatient to set the town right concerning the unfounded pretensions and the false reputation of certain men of standing. They are laboring harder to set the town right concerning themselves, and will certainly succeed. Suppress for a few days your criticism on the insufficiency of this or that teacher or experimenter, and he will have demonstrated his insufficiency to all men's eyes. In like manner, let a man fall into the divine circuits, and he is enlarged. Obedience to his genius is the only liberating influence. We wish to escape from subjection and a sense of inferiority, and we make self-denying ordinances, we drink water, we eat grass, we refuse the laws, we go to jail: it is all in vain; only by obedience to his genius, only by the freest activity in the way constitutional to him, does an angel seem to arise before a man and lead him by the hand out of all the wards of the prison.

That which befits us, embosomed in beauty and wonder as we are, is cheerfulness and courage, and the endeavor to realize our aspirations. The life of man is the true romance, which when it is valiantly conducted will yield the imagination a higher joy than any fiction. All around us what powers are wrapped up under the coarse mattings of custom, and all wonder prevented. It is so wonderful to our neurologists that a man can see without his eyes, that it does not occur to them that it is just as wonderful that he should see with them; and that is ever the difference between the wise and the unwise: the latter wonders at what is unusual, the wise man wonders at the usual. Shall not the heart which has received so much, trust the Power by which it lives? May it not quit other leadings, and listen to the Soul that has guided it so gently and taught it so much,

secure that the future will be worthy of the past?

Oliver Wendell Holmes
✳ 1809-1894

Oliver Wendell Holmes, physician and wit, is remembered as poet for "Old Ironsides," "The Chambered Nautilus," and "The Deacon's Masterpiece" which tells of "the wonderful one-hoss shay," as essayist for his three Breakast Table series which appeared after 1857 for many years in many issues of the AT-LANTIC MONTHLY and then in widely admired volumes, and as writer of fiction for "medicated novels" in which he discussed in story form such subjects of scientific and moral significance as the inheritance of acquired characteristics and the relation of unconscious mind to freedom of the will. His remarks on "The Brahmin Caste of New England," which speak more directly to a point than many of his discursive essays, form part of the opening chapter of the first of these novels, ELSIE VENNER, which first appeared in the ATLANTIC MONTHLY in 1860 as "The Professor's Story."

The Brahmin Caste of New England

There is nothing in New England corresponding at all to the feudal aristocracies of the Old World. Whether it be owing to the stock from which we were derived, or to the practical working of our institutions, or to the abrogation of the technical "law of honor," which draws a sharp line between the personally responsible class of "gentlemen" and the unnamed multitude of those who are not expected to risk their lives for an abstraction,—whatever be the cause, we have no such aristocracy here as that which grew up out of the military systems of the Middle Ages.

What we mean by "aristocracy" is merely the richer part of the community, that live in the tallest houses, drive real carriages, (not "kerridges,") kid-glove their hands, and French-bonnet their ladies' heads, give parties where the persons who call them by the above title are not invited, and have a provokingly easy way of dressing, walking, talking, and nodding to people, as if they felt entirely at home, and would not be embarrassed in the least, if they met the Governor, or even the President of the United States, face to face. Some of these great folks are really well-bred, some of them are only purse-proud and assuming,—but they form a class, and are named as above in the common speech.

It is in the nature of large fortunes to diminish rapidly, when subdivided and distributed. A million is the unit of wealth, now and here in America. It splits into four handsome properties; each of these into four good inheritances; these, again, into scanty competences for four ancient maidens,—with whom it is best the family should die out, unless it can begin again as its great-grandfather did. Now a million is a kind of golden cheese, which represents in a compendious form the summer's growth of a fat meadow of craft or commerce; and as this kind of meadow rarely bears more than one crop, it is pretty certain that sons and grandsons will not get another golden cheese out of it, whether they milk the same cows or turn in new ones. In other words, the millionocracy, considered in a large way, is not at all an affair of persons and families, but a perpetual fact of money with a variable human element, which a philosopher

might leave out of consideration without falling into serious error. Of course, this trivial and fugitive fact of personal wealth does not create a permanent class, unless some special means are taken to arrest the process of disintegration in the third generation. This is so rarely done, at least successfully, that one need not live a very long life to see most of the rich families he knew in childhood more or less reduced, and the millions shifted into the hands of the country-boys who were sweeping stores and carrying parcels when the now decayed gentry were driving their chariots, eating their venison over silver chafing-dishes, drinking Madeira chilled in embossed coolers, wearing their hair in powder, and casing their legs in long boots with silken tassels.

There is, however, in New England, an aristocracy, if you choose to call it so, which has a far greater character of permanence. It has grown to be a *caste*, —not in any odious sense,—but, by the repetition of the same influences, generation after generation, it has acquired a distinct organization and physiognomy, which not to recognize is mere stupidity, and not to be willing to describe would show a distrust of the good-nature and intelligence of our readers, who like to have us see all we can and tell all we see.

If you will look carefully at any class of students in one of our colleges, you will have no difficulty in selecting specimens of two different aspects of youthful manhood. Of course I shall choose extreme cases to illustrate the contrast between them. In the first, the figure is perhaps robust, but often otherwise,— inelegant, partly from careless attitudes, partly from ill-dressing,—the face is uncouth in feature, or at least common,— the mouth coarse and unformed,—the eye unsympathetic, even if bright,—the movements of the face are clumsy, like those of the limbs,—the voice is unmusical,—and the enunciation as if the words were coarse castings, instead of fine carvings. The youth of the other aspect is commonly slender,—his face is smooth, and apt to be pallid,—his features are regular and of a certain delicacy, —his eye is bright and quick,—his lips play over the thought he utters as a pianist's fingers dance over their music,— and his whole air, though it may be timid, and even awkward, has nothing clownish. If you are a teacher, you know what to expect from each of these young men. With equal willingness, the first will be slow at learning; the second will take to his books as a pointer or a setter to his field-work.

The first youth is the common country-boy, whose race has been bred to bodily labor. Nature has adapted the family organization to the kind of life it has lived. The hands and feet by constant use have got more than their share of development,—the organs of thought and expression less than their share. The finer instincts are latent and must be developed. A youth of this kind is raw material in its first stage of elaboration. You must not expect too much of any such. Many of them have force of will and character, and become distinguished in practical life; but very few of them ever become great scholars. A scholar is, in a large proportion of cases, the son of scholars or scholarly persons.

That is exactly what the other young man is. He comes of the *Brahmin caste of New England*. This is the harmless, inoffensive, untitled aristocracy referred to, and which many readers will at once acknowledge. There are races of scholars among us, in which aptitude for learning, and all these marks of it I have spoken of, are congenital and hereditary. Their names are always on some college catalogue or other. They break out every generation or two in some learned labor which calls them up after they seem to have died out. At last some newer name takes their place, it may be,—but you inquire a little and you find it is the blood of the Edwardses or the Chauncys or the Ellerys or some of the old historic scholars, disguised under the altered name of a female descendant.

There probably is not an experienced instructor anywhere in our Northern States who will not recognize at once the truth of this general distinction. But the reader who has never been a teacher will very probably object, that some of our most illustrious public men have come direct from the homespun-clad class of the people,—and he may, perhaps, even find a noted scholar or two whose parents were masters of the English alphabet, but of no other.

It is not fair to pit a few chosen families against the great multitude of those who are continually working their way up into the intellectual classes. The results which are habitually reached by hereditary training are occasionally brought about without it. There are natural filters as well as artificial ones; and though the great rivers are commonly more or less turbid, if you will look long enough, you may find a spring that sparkles as no water does which drips through your apparatus of sands and sponges. So there are families which refine themselves into intellectual aptitude without having had much opportunity for intellectual acquirements. A series of felicitous crosses develops an improved strain of blood, and reaches its maximum perfection at last in the large uncombed youth who goes to college and startles the hereditary class-leaders by striding past them all. That is Nature's republicanism; thank God for it, but do not let it make you illogical. The race of the hereditary scholar has exchanged a certain portion of its animal vigor for its new instincts, and it is hard to lead men without a good deal of animal vigor. The scholar who comes by Nature's special grace from an unworn stock of broad-chested sires and deep-bosomed mothers must always overmatch an equal intelligence with a compromised and lowered vitality. A man's breathing and digestive apparatus (one is tempted to add *muscular*) are just as important to him on the floor of the Senate as his thinking organs. You broke down in your great speech, did you? Yes, your grandfather had an attack of dyspepsia in '82, after working too hard on his famous Election Sermon. All this does not touch the main fact: our scholars come chiefly from a privileged order, just as our best fruits come from well-known grafts,—though now and then a seedling apple, like the Northern Spy, or a seedling pear, like the Seckel, springs from a nameless ancestry and grows to be the pride of all the gardens in the land.

Henry Adams
✳ 1838-1918

The Brahmin Caste of which Dr. Holmes wrote has had perhaps no more characteristic a member than Henry Adams, descended from two presidents of the United States, but destined himself to become an observer rather than a leader. His achievement as formal historian, especially of the administrations which separated those of John Adams and John Quincy Adams, is overshadowed by two books published late in life, MONT-SAINT-MICHEL AND CHARTRES *in* 1904 *and* THE EDUCATION OF HENRY ADAMS *in* 1907, *which contrast the confusing multiplicity of Adams's time with the more unified serenity of the Middle Ages. The following preliminary explanation of the dilemma which faced him is* *drawn from the opening chapter of the second of those books.*

The Education of Henry Adams

Under the shadow of Boston State House, turning its back on the house of John Hancock, the little passage called Hancock Avenue runs, or ran, from Beacon Street, skirting the State House grounds, to Mount Vernon Street, on the summit of Beacon Hill; and there, in the third house below Mount Vernon Place, February 16, 1838, a child was born, and christened later by his uncle, the minister of the First Church after the tenets of Boston Unitarianism, as Henry Brooks Adams.

Had he been born in Jerusalem under the shadow of the Temple and circumcised in the Synagogue by his uncle the high priest, under the name of Israel Cohen, he would scarcely have been more distinctly branded, and not much more heavily handicapped in the races of the coming century, in running for such stakes as the century had to offer; but, on the other hand, the ordinary traveller, who does not enter the field of racing, finds advantage in being, so to speak, ticketed through life, with the safeguards of an old, established traffic. Safeguards are often irksome, but sometimes convenient, and if one needs them at all, one is apt to need them badly. A hundred years earlier, such safeguards as his would have secured any young man's success; and although in 1838 their value was not very great compared with what they would have been in 1738, yet the mere accident of starting a twentieth-century career from a nest of associations so colonial—so troglodytic— as the First Church, the Boston State House, Beacon Hill, John Hancock and John Adams, Mount Vernon Street and Quincy, all crowded on ten pounds of unconscious babyhood, was so queer as to offer a subject of curious speculation to the baby long after he had witnessed the solution. What could become of such a child of the seventeenth and eighteenth centuries, when he should wake up to find himself required to play the game of the twentieth? Had he been consulted, would he have cared to play the game at all, holding such cards, as he held, and suspecting that the game was to be one of which neither he nor anyone else back to the beginning of time knew the rules or the risks or the stakes? He was not consulted and was not responsible, but had he been taken into the confidence of his parents, he would certainly have told them to change nothing as far as concerned him. He would have been astounded by his own luck. Probably no child, born in the year, held better cards than he. Whether life was an honest game of chance, or whether the cards were marked and forced, he could not refuse to play his excellent hand. He could never make the usual plea of irresponsibility. He accepted the situation as though he had been a party to it, and under the same circumstances would do it again, the more readily for knowing the exact values. To his life as a whole he was a consenting, contracting party, and partner from the moment he was born to the moment he died. Only with that understanding—as a consciously assenting member in full partnership with the society of his age—had his education an interest to himself or to others.

As it happened, he never got to the point of playing the game at all; he lost himself in the study of it, watching the errors of the players; but this is the only interest in the story, which otherwise has no moral and little incident. A story of education—seventy years of it—the practical value remains to the end in doubt, like other values about which

men have disputed since the birth of Cain and Abel; but the practical value of the universe has never been stated in dollars. Although every one cannot be a Gargantua-Napoleon-Bismarck and walk off with the great bells of Notre Dame, every one must bear his own universe, and most persons are moderately interested in learning how their neighbors have managed to carry theirs.

This problem of education started in 1838, went on for three years, while the baby grew, like other babies, unconsciously, as a vegetable, the outside world working as it never had worked before, to get his new universe ready for him. Often in old age he puzzled over the question whether, on the doctrine of chances, he was at liberty to accept himself or his world as an accident. No such accident had ever happened before in human experience. For him, alone, the old universe was thrown into the ash-heap and a new one created. He and his eighteenth-century, troglodytic Boston were suddenly cut apart—separated forever—in act if not in sentiment, by the opening of the Boston and Albany Railroad; the appearance of the first Cunard steamers in the bay; and the telegraphic messages which carried from Baltimore to Washington the news that Henry Clay and James K. Polk were nominated for the Presidency. This was in May, 1844; he was six years old; his new world was ready for use, and only fragments of the old met his eyes.

Of all this that was being done to complicate his education, he knew only the color of yellow. He first found himself sitting on a yellow kitchen floor in strong sunlight. He was three years old when he took his earliest step in education: a lesson in color. The second followed soon; a lesson in taste. On December 3, 1841, he developed scarlet fever. For several days he was as good as dead, reviving only under the careful nursing of his family. When he began to recover strength, about January 1, 1842, his hunger must have been stronger than any other pleasure or pain, for while in after life he retained not the faintest recollection of his illness, he remembered quite clearly his aunt entering the sick-room bearing in her hand a saucer with a baked apple.

The order of impressions retained by memory might naturally be that of color and taste, although one would rather suppose that the sense of pain would be first to educate. In fact, the third recollection of the child was that of discomfort. The moment he could be removed, he was bundled up in blankets and carried from the little house in Hancock Avenue to a larger one which his parents were to occupy in the neighboring Mount Vernon Street. The season was midwinter, January 10, 1842, and he never forgot his acute distress for want of air under his blankets, or the noises of moving furniture.

As a means of variation from a normal type, sickness in childhood ought to have a certain value not to be classed under any fitness or unfitness of natural selection; and especially scarlet fever affected boys seriously, both physically and in character, though they might through life puzzle themselves to decide whether it had fitted or unfitted them for success; but this fever of Henry Adams took greater and greater importance in his eyes, from the point of view of education, the longer he lived. At first, the effect was physical. He fell behind his brothers two or three inches in height, and proportionally in bone and weight. His character and processes of mind seemed to share in this fining-down process of scale. He was not good in a fight, and his nerves were more delicate than boys' nerves ought to be. He exaggerated these weaknesses as he grew older. The habit of doubt; of distrusting his own judgment and of totally rejecting the judgment of the world; the tendency to

regard every question as open; the hesitation to act except as a choice of evils; the shirking of responsibility; the love of line, form, quality; the horror of ennui; the passion for companionship and the antipathy to society—all these were well-known qualities of New England character in no way peculiar to individuals but in this instance they seemed to be stimulated by the fever, and Henry Adams could never make up his mind whether, on the whole, the change of character was morbid or healthy, good or bad for his purpose. His brothers were the type; he was the variation.

As far as the boy knew, the sickness did not affect him at all, and he grew up in excellent health, bodily and mental, taking life as it was given; accepting its local standards without a difficulty, and enjoying much of it as keenly as any other boy of his age. He seemed to think himself quite normal, and his companions seemed always to think him so. Whatever was peculiar about him was education, not character, and came to him, directly and indirectly, as the result of that eighteenth-century inheritance which he took with his name.

The atmosphere of education in which he lived was colonial, revolutionary, almost Cromwellian, as though he were steeped, from his greatest grandmother's birth, in the odor of political crime. Resistance to something was the law of New England nature; the boy looked out on the world with the instinct of resistance; for numberless generations his predecessors had viewed the world chiefly as a thing to be reformed, filled with evil forces to be abolished, and they saw no reason to suppose that they had wholly succeeded in the abolition; the duty was unchanged. That duty implied not only resistance to evil, but hatred of it. Boys naturally look on all force as an enemy, and generally find it so, but the New Englander, whether boy or man, in his long struggle with a stingy or hostile universe, had learned also to love the pleasure of hating; his joys were few. . . .

The magnificence of his grandfather Brooks' house in Pearl Street or South Street has long ago disappeared, but perhaps his country house at Medford may still remain to show what impressed the mind of a boy in 1845 with the idea of city splendor. The President's house at Quincy was the larger and far more interesting of the two; but the boy felt at once its inferiority in fashion. It showed plainly enough its want of wealth. It smacked of colonial age, but not of Boston style or plush curtains. To the end of his life he never quite overcame the prejudice thus drawn in with his childish breath. He never could compel himself to care for nineteenth-century style. He was never able to adopt it, any more than his father or grandfather or great-grandfather had done. Not that he felt it as particularly hostile, for he reconciled himself to much that was worse; but because, for some remote reason, he was born an eighteenth-century child. . . .

The attachment to Quincy was not altogether sentimental or wholly sympathetic. Quincy was not a bed of thornless roses. Even there the curse of Cain set its mark. There as elsewhere a cruel universe combined to crush a child. As though three or four vigorous brothers and sisters, with the best will, were not enough to crush any child, every one else conspired toward an education which he hated. From cradle to grave this problem of running order through chaos, direction through space, discipline through freedom, unity through multiplicity, has always been, and must always be, the task of education, as it is the moral of religion, philosophy, science, art, politics, and economy; but a boy's will is his life, and he dies when it is broken, as the colt dies in harness, taking a new nature in becoming tame.

Rarely has a boy felt kindly toward his tamers. Between him and his masters has always been a war. Henry Adams never knew a boy of his generation to like a master, and the task of remaining on friendly terms with one's own family, in such a relation, was never easy. . . . The tone of Boston society was colonial. The true Bostonian always knelt in self-abasement before the majesty of English standards; far from concealing it as a weakness, he was proud of it as his strength. The eighteenth century ruled society long after 1850. Perhaps the boy began to shake it off rather earlier than most of his mates.

Indeed this prehistoric stage of education ended rather abruptly with his tenth year. . . . Even then he felt that something was wrong, but he concluded that it must be Boston. Quincy had always been right, for Quincy represented a moral principle—the principle of resistance to Boston. His Adams ancestors must have been right, since they were always hostile to State Street. If State Street was wrong, Quincy must be right! Turn the dilemma as he pleased, he still came back to the eighteenth century and the law of Resistance; of Truth; of Duty, and of Freedom.

Philip Rahv
✴ 1908-

Philip Rahv, editor, critic, and teacher for many years at New York University, collected some of his literary essays in IMAGES AND IDEA *in 1949, expanded in 1955. He was one of the founders of the* PARTISAN REVIEW *and has edited* THE DISCOVERY OF EUROPE: THE STORY OF AMERICAN EXPERIENCE IN THE OLD WORLD (1947) *and* LITERATURE IN

AMERICA; AN ANTHOLOGY OF LITERARY
CRITICISM (1957). *"Attitudes toward
Henry James"* first appeared in the NEW
REPUBLIC *in 1943.*

Attitudes toward Henry James

Henry James is at once the most and
least appreciated figure in American
writing. His authority as a novelist of
unique quality and as an archetypal
American has grown immeasurably in the
years since his death, and in some literary circles his name has of late been
turned into the password of a cult. But
at the same time he is still regarded, in
those circles that exert the major influence on popular education and intelligence, with the coldness and even derision that he encountered in the most
depressed period of his career, when his
public deserted him and he found himself almost alone.

To illustrate the extent to which he is
even now misunderstood, let me cite the
opening gambit of the section on James
in the *College Book of American Literature,* a text used in many schools. "It is
not certain that Henry James really belongs to American literature, for he was
critical of America and admired Europe."
The attitude so automatically expressed
by the editors of this academic volume
obviously borders on caricature. The responsibility for it, however, must be laid
at the door of all those critics and historians who, in response to a deep anti-
intellectual compulsion or at the service
of some blindly nationalistic or social
creed, are not content merely to say no
to the claims made in James's behalf but
must ever try to despoil him utterly. The
strategy is simple: James was nothing
but a self-deluded, expatriate snob, a
concoctor of elegant if intricate trifles,
a fugitive from "reality," etc., etc. Professor Pattee, a run-of-the-mill historian

of American writing permits himself the
remark that James's novels "really accomplish nothing." Ludwig Lewisohn is
likewise repelled by the novels—"cathedrals of frosted glass" he calls them; in
his opinion only the shorter narratives are
worth reading. In his *Main Currents in
American Thought* Parrington gives two
pages to James against eleven to James
Branch Cabell, and he has the further
temerity (and/or innocence) to round
out his two pages with comparing James
—much to his disadvantage, of course
—to Sherwood Anderson. And Van Wyck
Brooks does all he can, in *New England:
Indian Summer,* to promote once more
the notoriously low estimate of the later
James to which he committed himself in
The Pilgrimage of Henry James. Brooks
may well believe that the Jamesian attachment is to be counted among the
fixed ideas of our native "coterie writers"
—and plainly the best cure for a fixed
idea is to stamp on it.

This deprecation of James is prepared
for by some of the leading assumptions
of our culture. The attitude of Parrington, for example, is formed by the Populist spirit of the West and its open-air
poetics, whereas that of Brooks is at
bottom formed by the moralism of New
England—a moralism to which he has
reverted, even though in practice he applies it in a more or less impressionistic
and sentimental manner, with all the
vehemence of a penitent atoning for
his backsliding in the past. And the difference between such typical attitudes
is mainly this: that while Parrington—
like Whitman and Mark Twain before
him—rejects James entirely, Brooks at
least recognizes the value and fidelity to
life of his earlier novels. Yet if James can
be named, in T. S. Eliot's phrase, "a
positive continuator of the New England
genius," then surely Brooks must be
aware of it as well as any of us; for he is
nothing if not a pious servitor of this
genius; after all, he, too, is a paleface.

But still he scoffs at the more complex and, so to speak, ultimate James. And this Brooks does essentially for the same reasons, I think, that the Boston public of the 1870's scoffed at the works he now admits into his canon. We know that when the first of James's books appeared in America, they were actively disliked in Boston: Mrs. Fields (the wife of the publisher) relates that they were thought "self-conscious, artificial and shallow." A like animus is now betrayed in Brooks's statement of such novels as *The Spoils of Poynton, The Wings of the Dove,* and *The Golden Bowl:*

Magnificent pretensions, petty perform-ances!—the fruits of an irresponsible imagination, of a deranged sense of value, of a mind working in a void, uncorrected by any clear consciousness of human cause and effect (*The Pilgrimage of Henry James*).

There was scarcely enough substance in these great ghosts of novels. . . . What concerned him now was form, almost regardless of content, the problems of calculation and construction. . . . His American characters might be nobler, but, if the old world was corrupt, its glamor outweighed its corruption in his mind . . . so that he later pictured people, actually base, as eminent, noble and great (*New England: Indian Summer*).

What are such extreme statements if not critical rationalizations of the original Boston prejudice? Brooks begins by magnifying the distinctions between James's early and late manner into an absolute contradiction, and ends by invoking the charge of degeneracy. But the fact is that the changes in James's work mark no such gap as Brooks supposes but are altogether implicit in the quality of his vision, flowing from the combined release and elaboration of his basic tendency. Moreover, these changes, far from justifying the charge of degeneracy, define for a good many of his readers the one salient example in our literature of a novelist who, not exhausted by his initial assertion of power, learned how to nourish his gifts and grow to full maturity. To me he is the only really fine American writer of the nineteenth century who can truly be said to have mastered that "principle of growth," to the failure of which in our creative life Brooks has himself repeatedly called attention in his earlier preachments.

For what is to be admired in a late narrative like *The Wings of The Dove* is James's capacity to lift the nuclear theme of his first period—the theme of the American innocent's penetration into the "rich and deep and dark" hive of Europe—to a level of conscious experience and aesthetic possession not previously attained. James orders his world with consummate awareness in this narrative, applying successfully his favorite rule of an "exquisite economy" in composition. There are brilliant scenes in it of London and Venice, and strongly contrasted symbols of social glamor and decay; it is invigorated, too, by an unflagging realism in the plotting of act and motive and by the large movement of the characters. No literary standpoint that allows for the dismissal of this creation as a "petty performance" can possibly be valid. Is its heroine, Milly Theale, a character without reality? She remains in our mind, writes Edmund Wilson, "as a personality independent of the novel, the kind of personality, deeply felt, invested with poetic beauty and unmistakably individualized, which only the creators of the first rank can give life to."

James suffers from a certain one-sidedness, to be sure. This tends to throw off balance such readers as are unable to see it for what it is—the price he paid, given the circumstances of his career, for being faithful to his own genius. For James could continue to develop and sustain his "appeal to a high refinement and a handsome wholeness of effect" only through intensively exploiting his very limitations, through submitting himself to a process of creative yet cruel self-exaggeration. The strain shows in the stylization of his language, a stylization so rich that it turns into an intellectual quality of rare value, but which at times is apt to become overwrought and drop into unconscious parody. It is further shown in his obsessive refinement—a veritable delirium of refinement—which again serves at times to remove us from the actuality of the represented experience. This should be related to his all-too-persistent attempts, as Yvor Winters has observed, to make the sheer *tone* of speech and behavior "carry vastly more significance than is proper to it." It is true that, for instance, in novels like *The Sense of the Past* and *The Awkward Age,* he pushes his feelings for nuances and discriminations to an unworkable extreme. But such distortions, inflated into awful vices by his detractors, are of the kind which in one form or another not only James but most of the considerable modern artists are forced to cultivate as a means of coping with the negative environment that confines them. To regard such distortions as the traits of a willful coterie is utterly naïve. They are the traits, rather, of an art which, if it is to survive at all in a society inimical to all interests that are pure, gratuitous, and without cash value, has no other recourse save constantly to "refine its singularities" and expose itself more and more to the ravages of an unmitigated individualism.

But in all this I do not mean to imply that I agree with those enthusiasts who see no moral defects whatsoever in James. From the viewpoint of social criticism, there is a good deal of justice in Ferner Nuhn's mordant analysis of *The Golden Bowl.* Nuhn shows up one such defect in James's close identification with Adam and Maggie Verver's upper-class American illusions and self-righteousness. (One is persuaded of this view by the evidence of the tone and the inner manipulation of the scale of value, for here too the author makes the story "tell itself.") Nuhn fails to bring out, however, the enormous assets with which this novel is otherwise endowed. There is a use of symbols in it and a scenic and dramatic power scarcely equaled, to my mind, anywhere in American prose. Furthermore, whatever one may think of the millionaire self-indulgence of the Ververs, this is a far cry from the charge that his long exile put James into such a bad state that he could no longer distinguish between the noble and the base. This sort of charge is answered once and for all, it seems to me, by Stephen Spender in his study, *The Destructive Element:*

The morality of the heroes and heroines [in the last great novels] is to "suffer generously." What they have to suffer from is being more intelligent than the other characters. Also, there are no villains. It is important to emphasize this, because in these really savage novels the behavior of some of the characters is exposed in its most brutal form. But the wickedness of the characters lies primarily in their situation. Once the situation is provided, the actors cannot act otherwise. Their only compensation is that by the use of their intelligence, by their ability to understand, to love and to suffer, they may to some extent atone for the evil which is simply the evil of the modern world.

As against the sundry moralizers and nationalists who belittle James, there are the cultists who go to the other extreme in presenting him as a kind of culture hero, an ideal master whose perfection of form is equaled by his moral insight and stanch allegiance to "tradition." This image is, no doubt, of consolatory value to some high-minded literary men. It contributes, however, to the misunderstanding of James, in that it is so impeccable, one might say transcendent, that it all but eliminates the contradictions in him—and in modern literature, which bristles with anxieties and ideas of isolation, it is above all the creativity, the depth and quality of the contradictions that a writer unites within himself, that gives us the truest measure of his achievement. And this is not primarily a matter of the solutions, if any, provided by the writer—for it is hardly the writer's business to stand in for the scientist or philosopher—but of his force and integrity in reproducing these contradictions as felt experience. Very few of us would be able to appreciate Dostoevski, for instance, if we first had to accept his answer to the problem of the Christian man, or Proust if we first had to accept his answer to the problem of the artist. We appreciate these novelists because they employ imaginative means that convince us of the reality of their problems, which are not *necessarily* ours.

T. S. Eliot was surely right in saying that the soil of James's origin imparted a "flavor" that was "precisely improved and given its chance, not worked off" by his living in Europe. Now James differs radically in his contradictions from European novelists—that is why readers lacking a background in American or at least Anglo-Saxon culture make so little of him. And the chief contradiction is that his work represents a positive and ardent search for "experience" and simultaneously a withdrawal from it, or rather a dread of approaching it in its natural state. Breaking sharply with the then still dominant American morality of abstention, he pictures "experience" as the "real taste of life," as a longed-for "presence" at once "vast, vague, and dazzling —an irradiation of light from objects undefined, mixed with the atmosphere of Paris and Venice." Nevertheless, to prove truly acceptable, it must first be Americanized as it were, that is to say, penetrated by the new-world conscience and cleansed of its taint of "evil." This tension between the impulse to plunge into "experience" and the impulse to re-

nounce it is the chief source of the internal yet astonishingly abundant Jamesian emotion; and because the tension is not always adequately resolved, we sometimes get that effect, so well described by Glenway Wescott, of "embarrassed passion and hinted meaning in excess of the narrated facts; the psychic content is too great for its container of elegantly forged happenings; it all overflows and slops about and is magnificently wasted." On this side of James we touch upon his relationship to Hawthorne, whose characters, likewise tempted by "experience," are held back by the fear of sin. And Hawthorne's ancestral idea of sin survives in James, though in a secularized form. It has entered the sensibility and been translated into a revulsion, an exasperated feeling, almost morbid in its sensitiveness, against any conceivable crudity of scene or crudity of conduct. (The trouble with American life, he wrote, is not that it is "ugly"—the ugly can be strange and grotesque—but that it is "plain"; "even nature, in the western world, has the peculiarity of seeming rather crude and immature.") Any failure of discrimination is sin, whereas virtue is a compound of intelligence, moral delicacy, and the sense of the past.

And Hawthorne's remembrance of the religious mythology of New England and his fanciful concern with it is replaced in James—and this too is a kind of transmutation—by the remembrance and fanciful concern with history. It was for the sake of Europe's historical "opulence" that he left his native land. Yet this idea is also managed by him in a contradictory fashion, and for this reason W. C. Brownell was able to say that he showed no real interest in the "course of history." Now, as a critic, Brownell had no eye for James's historical picture of the American experience in Europe; but it is true that on the whole James's sense of history is restricted by the point of view of the "passionate pilgrim" who comes to enrich his personality. Thus there is produced the Jamesian conception of history as a static yet irreproachable standard, a beautiful display, a treasured background, whose function is at once to adorn and lend perspective to his well-nigh metaphysical probing of personal relations, of the private life. There never was a writer so immersed in personal relations, and his consistency in this respect implies an antihistorical attitude. This helps to explain the peculiarities of his consciousness, which is intellectual yet at the same time indifferent to general ideas, deeply comprehensive yet unattached to any open philosophical motive.

These contradictions in James—and there are others besides those I have mentioned—are chiefly to be accounted for in terms of his situation as an American writer who experienced his nationality and the social class to which he belonged at once as an ordeal and as an inspiration. His characteristic themes all express this doubleness. The "great world" is corrupt, yet it represents an irresistible goal. Innocence points to all the wanted things one has been deprived of, yet it is profound in its good faith and not to be tampered with without loss. History and culture are the supreme ideal, but why not make of them a strictly private possession? Europe is romance and reality and civilization, but the spirit resides in America. James never faltered in the maze of these contraries; he knew how to take hold of them creatively and weave them into the web of his art. And the secret of their combination is the secret of his irony, and of his humor.

POETRY

Ralph Waldo Emerson

✳ 1803-1882

Emerson's conception of the poet is not greatly different from that held by such slightly older English contemporaries as Wordsworth, Coleridge, and Shelley: truth, goodness, and beauty were aspects of a single whole, so that Keats, for example, could say with confidence that beauty was truth. The poet is a seer who through the magic of words expresses truths which have always existed but which have not been revealed before. "The Poet" opens Emerson's 1844 collection of ESSAYS: SECOND SERIES.

The Poet

A moody child and wildly wise
Pursued the game with joyful eyes,
Which chose, like meteors, their way,
And rived the dark with private ray:
They overleapt the horizon's edge,
Searched with Apollo's privilege;
Through man, and woman, and sea, and
   star
Saw the dance of nature forward far;
Through worlds, and races, and terms,
   and times
Saw musical order, and pairing rhymes.

Olympian bards who sung
   Divine ideas below,
Which always find us young,
   And always keep us so.

Those who are esteemed umpires of taste are often persons who have acquired some knowledge of admired pictures or sculptures, and have an inclination for whatever is elegant; but if you inquire whether they are beautiful souls, and whether their own acts are like fair pictures, you learn that they are selfish and sensual. Their cultivation is local, as if you should rub a log of dry wood in one spot to produce fire, all the rest remaining cold. Their knowledge of the fine arts is some study of rules and particulars, or some limited judgment of color or form, which is exercised for amusement or for show. It is a proof of the shallowness of the doctrine of beauty as it lies in the minds of our amateurs, that men seem to have lost the perception of the instant dependence of form upon soul. There is no doctrine of forms in our philosophy. We were put into our bodies, as fire is put into a pan to be carried about; but there is no accurate adjustment between the spirit and the organ, much less is the latter the germination of the former. So in regard to other forms, the intellectual men do not believe in any essential dependence of the material world on thought and volition. Theologians think it a pretty air-castle to talk of the spiritual meaning of a ship or a cloud, of a city or a contract, but they prefer to come again to the solid ground of historical evidence; and even the poets are contented with a civil and conformed manner of living, and to write poems from the fancy, at a safe distance from their own experience. But the highest minds of the world have never ceased to explore the double meaning, or shall I say the quadruple or the centuple or much more manifold meaning, of every sensuous fact; Orpheus, Empedocles, Heraclitus, Plato, Plutarch, Dante, Swedenborg, and the masters of sculpture, picture and poetry. For we are not pans and barrows, nor even porters of the fire and torch-bearers, but children of the fire, made of it, and only the same divinity transmuted and at two or three removes, when we know least about it. And this hidden truth, that the fountains whence all this river of Time and its creatures floweth are intrinsically ideal and beautiful, draws us to the consideration of the nature and functions of the Poet, or the man of Beauty; to the means and materials he uses, and to the general aspect of the art in the present time.

The breadth of the problem is great, for the poet is representative. He stands among partial men for the complete man, and apprises us not of his wealth, but of the common wealth. The young man reveres men of genius, because, to speak truly, they are more himself than he is. They receive of the soul as he also receives, but they more. Nature enhances her beauty, to the eye of loving men, from their belief that the poet is beholding her shows at the same time. He is isolated among his contemporaries by truth and by his art, but with this consolation in his pursuits, that they will draw all men sooner or later. For all men live by truth and stand in need of expression. In love, in art, in avarice, in politics, in labor, in games, we study to utter our painful secret. The man is only half himself, the other half is his expression.

Notwithstanding this necessity to be published, adequate expression is rare. I know not how it is that we need an interpreter, but the great majority of men seem to be minors, who have not yet come into possession of their own, or mutes, who cannot report the conversation they have had with nature. There is no man who does not anticipate a supersensual utility in the sun and stars, earth and water. These stand and wait to render him a peculiar service. But there is some obstruction or some excess of

phlegm in our constitution, which does not suffer them to yield the due effect. Too feeble fall the impressions of nature on us to make us artists. Every touch should thrill. Every man should be so much an artist that he could report in conversation what had befallen him. Yet, in our experience, the rays or appulses have sufficient force to arrive at the senses, but not enough to reach the quick and compel the reproduction of themselves in speech. The poet is the person in whom these powers are in balance, the man without impediment, who sees and handles that which others dream of, traverses the whole scale of experience, and is representative of man, in virtue of being the largest power to receive and to impart.

For the Universe has three children, born at one time, which reappear under different names in every system of thought, whether they be called cause, operation and effect; or, more poetically, Jove, Pluto, Neptune; or, theologically, the Father, the Spirit and the Son; but which we will call here the Knower, the Doer and the Sayer. These stand respectively for the love of truth, for the love of good, and for the love of beauty. These three are equal. Each is that which he is, essentially, so that he cannot be surmounted or analyzed, and each of these three has the power of the others latent in him and his own, patent.

The poet is the sayer, the namer, and represents beauty. He is a sovereign, and stands on the centre. For the world is not painted or adorned, but is from the beginning beautiful; and God has not made some beautiful things, but Beauty is the creator of the universe. Therefore the poet is not any permissive potentate, but is emperor in his own right. Criticism is infested with a cant of materialism, which assumes that manual skill and activity is the first merit of all men, and disparages such as say and do not, overlooking the fact that some men, namely poets, are natural sayers, sent into the world to the end of expression, and confounds them with those whose province is action but who quit it to imitate the sayers. But Homer's words are as costly and admirable to Homer as Agamemnon's victories are to Agamemnon. The poet does not wait for the hero or the sage, but, as they act and think primarily, so he writes primarily what will and must be spoken, reckoning the others, though primaries also, yet, in respect to him, secondaries and servants; as sitters or models in the studio of a painter, or as assistants who bring building-materials to an architect.

For poetry was all written before time was, and whenever we are so finely organized that we can penetrate into that region where the air is music, we hear those primal warblings and attempt to write them down, but we lose ever and anon a word or a verse and substitute something of our own, and thus miswrite the poem. The men of more delicate ear write down these cadences more faithfully, and these transcripts, though imperfect, become the songs of the nations. For nature is as truly beautiful as it is good, or as it is reasonable, and must as much appear as it must be done, or be known. Words and deeds are quite indifferent modes of the divine energy. Words are also actions, and actions are a kind of words.

The sign and credentials of the poet are that he announces that which no man foretold. He is the true and only doctor; he knows and tells; he is the only teller of news, for he was present and privy to the appearance which he describes. He is a beholder of ideas and an utterer of the necessary and causal. For we do not speak now of men of poetical talents, or of industry and skill in metre, but of the true poet. I took part in a conversation the other day concerning a recent writer of lyrics, a man of subtle mind, whose head appeared to be a music-box of delicate tunes and rhythms, and whose skill and command of language we could not sufficiently praise. But when the question arose whether he was not only a lyrist but a poet, we were obliged to confess that he is plainly a contemporary, not an eternal man. He does not stand out of our low limitations, like a Chimborazo under the line, running up from a torrid base through all the climates of the globe, with belts of the herbage of every latitude on its high and mottled sides; but this genius is the landscape-garden of a modern house, adorned with fountains and statues, with well-bred men and women standing and sitting in the walks and terraces. We hear, through all the varied music, the ground-tone of conventional life. Our poets are men of talents who sing, and not the children of music. The argument is secondary, the finish of the verses is primary.

For it is not metres, but a metre-making argument that makes a poem— a thought so passionate and alive that like the spirit of a plant or an animal it has an architecture of its own, and adorns nature with a new thing. The thought and the form are equal in the order of time, but in the order of genesis the thought is prior to the form. The poet has a new thought; he has a whole new experience to unfold; he will tell us how it was with him, and all men will be the richer in his fortune. For the experience of each new age requires a new confession, and the world seems always waiting for its poet. I remember when I was young how much I was moved one morning by tidings that genius had appeared in a youth who sat near me at table. He had left his work and gone rambling none knew whither, and had written hundreds of lines, but could not tell whether that which was in him was therein told; he could tell nothing but that all was changed—man, beast, heaven, earth and sea. How gladly we listened! how credulous! Society seemed to be compromised. We sat in the aurora of a sunrise which was to put out all the stars. Boston seemed to be at twice the distance it had the night before, or was much farther than that. Rome—what was Rome? Plutarch and Shakspeare were in the yellow leaf, and Homer no more should be heard of. It is much to know that poetry has been written this very day, under this very roof, by your side. What! that wonderful spirit has not expired! These stony moments are still sparkling and animated! I had fancied that the oracles were all silent, and nature had spent her fires; and behold! all night from every pore, these fine auroras have been streaming. Every one has some interest in the advent of the poet, and no one knows how much it may concern him. We know that the secret of the world is profound, but who or what shall be our interpreter, we know not. A mountain ramble, a new style of face, a new person, may put the key into our hands. Of course the value of genius to us is in the veracity of its report. Talent may frolic and juggle; genius realizes and adds. Mankind in good earnest have availed so far in understanding themselves and their work, that the foremost watchman on the peak announces his news. It is the truest word ever spoken, and the phrase will be the fittest, most musical, and the unerring voice of the world for that time.

All that we call sacred history attests that the birth of a poet is the principal event in chonology. Man, never so often deceived, still watches for the arrival of a brother who can hold him steady to a truth until he has made it his own. With what joy I begin to read a poem which I confide in as an inspiration! And now my chains are to be broken; I shall mount above these clouds and opaque airs in which I live—opaque, though they seem transparent—and from the heaven of truth I shall see and comprehend my relations. That will reconcile me to life and renovate nature, to see trifles animated by a tendency, and to know what I am doing. Life will no more be a noise; now I shall see men and women, and know the signs by which they may be discerned from fools and satans. This day shall be better than my birthday: then I became an animal; now I am invited into the science of the real. Such is the hope, but the fruition is postponed. Oftener it falls that this winged man, who will carry me into the heaven, whirls me into mists, then leaps and frisks about with me as it were from cloud to cloud, still affirming that he is bound heavenward; and I, being myself a novice, am slow in perceiving that he does not know the way into the heavens, and is merely bent that I should admire his skill to rise like a fowl or a flying fish, a little way from the ground or the water; but the all-piercing, all-feeding and ocular air of heaven that man shall never inhabit. I tumble down again soon into my old nooks, and lead the life of exaggerations as before, and have lost my faith in the possibility of any guide who can lead me thither where I would be.

But, leaving these victims of vanity, let us, with new hope, observe how nature, by worthier impulses, has insured the poet's fidelity to his office of announcement and affirming, namely by the beauty of things, which becomes a new and higher beauty when expressed. Nature offers all her creatures to him as a picture-language. Being used as a type, a second wonderful value appears in the object, far better than its old value; as the carpenter's stretched cord, if you hold your ear close enough, is musical in the breeze. "Things more excellent than every image," says Jamblichus, "are expressed through images." Things admit of being used as symbols because nature is a symbol, in the whole, and in every part. Every line we can draw in the sand has expression; and there is no body without its spirit or genius. All form is an effect of character; all condition, of the quality of the life; all harmony, of health; and for this reason a perception of beauty should be sympathetic, or proper only to the good. The beautiful rests on the foundations of the necessary. The soul makes the body, as the wise Spenser teaches:—

So every spirit, as it is more pure,
And hath in it the more of heavenly light,
So it the fairer body doth procure
To habit in, and it more fairly dight,
With cheerful grace and amiable sight.
For, of the soul, the body form doth take,
For soul is form, and doth the body make.

Here we find ourselves suddenly not in a critical speculation but in a holy place, and should go very warily and reverently. We stand before the secret of the world, there where Being passes into Appearance and Unity into Variety.

The Universe is the externization of the soul. Wherever the life is, that bursts into appearance around it. Our science is sensual, and therefore superficial. The earth and the heavenly bodies, physics and chemistry, we sensually treat, as if they were self-existent; but these are the retinue of that Being we have. "The mighty heaven," said Proclus, "exhibits, in its transfigurations, clear images of the splendor of intellectual perceptions; being moved in conjunction with the unapparent periods of intellectual natures." Therefore science always goes abreast with the just elevation of the man, keeping step with religion and metaphysics; or the state of science is an index of our self-knowledge. Since every thing in nature answers to a moral power, if any phenomenon remains brute and dark it is because the corresponding faculty in the observer is not yet active.

No wonder then, if these waters be so deep, that we hover over them with a religious regard. The beauty of the fable proves the importance of the sense; to the poet, and to all others; or, if you please, every man is so far a poet as to be susceptible of these enchantments of nature; for all men have the thoughts whereof the universe is the celebration. I find that the fascination resides in the symbol. Who loves nature? Who does not? Is it only poets, and men of leisure and cultivation, who live with her? No; but also hunters, farmers, grooms and butchers, though they express their affection in their choice of life and not in their choice of words. The writer wonders what the coachman or the hunter values in riding, in horses and dogs. It is not superficial qualities. When you talk with him he holds these at as slight a rate as you. His worship is sympathetic; he has no definitions, but he is commanded in nature by the living power which he feels to be there present. No imitation or playing of these things would content him; he loves the earnest of the north wind, of rain, of stone and wood and iron. A beauty not explicable is dearer than a beauty which we can see to the end of. It is nature the symbol, nature certifying the supernatural, body overflowed by life which he worships with coarse but sincere rites.

The inwardness and mystery of this attachment drive men of every class to the use of emblems. The schools of poets and philosophers are not more intoxicated with their symbols than the populace with theirs. In our political parties, compute the power of badges and emblems. See the great ball which they roll from Baltimore to Bunker Hill! In the political processions, Lowell goes in a loom, and Lynn in a shoe, and Salem in a ship. Witness the cider-barrel, the log-cabin, the hickory-stick, the palmetto, and all the cognizances of party. See the power of national emblems. Some stars, lilies, leopards, a crescent, a lion, an eagle, or other figure which came into credit God knows how, on an old rag of bunting, blowing in the wind on a fort at the ends of the earth, shall make the blood tingle under the rudest or the most conventional exterior. The people fancy they hate poetry, and they are all poets and mystics!

Beyond this universality of the symbolic language, we are appraised of the divineness of this superior use of things, whereby the world is a temple whose walls are covered with emblems, pictures and commandments of the Deity—in this, that there is no fact in nature which does not carry the whole sense of nature; and the distinctions which we make in events and in affairs, of low and high, honest and base, disappear when nature is used as a symbol. Thought makes everything fit for use. The vocabulary of an omniscient man would embrace words and images excluded from polite conversation. What would be base, or even obscene, to the obscene, becomes illustrious, spoken in a new connection of thought. The piety of the Hebrew prophets purges their grossness. The circumcision is an example of the power of poetry to raise the low and offensive. Small and mean things serve as well as great symbols. The meaner the type by which a law is expressed, the more pungent it is, and the more lasting in the memories of men; just as we choose the smallest box or case in which any needful utensil can be carried. Bare lists of words are found suggestive to an imaginative and excited mind; as it is related of Lord Chatham that he was accustomed to read in Bailey's Dictionary when he was preparing to speak in Parliament. The poorest experience is rich enough for all the purposes of expressing thought. Why covet a knowledge of new facts? Day and night, house and garden, a few books, a few actions serve us as well as would all trades and all spectacles. We are far from having exhausted the significance of the few symbols we use. We can come to use them yet with a terrible simplicity. It does not need that a poem should be long. Every word was once a poem. Every new relation is a new

word. Also we use defects and deformities to a sacred purpose, so expressing our sense that the evils of the world are such only to the evil eye. In the old mythology, mythologists observe, defects are ascribed to divine natures, as lameness to Vulcan, blindness to Cupid, and the like—to signify exuberances.

For as it is dislocation and detachment from the life of God that makes things ugly, the poet, who re-attaches things to nature and the Whole—re-attaching even artificial things and violation of nature, to nature, by a deeper insight—disposes very easily of the most disagreeable facts. Readers of poetry see the factory-village and the railway, and fancy that the poetry of the landscape is broken up by these; for these works of art are not yet consecrated in their reading; but the poet sees them fall within the great Order not less than the beehive or the spider's geometrical web. Nature adopts them very fast into her vital circles, and the gliding train of cars she loves like her own. Besides, in a centred mind, it signifies nothing how many mechanical inventions you exhibit. Though you add millions, and never so surprising, the fact of mechanics has not gained a grain's weight. The spiritual fact remains unalterable, by many or by few particulars; as no mountain is of any appreciable height to break the curve of the sphere. A shrewd country-boy goes to the city for the first time, and the complacent citizen is not satisfied with his little wonder. It is not that he does not see all the fine houses and know that he never saw such before, but he disposes of them as easily as the poet finds place for the railway. The chief value of the new fact is to enhance the great and constant fact of Life, which can dwarf any and every circumstance, and to which the belt of wampum and the commerce of America are alike.

The world being thus put under the mind for verb and noun, the poet is he who can articulate it. For though life is great, and fascinates and absorbs; and though all men are intelligent of the symbols through which it is named; yet they cannot originally use them. We are symbols and inhabit symbols; workmen, work, and tools, words and things, birth and death, all are emblems; but we sympathize with the symbols, and being infatuated with the economical uses of things, we do not know that they are thoughts. The poet, by an ulterior intellectual perception, gives them a power which makes their old use forgotten, and puts eyes and a tongue into every dumb and inanimate object. He perceives the independence of the thought on the symbol, the stability of the thought, the accidency and fugacity of the symbol. As the eyes of Lyncæus were said to see through the earth, so the poet turns the world to glass, and shows us all things in their right series and procession. For through that better perception he stands one step nearer to things, and sees the flowing or metamorphosis; perceives that thought is multiform; that within the form of every creature is a force impelling it to ascend into a higher form; and following with his eyes the life, uses the forms which express that life, and so his speech flows with the flowing of nature. All the facts of the animal economy, sex, nutriment, gestation, birth, growth, are symbols of the passage of the world into the soul of man, to suffer there a change and reappear a new and higher fact. He uses forms according to the life, and not according to the form. This is true science. The poet alone knows astronomy, chemistry, vegetation and animation, for he does not stop at these facts, but employs them as signs. He knows why the plain or meadow of space was strown with these flowers we call suns and moons and stars; why the great deep is adorned with animals, with men, and gods; for in every word he speaks he rides on them as the horses of thought.

By virtue of this science the poet is the Namer or Language-maker, naming things sometimes after their appearance, sometimes after their essence, and giving to every one its own name and not another's, thereby rejoicing the intellect, which delights in detachments or boundary. The poets made all the words, and therefore language is the archives of history, and, if we must say it, a sort of tomb of the muses. For though the origin of most of our words is forgotten, each word was at first a stroke of genius, and obtained currency because for the moment it symbolized the world to the first speaker and to the hearer. The etymologist finds the deadest word to have been once a brilliant picture. Language is fossil poetry. As the limestone of the continent consists of infinite masses of the shells of animalcules, so language is made up of images or tropes, which now, in their secondary use, have long ceased to remind us of their poetic origin. But the poet names the thing because he sees it, or comes one step nearer to it than any other. This expression or naming is not art, but a second nature, grown out of the first, as a leaf out of a tree. What we call nature is a certain self-regulated motion or change; and nature does all things by her own hands, and does not leave another to baptize her but baptizes herself; and this through the metamorphosis again. I remember that a certain poet described it to me thus:—

Genius is the activity which repairs the decays of things, whether wholly or partly of a material and finite kind. Nature, through all her kingdoms, insures herself. Nobody cares for planting the poor fungus; so she shakes down from the gills of one agaric countless spores, any one of which, being preserved, transmits new billions of spores to-morrow or next day. The new agaric of this hour has a chance which the old one had not. This atom of seed is thrown into a new place, not subject to the accidents which destroyed its parent two rods off. She makes a man; and having brought him to ripe age, she will no longer run the risk of losing this wonder at a blow, but she detaches from him a new self, that the kind may be safe from accidents to which the individual is exposed. So when the soul of the poet has come to ripeness of thought, she detaches and sends away from it its poems or songs—a fearless, sleepless, deathless progeny, which is not exposed to the accidents of the weary kingdom of time; a fearless, vivacious offspring, clad with wings (such was the virtue of the soul out of which they came) which carry them fast and far, and infix them irrecoverably into the hearts of men. These wings are the beauty of the poet's soul. The songs, thus flying immortal from their mortal parent, are pursued by clamorous flights of censures, which swarm in far greater numbers and threaten to devour them; but these last are not winged. At the end of a very short leap they fall plump down and rot, having received from the souls out of which they came no beautiful wings. But the melodies of the poet ascend and leap and pierce into the deeps of infinite time.

So far the bard taught me, using his freer speech. But nature has a higher end, in the production of new individuals, than security, namely *ascension,* or the passage of the soul into higher forms. I knew in my younger days the sculptor who made the statue of the youth which stands in the public garden. He was, as I remember, unable to tell directly what made him happy or unhappy, but by wonderful indirections he could tell. He rose one day, according to his habit, before the dawn, and saw the morning break, grand as the eternity out of which it came, and for many days after, he strove to express this tranquillity, and lo! his chisel had fashioned out of marble the form of a beautiful youth, Phosphorus, whose aspect is such that it is said all persons who look on it become silent. The poet also resigns himself to his mood, and that thought which agitated him is expressed, but *alter idem,* in a manner totally new. The expression is organic, or the new type which things themselves take when liberated. As, in the sun, objects paint their images on the retina of the eye, so they, sharing the

aspiration of the whole universe, tend to paint a far more delicate copy of their essence in his mind. Like the metamorphosis of things into higher organic forms is their change into melodies. Over everything stands its dæmon or soul, and, as the form of the thing is reflected by the eye, so the soul of the thing is reflected by a melody. The sea, the mountain-ridge, Niagara, and every flower-bed, pre-exist, or super-exist, in pre-cantations, which sail like odors in the air, and when any man goes by with an ear sufficiently fine, he overhears them and endeavors to write down the notes without diluting or depraving them. And herein is the legitimation of criticism, in the mind's faith that the poems are a corrupt version of some text in nature with which they ought to be made to tally. A rhyme in one of our sonnets should not be less pleasing than the iterated nodes of a sea-shell, or the resembling difference of a group of flowers. The pairing of the birds is an idyl, not tedious as our idyls are; a tempest is a rough ode, without falsehood or rant; a summer, with its harvest sown, reaped and stored, is an epic song, subordinating how many admirably executed parts. Why should not the symmetry and truth that modulate these, glide into our spirits, and we participate the invention of nature?

This insight, which expresses itself by what is called Imagination, is a very high sort of seeing, which does not come by study, but by the intellect being where and what it sees; by sharing the path or circuit of things through forms, and so making them translucid to others. The path of things is silent. Will they suffer a speaker to go with them? A spy they will not suffer; a lover, a poet, is the transcendency of their own nature—him they will suffer. The condition of true naming, on the poet's part, is his resigning himself to the divine *aura* which breathes through forms, and accompanying that.

It is a secret which every intellectual man quickly learns, that beyond the energy of his possessed and conscious intellect he is capable of a new energy (as of an intellect doubled on itself), by abandonment to the nature of things; that beside his privacy of power as an individual man, there is a great public power on which he can draw, by unlocking, at all risks, his human doors, and suffering the ethereal tides to roll and circulate through him; then he is caught up into the life of the Universe, his speech is thunder, his thought is law, and his words are universally intelligible as the plants and animals. The poet knows that he speaks adequately then only when he speaks somewhat wildly, or "with the flower of the mind"; not with the intellect used as an organ, but with the intellect released from all service and suffered to take its direction from its celestial life; or as the ancients were wont to express themselves, not with intellect alone but with the intellect inebriated by nectar. As the traveller who has lost his way throws his reins on his horse's neck and trusts to the instinct of the animal to find his road, so must we do with the divine animal who carries us through this world. For if in any manner we can stimulate this instinct, new passages are opened for us into nature; the mind flows into and through things hardest and highest, and the metamorphosis is possible.

This is the reason why bards love wine, mead, narcotics, coffee, tea, opium, the fumes of sandalwood and tobacco, or whatever other procurers of animal exhilaration. All men avail themselves of such means as they can, to add this extraordinary power to their normal powers; and to this end they prize conversation, music, pictures, sculpture, dancing, theatres, travelling, war, mobs, fires, gaming, politics, or love, or science, or animal intoxication—which are several coarser or finer *quasi*-mechanical substi-

tutes for the true nectar, which is the ravishment of the intellect by coming nearer to the fact. These are auxiliaries to the centrifugal tendency of a man, to his passage out into free space, and they help him to escape the custody of that body in which he is pent up, and of that jailyard of individual relations in which he is enclosed. Hence a great number of such as were professionally expressers of Beauty, as painters, poets, musicians and actors, have been more than others wont to lead a life of pleasure and indulgence; all but the few who received the true nectar; and, as it was a spurious mode of attaining freedom, as it was an emancipation not into the heavens but into the freedom of baser places, they were punished for that advantage they won, by a dissipation and deterioration. But never can any advantage be taken of nature by a trick. The spirit of the world, the great calm presence of the Creator, comes not forth to the sorceries of opium or of wine. The sublime vision comes to the pure and simple soul in a clean and chaste body. That is not an inspiration, which we owe to narcotics, but some counterfeit excitement and fury. Milton says that the lyric poet may drink wine and live generously, but the epic poet, he who shall sing of the gods and their descent unto men, must drink water out of a wooden bowl. For poetry is not 'Devil's wine,' but God's wine. It is with this as it is with toys. We fill the hands and nurseries of our children with all manner of dolls, drums and horses; withdrawing their eyes from the plain face and sufficing objects of nature, the sun and moon, the animals, the water and stones, which should be their toys. So the poet's habit of living should be set on a key so low that the common influences should delight him. His cheerfulness should be the gift of the sunlight; the air should suffice for his inspiration, and he should be tipsy with water. That spirit which suffices quiet hearts, which seems to come forth to such from every dry knoll of sere grass, from every pine stump and half-imbedded stone on which the dull March sun shines, comes forth to the poor and hungry, and such as are of simple taste. If thou fill thy brain with Boston and New York, with fashion and covetousness, and wilt stimulate thy jaded senses with wine and French coffee, thou shalt find no radiance of wisdom in the lonely waste of the pine woods.

If the imagination intoxicates the poet, it is not inactive in other men. The metamorphosis excites in the beholder an emotion of joy. The use of symbols has a certain power of emancipation and exhilaration for all men. We seem to be touched by a wand which makes us dance and run about happily, like children. We are like persons who come out of a cave or cellar into the open air. This is the effect on us of tropes, fables, oracles and all poetic forms. Poets are thus liberating gods. Men have really got a new sense, and found within their world another world, or nest of worlds; for, the metamorphosis once seen, we divine that it does not stop. I will not now consider how much this makes the charm of algebra and the mathematics, which also have their tropes, but it is felt in every definition; as when Aristotle defines *space* to be an immovable vessel in which things are contained; or when Plato defines a *line* to be a flowing point; or *figure* to be a bound of solid; and many the like. What a joyful sense of freedom we have when Vitruvius announces the old opinion of artists that no architect can build any house well who does not know something of anatomy. When Socrates, in Charmides, tells us that the soul is cured of its maladies by certain incantations, and that these incantations are beautiful reasons, from which temperance is generated in souls; when Plato calls the world an animal, and Timæus affirms that the plants also are animals; or af-

firms a man to be a heavenly tree, growing with his root, which is his head, upward; and, as George Chapman, following him, writes,

So in our tree of man, whose nervie root
Springs in his top;—

when Orpheus speaks of hoariness as "that white flower which marks extreme old age"; when Proclus calls the universe the statue of the intellect; when Chaucer, in his praise of 'Gentilesse,' compares good blood in mean condition to fire, which, though carried to the darkest house betwixt this and the mount of Caucasus, will yet hold its natural office and burn as bright as if twenty thousand men did it behold; when John saw, in the Apocalypse, the ruin of the world through evil, and the stars fall from heaven as the fig tree casteth her untimely fruit; when Aesop reports the whole catalogue of common daily relations through the masquerade of birds and beasts; we take the cheerful hint of the immortality of our essence and its versatile habit and escapes, as when the gypsies say of themselves "it is in vain to hang them, they cannot die."

The poets are thus liberating gods. The ancient British bards had for the title of their order, "Those who are free throughout the world." They are free, and they make free. An imaginative book renders us much more service at first, by stimulating us through its tropes, than afterward when we arrive at the precise sense of the author. I think nothing is of any value in books excepting the transcendental and extraordinary. If a man is inflamed and carried away by his thought, to that degree that he forgets the authors and the public and heeds only this one dream which holds him like an insanity, let me read his paper, and you may have all the arguments and histories and criticism. All the value which attaches to Pythagoras, Paracelsus, Cornelius Agrippa, Cardan, Kepler, Swedenborg,

Schelling, Oken, or any other who introduces questionable facts into his cosmogony, as angels, devils, magic, astrology, palmistry, mesmerism, and so on, is the certificate we have of departure from routine, and that there is a new witness. That also is the best success in conversation, the magic of liberty, which puts the world like a ball in our hands. How cheap even the liberty then seems; how mean to study, when an emotion communicates to the intellect the power to sap and upheave nature; how great the perspective! nations, times, systems, enter and disappear like threads in tapestry of large figure and many colors; dream delivers us to dream, and while the drunkenness lasts we will sell our bed, our philosophy, our religion, in our opulence.

There is good reason why we should prize this liberation. The fate of the poor shepherd, who, blinded and lost in the snowstorm, perishes in a drift within a few feet of his cottage door, is an emblem of the state of man. On the brink of the waters of life and truth, we are miserably dying. The inaccessibleness of every thought but that we are in, is wonderful. What if you come near to it; you are as remote when you are nearest as when you are farthest. Every thought is also a prison; every heaven is also a prison. Therefore we love the poet, the inventor, who in any form, whether in an ode or in an action or in looks and behavior, has yielded us a new thought. He unlocks our chains and admits us to a new scene.

This emancipation is dear to all men, and the power to impart it, as it must come from greater depth and scope of thought, is a measure of intellect. Therefore all books of the imagination endure, all which ascend to that truth that the writer sees nature beneath him, and uses it as his exponent. Every verse or sentence possessing this virtue will take care of its own immortality. The religions of the world are the ejaculations of a few imaginative men.

But the quality of the imagination is to flow, and not to freeze. The poet did not stop at the color or the form, but read their meaning; neither may he rest in this meaning, but he makes the same objects exponents of his new thought. Here is the difference betwixt the poet and the mystic, that the last nails a symbol to one sense, which was a true sense for a moment, but soon becomes old and false. For all symbols are fluxional; all language is vehicular and transitive, and is good, as ferries and horses are, for conveyance, not as farms and houses are, for homestead. Mysticism consists in the mistake of an accidental and individual symbol for an universal one. The morning-redness happens to be the favorite meteor to the eyes of Jacob Behmen, and comes to stand to him for truth and faith; and, he believes, should stand for the same realities to every reader. But the first reader prefers as naturally the symbol of a mother and child, or a gardener and his bulb, or a jeweller polishing a gem. Either of these, or of a myriad more, are equally good to the person to whom they are significant. Only they must be held lightly, and be very willingly translated into the equivalent terms which others use. And the mystic must be steadily told—All that you say is just as true without the tedious use of that symbol as with it. Let us have a little algebra, instead of this trite rhetoric —universal signs, instead of these village symbols—and we shall both be gainers. The history of hierarchies seems to show that all religious error consisted in making the symbol too stark and solid, and was at last nothing but an excess of the organ of language.

Swedenborg, of all men in the recent ages, stands eminently for the translator of nature into thought. I do not know the man in history to whom things stood so uniformly for words. Before him the metamorphosis continually plays. Everything on which his eye rests, obeys the impulses of moral nature. The figs become grapes whilst he eats them. When some of his angels affirmed a truth, the laurel twig which they held blossomed in their hands. The noise which at a distance appeared like gnashing and thumping, on coming nearer was found to be the voice of disputants. The men in one of his visions, seen in heavenly light, appeared like dragons, and seemed in darkness; but to each other they appeared as men, and when the light from heaven shone into their cabin, they complained of the darkness, and were compelled to shut the window that they might see.

There was this perception in him which makes the poet or seer an object of awe and terror, namely that the same man or society of men may wear one aspect to themselves and their companions, and a different aspect to higher intelligences. Certain priests, whom he describes as conversing very learnedly together, appeared to the children who were at some distance, like dead horses; and many the like misappearances. And instantly the mind inquires whether these fishes under the bridge, yonder oxen in the pasture, those dogs in the yard, are immutably fishes, oxen and dogs, or only so appear to me, and perchance to themselves appear upright men; and whether I appear as a man to all eyes. The Brahmins and Pythagoras propounded the same question, and if any poet has witnessed the transformation he doubtless found it in harmony with various experiences. We have all seen changes as considerable in wheat and caterpillars. He is the poet and shall draw us with love and terror, who sees through the flowing vest the firm nature, and can declare it.

I look in vain for the poet whom I describe. We do not with sufficient plainness or sufficient profoundness address ourselves to life, nor dare we chaunt our own times and social circumstance. If we filled the day with bravery, we should not shrink from celebrating it. Time and nature yield us many gifts, but not yet the timely man, the new religion, the reconciler, whom all things await. Dante's praise is that he dared to write his autobiography in colossal cipher, or into universality. We have yet had no genius in America, with tyrannous eye, which knew the value of our incomparable materials, and saw, in the barbarism and materialism of the times, another carnival of the same gods whose picture he so much admires in Homer; then in the Middle Age; then in Calvinism. Banks and tariffs, the newspaper and caucus, Methodism and Unitarianism, are flat and dull to dull people, but rest on the same foundations of wonder as the town of Troy and the temple of Delphi, and are as swiftly passing away. Our log-rolling, our stumps and their politics, our fisheries, our Negroes and Indians, our boats and our repudiations, the wrath of rogues and the pusillanimity of honest men, the northern trade, the southern planting, the western clearing, Oregon and Texas, are yet unsung. Yet America is a poem in our eyes; its ample geography dazzles the imagination, and it will not wait long for metres. If I have not found that excellent combination of gifts in my countrymen which I seek, neither could I aid myself to fix the idea of the poet by reading now and then in Chalmers's collection of five centuries of English poets. These are wits more than poets, though there have been poets amoung them. But when we adhere to the ideal of the poet, we have our difficulties even with Milton and Homer. Milton is too literary, and Homer too literal and historical.

But I am not wise enough for a national criticism, and must use the old largeness a little longer, to discharge my errand from the muse to the poet concerning his art.

Art is the path of the creator to his

work. The paths or methods are ideal and eternal, though few men ever see them; not the artist himself for years, or for a lifetime, unless he come into the conditions. The painter, the sculptor, the composer, the epic rhapsodist, the orator, all partake one desire, namely to express themselves symmetrically and abundantly, not dwarfishly and fragmentarily. They found or put themselves in certain conditions, as, the painter and sculptor before some impressive human figures; the orator into the assembly of the people; and the others in such scenes as each has found exciting to his intellect; and each presently feels the new desire. He hears a voice, he sees a beckoning. Then he is apprised, with wonder, what herds of dæmons hem him in. He can no more rest; he says, with the old painter, "By God it is in me and must go forth of me." He pursues a beauty, half seen, which flies before him. The poet pours out verses in every solitude. Most of the things he says are conventional, no doubt; but by and by he says something which is original and beautiful. That charms him. He would say nothing else but such things. In our way of talking we say 'That is yours, this is mine,' but the poet knows well that it is not his; that it is as strange and beautiful to him as to you; he would fain hear the like eloquence at length. Once having tasted this immortal ichor, he cannot have enough of it, and as an admirable creative power exists in these intellections, it is of the last importance that these things get spoken. What a little of all we know is said! What drops of all the sea of our science are baled up! and by what accident it is that these are exposed, when so many secrets sleep in nature! Hence the necessity of speech and song; hence these throbs and heart-beatings in the orator, at the door of the assembly, to the end namely that thought may be ejaculated as Logos, or Word.

Doubt not, O poet, but persist. Say 'It is in me, and shall out.' Stand there, balked and dumb, stuttering and stammering, hissed and hooted, stand and strive, until at last rage draw out of thee that *dream*-power which every night shows thee is thine own; a power transcending all limit and privacy, and by virtue of which a man is the conductor of the whole river of electricity. Nothing walks, or creeps, or grows, or exists, which must not in turn arise and walk before him as exponent of his meaning. Comes he to that power, his genius is no longer exhaustible. All the creatures by pairs and by tribes pour into his mind as into a Noah's ark, to come forth again to people a new world. This is like the stock of air for our respiration or for the combustion of our fireplace; not a measure of gallons, but the entire atmosphere if wanted. And therefore the rich poets, as Homer, Chaucer, Shakespeare, and Raphael, have obviously no limits to their works except the limits of their lifetime, and resemble a mirror carried through the street, ready to render an image of every created thing.

O poet! a new nobility is conferred in groves and pastures, and not in castles or by the sword blade any longer. The conditions are hard, but equal. Thou shalt leave the world, and know the muse only. Thou shalt not know any longer the times, customs, graces, politics, or opinions of men, but shalt take all from the muse. For the time of towns is tolled from the world by funereal chimes, but in nature the universal hours are counted by succeeding tribes of animals and plants, and by growth of joy on joy. God wills also that thou abdicate a manifold and duplex life, and that thou be content that others speak for thee. Others shall be thy gentlemen and shall represent all courtesy and worldly life for thee; others shall do the great and resounding actions also. Thou shalt lie close hid with nature, and canst not be afforded to the Capitol or the Exchange. The world is full of renunciations and apprenticeships, and this is thine; thou must pass for a fool and a churl for a long season. This is the screen and sheath in which Pan has protected his well-beloved flower, and thou shalt be known only to thine own, and they shall console thee with tenderest love. And thou shalt not be able to rehearse the names of thy friends in thy verse, for an old shame before the holy ideal. And this is the reward; that the ideal shall be real to thee, and the impressions of the actual world shall fall like summer rain, copious, but not troublesome to thy invulnerable essence. Thou shalt have the whole land for thy park and manor, the sea for thy bath and navigation, without tax and without envy; the woods and the rivers thou shalt own, and thou shalt possess that wherein others are only tenants and boarders. Thou true land-lord! sea-lord! air-lord! Wherever snow falls or water flows or birds fly, wherever day and night meet in twilight, wherever the blue heaven is hung by clouds or sown by stars, wherever are forms with transparent boundaries, wherever are outlets into celestial space, wherever is danger, and awe, and love—there is Beauty, plenteous as rain, shed for thee, and though thou shouldst walk the world over, thou shalt not be able to find a condition inopportune or ignoble.

Edgar Allan Poe

❋ 1809-1849

Poe agreed with Coleridge that poetry was rhythmical creation of beauty and that it was meant to suggest more than it said. Its essence was indefiniteness, its achievement the establishment of a mood wherein the reader would experience what the poet had experienced or what the poet wished him to experience. The effect could be contrived, as Poe in "The Philosophy of Composition" said he contrived "The Raven" by choosing dolorous sounds for its refrain, but it must result in a reaching toward what he called supernal beauty. It became true then, according to the rubric of his time, because it was beautiful. But these two should not be confused: "It's sole arbiter," Poe said, "was Taste. With the Intellect or with Conscience, it has only collateral relations. Unless incidentally, it has no concern whatever either with Duty or with Truth." These sentences are from Poe's lecture in 1849 on "The Poetic Principle," as are also his following remarks on "The Heresy of the Didactic."

The Heresy of the Didactic

. . . It has been assumed, tacitly and avowedly, directly and indirectly, that the ultimate object of all Poetry is Truth. Every poem, it is said, should inculcate a moral; and by this moral is the poetical merit of the work to be adjudged. We Americans especially have patronized this happy idea; and we Bostonians, very especially, have developed it in full. We have taken it into our heads that to write a poem simply for the poem's sake, and to acknowledge such to have been our design, would be to confess ourselves radically wanting in the true Poetic dignity and force:—but the simple fact is, that, would we permit ourselves to look into our own souls, we should immediately there discover that under the sun there exists nor *can* exist any work more thoroughly dignified—more supremely noble than this very poem—this poem *per se*—this poem which is a poem and nothing more—this poem written solely for the poem's sake.

With as deep a reverence for the True

as ever inspired the bosom of man, I would, nevertheless, limit, in some measure, its modes of inculcation. I would limit to enforce them. I would not enfeeble them by dissipation. The demands of Truth are severe. She has no sympathy with the myrtles. All *that* which is so indispensable in Song, is precisely all *that* with which *she* has nothing whatever to do. It is but making her a flaunting paradox, to wreathe her in gems and flowers. In enforcing a truth, we need severity rather than efflorescence of language. We must be simple, precise, terse. We must be cool, calm, unimpassioned. In a word, we must be in that mood which, as nearly as possible, is the exact converse of the poetical. He must be blind indeed who does not perceive the radical and chasmal differences between the truthful and poetical modes of inculcation. He must be theory-mad beyond redemption who, in spite of these differences, shall still persist in attempting to reconcile the obstinate oils and waters of Poetry and Truth.

Dividing the world of the mind into its three most immediately obvious distinctions, we have the Pure Intellect, Taste, and the Moral Sense. I place Taste in the middle, because it is just this position which, in the mind, it occupies. It holds intimate relations with either extreme; but from the Moral Sense is separated by so faint a difference that Aristotle has not hesitated to place some of its operations among the virtues themselves. Nevertheless, we find the *offices* of the trio marked with a sufficient distinction. Just as the Intellect concerns itself with Truth, so Taste informs us of the Beautiful while the Moral Sense is regardful of Duty. Of this latter, while Conscience teaches the obligation, and Reason the expediency, Taste contents herself with displaying the charms:— waging war upon Vice solely on the ground of her deformity—her disproportion—her animosity to the fitting, to the appropriate, to the harmonious—in a word, to Beauty.

An immortal instinct, deep within the spirit of man, is thus, plainly, a sense of the Beautiful. This is what administers to his delight in the manifold forms, and sounds, and odors, and sentiments amid which he exists. And just as the lily is repeated in the lake, or the eyes of Amaryllis in the mirror, so is the mere oral or written repetition of these forms, and sounds, and colors, and odors, and sentiments, a duplicate source of delight. But this mere repetition is not poetry. He who shall simply sing, with however glowing enthusiasm, or with however vivid a truth of description, of the sights, and sounds, and odors, and colors, and sentiments, which greet *him* in common with all mankind—he, I say, has yet failed to prove his divine title. There is still a something in the distance which he has been unable to attain. We have still a thirst unquenchable, to allay which he has not shown us the crystal springs. This thirst belongs to the immortality of Man. It is at once a consequence and an indication of his perennial existence. It is the desire of the moth for the star. It is no mere appreciation of the Beauty before us—but a wild effort to reach the Beauty above. Inspired by an ecstatic presience of the glories beyond the grave, we struggle, by multiform combinations among the things and thoughts of Time, to attain a portion of Loveliness whose very elements, perhaps, appertain to eternity alone. And thus when by Poetry —or when by Music, the most entrancing of the Poetic moods—we find ourselves melted into tears—we weep then . . . through excess of pleasure, but through a certain, petulant, impatient sorrow at our inability to grasp *now*, wholly, here on earth, at once and forever, those divine and rapturous joys, of which *through* the poem, or *through* the music, we attain to but brief and indeterminate glimpses.

The struggle to apprehend the supernal Loveliness—this struggle, on the part of souls fittingly constituted—has given to the world all *that* which it (the world) has ever been enabled at once to understand and *to feel* as poetic.

The Poetic Sentiment, of course, may develop itself in various modes—in Painting, in Sculpture, in Architecture, in the Dance—very especially in Music —and very peculiarly, and with a wide field, in the composition of the Landscape Garden. Our present theme, however, has regard only to its manifestations in words. And here let me speak briefly on the topic of rhythm. Contenting myself with the certainty that Music, in its various modes of metre, rhythm, and rhyme, is of so vast a moment in Poetry as never to be wisely rejected—is so vitally important an adjunct, that he is simply silly who declines its assistance, I will not now pause to maintain its absolute essentiality. It is in Music, perhaps, that the soul most nearly attains the great end for which, when inspired by the Poetic Sentiment, it struggles— the creation of supernal Beauty. It *may* be, indeed, that here this sublime end is, now and then, attained *in fact*. We are often made to feel with a shivering delight, that from an earthly harp are stricken notes which *cannot* have been unfamiliar to the angels. And thus there can be little doubt that in the union of Poetry with Music in its popular sense, we shall find the widest field for the Poetic development. The old Bards and Minnesingers had advantages which we do not possess—and Thomas More, singing his own songs, was, in the most legitimate manner, perfecting them as poems.

To recapitulate, then:—I would define, in brief, the Poetry of words as *The Rhythmical Creation of Beauty*. Its sole arbiter is Taste. With the Intellect or with the Conscience, it has only collateral relations. Unless incidentally, it has no concern whatever with Duty or with Truth.

A few words, however, in explanation. *That* pleasure which is at once the most pure, the most elevating, and the most intense, is derived, I maintain, from the contemplation of the Beautiful. In the contemplation of Beauty we alone find it possible to attain that pleasurable elevation, or excitement, *of the soul*, which we recognize as the Poetic Sentiment, and which is so easily distinguished from Truth, which is the satisfaction of the Reason, or from Passion, which is the excitement of the heart. I make Beauty, therefore—using the word as inclusive of the sublime—I make Beauty the province of the poem, simply because it is an obvious rule of Art that effects should be made to spring as directly as possible from their causes: no one as yet having been weak enough to deny that the peculiar elevation in question is at least *most readily* attainable in the poem. It by no means follows, however, that the incitements of Passion, or the precepts of Duty, or even the Lessons of Truth, may not be introduced into a poem, and with advantage; for they may subserve, incidentally, in various ways, the general purposes of the work:—but the true artist will always contrive to tone them down in proper subjection to that *Beauty* which is the atmosphere and the real essence of the poem.

Walt Whitman

✳ 1819-1892

Whitman would not define poetry, but he tried often to tell what the poet should be. Like Emerson, he thought of the poet as a prophet, and became increasingly convinced that his function was religious rather than merely literary. Certainly he had no conception of pure beauty of the kind which Poe tried so often to describe. For several years at the end of his life Whitman worked over versions of a final statement of his own intention as poet. The following is from "A Backward Glance O'er Travel'd Roads" which in 1888 he presented as a preface to the collection of late poems called NOVEMBER BOUGHS.

A Backward Glance

. . . Let me not dare, here or anywhere, for my own purposes, or any purposes, to attempt the definition of Poetry, nor answer the question what it is. Like Religion, Love, Nature, while those terms are indispensable, and we all give a sufficiently accurate meaning to them, in my opinion no definition that has ever been made sufficiently encloses the name Poetry; nor can any rule or convention ever so absolutely obtain but some great exception may arise and disregard and overturn it.

And it must be carefully remember'd that first-class literature does not shine by any luminosity of its own; nor do its poems. They grow of circumstances, and are evolutionary. The actual living light is always curiously from elsewhere—follows unaccountable sources, and is lunar and relative at the best. There are, I know, certain controlling themes that seem endlessly appropriated to the poets —as war, in the past—in the Bible, religious rapture and adoration—always love, beauty, some fine plot, or pensive or other emotion. But, strange as it may sound at first, I will say there is something striking far deeper and towering far higher than those themes for the best elements of modern song.

Just as all the old imaginative works rest, after their kind, on long trains of

presuppositions, often entirely unmention'd by themselves, yet supplying the most important bases of them, and without which they could have no reason for being, so Leaves of Grass, before a line was written, presupposed something different from any other, and, as it stands, is the result of such presupposition. I should say, indeed, it were useless to attempt reading the book without first carefully tallying that preparatory background and quality in the mind. Think of the United States today—the facts of these thirty-eight or forty empires solder'd in one—sixty or seventy millions of equals with their lives, their passions, their future—these incalculable, modern, American, seething multitudes around us, of which we are inseparable parts! Think, in comparison, of the petty environage and limited area of the poets of past or present Europe, no matter how great their genius. Think of the absence and ignorance in all cases hitherto, of the multitudinousness, vitality, and the unprecedented stimulants of today and here. It almost seems as if a poetry with cosmic and dynamic features of magnitude and limitlessness suitable to the human soul were never possible before. It is certain that a poetry of absolute faith and equality for the use of the democratic masses never was.

In estimating first-class song, a sufficient Nationality, or, on the other hand, what may be call'd the negative and lack of it, (as in Goethe's case, it sometimes seems to me,) is often, if not always, the first element. One needs only a little penetration to see, at more or less removes, the material facts of their country and radius, with the coloring of the moods of humanity at the time, and its gloomy or hopeful prospects, behind all poets and each poet, and forming their birthmarks. I know very well that my *Leaves* could not possibly have emerged or been fashion'd or completed, from any other era than the latter half of the

Nineteenth Century, nor any other land than democratic America, and from the absolute triumph of the National Union arms.

And whether my friends claim it for me or not, I know well enough, too, that in respect to pictorial talent, dramatic situations, and especially in verbal melody and all the conventional technique of poetry, not only the divine works that today stand ahead in the world's reading but dozens more, transcend (some of them immeasurably transcend) all I have done, or could do. But it seem'd to me, as the objects in Nature, the themes of estheticism, and all special exploitations of the mind and soul, involve not only their own inherent quality, but the quality, just as inherent and important, of *their point of view,* the time had come to reflect all themes and things, old and new, in the lights thrown on them by the advent of America and democracy— to chant those themes through the utterance of one, not only the grateful and reverent legatee of the past, but the born child of the New World—to illustrate all through the genesis and ensemble of today; and that such illustration and ensemble are the chief demands of America's prospective imaginative literature. Not to carry out, in the approved style, some choice plot of fortune or misfortune, or fancy, or fine thoughts, or incidents, or courtesies—all of which has been done overwhelmingly and well. Probably never to be excell'd—but that while in such aesthetic presentation of objects, passions, plots, thoughts, etc., our lands and days do not want, and probably will never have, anything better than they already possess from the bequests of the past, it still remains to be said that there is even toward all those a subjective and contemporary point of view appropriate to ourselves alone, and to our new genius and environments, different from anything hitherto; and that such conception of current or gone-by life and art is for us

the only means of their assimilation consistent with the Western world.

Indeed, and anyhow, to put it specifically, has not the time arrived when, (it must be plainly said, for democratic America's sake, if for no other) there must imperatively come a readjustment of the whole theory and nature of Poetry? The question is important, and I may turn the argument over and repeat it: Does not the best thought of our day and Republic conceive of a birth and spirit of song superior to anything past or present? To the effectual and moral consolidation of our lands (already, as materially establish'd, the greatest factors in known history, and far, far greater through what they prelude and necessitate, and are to be in the future)—to conform with and build on the concrete realities and theories of the universe furnish'd by science, and henceforth the only irrefragable basis for anything, verse included—to root both influence in the emotional and imaginative action of modern time, and dominate all that precedes or opposes them—is not either a radical advance and step forward, or a new verteber of the best song indispensable?

The New World receives with joy the poems of the antique, with European feudalism's rich fund of epics, plays, ballades—seeks not in the least to deaden or displace those voices from our ear and area—holds them indeed as indispensable studies, influences, records, comparisons. But though the dawn-dazzle of the sun of literature is in those poems for us of today—though perhaps the best parts of current character in nations, social groups, or any man's or woman's individuality, Old World or New, are from them—and though if I were ask'd to name the most precious bequest to current American civilization from all the hitherto ages, I am not sure but I would name those old and less old songs ferried hither from east and west—some serious words and debits remain; some acrid considerations demand a hearing. Of the great poems receiv'd from abroad and from the ages, and today enveloping and penetrating America, is there one that is consistent with these United States, or essentially applicable to them as they are and are to be? What a comment it forms, anyhow, on this era of literary fulfillment, with the splendid day-rise of science and resuscitation of history, that our chief religious and poetical works are not our own, nor adapted to our light, but have been furnish'd by far-back ages out of their arriere and darkness, or, at most, twilight dimness! What is there in those works that so imperiously and scornfully dominates all our advanced civilization, and culture?

Even Shakespeare, who so suffuses current letters and art (which indeed have in most degrees grown out of him,) belongs essentially to the buried past. Only he holds the proud distinction for certain important phases of that past, of being the loftiest of singers life has yet given voice to. All, however, relate to and rest upon conditions, standards, politics, sociologies, ranges of belief, that have been quite eliminated from the Eastern hemisphere, and never existed at all in the Western. As authoritative types of song they belong in America just about as much as the persons and institutes they depict. True, it may be said, the emotional, moral, and aesthetic natures of humanity have not radically changed—that in these the old poems apply to our times and all times, irrespective of date; and that they are of incalculable value as pictures of the past. I willingly make those admissions and to their fullest extent; then advance the points herewith as of serious, even paramount importance.

I have indeed put on record elsewhere my reverence and eulogy for those never-to-be-excell'd poetic bequests, and their indescribable preciousness as heirlooms for America. Another and separate point must now be candidly stated. If I had not stood before those poems with uncover'd head, fully aware of their colossal grandeur and beauty of form and spirit, I could not have written *Leaves of Grass*. My verdict and conclusions as illustrated in its pages are arrived at through the temper and inculcation of the old works as much as through anything else—perhaps more than through anything else. As America fully and fairly construed is the legitimate result and evolutionary outcome of the past, so I would dare to claim for my verse. Without stopping to qualify the averment, the Old World has had the poems of myths, fictions, feudalism, conquest, caste, dynastic wars, and splendid exceptional characters and affairs, which have been great; but the New World needs the poems of realities and science and of the democratic average and basic equality, which shall be greater. In the center of all, and object of all, stands the Human Being, toward whose heroic and spiritual evolution poems and everything directly or indirectly tend, Old World or New. . . .

But I set out with the intention also of indicating or hinting some point-characteristics which I since see (though I did not then, at least not definitely) were bases and object-urgings toward those *Leaves* from the first. The word I myself put primarily for the description of them as they stand at last, is the word Suggestiveness. I round and finish little, if anything; and could not, consistently with my scheme. The reader will always have his or her part to do, just as much as I have had mine. I seek less to state or display any theme or thought, and more to bring you, reader, into the atmosphere of the theme or thought—there to pursue your own flight. Another impetus-word is Comradeship as for all lands, and in more commanding and acknowledg'd sense than hitherto. Other word signs would be Good Cheer, Content, and Hope.

The chief trait of any given poet is always the spirit he brings to the observation of Humanity and Nature—the mood out of which he contemplates his subjects. What kind of temper and what amount of faith report these things? Up to how recent a date is the song carried? What the equipment, and special raciness of the singer—what his tinge of coloring? The last value of artistic expressers, past and present—Greek aesthetics, Shakespeare—or in our own day Tennyson, Victor Hugo, Carlyle, Emerson—is certainly involv'd in such questions. I say the profoundest service that poems or any other writings can do for their reader is not merely to satisfy the intellect, or supply something polish'd and interesting, nor even to depict great passions, or persons or events, but to fill him with vigorous and clean manliness, religiousness, and give him *good heart* as a radical possession and habit. The educated world seems to have been growing more and more ennuyed for ages, leaving to our time the inheritance of it all. Fortunately there is the original inexhaustible fund of buoyancy, normally resident in the race, forever eligible to be appeal'd to and relied on.

As for native American individuality, though certain to come, and on a large scale, the distinctive and ideal type of Western character (as consistent with the operative political and even money-making features of United States' humanity in the Nineteenth Century as chosen knights, gentlemen and warriors for the ideals of the centuries of European feudalism) it has not yet appear'd. I have allow'd the stress of my poems from beginning to end to bear upon American individuality and assist it—not only because that is a great lesson in Nature, amid all her generalizing laws, but as counterpoise to the leveling tendencies of Democracy—and for other reasons. Defiant of ostensible literary and other conventions, I avowedly chant "the great pride of man in himself," and per-

mit it to be more or less a *motif* of nearly all my verse. I think it not inconsistent with obedience, humility, deference, and self-questioning. . . .

Leaves of Grass indeed (I cannot too often reiterate) has mainly been the outcropping of my own emotional and other personal nature—an attempt, from first to last, to put a *Person*, a human being (myself, in the latter half of the Nineteenth Century, in America,) freely, fully and truly on record. I could not find any similar personal record in current literature that satisfied me. But it is not on *Leaves of Grass* distinctively as *literature*, or a specimen thereof, that I feel to dwell, or advance claims. No one will get at my verses who insists upon viewing them as a literary performance, or attempt at such performance, or as aiming mainly toward art or aestheticism.

I say no land or people or circumstances ever existed so needing a race of singers and poems differing from all others, and rigidly their own, as the land and people and circumstances of our United States need such singers and poems today, and for the future. Still further, as long as the States continue to absorb and be dominated by the poetry of the Old World, and remain unsupplied with autochthonous song, to express, vitalize and give color to and define their material and political success, and minister to them distinctively, so long will they stop short of first-class Nationality and remain defective. . . .

George Santayana
✳ 1863-1952

George Santayana, born in Spain but educated at Harvard where he taught for many years, was a poet and novelist

as well as a formal philosopher. His
writings in prose, beginning with THE
SENSE OF BEAUTY in 1896 and culminating in the three volumes of his autobiography, PERSONS AND PLACES in the 1940s,
mirror much of the more serious thinking of the first half of our century.
Though many readers find the five volumes of his THE LIFE OF REASON, published in 1905 and 1906, too tightly tex-
tured for their taste, it remains one of the
masterworks of our time, the groundplan
on which such later writings as CHAR-
ACTER AND OPINION IN THE UNITED
STATES, in 1920, PLATONISM AND THE
SPIRITUAL LIFE, in 1927, and THE GEN-
TEEL TRADITION AT BAY, in 1931, are
based. Something of the essence of Santayana's thought is attractively set forth
in THE LAST PURITAN, a novel published
in 1935. The following essay first appeared in INTERPRETATIONS OF POETRY
AND RELIGION in 1900.

The Elements and Function
of Poetry

If a critic, in despair of giving a serious
definition of poetry, should be satisfied
with saying that poetry is metrical discourse, he would no doubt be giving an
inadequate account of the matter, yet
not one of which he need be ashamed or
which he should regard as superficial.
Although a poem be not made by counting of syllables upon the fingers, yet
"numbers" is the most poetical synonym
we have for verse, and "measure" the
most significant equivalent for beauty,
for goodness, and perhaps even for truth.
Those early and profound philosophers,
the followers of Pythagoras, saw the essence of all things in number, and it was
by weight, measure, and number, as we
read in the Bible, that the Creator first
brought Nature out of the void. Every
human architect must do likewise with

his edifice; he must mould his bricks or
hew his stones into symmetrical solids
and lay them over one another in regular
strata, like a poet's lines.

Measure is a condition of perfection,
for perfection requires that order should
be pervasive, that not only the whole
before us should have a form, but that
every part in turn should have a form of
its own, and that those parts should be
coördinated among themselves as the
whole is coördinated with the other parts
of some greater cosmos. Leibnitz lighted
in his speculations upon a conception of
organic nature which may be false as a
fact, but which is excellent as an ideal;
he tells us that the difference between
living and dead matter, between animals
and machines, is that the former are
composed of parts that are themselves
organic, every portion of the body being
itself a machine, and every portion of
that machine still a machine, and so *ad
infinitum;* whereas, in artificial bodies the
organization is not in this manner infinitely deep. Fine Art, in this as in all
things, imitates the method of Nature
and makes its most beautiful works out
of materials that are themselves beautiful. So that even if the difference between verse and prose consisted only in
measure, that difference would already
be analogous to that between jewels and
clay.

The stuff of language is words, and the
sensuous material of words is sound; if
language therefore is to be made perfect,
its materials must be made beautiful by
being themselves subjected to a measure,
and endowed with a form. It is true that
language is a symbol for intelligence
rather than a stimulus to sense, and accordingly the beauties of discourse which
commonly attract attention are merely
the beauties of the objects and ideas signified; yet the symbols have a sensible
reality of their own, a euphony which
appeals to our senses if we keep them
open. The tongue will choose those

forms of utterance which have a natural grace as mere sound and sensation; the memory will retain these catches, and they will pass and repass through the mind until they become types of instinctive speech and standards of pleasing expression.

The highest form of such euphony is song; the singing voice gives to the sounds it utters the thrill of tonality,— a thrill itself dependent, as we know, on the numerical proportions of the vibrations that it includes. But this kind of euphony and sensuous beauty, the deepest that sounds can have, we have almost wholly surrendered in our speech. Our intelligence has become complex, and language, to express our thoughts, must commonly be more rapid, copious, and abstract than is compatible with singing. Music at the same time has become complex also, and when united with words, at one time disfigures them in the elaboration of its melody, and at another overpowers them in the volume of its sound. So that the art of singing is now in the same plight as that of sculpture,— an abstract and conventional thing surviving by force of tradition and of an innate but now impotent impulse, which under simpler conditions would work itself out into the proper forms of those arts. The truest kind of euphony is thus denied to our poetry. If any verses are still set to music, they are commonly the worst only, chosen for the purpose by musicians of specialized sensibility and inferior intelligence, who seem to be attracted only by tawdry effects of rhetoric and sentiment.

When song is given up, there still remains in speech a certain sensuous quality, due to the nature and order of the vowels and consonants that compose the sounds. This kind of euphony is not neglected by the more dulcet poets, and is now so studied in some quarters that I have heard it maintained by a critic of relative authority that the beauty of poetry consists entirely in the frequent utterance of the sound of "j" and "sh," and the consequent copious flow of saliva in the mouth. But even if saliva is not the whole esssence of poetry, there is an unmistakable and fundamental diversity of effect in the various vocalization of different poets, which bccomes all the more evident when we compare those who use different languages. One man's speech, or one nation's, is compact, crowded with consonants, rugged, broken with emphatic beats; another man's, or nation's, is open, tripping, rapid, and even. So Byron, mingling in his boyish fashion burlesque with exquisite sentiment, contrasts English with Italian speech:—

I love the language, that soft bastard Latin
Which melts like kisses from a female mouth
And sounds as if it should be writ on satin
With syllables which breathe of the sweet
    South,
And gentle liquids gliding all so pat in
That not a single accent seems uncouth,
Like our harsh Northern whistling, grunting
    guttural
Which we're obliged to hiss and spit and
    sputter all.

And yet these contrasts, strong when we compare extreme cases, fade from our consciousness in the actual use of a mother-tongue. The function makes us unconscious of the instrument, all the more as it is an indispensable and almost invariable one. The sense of euphony accordingly attaches itself rather to another and more variable quality; the tune, or measure, or rhythm of speech. The elementary sounds are prescribed by the language we use, and the selection we may make among those sounds is limited; but the arrangement of words is still undetermined, and by casting our speech into the moulds of metre and rhyme we can give it a heightened power, apart from its significance. A tolerable definition of poetry, on its formal side, might be found in this: that poetry is speech in which the instrument counts as well as the meaning—poetry is speech for its own sake and for its own sweetness. As common windows are intended only to admit the light, but painted windows also to dye it, and to be an object of attention in themselves as well as a cause of visibility in other things, so, while the purest prose is a mere vehicle of thought, verse, like stained glass, arrests attention in its own intricacies, confuses it in its own glories, and is even at times allowed to darken and puzzle in the hope of casting over us a supernatural spell.

Long passages in Shelley's "Revolt of Islam" and Keats' "Endymion" are poetical in this sense; the reader gathers, probably, no definite meaning, but is conscious of a poetic medium, of speech euphonious and measured, and redolent of a kind of objectless passion which is little more than the sensation of the movement and sensuous richness of the lines. Such poetry is not great; it has, in fact, a tedious vacuity, and is unworthy of a mature mind; but it is poetical, and could be produced only by a legitimate child of the Muse. It belongs to an apprenticeship, but in this case the apprenticeship of genius. It bears that relation to great poems which scales and aimless warblings bear to great singing—they test the essential endowment and fineness of the organ which is to be employed in the art. Without this sensuous background and ingrained predisposition to beauty, no art can reach the deepest and most exquisite effects; and even without an intelligible superstructure these sensuous qualities suffice to give that thrill of exaltation, that suggestion of an ideal world, which we feel in the presence of any true beauty.

The sensuous beauty of words and their utterance in measure suffice, therefore, for poetry of one sort—where these are, there is something unmistakably poetical, although the whole of poetry, or

the best of poetry, be not yet there. Indeed, in such works as "The Revolt of Islam" or "Endymion" there is already more than mere metre and sound; there is the colour and choice of words, the fanciful, rich, or exquisite juxtaposition of phrases. The vocabulary and the texture of the style are precious; affected, perhaps, but at any rate refined.

This quality, which is that almost exclusively exploited by the Symbolist, we may call euphuism—the choice of coloured words and rare and elliptical phrases. If great poets are like architects and sculptors, the euphuists are like goldsmiths and jewellers; their work is filigree in precious metals, encrusted with glowing stones. Now euphuism contributes not a little to the poetic effect of the tirades of Keats and Shelley; if we wish to see the power of versification without euphuism we may turn to the tirades of Pope, where metre and euphony are displayed alone, and we have the outline or skeleton of poetry without the filling

In spite of pride, in erring reason's spite,
One truth is clear, Whatever is, is right.

We should hesitate to say that such writing was truly poetical; so that some euphuism would seem to be necessary as well as metre, to the formal essence of poetry.

An example of this sort, however, takes us out of the merely verbal into the imaginative region; the reason that Pope is hardly poetical to us is not that he is inharmonious,—not a defect of euphony, —but that he is too intellectual and has an excess of mentality. It is easier for words to be poetical without any thought, when they are felt merely as sensuous and musical, than for them to remain so when they convey an abstract notion,—especially if that notion be a tart and frigid sophism, like that of the couplet just quoted. The pyrotechnics of the intellect then take the place of the glow of sense, and the artifice of thought chills the pleasure we might have taken in the grace of expression.

If poetry in its higher reaches is more philosophical than history, because it presents the memorable types of men and things apart from unmeaning circumstances, so in its primary substance and texture poetry is more philosophical than prose because it is nearer to our immediate experience. Poetry breaks up the trite conceptions designated by current words into the sensuous qualities out of which those conceptions were originally put together. We name what we conceive and believe in, not what we see; things, not images; souls, not voices and silhouettes. This naming, with the whole education of the senses which it accompanies, subserves the uses of life; in order to thread our way through the labyrinth of objects which assault us, we must make a great selection in our sensuous experience; half of what we see and hear we must pass over as insignificant, while we piece out the other half with such an ideal complement as is necessary to turn it into a fixed and well-ordered world. This labour of perception and understanding, this spelling of the material meaning of experience is enshrined in our work-a-day language and ideas; ideas which are literally poetic in the sense that they are "made" (for every conception in an adult mind is a fiction), but which are at the same time prosaic because they are made economically, by abstraction, and for use.

When the child of poetic genius, who has learned this intellectual and utilitarian language in the cradle, goes afield and gathers for himself the aspects of Nature, he begins to encumber his mind with the many living impressions which the intellect rejected, and which the language of the intellect can hardly convey; he labours with his nameless burden of perception, and wastes himself in aimless impulses of emotion and revery, until finally the method of some art offers a vent to his inspiration, or to such part of it as can survive the test of time and the discipline of expression.

The poet retains by nature the innocence of the eye, or recovers it easily; he disintegrates the fictions of common perception into their sensuous elements, gathers these together again into chance groups as the accidents of his environment or the affinities of his temperament may conjoin them; and this wealth of sensation and this freedom of fancy, which make an extraordinary ferment in his ignorant heart, presently bubble over into some kind of utterance.

The fulness and sensuousness of such effusions bring them nearer to our actual perceptions than common discourse could come; yet they may easily seem remote, overloaded, and obscure to those accustomed to think entirely in symbols, and never to be interrupted in the algebraic rapidity of their thinking by a moment's pause and examination of heart, nor ever to plunge for a moment into that torrent of sensation and imagery over which the bridge of prosaic associations habitually carries us safe and dry to some conventional act. How slight that bridge commonly is, how much an affair of trestles and wire, we can hardly conceive until we have trained ourselves to an extreme sharpness of introspection. But psychologists have discovered, what laymen generally will confess, that we hurry by the procession of our mental images as we do by the traffic of the street, intent on business, gladly forgetting the noise and movement of the scene, and looking only for the corner we would turn or the door we would enter. Yet in our alertest moment the depths of the soul are still dreaming; the real world stands drawn in bare outline against a background of chaos and unrest. Our logical thoughts dominate experience only as the parallels and meridians make a checkerboard of the sea. They guide our voyage without controlling the waves, which toss for ever in spite of our ability to ride over them to our chosen ends. Sanity is a madness put to good uses; waking life is a dream controlled.

Out of the neglected riches of this dream the poet fetches his wares. He dips into the chaos that underlies the rational shell of the world and brings up some superfluous image, some emotion dropped by the way, and reattaches it to the present object; he reinstates things unnecessary, he emphasizes things ignored, he paints in again into the landscape the tints which the intellect has allowed to fade from it. If he seems sometimes to obscure a fact, it is only because he is restoring an experience. We may observe this process in the simplest cases. When Ossian, mentioning the sun, says it is round as the shield of his fathers, the expression is poetical. Why? Because he has added to the word sun, in itself sufficient and unequivocal, other words, unnecessary for practical clearness, but serving to restore the individuality of his perception and its associations in his mind. There is no square sun with which the sun he is speaking of could be confused; to stop and call it round is a luxury, a halting in the sensation for the love of its form. And to go on to tell us, what is wholly impertinent, that the shield of his fathers was round also, is to invite us to follow the chance wanderings of his fancy, to give us a little glimpse of the stuffing of his own brain, or, we might almost say, to turn over the pattern of his embroidery and show us the loose threads hanging out on the wrong side. Such an escapade disturbs and interrupts the true vision of the object, and a great poet, rising to a perfect conception of the sun and forgetting himself, would have disdained to make it; but it has a romantic and pathological interest, it restores an experience, and is in that measure poetical. We have been made to halt at the sensation, and to penetrate for a moment into its background of dream.

But it is not only thoughts or images that the poet draws in this way from the store of his experience, to clothe the bare form of conventional objects: he often adds to these objects a more subtle ornament, drawn from the same source. For the first element which the intellect rejects in forming its ideas of things is the emotion which accompanies the perception; and this emotion is the first thing the poet restores. He stops at the image, because he stops to enjoy. He wanders into the by-paths of association because the by-paths are delightful. The love of beauty which made him give measure and cadence to his words, the love of harmony which made him rhyme them, reappear in his imagination and make him select there also the material that is itself beautiful, or capable of assuming beautiful forms. The link that binds together the ideas, sometimes so wide apart, which his wit assimilates, is most often the link of emotion; they have in common some element of beauty or of horror.

The poet's art is to a great extent the art of intensifying emotions by assembling the scattered objects that naturally arouse them. He sees the affinities of things by seeing their common affinities with passion. As the guiding principle of practical thinking is some interest, so that only what is pertinent to that interest is selected by the attention; as the guiding principle of scientific thinking is some connection of things in time or space, or some identity of law; so in poetic thinking the guiding principle is often a mood or a quality of sentiment. By this union of disparate things having a common overtone of feeling, the feeling is itself evoked in all its strength; nay, it is often created for the first time, much as by a new mixture of old pigments Perugino could produce the unprecedented limpidity of his colour, or Titian the unprecedented glow of his. Poets can thus arouse sentiments finer than any which they have known, and in the act of composition become discoverers of new realms of delightfulness and grief. Expression is a misleading term which suggests that something previously known is rendered or imitated; whereas the expression is itself an original fact, the values of which are then referred to the thing expressed, much as the honours of a Chinese mandarin are attributed retroactively to his parents. So the charm which a poet, by his art of combining images and shades of emotion, casts over a scene or an action, is attached to the principal actor in it, who gets the benefit of the setting furnished him by a well-stocked mind.

The poet is himself subject to this illusion, and a great part of what is called poetry, although by no means the best part of it, consists in this sort of idealization by proxy. We dye the world of our own colour; by a pathetic fallacy, by a false projection of sentiment, we soak Nature with our own feeling, and then celebrate her tender sympathy with our moral being. This aberration, as we see in the case of Wordsworth, is not inconsistent with a high development of both the faculties which it confuses,—I mean vision and feeling. On the contrary, vision and feeling, when most abundant and original, most easily present themselves in this undivided form. There would be need of a force of intellect which poets rarely possess to rationalize their inspiration without diminishing its volume: and if, as is commonly the case, the energy of the dream and the passion in them is greater than that of the reason, and they cannot attain true propriety and supreme beauty in their works, they can, nevertheless, fill them with lovely images and a fine moral spirit.

The pouring forth of both perceptive and emotional elements in their mixed and indiscriminate form gives to this kind of imagination the directness and truth which sensuous poetry possesses on a lower level. The outer world bathed in the hues of human feeling, the inner world expressed in the forms of things,—that is the primitive condition of both before intelligence and the prosaic classification of objects have abstracted them and assigned them to their respective spheres. Such identifications, on which a certain kind of metaphysics prides itself also, are not discoveries of profound genius; they are exactly like the observation of Ossian that the sun is round and that the shield of his fathers was round too; they are disintegrations of conventional objects, so that the original associates of our perceptions reappear; then the thing and the emotion which chanced to be simultaneous are said to be one, and we return, unless a better principle of organization is substituted for the principle abandoned, to the chaos of a passive animal consciousness, where all is mixed together, projected together, and felt as an unutterable whole.

The pathetic fallacy is a return to that early habit of thought by which our ancestors peopled the world with benevolent and malevolent spirits; what they felt in the presence of objects they took to be a part of the objects themselves. In returning to this natural confusion, poetry does us a service in that she recalls and consecrates those phases of our experience which, as useless to the understanding of material reality, we are in danger of forgetting altogether. Therein is her vitality, for she pierces to the quick and shakes us out of our servile speech and imaginative poverty; she reminds us of all we have felt, she invites us even to dream a little, to nurse the wonderful spontaneous creations which at every waking moment we are snuffing out in our brain. And the indulgence is no mere momentary pleasure; much of its exuberance clings afterward to our ideas; we see the more and feel the more for that exercise; we are capable of finding greater entertainment in the common aspects of Nature and life. When the veil of convention is once removed from our eyes by the poet, we are better able to dominate any particular experience and, as it were, to change its scale, now losing ourselves in its infinitesimal texture, now in its infinite ramifications.

If the function of poetry, however, did not go beyond this recovery of sensuous and imaginative freedom, at the expense of disrupting our useful habits of thought, we might be grateful to it for occasionally relieving our numbness, but we should have to admit that it was nothing but a relaxation; that spiritual discipline was not to be gained from it in any degree, but must be sought wholly in that intellectual system that builds the science of Nature with the categories of prose. So conceived, poetry would deserve the judgment passed by Plato on all the arts of flattery and entertainment; it might be crowned as delightful, but must be either banished altogether as meretricious or at least confined to a few forms and occasions where it might do little harm. The judgment of Plato has been generally condemned by philosophers, although it is eminently rational, and justified by the simplest principles of morals. It has been adopted instead, although unwittingly, by the practical and secular part of mankind, who look upon artists and poets as inefficient and brain-sick people under whose spell it would be a serious calamity to fall, although they may be called in on feast days as an ornament and luxury together with the cooks, hairdressers, and florists.

Several circumstances, however, might suggest to us the possibility that the greatest function of poetry may be still to find. Plato, while condemning Homer, was a kind of poet himself; his quarrel with the followers of the Muse was not a quarrel with the goddess; and the good people of Philistia, distrustful as they may be of profane art, pay undoubting

honour to religion, which is a kind of poetry as much removed from their sphere as the midnight revels upon Mount Citheron, which, to be sure, were also religious in their inspiration. Why, we may ask, these apparent inconsistencies? Why do our practical men make room for religion in the background of their world? Why did Plato, after banishing the poets poetize the universe in his prose? Because the abstraction by which the world of science and of practice is drawn out of our experience is too violent to satisfy even the thoughtless and vulgar; the ideality of the machine we call Nature, the conventionality of the drama we call the world, are too glaring not to be somehow perceived by all. Each must sometimes fall back upon the soul; he must challenge this apparition with the thought of death; he must ask himself for the mainspring and value of his life. He will then remember his stifled loves; he will feel that only his illusions have ever given him a sense of reality, only his passions the hope and the vision of peace. He will read himself through and almost gather a meaning from his experience; at least he will half believe that all he has been dealing with was a dream and a symbol, and raise his eyes toward the truth beyond.

This plastic moment of the mind, when we become aware of the artificiality and inadequacy of what common sense perceives, is the true moment of poetic opportunity,—an opportunity, we may hasten to confess, which is generally missed. The strain of attention, the concentration and focussing of thought on the unfamiliar immediacy of things, usually brings about nothing but confusion. We are dazed, we are filled with a sense of unutterable things, luminous yet indistinguishable, many yet one. Instead of rising to imagination, we sink into mysticism.

To accomplish a mystical disintegration is not the function of any art; if any art seems to accomplish it, the effect is only incidental, being involved, perhaps, in the process of constructing the proper object of that art, as we might cut down trees and dig them up by the roots to lay the foundations of a temple. For every art looks to the building up of something. And just because the world built up by common sense and natural science is an inadequate world (a skeleton which needs the filling of sensation before it can live), therefore the moment when we realize its inadequacy is the moment when the higher arts find their opportunity. When the world is shattered to bits they can come and "build it nearer to the heart's desire."

The great function of poetry, which we have not yet directly mentioned, is precisely this: to repair to the material of experience, seizing hold of the reality of sensation and fancy beneath the surface of conventional ideas, and then out of that living but indefinite material to build new structures, richer, finer, fitter to the primary tendencies of our nature, truer to the ultimate possibilities of the soul. Our descent into the elements of our being is then justified by our subsequent freer ascent toward its goal; we revert to sense only to find food for reason; we destroy conventions only to construct ideals.

Such analysis for the sake of creation is the essence of all great poetry. Science and common sense are themselves in their way poets of no mean order, since they take the material of experience and make out of it a clear, symmetrical, and beautiful world; the very propriety of this art, however, has made it common. Its figures have become mere rhetoric and its metaphors prose. Yet, even as it is, a scientific and mathematical vision has a higher beauty than the irrational poetry of sensation and impulse, which merely tickles the brain, like liquor, and plays upon our random, imaginative lusts. The imagination of a great poet, on the con-

trary, is as orderly as that of an astronomer, and as large; he has the naturalist's patience, the naturalist's love of detail and eye trained to see fine gradations and essential lines; he knows no hurry; he has no pose, no sense of originality; he finds his effects in his subject, and his subject in his inevitable world. Resembling the naturalist in all this, he differs from him in the balance of his interests; the poet has the concreter mind; his visible world wears all its colours and retains its indwelling passion and life. Instead of studying in experience its calculable elements, he studies its moral values, its beauty, the openings it offers to the soul: and the cosmos he constructs is accordingly an ideal theatre for the spirit in which its noblest potential drama is enacted and its destiny resolved.

This supreme function of poetry is only the consummation of the method by which words and imagery are transformed into verse. As verse breaks up the prosaic order of syllables and subjects them to a recognizable and pleasing measure, so poetry breaks up the whole prosaic picture of experience to introduce into it a rhythm more congenial and intelligible to the mind. And in both these cases the operation is essentially the same as that by which, in an intermediate sphere, the images rejected by practical thought, and the emotions ignored by it, are so marshalled as to fill the mind with a truer and intenser consciousness of its memorable experience. The poetry of fancy, of observation, and of passion moves on this intermediate level; the poetry of mere sound and virtuosity is confined to the lower sphere; and the highest is reserved for the poetry of the creative reason. But one principle is present throughout,—the principle of Beauty,—the art of assimilating phenomena, whether words, images, emotions, or systems of ideas, to the deeper innate cravings of the mind.

Let us now dwell a little on this higher function of poetry and try to distinguish some of its phases.

The creation of characters is what many of us might at first be tempted to regard as the supreme triumph of the imagination. If we abstract, however, from our personal tastes and look at the matter in its human and logical relations, we shall see, I think, that the construction of characters is not the ultimate task of poetic fiction. A character can never be exhaustive of our materials: for it exists by its idiosyncrasy, by its contrast with other natures, by its development of one side, and one side only, of our native capacities. It is, therefore, not by characterization as such that the ultimate message can be rendered. The poet can put only a part of himself into any of his heroes, but he must put the whole into his noblest work. A character is accordingly only a fragmentary unity; fragmentary in respect to its origin,—since it is conceived by enlargement, so to speak, of a part of our own being to the exclusion of the rest,—and fragmentary in respect to the object it presents, since a character must live in an environment and be appreciated by contrast and by the sense of derivation. Not the character, but its effects and causes, is the truly interesting thing. Thus in master poets, like Homer and Dante, the characters, although well drawn, are subordinate to the total movement and meaning of the scene. There is indeed something pitiful, something comic, in any comprehended soul; souls, like other things, are only definable by their limitations. We feel instinctively that it would be insulting to speak of any man to his face as we should speak of him in his absence, even if what we say is in the way of praise: for absent he is a character understood, but present he is a force respected.

In the construction of ideal characters, then, the imagination is busy with material,—particular actions and thoughts, —which suggest their unification in persons; but the characters thus conceived can hardly be adequate to the profusion of our observations, nor exhaustive, when all personalities are taken together, of the interest of our lives. Characters are initially imbedded in life, as the gods themselves are originally imbedded in Nature. Poetry must, therefore, to render all reality, render also the background of its figures, and the events that condition their acts. We must place them in that indispensable environment which the landscape furnishes to the eye and the social medium to the emotions.

The visible landscape is not a proper object for poetry. Its elements, and especially the emotional stimulation which it gives, may be suggested or expressed in verse; but landscape is not thereby represented in its proper form; it appears only as an element and associate of moral unities. Painting, architecture, and gardening, with the art of stage setting, have the visible landscape for their object, and to those arts we may leave it. But there is a sort of landscape larger than the visible, which escapes the synthesis of the eye; it is present to that topographical sense by which we always live in the consciousness that there is a sea, that there are mountains, that the sky is above us, even when we do not see it, and that the tribes of men, with their different degrees of blamelessness, are scattered over the broad-backed earth. This cosmic landscape poetry alone can render, and it is no small part of the art to awaken the sense of it at the right moment, so that the object that occupies the centre of vision may be seen in its true lights, coloured by its wider associations, and dignified by its felt affinities to things permanent and great. As the Italian masters were wont not to paint their groups of saints about the Virgin without enlarging the canvas, so as to render a broad piece of sky, some mountains and rivers, and nearer, perhaps, some decorative pile; so the poet of larger mind envelops his characters in the atmosphere of Nature and history, and keeps us constantly aware of the world in which they move.

The distinction of a poet—the dignity and humanity of his thought—can be measured by nothing, perhaps, so well as by the diameter of the world in which he lives; if he is supreme, his vision, like Dante's, always stretches to the stars. And Virgil, a supreme poet sometimes unjustly belittled, shows us the same thing in another form; his landscape is the Roman universe, his theme the sacred springs of Roman greatness in piety, constancy, and law. He has not written a line in forgetfulness that he was a Roman; he loves country life and its labours because he sees in it the origin and bulwark of civic greatness; he honours tradition because it gives perspective and momentum to the history that ensues; he invokes the gods, because they are symbols of the physical and moral forces by which Rome struggled to dominion.

Almost every classic poet has the topographical sense; he swarms with proper names and allusions to history and fable; if an epithet is to be thrown in anywhere to fill up the measure of a line, he chooses instinctively an appellation of place or family; his wine is not red, but Samian; his gorges are not deep, but are the gorges of Haemus; his songs are not sweet, but Pierian. We may deride their practice as conventional, but they could far more justly deride ours as insignificant. Conventions do not arise without some reason, and genius will know how to rise above them by a fresh appreciation of their rightness, and will feel no temptation to overturn them in favour of personal whimsies. The ancients found poetry not so much in sensible accidents as in essential forms and noble associations;

and this fact marks very clearly their superior education. They dominated the world as we no longer dominate it, and lived, as we are too distracted to live, in the presence of the rational and the important.

A physical and historical background, however, is of little moment to the poet in comparison with that other environment of his characters,—the dramatic situations in which they are involved. The substance of poetry is, after all, emotion; and if the intellectual emotion of comprehension and the mimetic one of impersonation are massive, they are not so intense as the appetites and other transitive emotions of life; the passions are the chief basis of all interests, even the most ideal, and the passions are seldom brought into play except by the contact of man with man. The various forms of love and hate are only possible in society, and to imagine occasions in which these feelings may manifest all their inward vitality is the poet's function,—one in which he follows the fancy of every child, who puffs himself out in his day-dreams into an endless variety of heroes and lovers. The thrilling adventures which he craves demand an appropriate theatre; the glorious emotions with which he bubbles over must at all hazards find or feign their correlative objects.

But the passions are naturally blind, and the poverty of the imagination, when left alone, is absolute. The passions may ferment as they will, they never can breed an idea out of their own energy. This idea must be furnished by the senses, by outward experience, else the hunger of the soul will gnaw its own emptiness for ever. Where the seed of sensation has once fallen, however, the growth, variations, and exuberance of fancy may be unlimited. Only we still observe (as in the child, in dreams, and in the poetry of ignorant or mystical poets) that the intensity of inwardly generated visions does not involve any real increase in their scope or dignity. The inexperienced mind remains a thin mind, no matter how much its vapours may be heated and blown about by natural passion. It was a capital error in Fichte and Schopenhauer to assign essential fertility to the will in the creation of ideas. They mistook, as human nature will do, even when at times it professes pessimism, an ideal for a reality: and because they saw how much the will clings to its objects, how it selects and magnifies them, they imagined that it could breed them out of itself. A man who thinks clearly will see that such self-determination of a will is inconceivable, since what has no external relation and no diversity of structure cannot of itself acquire diversity of functions. Such inconceivability, of course, need not seem a great objection to a man of impassioned inspiration; he may even claim a certain consistency in positing, on the strength of his preference, the inconceivable to be a truth.

The alleged fertility of the will is, however, disproved by experience, from which metaphysics must in the end draw its analogies and plausibility. The passions discover, they do not create, their occasions, a fact which is patent when we observe how they seize upon what objects they find, and how reversible, contingent, and transferable the emotions are in respect to their objects. A doll will be loved instead of a child, a child instead of a lover, God instead of everything. The differentiation of the passions, as far as consciousness is concerned, depends on the variety of the objects of experience,—that is, on the differentiation of the senses and of the environment which stimulates them.

When the "infinite" spirit enters the human body, it is determined to certain limited forms of life by the organs which it wears; and its blank potentiality becomes actual in thought and deed, according to the fortunes and relations of its organism. The ripeness of the passions may thus precede the information of the mind and lead to groping in by-paths without issue; a phenomenon which appears not only in the obscure individual whose abnormalities the world ignores, but also in the starved, half-educated genius that pours the whole fire of his soul into trivial arts or grotesque superstitions. The hysterical forms of music and religion are the refuge of an idealism that has lost its way; the waste and failures of life flow largely in those channels. The carnal temptations of youth are incidents of the same maladaptation, when passions assert themselves before the conventional order of society can allow them physical satisfaction, and long before philosophy or religion can hope to transform them into fuel for its own sacrificial flames.

Hence flows the greatest opportunity of fiction. We have, in a sense, an infinite will; but we have a limited experience, an experience sadly inadequate to exercise that will either in its purity or its strength. To give form to our capacities nothing is required but the appropriate occasion; this the poet, studying the world, will construct for us out of the materials of his observations. He will involve us in scenes which lie beyond the narrow lane of our daily ploddings; he will place us in the presence of important events, that we may feel our spirit rise momentarily to the height of his great argument. The possibilities of love or glory, of intrigue and perplexity, will be opened up before us; if he gives us a good plot, we can readily furnish the characters, because each of them will be the realization of some stunted potential self of our own. It is by the plot, then, that the characters will be vivified, because it is by the plot that our own character will be expanded into its latent possibilities.

The description of an alien character can serve this purpose only very imperfectly; but the presentation of the circumstances in which that character manifests itself will make description unnecessary, since our instinct will supply all that is requisite for the impersonation. Thus it seems that Aristotle was justified in making the plot the chief element in fiction: for it is by virtue of the plot that the characters live, or, rather, that we live in them, and by virtue of the plot accordingly that our soul rises to that imaginative activity by which we tend at once to escape from the personal life and to realize its ideal. This idealization is, of course, partial and merely relative to the particular adventure in which we imagine ourselves engaged. But in some single direction our will finds self-expression, and understands itself; runs through the career which it ignorantly coveted, and gathers the fruits and the lesson of that enterprise.

This is the essence of tragedy: the sense of the finished life, of the will fulfilled and enlightened: that purging of the mind so much debated upon, which relieves us of pent-up energies, transfers our feelings to a greater object, and thus justifies and entertains our dumb passions, detaching them at the same time for a moment from their accidental occasions in our earthly life. An episode, however lurid, is not a tragedy in this nobler sense, because it does not work itself out to the end; it pleases without satisfying, or shocks without enlightening. This enlightenment, I need hardly say, is not a matter of theory or of moral maxims; the enlightenment by which tragedy is made sublime is a glimpse into the ultimate destinies of our will. This discovery need not be an ethical gain— Macbeth and Othello attain it as much as Brutus and Hamlet—it may serve to accentuate despair, or cruelty, or indifference, or merely to fill the imagination for a moment without much affecting the permanent tone of the mind. But without such a glimpse of the goal of a passion the passion has not been adequately

read, and the fiction has served to amuse us without really enlarging the frontiers of our ideal experience. Memory and emotion have been played upon, but imagination has not brought anything new to the light.

The dramatic situation, however, gives us the environment of a single passion, of life in one of its particular phases; and although a passion, like Romeo's love, may seem to devour the whole soul, and its fortunes may seem to be identical with those of the man, yet much of the man, and the best part of him, goes by the board in such a simplification. If Leonardo da Vinci, for example, had met in his youth with Romeo's fate, his end would have been no more ideally tragic than if he had died at eighteen of a fever; we should be touched rather by the pathos of what he had missed, than by the sublimity of what he had experienced. A passion like Romeo's, compared with the ideal scope of human thought and emotion, is a thin dream, a pathological crisis.

Accordingly Aristophanes, remembering the original religious and political functions of tragedy, blushes to see upon the boards a woman in love. And we should readily agree with him, but for two reasons,—one, that we abstract too much, in our demands upon art, from nobility of mind, and from the thought of totality and proportion; the other, that we have learned to look for a symbolic meaning in detached episodes, and to accept the incidental emotions they cause, because of their violence and our absorption in them, as in some sense sacramental and representative of the whole. Thus the picture of an unmeaning passion, of a crime without an issue, does not appear to our romantic apprehension as the sorry farce it is, but rather as a true tragedy. Some have lost even the capacity to conceive of a true tragedy, because they have no idea of a cosmic order, of general laws of life, or of an impersonal religion. They measure the profundity of feeling by its intensity, not by its justifying relations; and in the radical disintegration of their spirit, the more they are devoured the more they fancy themselves fed. But the majority of us retain some sense of a meaning in our joys and sorrows, and even if we cannot pierce to their ultimate object, we feel that what absorbs us here and now has a merely borrowed or deputed power; that it is a symbol and foretaste of all reality speaking to the whole soul. At the same time our intelligence is too confused to give us any picture of that reality, and our will too feeble to marshal our disorganized loves into a religion consistent with itself and harmonious with the comprehended universe. A rational ideal eludes us, and we are the more inclined to plunge into mysticism.

Nevertheless, the function of poetry, like that of science, can only be fulfilled by the conception of harmonies that become clearer as they grow richer. As the chance note that comes to be supported by a melody becomes in that melody determinate and necessary, and as the melody, when woven into a harmony, is explicated in that harmony and fixed beyond recall, so the single emotion, the fortuitous dream, launched by the poet into the world of recognizable and immortal forms, looks in that world for its ideal supports and affinities. It must find them or else be blown back among the ghosts. The highest ideality is the comprehension of the real. Poetry is not at its best when it depicts a further possible experience, but when it initiates us, by feigning something which as an experience is impossible, into the meaning of the experience which we have actually had.

The highest example of this kind of poetry is religion; and although disfigured and misunderstood by the simplicity of men who believe in it without being capable of that imaginative interpretation of life in which its truth consists, yet this religion is even then often beneficent, because it colours life harmoniously with the ideal. Religion may falsely represent the ideal as a reality, but we must remember that the ideal, if not so represented, would be despised by the majority of men, who cannot understand that the value of things is moral, and who therefore attribute to what is moral a natural existence, thinking thus to vindicate its importance and value. But value lies in meaning, not in substance; in the ideal which things approach, not in the energy which they embody.

The highest poetry, then, is not that of the versifiers, but that of the prophets, or of such poets as interpret verbally the visions which the prophets have rendered in action and sentiment rather than in adequate words. That the intuitions of religion are poetical, and that in such intuitions poetry has its ultimate function, are truths of which both religion and poetry become more conscious the more they advance in refinement and profundity. A crude and superficial theology may confuse God with the thunder, the mountains, the heavenly bodies, or the whole universe; but when we pass from these easy identifications to a religion that has taken root in history and in the hearts of men, and has come to flower, we find its objects and its dogmas purely ideal, transparent expressions of moral experience and perfect counterparts of human needs. The evidence of history or of the senses is left far behind and never thought of; the evidence of the heart, the value of the idea, are alone regarded.

Take, for instance, the doctrine of transubstantiation. A metaphor here is the basis of a dogma, because the dogma rises to the same subtle region as the metaphor, and gathers its sap from the same soil of emotion. Religion has here rediscovered its affinity with poetry, and in insisting on the truth of its mystery it unconsciously vindicates the ideality of its truth. Under the accidents of bread and wine lies, says the dogma, the substance of Christ's body, blood, and divinity. What is that but to treat facts as an appearance, and their ideal import as a reality? And to do this is the very essence of poetry, for which everything visible is a sacrament—an outward sign of that inward grace for which the soul is thirsting.

In this same manner, where poetry rises from its elementary and detached expressions in rhythm, euphuism, characterization, and story-telling, and comes to the consciousness of its highest function, that of portraying the ideals of experience and destiny, then the poet becomes aware that he is essentially a prophet, and either devotes himself, like Homer or Dante, to the loving expression of the religion that exists, or like Lucretius or Wordsworth, to the heralding of one which he believes to be possible. Such poets are aware of their highest mission; others, whatever the energy of their genius, have not conceived their ultimate function as poets. They have been willing to leave their world ugly as a whole, after stuffing it with a sufficient profusion of beauties. Their contemporaries, their fellow-countrymen for many generations, may not perceive this defect, because they are naturally even less able than the poet himself to understand the necessity of so large a harmony. If he is short-sighted, they are blind, and his poetic world may seem to them sublime in its significance, because it may suggest some partial lifting of their daily burdens and some partial idealization of their incoherent thoughts.

Such insensibility to the highest poetry is no more extraordinary than the corresponding indifference to the highest religion; nobility and excellence, however, are not dependent on the suffrage of half-baked men, but on the original disposition of the clay and the potter; I mean on the conditions of the art and the ideal capacities of human nature. Just as a note is better than a noise because, its beats being regular, the ear and brain can react with pleasure on that regularity, so all the stages of harmony are better than the confusion out of which they come, because the soul that perceives that harmony welcomes it as the fulfilment of her natural ends. The Pythagoreans were therefore right when they made number the essence of the knowable world, and Plato was right when he said harmony was the first condition of the highest good. The good man is a poet whose syllables are deeds and make a harmony in Nature. The poet is a rebuilder of the imagination, to make a harmony in that. And he is not a complete poet if his whole imagination is not attuned and his whole experience composed into a single symphony.

For his complete equipment, then, it is necessary, in the first place, that he sing; that his voice be pure and well pitched, and that his numbers flow; then, at a higher stage, his images must fit with one another; he must be euphuistic, colouring his thoughts with many reflected lights of memory and suggestion, so that their harmony may be rich and profound; again, at a higher stage, he must be sensuous and free, that is, he must build up his world with the primary elements of experience, not with the conventions of common sense or intelligence; he must draw the whole soul into his harmonies, even if in doing so he disintegrates the partial systematizations of experience made by abstract science in the categories of prose. But finally, this disintegration must not leave the poet weltering in a chaos of sense and passion; it must be merely the ploughing of the ground before a new harvest, the kneading of the clay before the modelling of a more perfect form. The expression of emotion should be rationalized by derivation from character and by reference to the real objects that arouse it—to Nature, to history, and to the universe of truth; the experience imagined should be conceived as a destiny, governed by principles, and issuing in the discipline and enlightenment of the will. In this way alone can poetry become an interpretation of life and not merely an irrelevant excursion into the realm of fancy, multiplying our images without purpose, and distracting us from our business without spiritual gain.

If we may then define poetry, not in the formal sense of giving the minimum of what may be called by that name, but in the ideal sense of determining the goal which it approaches and the achievement in which all its principles would be fulfilled, we may say that poetry is metrical and euphuistic discourse, expressing thought which is both sensuous and ideal.

Such is poetry as a literary form; but if we drop the limitation to verbal expression, and think of poetry as that subtle fire and inward light which seems at times to shine through the world and to touch the images in our minds with ineffable beauty, then poetry is a momentary harmony in the soul amid stagnation or conflict,—a glimpse of the divine and an incitation to a religious life.

Religion is poetry become the guide of life, poetry substituted for science or supervening upon it as an approach to the highest reality. Poetry is religion allowed to drift, left without points of application in conduct and without an expression in worship and dogma; it is religion without practical efficacy and without metaphysical illusion. The ground of this abstractness of poetry, however, is usually only its narrow scope; a poet who plays with an idea for half an hour, or constructs a character to which he gives no profound moral significance, forgets his own thought, or remembers it only as a fiction of his leisure, because he has not dug his well deep enough to tap the subterranean springs of his own life. But when the poet enlarges his theatre and puts into his rhapsodies the true visions of his people and of his soul, his poetry is the consecration of his deepest convictions, and contains the whole truth of his religion. What the religion of the vulgar adds to the poet's is simply the inertia of their limited apprehension, which takes literally what he meant ideally, and degrades into a false extension of this world on its own level what in his mind was a true interpretation of it upon a moral plane.

This higher plane is the sphere of significant imagination, of relevant fiction, of idealism become the interpretation of the reality it leaves behind. Poetry raised to its highest power is then identical with religion grasped in its inmost truth; at their point of union both reach their utmost purity and beneficence, for then poetry loses its frivolity and ceases to demoralize, while religion surrenders its illusions and ceases to deceive.

Amy Lowell

✳ 1874-1925

It has been said that Ezra Pound fathered and Amy Lowell mothered the Imagist movement which in the second decade of this century labored to rescue poetry from the superficiality to which the facile rhythms and timid vision of a genteel tradition had brought it. In 1915 in the first of several annual volumes called SOME IMAGIST POETS, *she presented a manifesto which called for the use by poets of the language of common speech, the creation of fresh rhythms, and the presentation of images which were hard and clear, not blurred or indefinite: "most of us believe that concentration is of the essence in poetry." Her Poe-like remarks on the poet's trade appear in 1914 as part of the Preface to a collection of her own poetry called* SWORD BLADES AND POPPY SEEDS.

The Poet's Trade

No one expects a man to make a chair without first learning how, but there is a popular impression that the poet is born, not made, and that his verses burst from his overflowing heart of themselves. As a matter of fact, the poet must learn his trade in the same manner, and with the same painstaking care, as the cabinet-maker. His heart may overflow with high thoughts and sparkling fancies, but if he cannot convey them to his reader by means of the written word he has no claim to be considered a poet. A work-man may be pardoned, therefore, for spending a few moments to explain and describe the technique of his trade. A work of beauty which cannot stand an intimate examination is a poor and jerry-built thing.

In the first place, I wish to state my firm belief that poetry should not try to teach, that it should exist simply because it is a created beauty, even if sometimes the beauty of a gothic grotesque. We do not ask the trees to teach us moral lessons, and only the Salvation Army feels it necessary to pin texts upon them. We know that these texts are ridiculous, but many of us do not yet see that to write an obvious moral all over a work of art, picture, statue, or poem, is not only ridiculous, but timid and vulgar. We distrust a beauty we only half understand, and rush in with our impertinent suggestions. How far are we from "admitting the Universe"! The Universe, which flings down its continents and seas, and leaves them without comment. Art is as much

a function of the Universe as an Equinoctial gale, or the Law of Gravitation; and we insist upon considering it merely a little scroll-work, of no great importance unless it be studded with nails from which pretty and uplifting sentiments may be hung!

H. L. Mencken
✳ 1880-1956

Mencken could not have been expected to approve the kind of poetry for which Amy Lowell called, and with few, often tongue-in-cheek exceptions, he was unimpressed by any of the new poetry of his time. His complaint was against its bloodlessness and the private coteries it encouraged. His bellicose pronouncements, a sample of which is here reprinted from his sixth series of PREJUDICES, *published in 1927, have had little effect on poets or on public taste, but have been provocative or amusing to readers who like thoughts well dressed.*

Poetry in America

The New Poetry movement in America, so full of life and even of malicious animal magnetism a dozen years ago, is now obviously down with cholelithiasis, and no literary pathologist of genuine gifts would be surprised to hear, at any moment, of its death. Most of its former ornaments, indeed, begin to flee its bedside. Miss Lowell, in her last years, devoted herself to prose, and Masters goes the same way. Vachel Lindsay and Robert Frost take to college professing. Carl Sandburg has joined the minstrels. All the principal Greenwich Village poets, harassed by the morals squad, fled long ago to Paris, where landlords are less prying, and even artists may lead their own lives.

This slackening of effort is visible in all the little poetry magazines. Most of them continue to come out, and in the backwaters of the Republic, where all varieties of human progress are behind schedule, there are even occasional appearances of new ones, but there is little in any of them that is worth reading, and almost no actual poetry. What they print, in the main, is simply a series of exercises in the new prosody. It turns out, on examination, to be quite as tight and arbitrary as the old kind. For one thing that a poet of 1885 could not do there are ten things that a poet of 1927 cannot do. Thus the revolt against form expires in a new and worse formalism. The fact is most visible, of course, on the edges of the movement—that is, among the poets of Greenwich Village. What one observes in the advanced and atrabilious magazines which they publish is simply a sort of organized imbecility. The poet is strictly forbidden to make use of any of the traditional materials of his craft, or to concede anything to its traditional idioms. He must eschew all rhyme that really rhymes, he must eschew all the orthodox rhythms, and he must eschew all direct attack upon the emotions. In other words, he must eschew poetry. What he writes, it must be confessed, is sometimes very interesting, in its bizarre, unearthly way—just as a college yell, say, is interesting, or an act of Congress. But it is no more poetry than the college yell is music or the act of Congress wisdom.

The trouble with most of the new poets, whether in or out of Greenwich Village, is that they are too cerebral—that they attack the problems of a fine art with the methods of science. That error runs through all their public discussions of the business. Those discussions are full of theories, by the new psychology out of the cant of the studios, that do not work and are not true. The old-time poet did not bother with theories. When the urge to write was upon him, he simply got himself into a lather, tied a towel around his head, and then tried to reduce his feelings to paper. If he had any skill the result was poetry; if he lacked skill it was nonsense. But even his worst failure still had something natural and excusable about it—it was the failure of a man admittedly somewhat feverish, with purple paint on his nose and vine-leaves in his hair. The failure of the new poet is the far more grotesque failure of a scientist who turns out to be a quack—of a mathematician who divides 20 by 4 and gets 6, of a chiropractor who looks in the vertebræ for the cause of cross-eyes, of a cook who tries to make an omelette of china doorknobs. Poetry can never be concocted by any purely intellectual process. It has nothing to do with the intellect; it is, in fact, a violent and irreconcilable enemy to the intellect. Its purpose is not to establish facts, but to evade and deny them. What it essays to do is to make life more bearable in an intolerable world by concealing and obliterating all the harsher realities. Its message is that all will be well tomorrow, or, at the latest, next Tuesday, that the grave is not cold and damp but steam-heated and lined with roses, that serving in the trenches is far more amusing and comfortable than serving in the United States Senate, that a girl is not a viviparous mammal, full of pathogenic organisms and enlightened self-interest, but an angel with bobbed wings and a heart of gold. Take this denial of the bald and dreadful facts out of poetry— make it scientific and sensible—and it simply ceases to be what it pretends to be. It may remain good prose; it may even remain beautiful prose. But it cannot stir the blood as true poetry does; it cannot offer that soothing consolation, that escape from reality, that sovereign balm for every spiritual itch and twinge which is the great gift of poetry to man. The best poetry is always palpably untrue; it is its eloquent untruth that makes it so lovely. The other day I read of a gentleman, condemned to death in one of the Southern States, who went to the electric chair reciting the Twenty-third Psalm. It is a pity he had to die; he would have made an excellent critic, for he understood perfectly the nature and purpose of poetry.

The new poets, now passing into the shadows, not only made the mistake of trying to rationalize poetry, an enterprise comparable to trying to rationalize necking, drunkenness or the use of hasheesh; they also tried to detach themselves from the ordinary flow of American ideas, and to convert themselves into an intellectual aristocracy. Some of them, true enough, quickly found the thing impossible, and so turned back, notably Sandburg and Lindsay, but nearly all at least made the attempt. Miss Lowell, perhaps, went furthest; there was a time when even Boston felt bucolic and loutish, and hence very uneasy, in her presence. The result was that nine-tenths of the compositions the fraternity produced simply shot into space. The great heart of the folk reacted to them as feebly as it might have reacted to polemics between astronomers. When poetry fails in this way it fails all over. I do not argue that it ought to reach and soothe the nether herd, though some of the very best poetry ever written actually does—for example, the poetry in the Bible. All I contend is that it ought to reach the generality of the literate. If literary pastors are not moved by it, if it fails to supply phrases for editorial writers, if it is not quoted by stewed Congressmen at the endless memorial services on Capitol Hill, then it has obviously missed fire. Of all the stuff produced by the new poets precious little has ever gone that far. I can recall a few poems by Sandburg and Lindsay, perhaps one or two by Frost, and none other. The whole body of verse of Miss Lowell is as dead as if it had been written in Choctaw. Meanwhile, certain old-fashioned poets, notably Miss Reese and Miss Teasdale, have written things that will probably live. They will live because they are alive.

I sometimes think, indeed, that the real poetry of our era has been written, not by poets at all, but by men who would be as indignant, if you called them poets, as if you called them kidnapers, violoncellists or Socialists. I allude to the earnest rhetoricians who roam the chautauquas and the Kiwanis Clubs, waving the banner of idealism. What these fellows say is almost always nonsense, but it is at least the sort of nonsense that the American people yearn to cherish and believe in—it somehow fills their need. I point, for example, to their gabble about Service—already the source of phrases that Congressmen, clergymen, editorial writers and so on mouth every day. Here is the essential poetry of the Americano: his life is sordid, but he tries to escape from the fact by leering at the stars. It is a comprehensible impulse, and even worthy. The poets of his country have not helped him to attain his heart's desire. He has had to turn to traveling go-getters and forward-lookers.

Alas, whenever one thus discusses the nature and function of poetry—that is, whenever one tries to be realistic about it—one is sure to be accused of being an enemy to the art itself. But does this necessarily follow? I am sure it does not. The social value of poetry is not diminished in the slightest by looking at it without illusion. It still offers its old escape from reality; it still offers consolation to *Homo sapiens* in his woeful journey through this inclement vale. To denounce it out of hand would be as absurd as to denounce religion or anesthetics. The purpose of anesthetics is to get rid of the harsh torture of pain and substitute the sweet peace of sleep. The purpose of even the highest poetry is almost precisely the same. Chloroform tells a man that he is not having his leg cut off, but lying drunk on a feather-bed, with fireworks to entertain him. Poetry tells him that his girl is as beautiful as Venus and is marrying him without a single thought of his tenements and hereditaments, that his country is a Galahad among the nations and wholly devoid of the rascality prevailing everywhere else, that he himself is a noble fellow and will go to Heaven when he dies. All these things, I suspect, are false. But all of them make life more bearable. Poets are simply men who devote themselves to spreading them, often at great sacrifice of income. They are liars, but their lies, I believe, will be viewed very generously on the Resurrection Morn.

T. S. Eliot

* 1888-

Probably no one has had more pervasive an influence on writing and talking about writing in our century than Thomas Stearns Eliot, born in St. Louis, nurtured at Harvard, since 1914 a resident of England, and subsequently a British subject. His poetry has indelibly marked much of the poetry of our time, his literary analyses have stimulated our New Critics to challenge old notions of proper approaches to literature, and his plays have in recent years reached and pleased a larger audience. Eliot once defined his critical position as that of "an Anglo-Catholic in religion, a classicist in literature, and a royalist in politics." His essay on "Tradition and the Individual Talent," written in 1917, is often said to have ex-

erted influence in our time similar to that exerted after 1798 by Wordsworth and Coleridge's Preface to their LYRICAL BALLADS.

Tradition and the Individual Talent

In English writing we seldom speak of tradition, though we occasionally apply its name in deploring its absence. We cannot refer to "the tradition" or to "a tradition"; at most, we employ the adjective in saying that the poetry of So-and-so is "traditional" or even "too traditional." Seldom, perhaps, does the word appear except in a phrase of censure. If otherwise, it is vaguely approbative, with the implication, as to the work approved, of some pleasing archæological reconstruction. You can hardly make the word agreeable to English ears without this comfortable reference to the reassuring science of archæology.

Certainly the word is not likely to appear in our appreciations of living or dead writers. Every nation, every race, has not only its own creative, but its own critical turn of mind; and is even more oblivious of the shortcomings and limitations of its critical habits than of those of its creative genius. We know, or think we know, from the enormous mass of critical writing that has appeared in the French language the critical method or habit of the French; we only conclude (we are such unconscious people) that the French are "more critical" than we, and sometimes even plume ourselves a little with the fact, as if the French were the less spontaneous. Perhaps they are; but we might remind ourselves that criticism is as inevitable as breathing, and that we should be none the worse for articulating what passes in our minds when we read a book and feel an emotion about it, for criticizing our own minds in their work of criticism. One of the facts that might come to light in this process is our tendency to insist, when we praise a poet, upon those aspects of his work in which he least resembles any one else. In these aspects or parts of his work we pretend to find what is individual, what is the peculiar essence of the man. We dwell with satisfaction upon the poet's difference from his predecessors, especially his immediate predecessors; we endeavour to find something that can be isolated in order to be enjoyed. Whereas if we approach a poet without this prejudice we shall often find that not only the best, but the most individual parts of his work may be those in which the dead poets, his ancestors, assert their immortality most vigorously. And I do not mean the impressionable period of adolescence, but the period of full maturity.

Yet if the only form of tradition, of handing down, consisted in following the ways of the immediate generation before us in a blind or timid adherence to its successes, "tradition" should positively be discouraged. We have seen many such simple currents soon lost in the sand; and novelty is better than repetition. Tradition is a matter of much wider significance. It cannot be inherited, and if you want it you must obtain it by great labour. It involves, in the first place, the historical sense, which we may call nearly indispensable to any one who would continue to be a poet beyond his twenty-fifth year; and the historical sense involves a perception, not only of the pastness of the past, but of its presence; the historical sense compels a man to write not merely with his own generation in his bones, but with a feeling that the whole of the literature of Europe from Homer and within it the whole of the literature of his own country has a simultaneous existence and composes a simultaneous order. This historical sense, which is a sense of the timeless as well as of the temporal and of the timeless and of the temporal together, is what makes a writer traditional. And it is at the same time what makes a writer most acutely conscious of his place in time, of his own contemporaneity.

No poet, no artist of any art, has his complete meaning alone. His significance, his appreciation is the appreciation of his relation to the dead poets and artists. You cannot value him alone; you must set him, for contrast and comparison, among the dead. I mean this as a principle of æsthetic, not merely historical, criticism. The necessity that he shall conform, that he shall cohere, is not one-sided; what happens when a new work of art is created is something that happens simultaneously to all the works of art which preceded it. The existing monuments form an ideal order among themselves, which is modified by the introduction of the new (the really new) work of art among them. The existing order is complete before the new work arrives; for order to persist after the supervention of novelty, the *whole* existing order must be, if ever so slightly, altered; and so the relations, proportions, values of each work of art toward the whole are readjusted; and this is conformity between the old and the new. Whoever has approved this idea of order, of the form of European, of English literature will not find it preposterous that the past should be altered by the present as much as the present is directed by the past. And the poet who is aware of this will be aware of great difficulties and responsibilities.

In a peculiar sense he will be aware also that he must inevitably be judged by the standards of the past. I say judged, not amputated, by them; not judged to be as good as, or worse or better than, the dead; and certainly not judged by the canons of dead critics. It is a judgment, a comparison, in which two things are measured by each other. To conform merely would be for the new work not really to conform at all; it would not be new, and would therefore not be a work of art. And we do not quite say that the new is more valuable because it fits in; but its fitting in is a test of its value— a test, it is true, which can only be slowly and cautiously applied, for we are none of us infallible judges of conformity. We say: it appears to conform, and is perhaps individual, or it appears individual, and may conform; but we are hardly likely to find that it is one and not the other.

To proceed to a more intelligible exposition of the relation of the poet to the past: he can neither take the past as a lump, an indiscriminate bolus, nor can he form himself wholly on one or two private admirations, nor can he form himself wholly upon one preferred period. The first course is inadmissible, the second is an important experience of youth, and the third is a pleasant and highly desirable supplement. The poet must be very conscious of the main current, which does not at all flow invariably through the most distinguished reputations. He must be quite aware of the obvious fact that art never improves, but that the material of art is never quite the same. He must be aware that the mind of Europe—the mind of his own country—a mind which he learns in time to be much more important than his own private mind—is a mind which changes, and that this change is a development which abandons nothing *en route,* which does not superannuate either Shakespeare, or Homer, or the rock drawing of the Magdalenian draughtsmen. That this development, refinement perhaps, complication certainly, is not, from the point of view of the artist, any improvement. Perhaps not even an improvement from the point of view of the psychologist or not to the extent which we imagine; perhaps only in the end

based upon a complication in economics and machinery. But the difference between the present and the past is that the conscious present is an awareness of the past in a way and to an extent which the past's awareness of itself cannot show.

Some one said: "The dead writers are remote from us because we *know* so much more than they did." Precisely, and they are that which we know.

I am alive to a usual objection to what is clearly part of my programme for the *métier* of poetry. The objection is that the doctrine requires a ridiculous amount of erudition (pedantry), a claim which can be rejected by appeal to the lives of poets in any pantheon. It will even be affirmed that much learning deadens or perverts poetic sensibility. While, however, we persist in believing that a poet ought to know as much as will not encroach upon his necessary receptivity and necessary laziness, it is not desirable to confine knowledge to whatever can be put into a useful shape for examinations, drawing-rooms, or the still more pretentious modes of publicity. Some can absorb knowledge, the more tardy must sweat for it. Shakespeare acquired more essential history from Plutarch than most men could from the whole British Museum. What is to be insisted upon is that the poet must develop or procure the consciousness of the past and that he should continue to develop this consciousness throughout his career.

What happens is a continual surrender of himself as he is at the moment to something which is more valuable. The progress of an artist is a continual self-sacrifice, a continual extinction of personality.

There remains to define this process of depersonalization and its relation to the sense of tradition. It is in this depersonalization that art may be said to approach the condition of science. I, therefore, invite you to consider, as a suggestive analogy, the action which takes place when a bit of finely filiated platinum is introduced into a chamber containing oxygen and sulphur dioxide.

2

Honest criticism and sensitive appreciation are directed not upon the poet but upon the poetry. If we attend to the confused cries of the newspaper critics and the *susurrus* [murmuring] of popular repetition that follows, we shall hear the names of poets in great numbers; if we seek not Bluebook knowledge but the enjoyment of poetry, and ask for a poem, we shall seldom find it. I have tried to point out the importance of the relation of the poem to other poems by other authors, and suggested the conception of poetry as a living whole of all the poetry that has ever been written. The other aspect of this Impersonal theory of poetry is the relation of the poem to its author. And I hinted, by an analogy, that the mind of the mature poet differs from that of the immature one not precisely in any valuation of "personality," not being necessarily more interesting, or having "more to say," but rather by being a more finely perfected medium in which special, or very varied, feelings are at liberty to enter into new combinations.

The analogy was that of the catalyst. When the two gasses previously mentioned are mixed in the presence of a filament of platinum, they form sulphurous acid. The combination takes place only if the platinum is present; nevertheless the newly formed acid contains no trace of platinum, and the platinum itself is apparently unaffected; has remained inert, neutral, and unchanged. The mind of the poet is the shred of platinum. It may partly or exclusively operate upon the experience of the man himself; but, the more perfect the artist, the more completely separate in him will be the man who suffers and the mind which creates; the more perfectly will the mind digest and transmute the passions which are its material.

The experience, you will notice, the elements which enter the presence of the transforming catalyst, are of two kinds: emotions and feelings. The effect of a work of art upon the person who enjoys it is an experience different in kind from any experience not of art. It may be formed out of one emotion, or may be a combination of several; and various feelings, inhering for the writer in particular words or phrases or images, may be added to compose the final result. Or great poetry may be made without the direct use of any emotion whatever: composed out of feelings solely. Canto XV of the *Inferno* (Brunetto Latini) is a working up of the emotion evident in the situation; but the effect, though single as that of any work of art, is obtained by considerable complexity of detail. The last quatrain gives an image, a feeling attaching to an image, which "came," which did not develop simply out of what precedes, but which was probably in suspension in the poet's mind until the proper combination arrived for it to add itself to. The poet's mind is in fact a receptacle for seizing and storing up numberless feelings, phrases, images, which remain there until all the particles which can unite to form a new compound are present together.

If you compare several representative passages of the greatest poetry you see how great is the variety of types of combination, and also how completely any semi-ethical criterion of "sublimity" misses the mark. For it is not the "greatness," the intensity, of the emotions, the components, but the intensity of the artistic process, the pressure, so to speak, under which the fusion takes place, that counts. The episode of Paolo and Francesca employs a definite emotion, but the intensity of the poetry is something quite different from whatever intensity in the supposed experience it may give the impression of. It is no more intense, further-more, than Canto XXVI, the voyage of Ulysses, which has not the direct de-pendence upon an emotion. Great variety is possible in the process of transmuta-tion of emotion: the murder of Agamem-non, or the agony of Othello, gives an artistic effect apparently closer to a pos-sible original than the scenes from Dante. In the *Agamemnon,* the artistic emotion approximates to the emotion of an actual spectator; in *Othello* to the emotion of the protagonist himself. But the differ-ence between art and the event is always absolute; the combination which is the murder of Agamemnon is probably as complex as that which is the voyage of Ulysses. In either case there has been a fusion of elements. The ode of Keats con-tains a number of feelings which have nothing particular to do with the nightin gale, but which the nightingale, partly, perhaps, because of its attractive name, and partly because of its reputation, served to bring together.

The point of view which I am strug-gling to attack is perhaps related to the metaphysical theory of the substantial unity of the soul: for my meaning is, that the poet has, not a "personality" to ex-press, but a particular medium, which is only a medium and not a personality, in which impressions and experiences com-bine in peculiar and unexpected ways. Impressions and experiences which are important for the man may take no place in the poetry, and those which be-come important in the poetry may play quite a negligible part in the man, the personality.

I will quote a passage which is un-familiar enough to be regarded with fresh attention in the light—or darkness—of these observations:

And now methinks I could e'en chide myself
For doating on her beauty, though her death
Shall be revenged after no common action.
Does the silkworm expend her yellow labours
For thee? For thee does she undo herself?

Are lordships sold to maintain ladyships
For the poor benefit of a bewildering minute?
Why does yon fellow falsify highways,
And put his life between the judge's lips,
To refine such a thing—keep horse and men
To beat their valours for her? . . .[1]

In this passage (as is evident if it is taken in its context) there is a combina-tion of positive and negative emotions: an intensely strong attraction toward beauty and an equally intense fasci-nation by the ugliness which is con-trasted with it and which destroys it. This balance of contrasted emotion is in the dramatic situation to which the speech is pertinent, but that situation alone is inadequate to it. This is, so to speak, the structural emotion, provided by the drama. But the whole effect, the dom-inant tone, is due to the fact that a number of floating feelings, having an affinity to this emotion by no means su-perficially evident, have combined to give us a new art emotion.

It is not in his personal emotions, the emotions provoked by particular events in his life, that the poet is in any way re-markable or interesting. His particular emotions may be simple, or crude, or flat. The emotion in his poetry will be a very complex thing, but not with the complexity of the emotions of people who have very complex or unusual emo-tions in life. One error, in fact, of ec-centricity in poetry is to seek for new human emotions to express; and in this search for novelty in the wrong place it discovers the perverse. The business of the poet is not to find new emotions, but to use the ordinary ones and, in work-ing them up into poetry, to express feel-ings which are not in actual emotions at all. And emotions which he has never experienced will serve his turn as well as those familiar to him. Consequently, we must believe that "emotion recol-

[1] From *The Revenger's Tragedy,* Act III, Scene v, by the Elizabethan dramatist, Cyril Tourneur.

lected in tranquillity" is an inexact formula. For it is neither emotion, nor recollection, nor, without distortion of meaning, tranquillity. It is a concentration, and a new thing resulting from the concentration, of a very great number of experiences which to the practical and active person would not seem to be experiences at all; it is a concentration which does not happen consciously or of deliberation. These experiences are not "recollected," and they finally unite in an atmosphere which is "tranquil" only in that it is a passive attending upon the event. Of course this is not quite the whole story. There is a great deal, in the writing of poetry, which must be conscious and deliberate. In fact, the bad poet is usually unconscious where he ought to be conscious, and conscious where he ought to be unconscious. Both errors tend to make him "personal." Poetry is not a turning loose of emotion, but an escape from emotion; it is not the expression of personality, but an escape from personality. But, of course, only those who have personality and emotions know what it means to want to escape from these things.

3

ὁ δὲ νοῦς ἴσως θειότερόν τι καὶ ἀπαθές ἐστιν.[2]

This essay proposes to halt at the frontier of metaphysics or mysticism, and confine itself to such practical conclusions as can be applied by the reasonable person interested in poetry. To divert interest from the poet to the poetry is a laudable aim: for it would conduce to a juster estimation of actual poetry, good and bad. There are many people who appreciate the expression of sincere emotion in verse, and there is a smaller number of people who can appreciate tech-

[2] Possibly the mind is too divine, and is therefore unaffected.

nical excellence. But very few know when there is an expression of *significant* emotion, emotion which has its life in the poem and not in the history of the poet. The emotion of art is impersonal. And the poet cannot reach this impersonality without surrendering himself wholly to the work to be done. And he is not likely to know what is to be done unless he lives in what is not merely the present, but the present moment of the past, unless he is conscious, not of what is dead, but of what is already living.

Robert Frost
✳ 1874-

Unlike Mr. Eliot, Robert Frost is a poet who has written little about his craft, though he has talked of it often informally to audiences whom he has delighted with homely observations on what he has done and why he did it. How he did it or what he intended is another matter, and Mr. Frost speaks less willingly on that, because he is not sure that the poet ever really knows. His eye is turned and his ear is tuned to poetry which delights by surprise rather than puzzles. Sometimes he speaks of his own poems as his "little jokes," which is a deceptively leisurely manner of describing them. But Mr. Frost, in verse or prose, is deceptive, even in his seriousness, which people who are too serious sometimes fail to recognize. In speaking of wildness in poetry, he links himself to some attitudes expressed by such New England predecessors as Emerson and Thoreau. "The Figure a Poem Makes" appears as a preface to the COMPLETE POEMS OF ROBERT FROST.

The Figure a Poem Makes

Abstraction is an old story with the philosophers, but it has been like a new toy in the hands of the artists of our day. Why can't we have any one quality of poetry we choose by itself? We can have in thought. Then it will go hard if we can't in practice. Our lives for it.

Granted no one but a humanist much cares how sound a poem is if it is only *a* sound. The sound is the gold in the ore. Then we will have the sound out alone and dispense with the inessential. We do till we make the discovery that the object in writing poetry is to make all poems sound as different as possible from each other, and the resources for that of vowels, consonants, punctuation, syntax, words, sentences, meter are not enough. We need the help of context—meaning —subject matter. That is the greatest help towards variety. All that can be done with words is soon told. So also with meters—particularly in our language where there are virtually but two, strict iambic and loose iambic. The ancients with many were still poor if they depended on meters for all tune. It is painful to watch our sprung-rhythmists straining at the point of omitting one short from a foot for relief from monotony. The possibilities for tune from the dramatic tones of meaning struck across the rigidity of a limited meter are endless. And we are back in poetry as merely one more art of having something to say, sound or unsound. Probably better if sound, because deeper and from wider experience.

Then there is this wildness whereof it is spoken. Granted again that it has an equal claim with sound to being a poem's better half. If it is a wild tune, it is a poem. Our problem then is, as modern abstractionists, to have the wildness pure; to be wild with nothing to be wild about. We bring up as aberrationists, giving way to undirected associations and kicking ourselves from one chance suggestion to another in all directions as of a hot afternoon in the life of a grasshopper. Theme alone can steady us down. Just as the first mystery was how a poem could have a tune in such a straightness as meter, so the second mystery is how a poem can have wildness and at the same time a subject that shall be fulfilled.

It should be of the pleasure of a poem itself to tell how it can. The figure a poem makes. It begins in delight and ends in wisdom. The figure is the same as for love. No one can really hold that the ecstasy should be static and stand still in one place. It begins in delight, it inclines to the impulse, it assumes direction with the first line laid down, it runs a course of lucky events, and ends in a clarification of life—not necessarily a great clarification, such as sects and cults are founded on, but in a momentary stay against confusion. It has denouement. It has an outcome that though unforeseen was predestined from the first image of the original mood—and indeed from the very mood. It is but a trick poem and no poem at all if the best of it was thought of first and saved for the last. It finds its own name as it goes and discovers the best waiting for it in some final phrase at once wise and sad—the happy-sad blend of the drinking song.

No tears in the writer, no tears in the reader. No surprise for the writer, no surprise for the reader. For me the initial delight is in the surprise of remembering something I didn't know I knew. I am in a place, in a situation, as if I had materialized from cloud or risen out of the ground. There is a glad recognition of the long lost and the rest follows. Step by step the wonder of unexpected supply keeps growing. The impressions most useful to my purpose seem always those

I was unaware of and so made no note of at the time when taken, and the conclusion is come to that like giants we are always hurling experience ahead of us to pave the future with against the day when we may want to strike a line of purpose across it for somewhere. The line will have the more charm for not being mechanically straight. We enjoy the straight crookedness of a good walking stick. Modern instruments of precision are being used to make things crooked as if by eye and hand in the old days.

I tell how there may be a better wildness of logic than of inconsequence. But the logic is backward, in retrospect, after the act. It must be more felt than seen ahead like prophecy. It must be a revelation, or a series of revelations, as much for the poet as for the reader. For it to be that there must have been the greatest freedom of the material to move about in it and to establish relations in it regardless of time and space, previous relation, and everything but affinity. We prate of freedom. We call our schools free because we are not free to stay away from them till we are sixteen years of age. I have given up my democratic prejudices and now willingly set the lower classes free to be completely taken care of by the upper classes. Political freedom is nothing to me. I bestow it right and left. All I would keep for myself is the freedom of my material—the condition of body and mind now and then to summons aptly from the vast chaos of all I have lived through.

Scholars and artists thrown together are often annoyed at the puzzle of where they differ. Both work from knowledge; but I suspect they differ most importantly in the way their knowledge is come by. Scholars get theirs with conscientious thoroughness along projected lines of logic; poets theirs cavalierly and as it happens in and out of books. They stick

to nothing deliberately, but let what will stick to them like burrs where they walk in the fields. No acquirement is on assignment, or even self-assignment. Knowledge of the second kind is much more available in the wild free ways of wit and art. A schoolboy may be defined as one who can tell you what he knows in the order in which he learned it. The artist must value himself as he snatches a thing from some previous order in time and space into a new order with not so much as a ligature clinging to it of the old place where it was organic.

More than once I should have lost my soul to radicalism if it had been the originality it was mistaken for by its young converts. Originality and initiative are what I ask for my country. For myself the originality need be no more than the freshness of a poem run in the way I have described: from delight to wisdom. The figure is the same as for love. Like a piece of ice on a hot stove the poem must ride on its own melting. A poem may be worked over once it is in being, but may not be worried into being. Its most precious quality will remain its having run itself and carried away the poet with it. Read it a hundred times: it will forever keep its freshness as a metal keeps its fragrance. It can never lose its sense of a meaning that once unfolded by surprise as it went.

E. B. White

✳ 1899-

Elwyn Brooks White is another poet, though a minor one, who prefers to allow poetry to be what it will rather than what he would like it to be. As the almost anonymous stylist who for years is said to have manicured the paragraphs which make up the "Talk of the Town" section of the NEW YORKER, *he has become something of a legend among his admirers, though frowned on by others because he refuses to be pinned down. Among his books are* IS SEX NECESSARY?, *done in collaboration with James Thurber, in 1929,* ALICE THROUGH THE CELLOPHANE *in 1933, a witty discussion of what were then considered modern trends,* QUO VADIS? OR, THE CASE FOR THE BICYCLE *in 1939, which talked of the complex absurdities of urban and suburban life, and* ONE MAN'S MEAT *in 1942, from which this essay on poetry is reprinted.*

Poetry

"I wish poets could be clearer," shouted my wife angrily from the next room.

Hers is a universal longing. We would all like it if the bards would make themselves plain, or we think we would. The poets, however, are not easily diverted from their high mysterious ways. A poet dares to be just so clear and no clearer; he approaches lucid ground warily, like a mariner who is determined not to scrape his bottom on anything solid. A poet's pleasure is to withhold a little of his meaning, to intensify by mystification. He unzips the veil from beauty, but does not remove it. A poet utterly clear is a trifle glaring.

The subject is a fascinating one. I think poetry is the greatest of the arts. It combines music and painting and story-telling and prophecy and the dance. It is religious in tone, scientific in attitude. A true poem contains a seed of wonder; but a bad poem, egg-fashion, stinks. I think there is no such thing as a long poem. If it is long it isn't a poem: it is something else. A book like *John Brown's Body*, for instance, is not a poem—it is a series of poems tied together with a cord. Poetry is intensity, and nothing is intense for long.

Some poets are naturally clearer than others. To achieve great popularity or great fame it is of some advantage to be either extremely clear (like Edgar Guest) or thoroughly opaque (like Gertrude Stein). The first poet in the land—if I may use the word poet loosely—is Edgar Guest. He is the singer who, more than any other, gives to Americans the enjoyment of rhyme and meter. Whether he gives also to any of his satisfied readers that blinding, aching emotion which I get from reading certain verses by other writers is a question which interests me very much. Being democratic, I am content to have the majority ruling in everything, it would seem, but literature.

There are many types of poetical obscurity. There is the obscurity which results from the poet's being mad. This is rare. Madness in poets is as uncommon as madness in dogs. A discouraging number of reputable poets are sane beyond recall. There is also the obscurity which is the result of the poet's wishing to appear mad. This is rather common and rather dreadful. I know of nothing more distasteful than the work of a poet who has taken leave of his reason deliberately, as a commuter might of his wife.

Then there is the unintentional obscurity, or muddiness, which comes from the inability of some writers to express even a simple idea without stirring up the bottom. And there is the obscurity which results when a fairly large thought is crammed into a three- or four-foot line. The function of poetry is to concentrate; but sometimes over-concentration occurs, and there is no more comfort in such a poem than there is in the subway at peak hour.

Sometimes a poet becomes so completely absorbed in the lyrical possibilities of certain combinations of sounds that he forgets what he started out to say, if anything, and here again a nasty tangle results. This type of obscurity is one which I have great sympathy for: I know that quite frequently in the course of delivering himself of a poem a poet will find himself in possession of a lyric bauble—a line as smooth as velvet to the ear, as pretty as a feather to the eye, yet a line definitely out of plumb with the frame of the poem. What to do with a trinket like this is always troubling to a poet, who is naturally grateful to his Muse for small favors. Usually he just drops the shining object into the body of the poem somewhere and hopes it won't look too giddy. (I sound as though I were contemptuous of poets; the fact is I am jealous of them. I would rather be one than anything.)

My quarrel with poets (who will be surprised to learn that a quarrel is going on) is not that they are unclear but that they are too diligent. Diligence in a poet is the same as dishonesty in a bookkeeper. There are rafts of bards who are writing too much, too diligently, and too slyly. Few poets are willing to wait out their pregnancy—they prefer to have a premature baby and allow it to incubate after being laid in Caslon Old Style.

I think Americans, perhaps more than other people, are impressed by what they don't understand, and the poets take advantage of this. Gertrude Stein has had an amazing amount of newspaper space, out of all proportion to the pleasure she has given people by her writings, it seems to me, although I am just guessing. Miss Stein is preoccupied with an experimental sort of writing which she finds diverting and exciting and which is all right by me. Her deep interest in the sound that words make is laudable; too little attention is paid by most writers to sound, and too many writers are completely tone-deaf. But on the other hand I am not ready to believe that any writer,

except with dogged premeditation, would always work in so elegantly obscure and elliptical a fashion as the author of "A rose is a rose"—never in a more conventional manner. To be one hundred per cent roundabout one must be pure genius —and nobody is that good.

On the whole, I think my wife is right: the poets could be a little clearer and still not get over on to ground which is unsuitably solid. I am surprised that I have gone on this way about them. I too am cursed with diligence. I bite my pencil and stare at a marked calendar.

W. H. Auden
✳ 1907-

Born in England and educated at Oxford, Wystan Hugh Auden came to the United States in the 1930s, and has become a prominent and influential member of our literary society. Having written and published verse here and in England, he was well equipped to provide for the ANCHOR REVIEW *in 1957 this informed estimate of the differences between poetry composed in his homeland and his adopted country.*

The Anglo-American Difference

One often hears it said that only in this century have the writers of the United States learned to stand on their own feet and be truly American, that, previously, they were slavish imitators of British literature. Applied to the general reading public and academic circles this has a certain amount of truth, but so far as the writers themselves are concerned it is quite false. From Bryant on there is scarcely one American poet whose work, if unsigned, could be mistaken for that of an Englishman. What English poet, for example, in need of emotive place names for a serious poem, would have employed neither local names nor names famous in history or mythology, but names made up by himself as Poe did in *Ulalume?* Would an English poet have conceived the idea of writing a scientific cosmological prose poem and of prefacing it thus: "I offer this Book of Truths, not in its character of truth-teller, but for the Beauty that abounds in its Truth, constituting it true. . . . *What I here propound is true:* therefore it cannot die. . . . Nevertheless it is as a Poem only that I wish this work to be judged after I am dead." (Poe: Preface to *Eureka*.)

In the same year, 1855, appeared *Maud, The Song of Hiawatha,* and the first edition of *Leaves of Grass:* no two poets could have been more unlike each other than Longfellow and Whitman—such diversity is in itself an American phenomenon—yet, when compared with Tennyson, each in his own way shows characteristics of the New World. Tennyson and Longfellow were both highly skillful technicians in conventional forms and both were regarded by their countrymen as the respectable mouthpieces of their age, and yet, how different they are. There is much in Tennyson that Longfellow would never have dared to write, for the peculiar American mixture of Puritan conscience and democratic license can foster in some cases a genteel horror of the coarse for which no Englishman has felt the need. On the other hand Longfellow had a curiosity about the whole of European literature compared with which Tennyson, concerned only with the poetry of his own land and the classical authors on whom he was educated, seems provincial. Even if there had been Red Indians roaming the North of Scotland, unsubjugated and un-

assimilable, one cannot imagine Tennyson sitting down to write a long poem about them and choosing for it a Finnish meter. Leaving aside all questions of style, there is a difference between Tennyson's *Ode on the Death of the Duke of Wellington* and Whitman's elegy for President Lincoln *When Lilacs Last in the Door-yard Bloom'd* which is significant. Tennyson, as one would expect from the title of his poem, mourns for a great public official figure, but it would be very hard to guess from the words of Whitman's poem that the man he is talking about was the head of a State; one would naturally think that he was some close personal friend, a private individual.

To take one more example: two poets, contemporaries, both women, both religious, both introverts preoccupied with renunciation—Christina Rossetti and Emily Dickinson—could anyone imagine either of them in the country of the other? When I try to fancy such translations, the only Americans I could possibly imagine as British are minor poets with a turn for light verse like Lowell and Holmes, and the only British poets who could conceivably have been Americans are eccentrics like Blake and Hopkins.

Normally, in comparing the poetry of two cultures, the obvious and easiest point at which to start is with a comparison of the peculiar characteristics, grammatical, rhetorical, rhythmical, of their respective languages, for even the most formal and elevated styles of poetry are more conditioned by the spoken tongue, the language really used by the men of that country, than by anything else. In the case of British and American poetry, however, this is the most subtle difference of all, and the hardest to define. Any Englishman, with a little effort, can learn to pronounce "the letter *a* in psalm and calm . . . with the sound of *a* in candle," to say *thumbtacks* instead of *drawing pins* or twenty-*of*-one instead of twenty-*to*-one, and discover that, in the Middle West, *bought* rhymes with *hot;* but he will be as far from speaking American English as his Yankee cousin who comes to England will be from speaking the King's. No dramatist in either country who has introduced a character from the other side, has, to my knowledge, been able to make his speech convincing. What the secret of the differences is I cannot put my finger on; William Carlos Williams who has thought more than most about this problem, says that "Pace is one of its most important manifestations," and to this one might add another, Pitch. If undefinable, the difference is, however, immediately recognizable by the ear, even in verse where the formal conventions are the same.

He must have had a father and a mother—
In fact I've heard him say so—and a dog,
As a boy should, I venture; and the dog
Most likely, was the only man who knew
    him.
A dog, for all I know, is what he needs
As much as anything right here today
To counsel him about his disillusions,
Old aches, and parturitions of what's com-
    ing,—
A dog of orders, an emeritus,
To wag his tale at him when he comes home,
And then to put his paws up on his knees
And say, "For God's sake, what's it all
    about?"

    E. A. ROBINSON
    *Ben Jonson Entertains a Man from
    Stratford*

Whatever this may owe to Browning, the fingering is quite different and un-British. Again, how American in rhythm as well as in sensibility is this stanza by Robert Frost.

    But no, I was out for stars:
    I would not come in.
    I meant not even if asked;
    And I hadn't been.

Until quite recently an English writer, like one of any European country, could presuppose two conditions, a nature which was mythologized, humanized, on the whole friendly, and a human society which had become in time, whatever succession of invasions it may have suffered in the past, in race and religion more or less homogeneous and in which most people lived and died in the locality where they were born.

Christianity might have deprived Aphrodite, Apollo, the local genius, of their divinity, but as figures for the forces of nature, as a mode of thinking about the creation, they remained valid for poets and their readers alike. Descartes might reduce the non-human universe to a mechanism, but the feelings of Europeans about the sun and moon, the cycle of the seasons, the local landscape remained unchanged. Wordsworth might discard the mythological terminology, but the kind of relation between nature and man which he described was the same personal one. Even when nineteenth-century biology began to trouble men's minds with the thought that the universe might be without moral values, their immediate experience was still of a friendly and lovable nature. Whatever their doubts and convictions about the purpose and significance of the universe as a whole, Tennyson's Lincolnshire or Hardy's Dorset were places where they felt completely at home, landscapes with faces of their own which a human being could recognize and trust.

But in America, neither the size, condition, nor climate of the continent encourage such intimacy. It is an unforgettable experience for anyone born on the other side of the Atlantic to take a plane journey by night across the United States. Looking down he will see the lights of some town like a last outpost in a darkness stretching for hours ahead, and realize that, even if there is no longer an actual frontier, this is still a continent only partially settled and developed, where human activity seems a tiny thing in comparison to the magnitude of the earth, and the equality of men not some dogma of politics or jurisprudence but a self-evident fact. He will behold a wild nature compared with which the landscapes of Salvator Rosa are as cozy as Arcadia and which cannot possibly be thought of in human or personal terms. If Henry Adams could write:

When Adams was a boy in Boston, the best chemist in the place had probably never heard of Venus except by way of scandal, or of the Virgin except as idolatry. . . . The force of the Virgin was still felt at Lourdes, and seemed to be as potent as X-rays; but in America neither Venus nor Virgin ever had value as force—at most as sentiment. No American had ever been truly afraid of either.

the reason for this was not simply because the Mayflower carried iconophobic dissenters but also because the nature which Americans, even in New England, had every reason to fear could not possibly be imagined as a mother. A white whale whom man can neither understand nor be understood by, whom only a madman like Gabriel can worship, the only relationship with whom is a combat to the death by which a man's courage and skill are tested and judged, or the great buck who answers the poet's prayer for "someone else additional to him" in *The Most of It* are more apt symbols. Thoreau, who certainly tried his best to become intimate with nature, had to confess

> I walk in nature still alone
> And know no one,
> Discern no lineament nor feature
> Of any creature.
>
> Though all the firmament
> Is o'er me bent,
> Yet still I miss the grace
> Of an intelligent and kindred face.

> I still must seek the friend
> Who does with nature blend,
> Who is the person in her mask,
> He is the man I ask . . .

Many poets in the Old World have become disgusted with human civilization, but what the earth would be like if the race became extinct they cannot imagine; an American like Robinson Jeffers can quite easily, for he has seen with his own eyes country as yet untouched by history.

In a land which is fully settled, most men must accept their local environment or try to change it by political means; only the exceptionally gifted or adventurous can leave to seek his fortune elsewhere.

In America, on the other hand, to move on and make a fresh start somewhere else is still the normal reaction to dissatisfaction or failure. Such social fluidity has important psychological effects. Since movement involves breaking social and personal ties, the habit creates an attitude toward personal relationships in which impermanence is taken for granted.

One could find no better illustration of the difference between the Old and the New World than the respective conclusions of *Oliver Twist* and *Huckleberry Finn*, the heroes of which are both orphans. When Oliver is at last adopted by Mr. Brownlow, his fondest dream, to have a home, to be surrounded by familiar friendly faces, to receive an education, is realized. Huck is offered adoption too, significantly by a woman and not a man, but refuses because he knows she will try to "civilize" him, and lights out by himself for the West. Jim, who has been his "buddy" in friendship far closer than any employed by Oliver, is left behind like an old shoe, just as in *Moby Dick* Ishmael becomes a blood brother of Queequeg and then forgets all about him. Naturally the daydream of the lifelong comrade in adventure often appears in American literature:

Camerado, I give you my hand!
I give you my love more precious than money,
I give you myself before preaching or law;
Will you give me yourself? will you come travel with me?
Shall we stick by each other as long as we live?

WHITMAN
Song of the Open Road

But no American seriously expects such a dream to come true.

To be able at any time to break with the past, to move and keep on moving, lessens the significance not only of the past but also of the future, and minimizes the importance of political action. A European may be a conservative who thinks that the right form of society has been discovered already, or a liberal who believes it is in process of being realized, or a revolutionary who thinks that, by reason or force, he must convince the others that he is right; he may be an optimist about the future or a pessimist. None of these terms apply accurately to an American, for his profoundest feeling toward the future is not that it will be better or worse but that it is unpredictable, that all things, good and bad, will change. No failure is irredeemable, no success a final satisfaction. Democracy is the best form of government, not because men will necessarily lead better or happier lives under it, but because it permits constant experiment; a given experiment may fail, but the people have a right to make their own mistakes. America has always been a country of amateurs where the professional, that is to say, the man who claims authority as a member of an elite which knows the law in some field or other, is an object of distrust and resentment. (In the field with which we are here concerned, one symptom of this is that curious American phenomenon, the class of "Creative Writing.")

Amerika, du hast es besser
Als unser Kontinent, das alte,
Hast keine verfallene Schloesser
Und keine Basalte.

Goethe, I presume, was also thinking of the absence of violent political clashes. This is a subject about which, in relation to their histories, the English and the American cherish opposite fictions. Between 1533 and 1688 the English went through a succession of revolutions in which a church was imposed on them by the engines of the State, one king was executed and another deposed, yet they prefer to forget it and pretend that the social structure of England is the product of organic peaceful growth. The Americans on the other hand like to pretend that what was only a successful war of secession was a genuine revolution (1829, though bloodless, was a more revolutionary year than 1776). There is indeed an American mentality which is new and unique in the world, but it is the product less of conscious political action than of nature, of the new and unique environment of the American continent. Even the most revolutionary feature of the Constitution, the separation of Church and State, was a recognition of a condition which had existed since the first settlements were made by various religious denominations whose control of the secular authority could only be local. From the beginning America had been a pluralist state and pluralism is incompatible with an Established Church. The *Basalte* in American history, the Civil War, might indeed be called Counter-Revolution, for it was fought primarily on the issue not of slavery but for unity, that is, not for a freedom but for a limitation on freedom, to ensure that the United States should remain pluralist and not disintegrate into an anarchic heap of fragments. Pluralist and experimental: in place of *verfallene Schloesser* America has ghost towns and the relics of New Jerusalems which failed.

Whatever one may feel about Whitman's poetry, one is bound to admit that he was the first clearly to recognize what the conditions were with which any future American poet would have to come to terms.

Plenty of songs had been sung—beautiful, matchless songs—adjusted to other lands than these. . . . The Old World has had the poems of myths, fictions, feudalism, conquest, caste, dynastic wars, and splendid exceptional characters, which have been great; but the New World needs the poems of realities and science and of the democratic average and basic equality. . . . As for native American individuality, the distinctive and ideal type of Western character (as consistent with the operative and even money-making features of United States humanity as chosen knights, gentlemen and warriors were with the ideals of the centuries of European feudalism), it has not yet appeared. I have allowed the stress of my poems from beginning to end to bear upon American individuality and assist it —not only because that is a great lesson in Nature, amid all her generalising laws, but as counterpoise to the levelling tendencies of Democracy.

The last sentence makes it quite clear that by the "average" hero who was to replace the "knight" Whitman did not mean the mediocre, but the individual whose "exceptional character" is not derived from birth, education, or occupation, and that he is aware of how difficult it is for such an individual to appear without the encouragement which comes from membership in some elite.

What he does not say, and perhaps did not realize, is that in a democracy the status of the poet himself is changed. However fantastic in the light of present-day realities his notion may be, every European poet, I believe, still instinctively thinks of himself as a clerk, a member of a professional brotherhood, with a certain social status irrespective of the number of his readers (in his heart of hearts the audience he desires and expects are those who govern the country), and taking his place in an unbroken historical succession. Here in the States, poets have never had or imagined they had such a status, and it is up to each individual poet to justify his existence by offering a unique product. It would be grossly unjust to assert that there are fewer lovers of poetry in the New World than in the Old—in how many places abroad could a poet demand and receive a substantial sum for reading his work aloud?—but there is a tendency, perhaps, in the former, for audiences to be drawn rather by name than by a poem, and for a poet, on his side, to demand approval for his work not simply because it is good but because it is *his*. To some degree every American poet feels that the whole responsibility for contemporary poetry has fallen upon his shoulders, that he is a literary aristocracy of one. "Tradition," wrote T. S. Eliot in a famous essay, "cannot be inherited, and if you want it you must obtain it by great labour." I do not think that any European critic would have said just this. He would not, of course, deny that every poet must work hard, but the suggestion in the first half of the sentence that no sense of tradition is acquired except by conscious effort would seem strange to him.

There are advantages and disadvantages in both attitudes. A British poet can take writing more for granted and so write with a lack of strain and over-earnestness. American poetry has many tones, a man talking to himself or one intimate friend, a prophet crying in the wilderness, but the easy-going tone of a man talking to a group of his peers is rare; for a "serious" poet to write light verse is frowned on in America and if, when he is asked why he writes poetry, he replies, as any European poet would, "For fun," his audience is shocked. (In this Cambridge-on-the-Cam is perhaps a few leagues nearer Gambier, Ohio, than is Oxford-on-Thames.)

On the other hand the British poet is in much greater danger of becoming lazy, or academic, or irresponsible. (One comes across some passages, even in very fine English poetry which make one think; "Yes, very effective but does he believe what he is saying?"; in American poetry such passages are extremely rare.) The first thing that strikes a reader about the best American poets is how utterly unlike each other they are. Where else in the world, for example, could one find seven poets of approximately the same generation so different as Ezra Pound, W. C. Williams, Vachel Lindsay, Marianne Moore, Wallace Stevens, E. E. Cummings and Laura Riding? The danger for the American poet is not of writing like everybody else but of crankiness and a parody of his own manner.[1]

Plato said that when the modes of music change the walls of the city are shaken. It might be truer to say, perhaps, that a change in the modes gives warning of a shaking of the walls in the near future. The social strains which later break out in political action are first experienced by artists as a feeling that the current modes of expression are no longer

[1] The undeniable appearance in the States during the last fifteen years or so of a certain literary conformity, of a proper and authorized way to write poetry, is a new and disquieting symptom, which I cannot pretend to be able to explain fully. The role of the American college as a patron of poets has been discussed a good deal both here and in England. Those who criticize it, often with some reason, fail to suggest a better alternative. It would be nice if the colleges could ask no more from the poets in return for their keep than occasional pieces, a Commencement Day masque or an elegy on a deceased trustee; if that is too much to ask, then the poets themselves should at least demand that they give academic courses in the literature of the dead and refuse to have anything to do with modern literature or courses in writing. There has been a vast output of critical studies in contemporary poetry, some of them first-rate, but I do not think that, as a rule, a poet should read or write them.

capable of dealing with their real concerns. Thus, when one thinks of "modern" painting, music, fiction, or poetry, the names which immediately come to mind as its leaders and creators are those of persons who were born roughly between 1870 and 1890 and who began producing their "new" work before the outbreak of World War I in 1914, and in poetry and fiction, at least, American names are prominent.

When a revolutionary break with the past is necessary, it is an advantage not to be too closely identified with any one particular literature or any particular cultural group. Americans like Eliot and Pound, for example, could be as curious about French or Italian poetry as about English and could hear the poetry of the past, like the verse of Webster, freshly in a way that for an Englishman, trammeled by traditional notions of Elizabethan blank verse, would have been difficult.

Further, as Americans, they were already familiar with the dehumanized nature and the social leveling which a technological civilization was about to make universal and with which the European mentality was unprepared to deal. After his visit to America De Toqueville made a remarkable prophecy about the kind of poetry which a democratic society would produce.

I am persuaded that in the end democracy diverts the imagination from all that is external to man and fixes it on man alone. Democratic nations may amuse themselves for a while with considering the productions of nature, but they are excited in reality only by a survey of themselves. . . .

The poets who lived in aristocratic ages have been eminently successful in their delineations of certain incidents in the life of a people or a man; but none of them ever ventured to include within his performances the destinies of mankind, a task which poets writing in democratic ages may attempt. . . .

It may be forseen in like manner that poets living in democratic times will prefer the delineation of the passions and ideas to that of persons and achievements. The language, the dress, and the daily actions of men in democracies are repugnant to conceptions of the ideal. . . . This forces the poet constantly to search below the external surface which is palpable to the senses, in order to read the inner soul; and nothing lends itself more to the delineation of the idea than the scrutiny of the hidden depths in the immaterial nature of man. . . . The destinies of mankind, man himself taken aloof from his country and his age and standing in the presence of Nature and of God, with his passions, his doubts, his rare prosperities and inconceivable wretchedness, will become the chief, if not the sole, theme of poetry.

If this be an accurate description of the poetry we call modern, then one might say that America has never known any other kind.

Donald Hall

✳ 1928-

Donald Hall is a young poet, formerly a Junior Fellow at Harvard University and editor of the HARVARD ADVOCATE, *who now teaches at the University of Michigan. The following essay, subtitled "Notes on the Past Fifteen Years in America" first appeared in the* ANCHOR REVIEW *in 1955.*

The New Poetry

The old days are the best, and they are usually twenty or thirty years ago. They are the time when the men now in their vocal middle age were emerging from colleges and entering their professions. Today we worship the twenties; most undergraduates, following their intellec-

tual leaders, regret the disappearance of speakeasies, raccoon coats, and Jay Gatsby. Their teachers of poetry sometimes seem to consider that literature ended when Hart Crane drowned in the Gulf of Mexico. Though the new poets receive kindness and help, because they are poets, they are not thought to be very good. We are living, it is said, in an uncreative age.

All generations are not equally productive or intelligent, and perhaps in the perspective of a hundred years the creativity of the teens and the twenties will put the mid-century to shame. It is early to tell. Nevertheless, it seems probable that many men are blind to the virtues of contemporary literary effort merely because it does not accord with the styles of twenty or thirty years ago. Experimentalism has become a vested interest; now it is not Pound who shouts, "Make it new!", but the weekly news magazines. *Time*, which reported rumors that *The Waste Land* was a hoax when the poem was first printed, now displays T. S. Eliot on its cover; but in its book reviews *Time* shows that it has not really changed its philistine policy, for the new poets are scorned as "academic." Even a sympathetic critic like Malcolm Cowley, in *The Literary Situation*, can call poets "timid, formal, and correct," in comparison to the vigorous critics.

The new poetry in America seems to me an extremely impressive body of work. Not all the older generation have found it lacking. T. S. Eliot has published Robert Lowell and Richard Wilbur in England (Theodore Roethke has been published there by John Lehmann); he has printed the best, and avoided several undeserved reputations. Louise Bogan, as *The New Yorker's* poetry reviewer, has been both sympathetic and judicious. Perhaps some of the critics have simply failed to keep up. Cowley, who reports that "poetry seems to be retreating," mentions not a single new poet in his entire book, though he discusses novelist after novelist. He mentions Amy Lowell, but not Robert.

So let us look at what has been done in the last fifteen years and is being done now—the poetry which we are as inclined to overrate as our elders to underrate; the poetry which, in thirty years, we may well be lamenting the decline of— let us examine the contemporary period which will become the good old days.

2

Robert Lowell seems to me the best of the younger poets of the language. He was born in Boston in 1917, a member of the Lowell family which produced the poets Amy and James Russell, a president of Harvard, and many of the founders and conservatives of New England society. This heritage, and his break with it by his conversion to Catholicism, is the background against which many of his poems take place. His first book, *Land of Unlikeness*, was printed in an edition of 250 copies by the Cummington Press in 1944. His second book, *Lord Weary's Castle* (1946), was accorded the Pulitzer Prize. His most recent volume was *The Mills of the Kavanaughs* in 1951.

Lowell understands the world in terms of a fundamental opposition; Randall Jarrell's review of *Lord Weary's Castle* described it well. Always weighing on him are the constrictive forces of rigidity, sin, cruelty, the "Old Law," and his Puritan ancestors. But there exists, also, the possibility of freedom, of release, toward which the soul struggles. In the poems, the struggle is sometimes rewarded and sometimes frustrated. Even the Church, his scheme of liberation from capitalist-Protestant New England, sometimes is discovered to be the law and family again—like a nightmare in which the saving friend is the enemy in disguise. Though he can admire his ancestors, who "quartered the Leviathan's fat flanks/And fought the British Lion to his knees,"

these are the same men who "fenced their gardens with the Redman's bones," and their guilt has been inherited. The poet must say:

Mother, for these three hundred years or
    more
Neither our clippers nor our slavers reached
The haven of your peace in this Bay
    State . . .

and ask blessings from the Mother of God, blessings to raise him from the dead like Lazarus. Yet, unlike Lazarus, the poet is doomed to die and be raised again in a perpetual recurrence, as the opposition of constriction and release shifts from pole to pole.

Land of Unlikeness consisted of twenty-one poems. In *Lord Weary's Castle*, eight of these poems were revised and reprinted, and thirteen abandoned, mainly, it would seem, for metrical reasons. The growth, in technique and character, between the first book and the second is extraordinary. R. P. Blackmur's criticism of *Land of Unlikeness*, which was well taken, cannot be made of *Lord Weary's Castle;* the meter is no longer applied, but employed. Lowell is in control, and has established a kind of desperate equilibrium between the chaos of the world he usually hates and the loved form of the art by which he displays it.

As with most men, Lowell's occasional errors are only his felicities made extreme. The phrase about Mary's "scorched, blue thunderbreasts of love," which attempts passion but achieves bathos, is close to the genuinely intense emotions of these lines, from "New Year's Day":

In the snow
The kitten heaved its hindlegs, as if fouled,
And died. We bent it in a Christmas box
And scattered blazing weeds to scare the
    crow
Until the snake-tailed sea-winds coughed
    and howled

For alms outside the church whose double
  locks
Wait for St. Peter, the distorted key.
Under St. Peter's bell the parish sea

Swells with its smelt into the burlap shack
Where Joseph plucks his hand-lines like a
  harp,
And hears the fearful *Puer natus est*
Of Circumcision, and relives the wrack
And howls of Jesus whom he holds. How
  sharp
The burden of the Law before the beast:
Time and the grindstone and the knife of
  God.
The Child is born in blood, O child of blood.

where no word is even faintly out of
tone. Here is terror within decorum. The
cruelty which Lowell insists upon is
demonstrated by all the resources of his
technique.

Lowell's violence and individuality
come almost as much from prosody as
from imagery and idea. Though his syllabic regularity is extreme, his licenses
within the count of syllables are numerous. He is fond of the eccentric caesura;
time and again he ends a sentence after
the ninth syllable, and begins a new one
with the rhyme word. He is also fond of
medial inversion, and his enjambment,
often coupled with early or late caesura,
is more extreme than any other syllabic
English poet. His assonances abound:
"Time and the grindstone and the knife
of God." Harsh and consonantal mono-
syllables like "gouge" and "hacked," so
important to the obvious violence of his
diction, also serve to clot the line and
slow its pace. Initial inversion occurs in
about twenty per cent of the lines I have
counted, a relatively huge proportion.
One of the results of the combination of
eccentric caesura, enjambment, and initial
inversion is that the end rhymes are less
insistent, less hit by the voice; in writing
the run-over couplet, such a faculty is
valuable. Lowell's rhyming is extremely
skillful, and its origin is as much in his

metrical habits as in his avoidance of
rhyme clichés. His stanzas are often
rhymed irregularly, and he uses short
lines in a context of decasyllables most
effectively, in a manner sometimes reminiscent of "Lycidas." The master of
variation within rigidity, he can make his
lines rush, slow, hurtle, and come to a
quiet halt, always fully under his control.
It is pointless to list Lowell's best poems,
because the choice is too difficult.

"Between the Porch and the Altar,"
towards the end of *Lord Weary's Castle,*
begins a change in direction for Lowell's
verse. He had worked with the monologue before, but the speaker, even when
disguised, had spoken with a grandilo-
quence associated only with Robert
Lowell. The newer poem changes tone.
Lowell is not conversational, but the
bardic rhetoric, and the machinery of
Greek deities and Moby Dick, thin out
when he speaks under a dramatic mask.
Violence still exists, but now it is achieved
more in the action than in the diction;
his characteristic prosody changes little.
Monologue techniques, continued in most
of *The Mills of Kavanaughs,* are particularly expert in the third section of "Between the Porch and the Altar," which is
called "Katharine's Dream":

I walk through snow into St. Patrick's yard.
Black nuns with glasses smile and stand on
  guard
Before a bulkhead in a bank of snow,
Whose charred doors open, as good people
  go
Inside by twos to the confessor. One
Must have a friend to enter there, but none
Is friendless in this crowd, and the nuns
  smile.
I stand aside and marvel; for a while
The winter sun is pleasant and it warms
My heart with love for others, but the
  swarms
Of penitents have dwindled. I begin
To cry and ask God's pardon of our sin.
Where are you? You were with me and are
  gone.
All the forgiven couples hurry on

To dinner and their nights, and none will
stop.
I run about in circles till I drop
Against a padlocked bulkhead in a yard
Where faces redden and the snow is hard.

The Mills of the Kavanaughs contains
only seven poems, and the title poem
occupies over half of the volume. Without a flaw are two shorter narratives in
this book: "Mother Marie Therese" and
"Falling Asleep over the Aeneid." The
former is Lowell's most successful dramatic monologue, a true fulfillment of
that genre. A sequence of irregularly
rhymed sonnets, called "Crossing the
Alps," appeared in the *Kenyon Review*
in 1953, and is another of his best poems.
Other recent poems have been sonnets,
and there has been no narrative poem
since *The Mills of the Kavanaughs*. The
new lyrics resemble Lowell's later, narrative style more than his earlier short
poems.

Though I have noticed some changes
within Lowell's evolving style, its consistency is no less apparent. His prosody
does not change radically, and his work
as a whole remains poetic in a way
against which the vers librists rebelled
early in the century. It never does but
rhyme; the one unrhymed poem in *Land
of Unlikeness* disappeared. The verse is
rhetorical, and built on a firm syllabic
structure. Lowell repeats intricate stanza
forms, and employs sonnets and couplets.
Yet Lowell's success with tricks and
stage properties makes them cease to be
tricks and stage properties. We stop
watching the man on the stunt bar and
listen to the utterance of his individual
voice.

Lowell has much of the Old Law in
him. He could not write of it so well if
it were not digging its claws into him.
One might say that Lowell forces the
Law upon himself in his syllabic strictness, and within this rigidity, this self-
created confinement, hurls himself like
an animal at the bars, achieving the def-

inition of an emotion in the struggle of
interior opposites.

3

Many poets began publishing in the
forties and fifties who belong to no particular group, but whose work demands
attention. I regret that I lack the space to
attempt to do justice to the poetry of
Elizabeth Bishop, Jean Garrigue, and
Peter Viereck, each of whom requires
adequate discussion, or to mention the
work of E. L. Mayo, Hyam Plutzik,
Daniel G. Hoffman, or Howard Nemerov.
I can only list their names and hope that
the reader may seek them out. A few
others can be touched upon.

A very good poet is Theodore Roethke.
From the precise statements of *Open
House* (1941) through the sensuous wilderness of *Praise to the End!* (1951) he
has arrived at the wild precision of his
most recent verse. Many of Roethke's
new admirers tend to overlook the excellence of Roethke's first book. In it are
such finely worked stanzas as this, from
"The Adamant":

> Thought does not crush to stone.
> The great sledge drops in vain.
> Truth never is undone;
> Its shafts remain.

Some lyrics in *The Lost Son* (1948) are
written in the closely worked forms of the
earlier book, but they are different in
spirit. "My Papa's Waltz" has the stanza:

> The whiskey on your breath
> Could make a small boy dizzy;
> But I hung on like death:
> Such waltzing was not easy.

The looser feeling, the charm of "My
Papa's Waltz" was not present in the
earlier work, which is predominantly intellectual. More characteristic of *The Lost
Son* and *Praise to the End!* is a minute
attention to objects, usually flowers.
Roethke, who grew up in a greenhouse,
exercises negative capability and finds

himself inside the flower struggling down
with its roots and up with its leaves:

I can hear, underground, that sucking and
    sobbing,
In my veins, in my bones I feel it,—
The small waters seeping upward,
The tight grains parting at last.
When sprouts break out,
Slippery as fish,
I quail, lean to beginnings, sheath-wet.

Never, in Roethke's "free verse," is there
a hint of the arbitrary; every line is glued
in place, as fixed as in his regular forms.
The long poem "Praise to the End!" is
autobiographical; it is a snark hunt of a
poem, "an effort to be born." Roethke's
ear sustains it gloriously on an auditory
level; he is more accomplished outside
conventional forms than any poet since
Wallace Stevens. Too, there is description of sensuous fact, in this period of
Roethke's development, which no other
poet of recent years has approached; it is
like H. D., but it is better. His lyrics since
Praise to the End! have abandoned the
individualized forms of that poem, and
have returned to the strictness of *Open
House.* The difference, however, is that
Roethke is wilder within the exact form
than he was in 1941; his language is
more open to varied stylistic devices. A
recent poem, "Words for the Wind," appeared in *Botteghe Oscure,* and contained the stanza:

The shallow stream runs slack;
The wind creaks slowly by;
Out of a nestling's beak
Comes a tremulous cry
I cannot answer back;
A shape from deep in the eye,
That woman I saw in a stone,
Keeps pace when I walk alone.

It is one of his very best poems. *The
Waking* (1953) is a collection of the best
poems from Roethke's previous books,
and is extremely impressive. His work
has grown, and there is every reason to
believe that it will continue to grow.

J. V. Cunningham has written very
little, and there have been no radical
changes in his work. His tight, controlled,
intellectual, unassailable poems and epigrams have accrued slowly but for good
and all. Cunningham is a master of the
use of abstract language in poetry. Plain
statement, so bare that there can be nothing to detract from the poem's rational
progression, becomes powerful through
the honesty, compression and intensity of
the intelligence conveyed. He has written
many epigrams, some of them satirical,
and others personal statements. In the
latter category are these:

In whose will is our peace? Thou happiness,
Thou ghostly promise, to thee I confess
Neither in thine nor love's nor in that form
Disquiet hints at have I yet been warm;
And if I rest not till I rest in thee
Cold as thy grace, whose hand shall comfort
    me?

and:

On a cold night I came through the cold
    rain
and false snow to the wind shrill on your
    pane
With no hope and no anger and no fear:
Who are you? and with whom do you sleep
    here?

His three books of verse, *The Helmsman*
(1942), *The Judge Is Fury* (1947), and
Doctor Drink (1950), are not well
known, but his reputation will certainly
increase. At his best, he cannot be surpassed.

Part of the reason for the toleration,
rather than the appreciation, of the new
poetry in America, is the presence of
several reputations which have outgrown
the talents to which they are ascribed. I
am thinking especially of Randall Jarrell.
Jarrell's first publication was in New Direction's first number (1940) of the *Five
Young American Poets* series. John Berryman was in the same volume; Karl Shapiro, John Frederick Nims, and Jean
Garrigue were in subsequent issues. Jarrell's verse, like Berryman's, was prom-

ising. But it seems to me that the flaws in his early poems have become the mannerisms of his later work: a conscious sentimentality—flung, evidently, in the face of sophistication—and a conscious carelessness, a deliberate disregard of the means of control, whether in "free" or "regular" verse. His war poems have done the most to give him the reputation he now possesses, but it is difficult to understand why these particular verses have been so celebrated; perhaps they seem more realistic, concentrating as they do on the more obvious horrors. Bathos and sentimentality are what they contain for me. "The Death of the Ball Turret Gunner" is probably the best known American war poem, and yet the last line of this five-line poem is, "When I died they washed me out of the turret with a hose." His post-war poetry has not improved. Perhaps, in the careful use of a careless style, there is implicit an assumption that improvisation suggests sincerity, that artistry denies reality; Richard Wilbur's use of precision almost against reality seems to me productive of a much more pleasurable and intelligent body of poems. John Berryman has been overshadowed by Jarrell. He has published little in recent years, but the long "Homage to Mistress Bradstreet," which appeared in *Partisan Review* in 1953, is the best poem he has written, and a very good one. His next book is eagerly to be awaited.

4

Naming schools among contemporary poets is a dangerous and not altogether serious process. Still, it is a convenient way to organize material, and is reprehensible only when the metaphor is taken as more than a metaphor. The poets already discussed cannot be considered similar except in time and place, but some other poets of the last fifteen years have responded to their experience (of the world, of literature) in somewhat similar ways; mutual imitation is not implied, but

mutual stylistic ancestry often seems to exist.

The Wurlitzer Wits were a school which seems to have closed down. I am thinking of the early verse of John Ciardi, John Frederick Nims, John Malcolm Brinnin, and Karl Shapiro. The nickname seems apt for two reasons: the Wurlitzer style tried to include among its images, which were nearly always visual, the paraphernalia of ordinary life, especially, it sometimes seems, objects in the general class of jukeboxes; Wurlitzers were, a few years ago, the dominant machine of that sort. Also these poets' sensibilities resembled jukeboxes because it seemed possible to drop an impression in a slot and, after a pause for clicking and whirring, hear a poem step out in five-stress lines. Now the Wits have gone their separate ways, but until the late forties they were the most numerous school of poets. They were all Sons of Wystan; their witty descriptions of contemporary objects and events inside lyrical forms emanate from a side of Auden.

John Ciardi's first book, *Homeward to America*, was published in 1940, when the author was only twenty-four. *Other Skies* was published in 1947, and contained many war poems, perhaps the best war poetry so far written by an American who was in combat. In "V-J Day," "the dead were homing," and:

On the tallest day in time we saw them coming,
Wheels jammed and flaming on a metal sea.

Ciardi has published two more books of equal or greater quality, and a particularly accomplished translation of the *Inferno*. In his most recent book of poems, he is feeling his way toward a new style; like the other poets of the old school, he has seemed unsatisfied with his earlier methods. His poetry is becoming more apocalyptic, and he may be progressing toward his truest manner.

John Frederick Nims in his first book, *The Iron Pastoral,* wrote many amusing poems with subjects typical of the Wurlitzer Wits: "Dollar Bill" ("The feathered thing of silver-grey and jade"), "Penny Arcade," "Movie," "Colt Automatic," "Football Game," and a series called "Foto-Sonnets." These are poems of description, witty and enjoyable; yet each of them remains a tour de force, a literary curiosity. They never become more serious than their subject matter. Most of his second book, *A Fountain in Kentucky,* is the unsuccessful attempt to employ new methods of writing. John Malcolm Brinnin was capable of more variation in style than the others of his group, but he wrote often a kind of poem reminiscent of the contemporaries whom I have mentioned. In his early verse especially, he was more political than the others. Most of Brinnin's newer poems have moved away from wit and the celebration of contemporary objects into forms linguistically and intellectually more complex.

Karl Shapiro is the best of these poets, and one of the very best poets now writing. He alone of the poets originally Wurlitzer Wits seems to have endured the slump and emerged to write poems thoroughly better than his early work. *Poems 1940–1953* is an impressive selected volume, particularly in the most recent poems. A real growth is visible in his work, and he has demonstrated the extent of his talent by the skill of his change.

Most of Shapiro's early poems, like "Buick," "The Fly," and "Drug Store," display an exuberance of description which is attractive in energy and fertility, but not in intelligence or meaningful dexterity of poetic form. Shapiro at this time seemed anti-intellectual, and even anti-poetic; he wished to write amusingly about common objects, and he did. But when poets insist that poetry must include all manner of objects, even garbage cans, it generally means that they wish to write only about garbage cans. "The Fly" begins, "O hideous little bat, the size of snot. . . ." For many readers, the earlier style remains Shapiro's essence and achievement, but to others the poems seem as dated as 1941's Buick; their wit is sometimes childish, their exuberance undirected. Not all of Shapiro's early verse follows such a pattern, of course. In some he attempts serious statement, and sometimes he writes quieter poems closer to his more recent work, like "Six Religious Lyrics" from *Person, Place and Thing.* The early poem "Scyros" is deservedly well known and unlike any other poem by the author.

Shapiro's style began to change in *V-Letter* (1944). In his newest poems, those in *Trial of a Poet* and the previously uncollected poems in *Poems 1940–1953,* there is increased intellection, inwardness, and verbal decorum, words jump out of their context now by their supreme accuracy, not by shock or contrast. "Adam and Eve," "A Calder," "Boy-Man," "Recapitulations," "Ego," "The Minute," and "The Phenomenon" are all excellent examples of Shapiro's new wisdom and delicacy. Here is a part of "Glass Poem":

And I look up as one who looks through glass
And sees the thing his soul clearly desires,
Who stares until his vision flags and tires,
But from whose eye the image fails to pass;

Until a wish crashes the vitreous air
And comes to your real hands across this space,
Thief-like and deeply cut to touch your face,
Dearly, most bitterly to touch your hair. . . .

But the sun stands and the hours stare like brass
And day flows thickly into permanent time,
And toward your eyes my threatening wishes climb
Where you move through a sea of solid glass.

Shapiro's concentration on the intelligence seems to bring him closer to reality than his former nearsighted attention to Buicks and drugstores. His often elegant plainness is closer to the poetry being written by Richard Wilbur than it is to his earlier work.

5

Most of the good poems being written by the youngest poets today can be considered the products of a School of Elegance. In the novel, American letters has swung from the bare toughness of the early Hemingway to the ornament and compassion of William Styron; in poetry from the austerity of the vers librists to the lyrical elegance of Richard Wilbur. In Karl Shapiro's work there has been a shift from wit to artifice. Poets younger than Shapiro have often, like Wilbur, begun their writing with a pursuit of the defined and exquisite, the elegant and perfectly artificial construction. Characteristic of these poets, insofar as they are a group, are tight metrical and intellectual structures. Most of their poems are the development of an idea or a scene constructed to contain an idea; occasionally they will write a perfect simple lyric of the emotions, a kind of verse recently neglected in English. An example is Wilbur's "Then" of which the second stanza is:

> The leaf first learned of years
> One not forgotten fall;
> Of lineage now, and loss
> These latter singers tell,
> Of a year when birds now still
> Were all one choiring call
> Till the unreturning leaves
> Imperishably fell.

Richard Wilbur, born in 1921, is the youngest of the leading poets of the day; his reputation is exceeded only by Robert Lowell's. Critics who are irritated by his finesse usually reveal themselves to be the conservatives of experimentalism, or the romantics of imitative fragmentation. Wilbur's subject matter is often common ex-

perience; it is in the pose between the lines that we sense the erection of form as a statement about the world, a statement related to dandyism. He defends and attacks this position and its corollaries openly (the best defense is "Ceremony"), but remains effectively in the position all the same. To read Wilbur is to experience a tremendous delight in his precision, his unfailing decorum, his cleverness, and the subtle play of his mind. No one since Herrick has written more exactly.

When suffering is a subject in a Wilbur poem, it is understood and discussed, not presented in the act. Robert Lowell's poems often seem to have been squeezed out of him, foot by foot, by the pressure of his suffering. Wilbur's poems present us with the picture of the poet meditating on a problem; and the finished thought, formed so that it affirms its shape as a necessary part of its meaning, is the finished poem. The finished thought will not pretend to solve all our problems, but it may with both justice and neatness suggest our quandary. The cowboy-soldier Tywater dies:

> And what to say of him, God knows.
> Such violence. And such repose.

Wilbur's first book, *The Beautiful Changes*, was very nearly flawless, but the later *Ceremony* displayed a greater range within his style. His arch, conversational manner, in the beginning of "The Pardon," becomes intense and nearly apocalyptic when the action requires it. In "Then," he writes the pure lyric, and in many other poems he argues an idea to a logical conclusion. Objects, for Wilbur, are usually more true when imagined (or, in "Ceremony," "lightly hid") than when seen. "In the Elegy Season" has the lines:

> . . . And now the envious mind
>
> Which could not hold the summer in my head
> While bounded by that blazing circumstance

Parades these barrens in a golden trance,
Remembering the wealthy season dead,

And by an autumn inspiration makes
A summer all its own. . . .

In "Epistemology," Wilbur satirizes his position:

We milk the cow of the world, and as we do
We whisper in her ear, "You are not true."

And in "A World Without Objects Is a Sensible Emptiness," he calls the idealistic habits of his mind, "The tall camels of the spirit." He uses camels at first because they are images of self-denial, since they go without water for long periods; but at the end they become the camels plodding with the wise men toward Bethlehem, which here is a symbol of reality. Such careful "rigging" of his poems is customary. They are seldom discursive, though many of them pose as conversational; they are contrived toward their precise conclusion.

Like Lowell, and like the other members of his own school, Wilbur uses for his purposes mythological figures, inversions, and other old-fashioned poeticisms. Equally Wilbur can make use of slang, but somehow with inverted commas. The whole of speech is open to him, and yet within the artifice of his form his words take on a definite decorum. Wilbur has published many poems in magazines since *Ceremony*. Among the best are "Beasts," and "A Voice from Under the Table"; in the last especially there is a successful attempt to move away from the elegant pose. Much as we enjoy the elegant Wilbur, perhaps it is healthy for a poet to try new ways of speaking. Wherever he moves from here, Wilbur's survival as a poet of infinite delight is secure.

A number of young poets are writing in manners which may be called generally elegant, though most of them are distinct individuals. Barbara Howes and William Jay Smith are two, but there are several others less known or more necessary to discuss in limited space.

Howard Moss is an extremely fine craftsman, capable of a delicacy which is intellectually rigorous. *The Wound and the Weather*, his first book, contains little as excellent as the majority of the poems in *The Toy Fair* (1954). "A Balcony with Birds," in the latter, has these lines:

The eye must follow form, but from this height,
I see how softly summer parries weight
Till everything alive weighs less and less
And, thinly felt, the weighted consciousness,

No thicker than green leaves, or the meridian,
Grows thinner, even, to absorb the sun.

Moss is introspective; like Wilbur he is sometimes concerned with appearance and reality. He is less satisfying formally than Wilbur, but he is sometimes capable of a greater range. "Elegy for My Father" and "Venice" are particularly excellent poems from *The Toy Fair*, a book which has established Moss high among contemporary poets.

Anthony Hecht is most elegant of all elegants. *A Summoning of Stones*, which appeared in 1954, contains many fine poems which improvise, brilliantly, in the manner of a court jester; his words seem to come easily, and yet they are both apt and attractive. He adopts a subject and examines it and plays with it with the greatest skill. His discursive talents betray him sometimes into over-length, but for the most part, they produce only delight and delightful intelligence. *A Summoning of Stones* is the best first book of verse since Wilbur's *The Beautiful Changes*; there is no reason to believe that Hecht will not have the grace and adaptability to write successive volumes of an even greater quality.

James Merrill is a poet of a most elegant talent, but whose achievements are so far limited. Sometimes a lack of technical resources fails him; sometimes an unsupported claim of profundity hurts the poem's ending. His verbal gift is unsurpassed, and the power to sustain it may come later.

Adrienne Cecile Rich published her first book, *A Change of World*, at twenty-one. Though it was a good first book, it is not remarkable that her subsequent poems in the magazines have shown an impressive growth. What was an over-neatness in the book has become a justified precision of mind and technique in most of her later work. The poems are as formal as their predecesors, but now they include within themselves some of the terrors against which their form is addressed. "The Insomniacs" has the lines:

And each, wherever he has been,
Must know his hand before his face,
Must crawl back into his own skin
As in the darkness after crime
The thief can hear his breath again,
Resume the knowledge of his limbs,
And how the spasm goes and comes
Under the bones that cage his heart.

She will prove with her second book to have reached real stature as a poet. Cecil Hemley's *Porphyry's Journey* appeared in 1951. Still relatively unknown, his literary reputation, too, is due for a considerable advance. He is capable of elegant playfulness, à la Wilbur and Hecht, but most characteristic of his subject matter is serious religious commentary. "He Must Be Born Again" ends:

O Virgin, God is sucking at your breast,
But He will bring you little joy or rest.
O wise men, now divinity is here,
He has no Word to make His meaning clear.

Hemley and Rich share a tendency toward the rhetorically powerful, which does not characterize most of the poets with whom I have grouped them. They employ, within their precise forms, forceful diction without formalistic irony.

Louis Simpson's *The Arrivistes* was published in 1949. His second book will appear in the second volume of Scribner's *Poets of Today* series in September. It will probably be the best book of the year.

He has immense powers of stylistic variation, from the ballad swing of "The Ash and the Oak," through the quiet exactness of "The Battle," the triple meters of "The Hero," and the pure lyricism of "Song." The last stanza of "The Battle" is:

Most clearly of that battle I remember
The tiredness in eyes, how hands looked thin
Around a cigarette, and the bright ember
Would pulse with all the life there was
    within.

Perhaps Simpson will be the poet of the Second World War; it is a consistent subject. Like Auden he seems to enjoy the challenge of working in a variety of forms and tones. His range is wide, and his work consistently finished.

W. S. Merwin is the most celebrated of the very young poets, and deserves much of his acclaim. He is smooth and intelligent and careful. His two books, *A Mask for Janus* and *The Dancing Bears*, are even in quality. He retells myths, sometimes well, but sometimes he draws a final deduction which is forced. The quiet security of his language is admirable:

Was there truly in that afternoon
No sorcery, when the leaves between us
In the October garden fell like words
Through the long sun before the gathering
    winter . . . .

Technically, his work is extremely interesting. Unlike the other poets I have called elegant, his meter is not entirely syllabic. Many of his poems are accentual, and include a wide possibility of variation in short lines with much juxtaposition of stresses. These difficult meters are closely controlled, and he retains a pervasive refinement of tone.

6

A survey so short is bound to be unjust. Some poets who have not yet published volumes, but whose first books are sure to be very good, are Isabella Gardner,

James Wright, Edgar Bowers, and Philip Booth.

Attacks on the new poetry have three main resources. Poets are ridiculed as teachers: the patronage system established by the universities supports many of the poets I have mentioned. Is there any reason why an opium den is intrinsically more poetic than a Senior Common Room? In this attack is only the romantic cliché of the poet as starving revolutionary—a cliché contradicted by the contemporary poet who lives in a suburb and lectures to undergraduates.

The poets are sometimes accused of abandoning their native language, represented by William Carlos Williams, for the foreign ornaments of rhyme and meter. I am not sure that closeness to common speech is a test of the worth of poetry, but it seems to me that American speech, especially the more primitive, is characteristically ornamental. Little rhymes, alliteration, hyperbole, and other figures of speech abound; the austerity of much imagism, the deadness of anarchist verse like Kenneth Rexroth's, seem at least as far from common speech as the stanzas of Anthony Hecht.

The third attack is the most interesting. The poets are sometimes considered the practitioners of a decadent "magazine verse" for the sensible reason that most of them publish in magazines which formerly specialized in bad poetry. Yet it is the magazines that have raised their standards, not the poets who have lowered theirs. Because poetry now attempts clarity, and because popular taste has been educated to the point where it

wants to like good poetry, the big magazines are buying good poems. Especially *The New Yorker,* but also, the *Atlantic, Harper's, Mademoiselle, Harper's Bazaar,* and even *The Ladies' Home Journal* have bought poems by good American poets. The literary quarterlies, of course, continue their function, for some of the best poetry will never appear in the big magazines; Robert Lowell's best work has appeared in the *Kenyon Review. Poetry* exercises catholicity and is an invaluable institution. *New World Writing* and *discovery,* each selling over 100,000 copies, are an entirely new kind of literary magazine. The Yale Series of Younger Poets, whose long list is disappointing, has lately improved. Adrienne Rich and W. S. Merwin are both Yale Younger Poets.

The new poetry in America has already produced an extraordinary number of good poems; it is early to use the word great, but I am inclined to think that it would be justified. I think that the majority of Robert Lowell's poems will survive, along with the best poems of Richard Wilbur, Theodore Roethke, J. V. Cunningham, and Karl Shapiro; perhaps among the other poets I have mentioned is a talent which will surpass anything we have known. We are living in no uncreative age. A patronage system, in the universities and the foundations, helps keep the poets alive, and magazines compete to print them. There is the excitement of accomplishment and potential accomplishment in American poetry today. Maybe we are only at the beginning, and not at the end, of a poetic golden age.

PROSE FICTION

Edgar Allan Poe

✳ 1809-1849

Poe's review of the second edition of Hawthorne's TWICE TOLD TALES *in* GRAHAM'S MAGAZINE *for May, 1842, from which the following extract is reprinted, marks an important step in the development of the short story. Though not many of his contemporaries nor all of his successors responded to Poe's doctrine of single effect and controlled economy of words, it is remembered as our first attempt to explain the characteristics of a literary form in which, perhaps more than any other, American writers have excelled.*

The Tale Proper

The tale proper, in our opinion, affords unquestionably the fairest field for the exercise of the loftiest talent, which can be afforded by the wide domains of mere prose. Were we bidden to say how the highest genius could be most advantageously employed for the best display of its own powers, we should answer, without hesitation—in the composition of a rimed poem, not to exceed in length what might be perused in an hour. Within this limit alone can the highest order of true poetry exist. We need only here say, upon this topic, that, in almost all classes of composition, the unity of effect or impression is a point of the greatest importance. It is clear, moreover, that this unity cannot be thoroughly preserved in productions whose perusal cannot be completed at one sitting. We may continue the reading of a prose composition, from the very nature of prose itself, much longer than we can persevere, to any good purpose, in the perusal of a poem. This latter, if truly fulfilling the demands of the poetic sentiment, induces an exaltation of the soul which cannot be long sustained. All high excitements are necessarily transient. Thus a long poem is a paradox. And, without unity of impression, the deepest effects cannot be brought about. Epics were the offspring of an imperfect sense of Art, and their reign is no more. A poem *too* brief may produce a vivid, but never an intense or enduring impression. Without a certain continuity of effort—without a certain duration or repetition of purpose—the soul is never deeply moved. There must be the dropping of the water on the rock. . . . Extreme brevity will degenerate into epigrammatism; but the sin of extreme length is even more unpardonable *In medio tutissimus ibis* [You will go most safely in the middle course].

Were we called upon, however, to designate that class of composition which, next to such a poem as we have suggested, should best fulfil the demands of high genius—should offer it the most advantageous field of exertion—we should unhesitatingly speak of the prose tale. . . . We allude to the short prose narrative, requiring from a half-hour to one or two hours in its perusal. The ordinary novel is objectionable, from its length, for reasons already stated in substance. As it cannot be read at one sitting, it deprives itself, of course, of the immense force derivable from *totality*. Worldly interests intervening during the pauses of perusal, modify, annul, or counteract, in a greater or less degree, the impressions

229

of the book. But simple cessation in reading, would, of itself, be sufficient to destroy the true unity. In the brief tale, however, the author is enabled to carry out the fullness of his intention, be it what it may. During the hour of perusal the soul of the reader is at the writer's control. There are no external or extrinsic influences—resulting from weariness or interruption.

A skilful literary artist has constructed a tale. If wise, he has not fashioned his thoughts to accommodate his incidents: but having conceived, with deliberate care, a certain unique or single *effect* to be wrought out, he then invents such incidents—he then combines such events as may best aid him in establishing this preconceived effect. If his very initial sentence tend not to the outbringing of this effect, then he has failed in his first step. In the whole composition there should be no word written, of which the tendency, direct or indirect, is not to the one preëstablished design. And by such means, with such care and skill, a picture is at length painted which leaves in the mind of him who contemplates it with a kindred art, a sense of the fullest satisfaction. The idea of the tale has been presented unblemished, because undisturbed; and this is an end unattainable by the novel. Undue brevity is just as exceptionable here as in the poem; but undue length is yet more to be avoided.

We have said that the tale has a point of superiority even over the poem. In fact, while the *rhythm* of this latter is an essential aid in the development of the poet's highest idea—the idea of the Beautiful—the artificialities of this rhythm are an inseparable bar to the development of all points of thought or expression which have their basis in *Truth*. But Truth is often, and in very great degree, the aim of the tale. Some of the finest tales are tales of ratiocination. Thus the field of this species of composition, if not in so elevated a region on the mountain

of Mind, is a table-land of far vaster extent than the domain of the mere poem. Its products are never so rich, but infinitely more numerous, and more appreciable by the mass of mankind. The writer of the prose tale, in short, may bring to his theme a vast variety of modes or inflections of thought and expression—(the ratiocinative for example, the sarcastic, or the humorous) which are not only antagonistical to the nature of the poem, but absolutely forbidden by one of its most peculiar and indispensable adjuncts; we allude, of course, to rhythm. It may be added here, *par parenthèse*, that the author who aims at the purely beautiful in a prose tale is laboring at great disadvantage. For Beauty can be better treated in the poem. Not so with terror, or passion, or horror, or a multitude of such other points. And here it will be seen how full of prejudice are the usual animadversions against those *tales of effect*, many fine examples of which were found in the earlier numbers of Blackwood. The impressions produced were wrought in a legitimate sphere of action, and constituted a legitimate although sometimes an exaggerated interest. They were relished by every man of genius: although there were found many men of genius who condemned them without just ground. The true critic will but demand that the design intended be accomplished, to the fullest extent, by the means most advantageously applicable.

William Gilmore Simms
✳ 1806-1870

After Cooper, William Gilmore Simms of Charleston, South Carolina, was perhaps the best known writer of prose fiction in the United States before the Civil War. In thirty-some volumes he wrote historical romances of the colonial and Revolutionary periods and stirring fiction laid in the frontier border country of the Southern west. Best known of his romances is THE YEMASSEE *(1835) to which the following remarks were prefaced.*

The Romance as Epic

The question briefly is—What are the standards of the modern Romance? What is the modern Romance itself? The reply is immediate. The modern Romance is the substitute which the people of the present day offer for the ancient epic. The form is changed; the matter is very much the same; at all events, it differs much more seriously from the English novel than it does from the epic and the drama, because the difference is one of material, even more than fabrication. The reader who, reading Ivanhoe, keeps Richardson and Fielding beside him, will be at fault in every step of his progress. The domestic novel of those writers, confined to the felicitous narration of common and daily occurring events, and the grouping and delineation of characters in ordinary conditions of society, is altogether a different sort of composition; and if, in a strange doggedness, or simplicity of spirit, such a reader happens to pin his faith to such writers alone, circumscribing the boundless horizon of art to the domestic circle, the Romances of Maturin, Scott, Bulwer, and others of the present day, will be little better than rhapsodical and intolerable nonsense.

When I say that our Romance is the substitute in modern times for the epic or the drama, I do not mean to say that they are exactly the same things, and yet, examined thoroughly, the differences between them are very slight. These differences depend on the material employed, rather than upon the particular mode in which it is used. The Romance is of loftier origin than the Novel. It approximates the poem. It may be described as an amalgam of the two. It is only with those who are apt to insist upon poetry as verse, and to confound rhyme with poetry, that the resemblance is unapparent. The standards of the Romance—take such a story, for example, as the Ivanhoe of Scott, or the Salathiel of Croly—are very much those of the epic. It invests individuals with an absorbing interest—it hurries them rapidly through crowding and exacting events, in a narrow space of time—it requires the same unities of plan, of purpose, and of harmony of parts, and it seeks for its adventures among the wild and wonderful. It does not confine itself to what is known, or even what is probable. It grasps at the possible; and placing a human agent in hitherto untried situations, it exercises its ingenuity in extricating him from them, while describing his feelings and his fortunes in his progress. The task has been well or ill done, in proportion to the degree of ingenuity and knowledge which the romancer exhibits in carrying out the details, according to such proprieties as are called for by the circumstances of the story. These proprieties are the standards set up at his starting, and to which he is required religiously to confine himself.

Nathaniel Hawthorne
✳ 1804-1864

Though not, as we have seen, the first to make the distinction, Nathaniel Hawthorne spoke most effectively for his time of differences between the romance and the novel, a subject which we discover in Richard Chase's essay on pp. 270–279 below is with us still. Haw-

thorne wrote nowhere at length on the matter, but these four extracts from prefaces to what we think of as his novels, but which he preferred to call romances, present the substance of his ideas. The best way to understand them is to discover how he put them into practice in his own fiction.

The Romance and the Novel: Four Extracts

FROM "THE CUSTOM HOUSE," INTRODUCTION TO *The Scarlet Letter* (1850):

. . . It was a folly, with the materiality of this daily life pressing so intrusively upon me, to attempt to fling myself back into another age; or to insist on creating the semblance of a world out of airy matter, when, at every moment, the impalpable beauty of my soap-bubble was broken by the rude contact of some actual circumstance. The wiser effort would have been to diffuse thought and imagination through the opaque substance of today, and thus to make it a bright transparency; to spiritualize the burden that began to weigh so heavily; to seek, resolutely, the true and indestructible value that lay hidden in the petty and wearisome incidents, and ordinary characters, with which I was not conversant. The fault was mine. The page of life that was spread before me seemed dull and commonplace, only because I had not fathomed its deeper import. A better book than I shall ever write was there; leaf after leaf presenting itself to me, just as it was written out by the reality of the fleeting hour, and vanishing as fast as written, only because my brain wanted the insight and my hand the cunning to transcribe it. At some future day, it may be, I shall remember a few scattered fragments and broken paragraphs, and write them down, and find the letters turn to gold upon the page.

PREFACE TO *The House of the Seven Gables* (1851):

When a writer calls his work a Romance, it need hardly be observed that he wishes to claim a certain latitude, both as to its fashion and material, which he would not have felt himself entitled to assume had he professed to be writing a Novel. The latter form of composition is presumed to aim at a very minute fidelity, not merely to the possible, but to the probable and ordinary course of man's experience. The former—while, as a work of art, it must rigidly subject itself to laws, and while it sins unpardonably so far as it may swerve aside from the truth of the human heart—has fairly a right to present that truth under circumstances, to a great extent, of the writer's own choosing or creation. If he think fit, also, he may so manage his atmospherical medium as to bring out or mellow the lights and deepen and enrich the shadows of the picture. He will be wise, no doubt to make a very moderate use of the privileges here stated, and, especially, to mingle the Marvelous rather as a slight, delicate, and evanescent flavor, than as any portion of the actual substance of the dish offered to the public. He can hardly be said, however, to commit a literary crime even if he disregard this caution.

In the present work, the author has proposed to himself—but with what success, fortunately, it is not for him to judge —to keep undeviatingly within his immunities. The point of view in which this tale comes under the Romantic definition lies in the attempt to connect a bygone time with the very present which is flitting away from us. It is a legend prolonging itself, from an epoch now gray in the distance, down into our own broad daylight, and bringing along with it some of its legendary mist, which the reader, according to his pleasure, may either disregard, or allow it to float almost imperceptibly about the characters and events for the sake of a picturesque effect. The narrative, it may be, is woven of so humble a texture as to require this advantage, and, at the same time, to render it the more difficult of attainment.

PREFACE TO *The Blithedale Romance* (1852):

. . . In the old countries, with which fiction has long been conversant, a certain conventional privilege seems to be awarded to the romancer; his work is not put exactly side by side with nature; and he is allowed a license with regard to every-day probability, in view of the improved effects which he is bound to produce thereby. Among ourselves, on the contrary, there is as yet no such Faery Land, so like the real world, that, in a suitable remoteness, one cannot well tell the difference, but with an atmosphere of strange enchantment, beheld through which the inhabitants have a propriety of their own. This atmosphere is what the American romancer needs. In its absence, the beings of imagination are compelled to show themselves in the same category as actual living mortals; a necessity that generally renders the paint and pasteboard of their composition but too painfully discernible.

PREFACE TO *The Marble Faun* (1859):

. . . Italy, as the site of his Romance, was chiefly valuable to him as affording a sort of poetic or fairy precinct, where actualities would not be so terribly insisted upon as they are, and must needs be, in America. No author, without a trial, can conceive of the difficulty of writing a romance about a country where there is no shadow, no antiquity, no mystery, no picturesque and gloomy wrong, nor anything but a commonplace prosperity, in broad and simple daylight, as is happily the case with my dear native land. It will be very long, I trust, before

romance-writers may find congenial and easily handled themes, either in the annals of our stalwart republic, or in any characteristic and probable events of our individual lives. Romance and poetry, ivy, lichens, and wall-flowers, need ruin to make them grow.

Oliver Wendell Holmes
✳ 1809-1894

Dr. Holmes was a better appreciator than critic of literature. He knew what he liked and usually why he liked it. Remarks on tendencies among writers of his time are scattered through THE AUTOCRAT OF THE BREAKFAST TABLE *of 1858,* THE PROFESSOR AT THE BREAKFAST TABLE *of 1860, and* THE POET AT THE BREAKFAST TABLE *of 1872; the following, in which an aging man of polite letters considers what seem to him unfortunate trends set in motion by younger men, appeared in* OVER THE TEACUPS *in 1891.*

Realism in Literature

It seems to me . . . that the great additions which have been made by realism to the territory of literature consist largely of swampy, malarious, ill-smelling patches of soil which had previously been left to reptiles and vermin. It is perfectly easy to be original by violating the laws of decency and the canons of good taste. The general consent of civilized people was supposed to have banished certain subjects from the conversation of well bred people and the pages of respectable literature. There is no subject, or hardly any, which may not be treated of at the proper time, in the proper place, by the fitting person, for the right kind of listener or reader. But when the poet or the storyteller invades the province of the man of science, he is on dangerous ground. I need say nothing of the blunders he is pretty sure to make. The imaginative writer is after effects. The scientific man is after truth. Science is decent, modest; does not try to startle, but to instruct. The same scenes and objects which outrage every sense of delicacy in the storyteller's highly colored paragraph can be read without giving offense in the chaste language of the physiologist or the physician. . . . The subject which in the hands of the scientific student is handled decorously,—reverently, we might almost say,—becomes repulsive, shameful, and debasing in the unscrupulous manipulations of the low-bred man of letters.

I confess that I am a little jealous of certain tendencies in our American literature, which led one of the severest and most outspoken of our satirical fellow-countrymen, no longer living to be called to account for it, to say, in a moment of bitterness, that the mission of America was to vulgarize mankind. I myself have sometimes wondered at the pleasure some Old World critics have professed to find in the most lawless freaks of New World literature. I have questioned whether their delight was not like that of the Spartans in the drunken antics of their Helots. But I suppose I belong to another age, and must not attempt to judge the present by my old-fashioned standards.

Mark Twain

✴ 1835-1910

Mark Twain's notion of successful fiction was very different from Poe's, and seems to have lasted longer: Ernest Hemingway once said that all American literature begins with THE ADVENTURES OF HUCKLE-

BERRY FINN. *The first and the third of the extracts reprinted below are from "How to Tell a Story" and "What Paul Bourget Thinks of Us," both of which first appeared in the 1890s and were collected in the volume called* HOW TO TELL A STORY AND OTHER ESSAYS *in 1899; the second is from the first volume of* MARK TWAIN'S AUTOBIOGRAPHY, *published in 1924.*

Some Remarks on Fiction: Three Extracts

HOW TO TELL A STORY

I do not claim that I can tell a story as it ought to be told. I only claim to know how a story ought to be told, for I have been almost daily in the company of the most expert story-tellers for many years.

There are several kinds of stories, but only one difficult kind—the humorous. I will talk mainly about that one. The humorous story is American, the comic story is English, the witty story is French. The humorous story depends for its effect upon the *manner* of the telling; the comic story and the witty story upon the *matter*.

The humorous story may be spun out to great length, and may wander around as much as it pleases, and arrive nowhere in particular; but the comic and witty stories must be brief and end with a point. The humorous story bubbles gently along, the others burst.

The humorous story is strictly a work of art—high and delicate art—and only an artist can tell it; but no art is necessary in telling the comic and the witty story; anybody can do it. The art of telling a humorous story—understand, I mean by word of mouth, not print—was created in America, and has remained at home.

The humorous story is told gravely; the teller does his best to conceal the fact that he even dimly suspects there is anything funny about it; but the teller of the comic story tells you beforehand that this is one of the funniest things he has ever heard, then tells it with eager delight, and is the first person to laugh when he gets through. And sometimes, if he has had good success, he is so glad and happy that he will repeat the "nub" of it and glance around from face to face, collecting applause, and then repeat it again. It is a pathetic thing to see.

Very often, of course, the rambling and disjointed humorous story finishes with a nub, point, snapper, or whatever you like to call it. Then the listener must be alert, for in many cases the teller will divert attention from that nub by dropping it in a carefully casual and indifferent way, with the pretence that he does not know it is a nub. . . .

But the teller of the comic story does not slur the nub; he shouts it at you— every time. And when he prints it, in England, France, Germany, and Italy, he italicizes it, puts some whooping exclamation-points after it, and sometimes explains it in a parenthesis. All of which is very depressing, and makes me want to renounce joking and lead a better life. . . .

To string incongruities and absurdities together in a wandering and sometimes purposeless way, and seem innocently unaware that they are absurdities, is the basis of the American art. . . .

NARRATIVE IS A DIFFICULT ART

. . . With the pen in one's hand, narrative is a difficult art; narrative should flow as flows the brook down through the hills and the leafy woodlands, its course changed by every boulder it comes across and by every grass-clad gravelly spur that projects into its path; its surface broken, but its course not stayed by rocks and gravel on the bottom in the shoal places; a brook that never goes straight

for a minute, but *goes,* and goes briskly, sometimes ungrammatically, and sometimes fetching a horseshoe three-quarters of a mile around, and at the end of the circuit flowing within a yard of the path it traversed an hour before; but always *going,* and always following at least one law, always loyal to that law, the law of *narrative,* which *has no law.* Nothing to do but make the trip; the how of it is not important, so the trip is made.

With a pen in hand the narrative stream is a canal; it moves slowly, smoothly, decorously, sleepily, it has no blemish except that it is all blemish. It is too literary, too prim, too nice; the gait and style and movement are not suited to narrative. That canal stream is always reflecting; it is its nature, it can't help it. Its slick shiny surface is interested in everything it passes along the banks cows, foliage, flowers, everything. And so it wastes a lot of time in reflections.

THE NATIVE NOVELIST

. . . A foreigner can photograph the exteriors of a nation, but I think that is as far as he can get. I think that no foreigner can report its interior—its soul, its life, its speech, its thought. I think that a knowledge of these things is acquirable in only one way—not two or four or six —*absorption;* years and years of unconscious absorption; years and years of intercourse with the life concerned; of living it, indeed; sharing personally in its shames and prides, its joys and griefs, its loves and hates, its prosperities and reverses, its shows and shabbinesses, its deep patriotisms, its whirlwinds of political passion, its adorations—of flag, and heroic deed, and the glory of the national name. Observation? Of what real value is it? One learns peoples through the heart, not the eyes or the intellect.

There is only one expert who is qualified to examine the soul and the life of a people and make a valuable report—

the native novelist. This expert is so rare that the most populous country can never have fifteen conspicuously and confessedly competent ones in stock at one time. This native specialist is not qualified to begin work until he has been absorbing during twenty-five years. How much of his competency is derived from conscious "observation"? The amount is so slight that it counts for next to nothing in the equipment. Almost the whole capital of the novelist is the slow accumulation of *un*conscious observation—absorption. The native expert's intentional observation of manners, speech, character, and ways of life can have value, for the native knows what they mean without having to sipher out the meaning. But I should be astonished to see a foreigner get the right meanings, catch the elusive shades of these subtle things. Even the native novelist becomes a foreigner, with a foreigner's limitations, when he steps from the state whose life he has not lived. Bret Harte got his California and his Californians by unconscious absorption, and put them into his tales alive. But when he came from the Pacific to the Atlantic and tried to do Newport life from study—conscious observation—his failure was absolutely monumental. Newport is a disastrous place for the unacclimated observer, evidently.

To return to novel-building. Does the native novelist try to generalize the nation? No, he lays plainly before you the ways and speech and life of a few people grouped in a certain place—his own place—and that is one book. In time he and his brethren will report to you the life and the people of a whole nation—the life of a group in a New England village; in a New York village; in a Texan village; in an Oregon village; in villages in fifty states and territories; then the farm-life in fifty states and territories; a hundred patches of life and groups of people in a dozen widely separated cities. And the Indians will be attended to; and the cowboys; and the gold and silver miners; and the negroes; and the Idiots and Congressmen; and the Irish, the Germans, the Italians, the Swedes, the French, the Chinamen, the Greasers; and the Catholics, the Methodists, the Presbyterians, the Congregationalists, the Baptists, the Spiritualists, the Mormons, the Shakers, the Quakers, the Jews, the Campbellites, the infidels, the Christian Scientists, the Mind-Curists, the Faith-Curists, the Train-robbers, the White Caps, the Moonshiners. And when a thousand able novels have been written, *there* you have the soul of the people, the speech of the people; and not anywhere else can these be had. And the shadings of character, manners, ambitions, will be infinite.

William Dean Howells
✳ 1837-1920

Howells is sometimes remembered as the "reticent realist" because, though he spoke in critical essays of the necessity for literature to be true to life, his own novels presented nothing more exciting, one of his later contemporaries once said, than the romance of a broken teacup or the thrill of a walk down the block. Recent critics have understood him better, discovering that he had achieved a significant success in the difficult task of representing ordinary and uneventful life. The following remarks first appeared in HARPER'S MAGAZINE *and in 1891 were collected in a volume of essays called* CRITICISM AND FICTION.

Subjects For American Fiction

One of the great newspapers the other day invited the prominent American authors to speak their minds upon a point in the theory and practice of fiction which had already vexed some of them. It was the question of how much or how little the American novel ought to deal with certain facts of life which are not usually talked of before young people, and especially young ladies. Of course the question was not decided, and I forget just how far the balance inclined in favor of a larger freedom in the matter. But it certainly inclined that way; one or two writers of the sex which is somehow supposed to have purity in its keeping (as if purity were a thing that did not practically concern the other sex, preoccupied with serious affairs) gave it a rather vigorous tilt to that side. In view of this fact it would not be the part of prudence to make an effort to dress the balance; and indeed I do not know that I was going to make any such effort. But there are some things to say, around and about the subject, which I should like to have some one else say, and which I may myself possibly be safe in suggesting.

One of the first of these is the fact, generally lost sight of by those who censure the Anglo-Saxon novel for its prudishness, that it is really not such a prude after all; and that if it is sometimes apparently anxious to avoid those experiences of life not spoken of before young people, this may be an appearance only. Sometimes a novel which has this shuffling air, this effect of truckling to propriety, might defend itself, if it could speak for itself, by saying that such experiences happened not to come within its scheme, and that, so far from maiming or mutilating itself in ignoring them, it was all the more faithfully representative of the tone of modern life in dealing with love that was chaste, and with passion so honest that it could be openly spoken of before the tenderest society bud at dinner. It might say that the guilty intrigue, the betrayal, the extreme flirtation even, was the exceptional thing in life, and unless the scheme of the story necessarily involved it, that it would be bad art to lug it in, and as bad taste as to introduce such topics in a mixed company. It could say very justly that the novel in our civilization now always addresses a mixed company, and that the vast majority of the company are ladies, and that very many, if not most, of these ladies are young girls. If the novel were written for men and for married women alone, as in continental Europe, it might be altogether different. But the simple fact is that it is not written for them alone among us, and it is a question of writing, under cover of our universal acceptance, things for young girls to read which you would be put out-of-doors for saying to them, or frankly giving notice of your intention, and so cutting yourself off from the pleasure—and it is a very high and sweet one—of appealing to these vivid, responsive intelligences, which are none the less brilliant and admirable because they are innocent.

One day a novelist who liked, after the manner of other men, to repine at his hard fate, complained to his friend, a critic, that he was tired of the restriction he had put upon himself in this regard; for it is a mistake, as can be readily shown, to suppose that others impose it. "See how free those French fellows are!" he rebelled. "Shall we always be shut up to our tradition of decency?"

"Do you think it's much worse than being shut up to their tradition of indecency?" said his friend.

Then that novelist began to reflect, and he remembered how sick the invariable motive of the French novel made him. He perceived finally that, convention for convention, ours was not only more tolerable, but on the whole was truer to life, not only to its complexion, but also to its texture. No one will pretend that there is not vicious love beneath the surface of our society; if he did, the fetid explosions of the divorce trials would refute him; but if he pretended that it was in any just sense characteristic of our society, he could be still more easily refuted. Yet it exists, and it is unquestionably the material of tragedy, the stuff from which intense effects are wrought. The question, after owning this fact, is whether these intense effects are not rather cheap effects. I incline to think they are, and I will try to say why I think so, if I may do so without offence. The material itself, the mere mention of it, has an instant fascination; it arrests, it detains, till the last word is said, and while there is anything to be hinted. This is what makes a love intrigue of some sort all but essential to the popularity of any fiction. Without such an intrigue the intellectual equipment of the author must be of the highest, and then he will succeed only with the highest class of readers. But any author who will deal with a guilty love intrigue holds all readers in his hand, the highest with the lowest, as long as he hints the slightest hope of the smallest potential naughtiness. He need not at all be a great author; he may be a very shabby wretch, if he has but the courage or the trick of that sort of thing. The critics will call him "virile" and "passionate"; decent people will be ashamed to have been limned by him; but the low average will only ask another chance of flocking into his net. If he happens to be an able writer, his really fine and costly work will be unheeded, and the lure to the appetite will be chiefly remembered. There may be other qualities which make reputations for other men, but in his case they will count for nothing. He pays this penalty for his success in that kind; and every one pays some such penalty who deals with some such material. It attaches in like manner to the triumphs of the writers who now almost form a school among us, and who may be said to have established themselves in an easy popularity simply by the study of erotic shivers and fervors. They may find their account in the popularity, or they may not; there is no question of the popularity.

But I do not mean to imply that their case covers the whole ground. So far as it goes, though, it ought to stop the mouths of those who complain that fiction is enslaved to propriety among us. It appears that of a certain kind of impropriety it is free to give us all it will, and more. But this is not what serious men and women writing fiction mean when they rebel against the limitations of their art in our civilization. They have no desire to deal with nakedness, as painters and sculptors freely do in the worship of beauty; or with certain facts of life, as the stage does, in the service of sensation. But they ask why, when the conventions of the plastic and histrionic arts liberate their followers to the portrayal of almost any phase of the physical or of the emotional nature, an American novelist may not write a story on the lines of Anna Karenina or Madame Bovary. Sappho they put aside, and from Zola's work they avert their eyes. They do not condemn him or Daudet, necessarily, or accuse their motives; they leave them out of the question; they do not want to do that kind of thing. But they do sometimes wish to do another kind, to touch one of the most serious and sorrowful problems of life in the spirit of Tolstoi and Flaubert, and they ask why they may not. At one time, they remind us, the Anglo-Saxon novelist did deal with such problems—Defoe in his spirit, Richardson in his, Goldsmith in his. At what moment did our fiction lose this privilege? In what fatal hour did the Young Girl arise and seal the lips of Fiction, with a touch of her finger, to some of the most vital interests of life?

Whether I wished to oppose them in their aspiration for greater freedom, or whether I wished to encourage them, I should begin to answer them by saying that the Young Girl had never done anything of the kind. The manners of the novel have been improving with those of its readers; that is all. Gentlemen no longer swear or fall drunk under the table, or abduct young ladies and shut them in lonely country-houses, or so habitually set about the ruin of their neighbors' wives, as they once did. Generally, people now call a spade an agricultural implement; they have not grown decent without having also grown a little squeamish, but they have grown comparatively decent; there is no doubt about that. They require of a novelist whom they respect unquestionable proof of his seriousness, if he proposes to deal with certain phases of life; they require a sort of scientific decorum. He can no longer expect to be received on the ground of entertainment only; he assumes a higher function, something like that of a physician or a priest, and they expect him to be bound by laws as sacred as those of such professions; they hold him solemnly pledged not to betray them or abuse their confidence. If he will accept the conditions, they give him their confidence, and he may then treat to his greater honor, and not at all to his disadvantage, of such experiences, such relations of men and women as George Eliot treats in Adam Bede, in Daniel Deronda, in Romola, in almost all her books; such as Hawthorne treats in the Scarlet Letter; such as Dickens treats in David Copperfield; such as Thackeray treats in Pendennis, and glances at in every one of his fictions; such as most of the masters of English fiction have at some time treated more or less openly. It is quite false or quite mistaken to suppose that our novels have left untouched these most important realities of life. They have not only made them their stock in trade; they have kept a true perspective in regard to them; they have relegated them in their pictures of life to the space and place they occupy in life itself, as we know it in England and America. They have kept a correct proportion, knowing perfectly well that unless the novel is to be a map, with everything scrupulously laid down in it, a faithful record of life in far the

greater extent could be made to the exclusion of guilty love and all its circumstances and consequences.

I justify them in this view not only because I hate what is cheap and meretricious, and hold in peculiar loathing the cant of the critics who require "passion" as something in itself admirable and desirable in a novel, but because I prize fidelity in the historian of feeling and character. Most of these critics who demand "passion" would seem to have no conception of any passion but one. Yet there are several other passions: the passion of grief, the passion of avarice, the passion of pity, the passion of ambition, the passion of hate, the passion of envy, the passion of devotion, the passion of friendship; and all these have a greater part in the drama of life than the passion of love, and infinitely greater than the pasion of guilty love. Wittingly or unwittingly, English fiction and American fiction have recognized this truth, not fully, not in the measure it merits, but in greater degree than most other fictions.

Bret Harte
✳ 1836-1902

The effective literary career of Francis Bret Harte was extremely short, extending over the few years at the end of the 1860s when such stories as "The Luck of Roaring Camp" and "The Outcasts of Poker Flat" swept him to popularity which he was not able to maintain, but his influence on fiction, particularly in its most popular varieties, has extended even to the adult western on television today. In writing of "The Rise of the Short Story" for the London CORNHILL MAGAZINE *in 1899, he spoke with feeling and authority about a literary movement to which he had given important impetus.*

The Rise of the Short Story

As it has been the custom of good-natured reviewers to associate the present writer with the origin of the American "short story," he may have a reasonable excuse for offering the following reflections—partly the result of his own observations during the last thirty years, and partly from his experience in the introduction of this form of literature to the pages of the Western magazine, of which he was editor at the beginning of that period. But he is far from claiming the invention, or of even attributing its genesis to that particular occasion. The short story was familiar enough in form in America during the early half of the century; perhaps the proverbial haste of American life was some inducement to its brevity. It had been the medium through which some of the most characteristic work of the best American writers had won the approbation of the public. Poe—a master of the art, as yet unsurpassed—had written; Longfellow and Hawthorne had lent it the graces of the English classics. But it was not the American short story of today. It was not characteristic of American life, American habits nor American thought. It was not vital and instinct with the experience and observation of the average American; it made no attempt to follow his reasoning or to understand his peculiar form of expression—which it was apt to consider vulgar; it had no sympathy with those dramatic contrasts and surprises which are the wonders of American civilization; it took no account of the modifications of environment and of geographical limitations; indeed, it knew little of American geography. Of all that was distinctly American it was evasive—when it. was not apologetic. And even when graced by the style of the best masters, it was distinctly provincial.

It would be easier to trace the causes which produced this than to assign any distinct occasion or period for the change. What was called American literature was still limited to English methods and upon English models. The best writers either wandered far afield for their inspiration, or, restricted to home material, were historical or legendary; artistically contemplative of their own country, but seldom observant. Literature abode on a scant fringe of the Atlantic seaboard, gathering the drift from other shores, and hearing the murmur of other lands rather than the voices of its own; it was either expressed in an artificial treatment of life in the cities, or, as with Irving, was frankly satirical of provincial social ambition. There was much "fine" writing; there were American Addisons, Steeles, and Lambs—there were provincial *Spectators* and *Tatlers*. The sentiment was English. Even Irving in the pathetic sketch of "The Wife" echoed the style of "Rosamund Grey." They were sketches of American life in the form of the English Essayists, with no attempt to understand the American character. The literary man had little sympathy with the rough and half-civilised masses who were making his country's history; if he used them at all it was as a foil to bring into greater relief his hero of the unmistakable English pattern. In his slavish imitation of the foreigner, he did not, however, succeed in retaining the foreigner's quick appreciation of novelty. It took an Englishman to first develop the humor and picturesqueness of American or "Yankee" dialect, but Judge [Thomas] Haliburton succeeded better in reproducing "Sam Slick's" speech than his character. Dr. [Sylvester] Judd's "Margaret"—one of the earlier American stories—although a vivid picture of New England farm life and strongly marked with local color, was in incident and treatment a mere imitation of English rural tragedy. It would, indeed, seem that while the American people had shaken off the English yoke in government, politics, and national progression, while they had already startled the old world with invention and originality in practical ideas, they had never freed themselves from the trammels of English literary precedent. The old sneer "Who reads an American book?" might have been answered by another: "There are no *American* books."

But while the American literary imagination was still under the influence of English tradition, an unexpected factor was developing to diminish its power. It was *Humor*—of a quality as distinct and original as the country and civilisation in which it was developed. It was at first noticeable in the anecdote or "story," and, after the fashion of such beginnings, was orally transmitted. It was common in the bar-rooms, the gatherings in the country store, and finally at public meetings in the mouths of stump orators. Arguments were clinched, and political principles illustrated, by "a funny story." It invaded even the camp meeting and pulpit. It at last received the currency of the public press. But wherever met it was so distinctly original and novel, so individual and characteristic, that it was at once known and appreciated abroad as "an American story." Crude at first, it received a literary polish in the press, but its dominant quality remained. It was concise and condense, yet suggestive. It was delightfully extravagant—or a miracle of understatement. It voiced not only the dialect, but the habits of thought of a people or locality. It gave a new interest to slang. From a paragraph of a dozen lines it grew into a half column, but always retaining its conciseness and felicity of statement. It was a foe to prolixity of any kind, it admitted no fine writing nor affectation of style. It went directly to the point. It was burdened by no conscientiousness; it was often irreverent; it was devoid of all moral responsibility— but it was original! By degrees it developed character with its incident, often, in a few lines, gave a striking photograph of a community or a section, but always reached its conclusion without an unnecessary word. It became—and still exists—as an essential feature of newspaper literature. It was the parent of the American "short story."

But although these beginnings assumed more of a national character than American serious or polite literature, they were still purely comic, and their only immediate result was the development of a number of humorists in the columns of the daily press—all possessing the dominant national quality with a certain individuality of their own. For a while it seemed as if they were losing the faculty of story-telling in the elaboration of eccentric character—chiefly used as a vehicle for smart sayings, extravagant incident, or political satire. They were eagerly received by the public and, in their day, immensely popular, and probably were better known at home and abroad than the more academic but less national humorists of New York or Boston. The national note was always struck even in their individual variations, and the admirable portraiture of the shrewd and humorous showman in "Artemus Ward" survived his more mechanical bad spelling. Yet they did not invade the current narrative fiction; the short and long story-tellers went on with their old-fashioned methods, their admirable morals, their well-worn sentiments, their colorless heroes and heroines of the first ranks of provincial society. Neither did social and political convulsions bring anything new in the way of Romance. The Mexican war gave us the delightful satires of Hosea Biglow, but no dramatic narrative. The anti-slavery struggle before the War of the Rebellion produced a successful partisan political novel—on the old lines—with only the purely American characters of "Topsy," and the New England "Miss

Ophelia." The War itself, prolific as it was of poetry and eloquence, was barren of romance, except for Edward Everett Hale's artistic and sympathetic "The Man Without a Country." The tragedies enacted, the sacrifices offered, not only on the battle-field but in the division of families and households; the conflict of superb Quixotism and reckless gallantry against Reason and Duty fought out in quiet border farmhouses and plantations; the reincarnation of Puritan and Cavalier in a wild environment of trackless wastes, pestilential swamps and rugged mountains; the patient endurance of both the conqueror and the conquered: all these found no echo in the romance of the period. Out of the battle smoke that covered half a continent drifted into the pages of magazines shadowy but correct figures of blameless virgins of the North —heroines or fashionable belles—habited as hospital nurses, bearing away the deeply wounded but more deeply misunderstood Harvard or Yale graduate lover who had rushed to bury his broken heart in the conflict. It seems almost incredible that, until the last few years, nothing worthy of that tremendous episode has been preserved by the pen of the romancer.

But if the war produced no characteristic American story it brought the literary man nearer his work. It opened to him distinct conditions of life in his own country, of which he had no previous conceptions; it revealed communities governed by customs and morals unlike his own, yet intensely human and American. The lighter side of some of these he had learned from the humorists before alluded to; the grim realities of war and the stress of circumstances had suddenly given them a pathetic or dramatic reality. Whether he had acquired this knowledge of them with a musket or a gilded strap on his shoulder, or whether he was later a peaceful "carpet-bagger" into the desolate homes of the south and south-

west, he knew something personally of their romantic and picturesque value in story. Many cultivated aspirants for literature, as well as many seasoned writers for the press, were among the volunteer soldiery. Again, the composition of the army was heterogeneous: regiments from the West rubbed shoulders with regiments from the East; spruce city clerks hobnobbed with backwoodsmen, and the student fresh from college shared his rations with the half-educated western farmer. The Union, for the first time, recognised its component parts; the natives knew each other. The literary man must have seen heroes and heroines where he had never looked for them, situations that he had never dreamt of. Yet it is a mortifying proof of the strength of inherited literary traditions, that he never dared until quite recently to make a test of them. It is still more strange that he should have waited for the initiative to be taken by a still more crude, wild, and more western civilisation—that of California!

The gold discovery had drawn to the Pacific slope of the continent a still more heterogeneous and remarkable population. The immigration of 1849 and 1850 had taken farmers from the plow, merchants from their desks, and students from their books, while every profession was represented in the motley crowd of gold-seekers. Europe and her colonies had contributed to swell these adventurers—for adventurers they were whatever their purpose; the risks were great, the journey long and difficult—the nearest came from a distance of over a thousand miles; that the men were necessarily pre-equipped with courage, faith and endurance was a foregone conclusion. They were mainly young; a grey-haired man was a curiosity in the mines in the early days, and an object of rude respect and reverence. They were consequently free from the trammels of precedent or tradition in arranging their lives and making their rude homes. There was a singular fraternity in this ideal republic into which all men entered free and equal. Distinction of previous position or advantages was unknown, even record and reputation for ill or good were of little benefit or embarrassment to the possessor; men were accepted for what they actually were, and what they could do in taking their part in the camp or settlement. The severest economy, the direst poverty, the most menial labor carried no shame nor disgrace with it; individual success brought neither envy nor jealousy. What was one man's fortune to-day might be the luck of another to-morrow. Add to this Utopian simplicity of the people, the environment of magnificent scenery, a unique climate, and a vegetation that was marvellous in its proportions and spontaneity of growth; let it be further considered that the strongest relief was given to this picture by its setting among the crumbling ruins of early Spanish possession—whose monuments still existed in Mission and Presidio, and whose legitimate Castilian descendants still lived and moved in picturesque and dignified contrast to their energetic invaders—and it must be admitted that a condition of romantic and dramatic possibilities was created unrivalled in history.

But the earlier literature of the Pacific slope was, like that of the Atlantic seaboard, national and characteristic only in its humor. The local press sparkled with wit and satire, and, as in the East, developed its usual individual humorists. Of these should be mentioned the earliest pioneers of Californian humor—Lieut. [George H.] Derby, a U.S. army engineer officer, author of a series of delightful extravagances known as the "Squibob Papers," and the later and universally known "Mark Twain," who contributed "The Jumping Frog of Calaveras" to the columns of the weekly press. *The San Francisco News Letter,* whose

whilom contributor, Major [Ambrose] Bierce, has since written some of the most graphic romances of the Civil War; *The Golden Era,* in which the present writer published his earlier sketches, and *The Californian,* to which, as editor, in burlesque imitation of the enterprise of his journalistic betters, he contributed "The Condensed Novels," were the foremost literary weeklies. These were all more or less characteristically American, but it was again remarkable that the more literary, romantic, and imaginative romances had no national flavor. The better remembered serious work in the pages of the only literary magazine, *The Pioneer,* was a romance of spiritualism and psychological study, and a poem on the Chandos picture of Shakespeare!

With this singular experience before him, the present writer was called upon to take the editorial control of the *Overland Monthly,* a much more ambitious magazine venture than had yet appeared in California. The best writers had been invited to contribute to its pages. But in looking over his materials on preparing the first number, he was discouraged to find the same notable lack of characteristic fiction. There were good literary articles, sketches of foreign travel, and some essays in description of the natural resources of California—excellent from a commercial and advertising viewpoint. But he failed to discover anything of that wild and picturesque life which had impressed him, first as a truant schoolboy, and afterwards as a youthful schoolmaster among the mining population. In this perplexity he determined to attempt to make good the deficiency himself. He wrote "The Luck of Roaring Camp." However far short it fell of his ideal and his purpose, he conscientiously believed that he had painted much that "he saw, and part of which he was," that his subject and characters were distinctly Californian, as was equally his treatment of them. But an unexpected circumstance here intervened. The publication of the story was objected to by both printer and publisher, virtually for not being in the conventional line of subject, treatment, and morals! The introduction of the abandoned outcast mother of the foundling "Luck," and the language used by the characters, received a serious warning and protest. The writer was obliged to use his right as editor to save his unfortunate contribution from oblivion. When it appeared at last, he saw with consternation that the printer and publisher had really voiced the local opinion; that the press of California was still strongly dominated by the old conservatism and conventionalism of the East, and that when "The Luck of Roaring Camp" was not denounced as "improper" and "corrupting," it was coldly received as being "singular" and "strange." A still more extraordinary instance of the "provincial note" was struck in the criticism of a religious paper that the story was strongly "unfavorable to immigration" and decidedly unprovocative of the "investment of foreign capital." However, its instantaneousness and cordial acceptance as a new departure by the critics of the Eastern states and Europe, enabled the writer to follow it with other stories of a like character. More than that, he was gratified to find a disposition on the part of his contributors to shake off their conservative trammels, and in an admirable and original sketch of a wandering circus attendant called "Centerpole Bill," he was delighted to recognize and welcome a convert. The term "imitators," often used by the critics who, as previously stated, had claimed for the present writer the *invention* of this kind of literature, could not fairly apply to those who had cut loose from conventional methods, and sought to honestly describe the life around them, and he can only claim to have shown then that it could be done. How well it has since been done, what charm of individual flavor and style has been brought to it by such writers as

[Joel Chandler] Harris, [George Washington] Cable, [Thomas Nelson] Page, Mark Twain in *Huckleberry Finn,* the author of the *Prophet of the Great Smoky Mountains,* and Miss [Mary E.] Wilkins, the average reader need not be told. It would seem evident, therefore, that the secret of the American short story was the treatment of characteristic American life, with absolute knowledge of its peculiarities and sympathy with its methods; with no fastidious ignoring of its habitual expression, or the inchoate poetry that may be found even hidden in its slang; with no moral determination except that which may be the legitimate outcome of the story itself; with no more elimination than may be necessary for the artistic conception, and never from the fear of the "fetish" of conventionalism. Of such is the American short story of today—the germ of American literature to come.

Hamlin Garland
✳ 1860-1940

After Bret Harte discovered the West for fiction, other writers found in other areas of the expanding United States equivalent sources for stories of sentiment or romantic appeal. The resulting local color movement which swept through the 1870s and 1880s ran at mid career head on into an almost concurrent movement toward realism, and the juncture between them produced such realistic regional fiction as Edward Eggleston's THE HOOSIER SCHOOLMASTER *and Ed Howe's* THE STORY OF A COUNTRY TOWN. *Most continually vocal was Hamlin Garland who, from* MAIN-TRAVELLED ROADS *in 1891 to his Pulitzer Prize winning* A DAUGHTER OF THE MIDDLE BORDER *in*

1921, consistently attempted to combine objective realism with ethical idealism. Believing with Howells that fiction should tell the truth, in 1894 he set forth in a collection of essays called CRUMBLING IDOLS, *from which the following remarks are taken, a theory which he called "veritism," which would link realism for democratic purpose with individualism of a Whitman kind. Tell the harsh truth about life, he said, in order that men through individual effort may be moved to improve it.*

Local Color in Art

Local color in fiction is demonstrably the life of fiction. It is the native element, the differentiating element. It corresponds to the endless and vital charm of individual peculiarity. It is the differences which interest us; the similarities do not please, do not forever stimulate and feed as do the differences. Literature would die of dry rot if it chronicled the similarities only, or even largely.

Historically, the local color of a poet or dramatist is of the greatest value. The charm of Horace is the side light he throws on the manners and customs of his time. The vital in Homer lies, after all, in his local color, not in his abstractions. Because the sagas of the North delineate more exactly how men and women lived and wrought in those days, therefore they have always appealed to me with infinitely greater power than Homer.

Similarly it is the local color of Chaucer that interests us to-day. We yawn over his tales of chivalry which were in the manner of his contemporaries, but the Miller and the Priest interest us. Wherever the man of the past in literature showed us what he really lived and loved, he moves us. We understand him, and we really feel an interest in him.

Historically, local color has gained in beauty and suggestiveness and humanity from Chaucer down to the present day. Each age has embodied more and more of its actual life and social conformation until the differentiating qualities of modern art make the best paintings of Norway as distinct in local color as its fiction is vital and indigenous.

Every great moving literature to-day is full of local color. It is this element which puts the Norwegian and Russian almost at the very summit of modern novel writing, and it is the comparative lack of this distinctive flavor which makes the English and French take a lower place in truth and sincerity.

Everywhere all over the modern European world, men are writing novels and dramas as naturally as the grass or corn or flax grows. The Provençal, the Hun, the Catalonian, the Norwegian, is getting a hearing. This literature is not the literature of scholars; it is the literature of lovers and doers; of men who love the modern and who have not been educated to despise common things.

These men are speaking a new word. They are not hunting themes, they are struggling to express.

Conventional criticism does not hamper or confine them. They are rooted in the soil. They stand among the cornfields and they dig in the peat-bogs. They concern themselves with modern and very present words and themes, and they have brought a new word which is to divide in half the domain of beauty.

They have made art the re-creation of the beautiful *and the significant.* Mere beauty no longer suffices. Beauty is the world-old aristocrat who has taken for mate this mighty young plebeian Significance. Their child is to be the most human and humane literature ever seen.

It has taken the United States longer to achieve independence of English critics than it took to free itself from old-world political and economic rule. Its political freedom was won, not by its gentlemen and scholars, but by its yeomanry; and in the same way our national literature will come in its fulness when the common American rises spontaneously to the expression of his concept of life.

The fatal blight upon most American art has been, and is to-day, its imitative quality, which has kept it characterless and factitious,—as forced rose-culture rather than the free flowering of native plants.

Our writers despised or feared the home market. They rested their immortality upon the "universal theme," which was a theme of no interest to the public and of small interest to themselves.

During the first century and a half, our literature had very little national color. It was quite like the utterance of corresponding classes in England. But at length Bryant and Cooper felt the influence of our mighty forests and prairies. Whittier uttered something of New England boy-life, and Thoreau prodded about among newly discovered wonders, and the American literature got its first start.

Under the influence of Cooper came the stories of wild life from Texas, from Ohio, and from Illinois. The wild, rough settlements could not produce smooth and cultured poems or stories; they only furnished forth rough-and-ready anecdotes, but in these stories there were hints of something fine and strong and native.

As the settlements increased in size, as the pressure of the forest and the wild beast grew less, expression rose to a higher plane; men softened in speech and manner. All preparations were being made for a local literature raised to the level of art.

The Pacific slope was first in the line. By the exceptional interest which the world took in the life of the gold fields, and by the forward urge which seems always to surprise the pessimist and the scholiast, two young men [Bret Harte and Joaquin Miller] were plunged into

that wild life, led across the plains set in the shadow of Mount Shasta, and local literature received its first great marked, decided impetus.

To-day we have in America, at last, a group of writers who have no suspicion of imitation laid upon them. Whatever faults they may be supposed to have, they are at any rate, themselves. American critics can depend upon a characteristic American literature of fiction and the drama from these people.

The corn has flowered, and the cotton-boll has broken into speech.

Local color—what is it? It means that the writer spontaneously reflects the life which goes on around him. It is natural and unstrained art.

It is, in a sense, unnatural and artificial to find an American writing novels of Russia or Spain or the Holy Land. He cannot hope to do it so well as the native. The best he can look for is that poor word of praise, "He does it very well, considering he is an alien."

If a young writer complain that there are no themes at home, that he is forced to go abroad for prospective and romance, I answer there is something wrong in his education or his perceptive faculty. Often he is more anxious to win a money success than to be patiently one of art's unhurried devotees.

I can sympathize with him, however, for criticism has not helped him to be true. Criticism of the formal kind and spontaneous expression are always at war, like the old man and the youth. They may politely conceal it, but they are mutually destructive.

Old men naturally love the past; the books they read are the masterpieces; the great men are all dying off, they say; the young man should treat lofty and universal themes, as they used to do. These localisms are petty. These truths are disturbing. Youth annoys them. Spontaneousness is formlessness, and the criticisms that does not call for the abstract and the ideal and the beautiful is leading to destruction, these critics say.

And yet there is a criticism which helps, which tends to keep a writer at his best; but such criticism recognizes the dynamic force of a literature, and tries to spy out tendencies. This criticism to-day sees that local color means national character, and is aiding the young writer to treat his themes in the best art.

I assert it is the most natural thing in the world for a man to love his native land and his native, intimate surroundings. Born into a web of circumstances, enmeshed in common life, the youthful artist begins to think. All the associations of that childhood and the love-life of youth combine to make that web of common affairs, threads of silver and beads of gold; the near-at-hand things are the dearest and sweetest after all.

As the reader will see, I am using local color to mean something more than a forced study of the picturesque scenery of a State.

Local color in a novel means that it has such quality of texture and background that it could not have been written in any other place or by any one else than a native.

It means a statement of life as indigenous as the plant-growth. It means that the picturesque shall not be seen by the author,—that every tree and bird and mountain shall be dear and companionable and necessary, not picturesque; the tourist cannot write the local novel.

From this it follows that local color must not be put in for the sake of local color. It must go in, it *will* go in, because the writer naturally carries it with him half unconsciously, or conscious only of its significance, its interest to him.

He must not stop to think whether it will interest the reader or not. He must be loyal to himself, and put it in because he loves it. If he is an artist, he will make his reader feel it through his own emotion.

What we should stand for is not universality of theme, but beauty and strength of treatment, leaving the writer to choose his theme because he loves it.

Here is the work of the critic. Recognizing that the theme is beyond his control, let him aid the young writer to delineate simply and with unwavering strokes. Even here the critic can do little, if he is possessed of the idea that the young writer of to-day should model upon Addison or Macaulay or Swift.

There are new criterions to-day in writing as in painting, and individual expression is the aim. The critic can do much to aid the young writer to *not* copy an old master or any other master. Good criticism can aid him to be vivid and simple and unhackneyed in his technique, the subject is his own affair.

I agree with him who says, local art must be raised to the highest levels in its expression; but in aiding this perfection of technique we must be careful not to cut into the artist's spontaneity. To apply dogmas of criticism to our life and literature would be benumbing to artist and fatal to his art.

Frank Norris

❋ 1870-1902

Novelist Benjamin Franklin Norris is remembered in most literary histories as our first successful realist in fiction. His MCTEAGUE *in 1899 and* THE OCTOPUS *in 1901 seem influenced by the kind of objective observation and the attitude toward philosophic determinism which appeared in the writing of such novelists as Emil Zola in France. Indeed, there is argument still about whether Norris was a realist or a naturalist—and there is argument also about whether those two terms really represent exclusively differ-*

ent literary views. But Norris, revolting from the realism of Howells, preferred to call his writings romantic because they did not treat of ordinary people but of unusual people controlled by forces greater than they. Like Garland and most other writers in the United States, he believed that fiction had purpose beyond story, and he spoke of this and other things in THE RESPONSIBILITIES OF THE NOVELIST, *posthumously published in 1903, from which the following is extracted.*

The Novel with a Purpose

After years of indoctrination and expostulation on the part of the artists, the people who read appear at last to have grasped this one precept—"the novel must not preach," but "the purpose of the story must be subordinate to the story itself." It took a very long time for them to understand this, but once it became apparent they fastened upon it with a tenacity comparable only to the tenacity of the American schoolboy to the date "1492." "The novel must not preach," you hear them say.

As though it were possible to write a novel without a purpose, even if it is only the purpose to amuse. One is willing to admit that this savors a little of quibbling, for "purpose" and purpose to amuse are two different purposes. But every novel, even the most frivolous, must have some reason for the writing of it, and in that sense must have a "purpose."

Every novel must do one of three things—it must (1) tell something, (2) show something, or (3) prove something. Some novels do all three of these; some do only two; all must do at least one. The ordinary novel merely tells something, elaborates a complication, devotes itself primarily to *things*. In this class comes the novel of adventure, such

as *The Three Musketeers*. The second and better class of novel shows something, exposes the workings of a temperament, devotes itself primarily to the minds of human beings. In this class falls the novel of character, such as *Romola*. The third, and what we hold to be the best class, proves something, draws conclusions from a whole congeries of forces, social tendencies, race impulses, devotes itself not to the study of men but of man. In this class falls the novel with a purpose, such as *Les Miserables*.

And the reason we decide upon this last as the highest form of the novel is because that, though setting a great purpose before it as its task, it nevertheless includes, and is forced to include, both the other classes. It must tell something, must narrate vigorous incidents and show something, must penetrate deep into the motives and character of type-men, men who are composite pictures of a multitude of men. It must do this because of the nature of its subject, for it deals with elemental forces, motives that stir whole nations. These cannot be handled as abstractions in fiction. Fiction can find expression only in the concrete. The elemental forces, then, contribute to the novel with a purpose to provide it with vigorous action. In the novel, force can be expressed in no other way. The social tendencies must be expressed by means of analysis of the characters of the men and women who compose that society, and the two must be combined and manipulated to evolve the purpose—to find the value of x.

The production of such a novel is probably the most arduous task that the writer of fiction can undertake. Nowhere else is success more difficult; nowhere else is failure so easy. Unskilfully treated, the story may dwindle down and degenerate into mere special pleading, and the novelist become a polemicist, a pamphleteer, forgetting that, although his first consideration is to prove his case, his *means* must be living human beings, not statistics, and that his tools are not figures, but pictures from life as he sees it. The novel with a purpose *is*, one contends, a preaching novel. But it preaches by telling things and showing things. Only, the author selects from the great storehouse of actual life the things to be told and the things to be shown, which shall bear upon his problem, his purpose. The preaching, the moralizing, is the result not of direct appeal by the writer, but is made—should be made—to the reader by the very incidents of the story.

But here is presented a strange anomaly, a distinction as subtle as it is vital. Just now one has said that in the composition of the kind of novel under consideration the *purpose* is for the novelist the all-important thing, and yet it is impossible to deny that the *story*, as a mere story, is to the story-writer the one great object of attention. How reconcile then these two apparent contradictions?

For the novelist, the purpose of his novel, the problem he is to solve, is to his story what the keynote is to the sonata. Though the musician cannot exaggerate the importance of the keynote, yet the thing that interests him is the sonata itself. The keynote simply coordinates the music, systematizes it, brings all the myriad little rebellious notes under a single harmonious code. Thus, too, the purpose in the novel. It is important as an end and also as an ever-present guide. For the writer it is as important only as a note to which his work must be attuned. The moment, however, that the writer becomes really and vitally interested in his purpose his novel fails.

Here is the strange anomaly. Let us suppose that Hardy, say, should be engaged upon a story which had for purpose to show the injustices under which the miners of Wales were suffering. It is conceivable that he could write a story that would make the blood boil with indignation. But he himself, if he is to remain an artist, if he is to write his novel successfully, will, as a novelist, care very little about the iniquitous labour system of the Welsh coal-mines. It will be to him as impersonal a thing as the key is to the composer of a sonata. As a man Hardy may or may not be vitally concerned in the Welsh coal-miner. That is quite unessential. But as a novelist, as an artist, his sufferings must be for him a matter of the mildest interest. They are important, for they constitute his keynote. They are *not* interesting for the reason that the working out of his *story*, its people, episodes, scenes and pictures, is for the moment the most interesting thing in all the world to him, exclusive of everything else. Do you think that Mrs. Stowe was more interested in the slave question than she was in the writing of *Uncle Tom's Cabin?* Her book, her manuscript, the page-to-page progress of the narrative, were more absorbing to her than all the Negroes that were ever whipped or sold. Had it not been so, that great purpose novel never would have succeeded.

Consider the reverse—*Fécondité*, for instance. The purpose for which Zola wrote the book ran away with him. He really did care more for the depopulation of France than he did for his novel. Result—sermons on the fruitfulness of women, special pleading, a farrago of dry, dull incidents, overburdened and collapsing under the weight of a theme that should have intruded only indirectly.

This is preëminently a selfish view of the question, but it is assuredly the only correct one. It must be remembered that the artist has a double personality, himself as a man and himself as an artist. But, it will be urged, how account for the artist's sympathy in his fictitious characters, his emotion, the actual tears he sheds in telling of their griefs, their deaths, and the like?

The answer is obvious. As an artist his sensitiveness is quickened because they are characters in his novel. It does not at all follow that the same artist would be moved to tears over the report of parallel catastrophes in real life. As an artist, there is every reason to suppose he would welcome the news with downright pleasure. It would be for him "good material." He would see a story in it, a good scene, a great character. Thus the artist. What he would do, how he would feel as a man is quite a different matter.

To conclude, let us consider one objection urged against the novel with a purpose by the plain people who read. For certain reasons, difficult to explain, the purpose novel always ends unhappily. It is usually a record of suffering, a relation of tragedy. And the plain people say, "Ah, we see so much suffering in the world, why put it into novels? We do not want it in novels."

One confesses to very little patience with this sort. "We see so much suffering in the world already!" Do they? Is this really true? The people who buy novels are the well-to-do people. They belong to a class whose whole scheme of life is concerned solely with an aim to avoid the unpleasant. Suffering, the great catastrophes, the social throes, that annihilate whole communities, or that crush even isolated individuals—all these are as far removed from them as earthquakes and tidal-waves. Or, even if it were so, suppose that by some miracle these blind eyes were opened and the sufferings of the poor, the tragedies of the house around the corner, really were laid bare. If there is much pain in life, all the more reason that it should appear in a class of literature which, in its highest form, is a sincere transcription of life.

It is the complaint of the coward, this cry against the novel with a purpose, because it brings the tragedies and griefs of others to notice. Take this element from fiction, take from it the power and opportunity to prove that injustice, crime and inequality do exist, and what is left?

Just the amusing novels, the novels that entertain. The juggler in spangles, with his balancing-pole and gilt ball, does this. You may consider the modern novel from this point of view. It may be a flippant paper-covered thing of swords and cloaks, to be carried on a railway journey and to be thrown out the window when read, together with sucked oranges and peanut shells. Or it may be a great force, that works together with the pulpit and the universities for the good of the people, fearlessly proving that power is abused, that the strong grind the faces of the weak, that an evil tree is still growing in the midst of the garden, that undoing follows hard upon unrighteousness, that the course of Empire is not yet finished, and that the races of men have yet to work out their destiny in those great and terrible movements that crush and grind and rend asunder the pillars of the houses of the nations.

Fiction may keep pace with the Great March, but it will not be by dint of amusing the people. The muse is a teacher, not a trickster. Her rightful place is with the leaders, but in the last analysis that place is to be attained and maintained not by cap-and-bells, but because of a serious and sincere interest, such as inspires the great teachers, the great divines, the great philosophers, a well-defined, well-seen, courageously sought-for purpose.

Henry James
✳ 1843-1916

When the Victorian novelist and historian Walter Besant spoke in April, 1884, before the Royal Institute in London on the necessity of regarding fiction as one of the fine arts, he seemed to Henry James

to hem fiction in with too many restrictions. *Replying to Besant in September
in* LONGMAN'S MAGAZINE, *James spoke his
mind at length on what fiction might be.
Its first obligation, he said, was to be
interesting. Beyond that it was personal,
"a direct impression of life." But James's
idea of the novel cannot be simply condensed to a sentence or two. His conception of "The Art of Fiction," as reworked for inclusion among his* PARTIAL
PORTRAITS *in 1888, and reprinted here,
is as highly refined as are such novels as*
THE PORTRAIT OF A LADY *and* THE AM-
BASSADORS *in which he put large parts of
it to practice. James, as even those who
admire him most will tell you, is not
always easy to read, but it is difficult to
know how he could have said what he
has to say in any other manner.*

The Art of Fiction

I should not have fixed so comprehensive a title to these few remarks, necessarily wanting in any completeness upon
a subject the full consideration of which
would carry us far, did I not seem to discover a pretext for my temerity in the
interesting pamphlet lately published
under this name by Mr. Walter Besant.
Mr. Besant's lecture at the Royal Institution—the original form of his pamphlet
—appears to indicate that many persons
are interested in the art of fiction, and
are not indifferent to such remarks as
those who practise it may attempt to
make about it. I am therefore anxious not
to lose the benefit of this favourable association, and to edge in a few words under
cover of the attention which Mr. Besant
is sure to have excited. There is something very encouraging in his having put
into form certain of his ideas on the
mystery of story-telling.

It is a proof of life and curiosity—
curiosity on the part of the brotherhood

of novelists as well as on the part of their
readers. Only a short time ago it might
have been supposed that the English
novel was not what the French call
discutable. It had no air of having a
theory, a conviction, a consciousness of
itself behind it—of being the expression
of an artistic faith, the result of choice
and comparison. I do not say it was
necessarily the worse for that: it would
take much more courage than I possess
to intimate that the form of the novel as
Dickens and Thackeray (for instance)
saw it had any taint of incompleteness.
It was, however, *naïf* (if I may help myself out with another French word); and
evidently if it be destined to suffer in
any way for having lost its *naïveté* it has
now an idea of making sure of the corresponding advantages. During the period
I have alluded to there was a comfortable, good-humoured feeling abroad that
a novel is a novel, as a pudding is a pudding, and that our only business with it
could be to swallow it. But within a year
or two, for some reason or other, there
have been signs of returning animation
—the era of discussion would appear to
have been to a certain extent opened.
Art lives upon discussion, upon experiment, upon curiosity, upon variety of attempt, upon the exchange of views and
the comparison of standpoints; and there
is a presumption that those times when
no one has anything particular to say
about it, and has no reason to give for
practice or preference, though they may
be times of honour, are not times of development—are times, possibly, even a
little of dulness. The successful application of any art is a delightful spectacle,
but the theory too is interesting; and
though there is a great deal of the latter
without the former I suspect there has
never been a genuine success that has
not had a latent core of conviction. Discussion, suggestion, formulation, these
things are fertilising when they are frank
and sincere. Mr. Besant has set an excel-

lent example in saying what he thinks, for his part, about the way in which fiction should be written, as well as about the way in which it should be published; for his view of the "art," carried on into an appendix, covers that too. Other labourers in the same field will doubtless take up the argument, they will give it the light of their experience, and the effect will surely be to make our interest in the novel a little more what it had for some time threatened to fail to be—a serious, active, inquiring interest, under protection of which this delightful study may, in moments of confidence, venture to say a little more what it thinks of itself.

It must take itself seriously for the public to take it so. The old superstition about fiction being "wicked" has doubtless died out in England; but the spirit of it lingers in a certain oblique regard directed toward any story which does not more or less admit that it is only a joke. Even the most jocular novel feels in some degree the weight of the proscription that was formerly directed against literary levity: the jocularity does not always succeed in passing for orthodoxy. It is still expected, though perhaps people are ashamed to say it, that a production which is after all only a "make-believe" (for what else is a "story"?) shall be in some degree apologetic—shall renounce the pretension of attempting really to represent life. This, of course, any sensible, wide-awake story declines to do, for it quickly perceives that the tolerance granted to it on such a condition is only an attempt to stifle it disguised in the form of generosity. The old evangelical hostility to the novel, which was as explicit as it was narrow, and which regarded it as little less favourable to our immortal part than a stage-play, was in reality far less insulting. The only reason for the existence of a novel is that it does attempt to represent life. When it relinquishes this attempt, the same attempt that we see on the canvas of the painter, it will have arrived at a very strange pass. It is not expected of the picture that it will make itself humble in order to be forgiven; and the analogy between the art of the painter and the art of the novelist is, so far as I am able to see, complete. Their inspiration is the same, their process (allowing for the different quality of the vehicle) is the same, their success is the same. They may learn from each other, they may explain and sustain each other. Their cause is the same, and the honour of one is the honour of another. The Mahometans think a picture an unholy thing, but it is a long time since any Christian did, and it is therefore the more odd that in the Christian mind the traces (dissimulated though they may be) of a suspicion of the sister art should linger to this day. The only effectual way to lay it to rest is to emphasise the analogy to which I just alluded—to insist on the fact that as the picture is reality, so the novel is history. That is the only general description (which does it justice) that we may give of the novel. But history also is allowed to represent life; it is not, any more than painting, expected to apologise. The subject-matter of fiction is stored up likewise in documents and records, and, if it will not give itself away, as they say in California, it must speak with assurance, with the tone of the historian. Certain accomplished novelists have a habit of giving themselves away which must often bring tears to the eyes of people who take their fiction seriously. I was lately struck, in reading over many pages of Anthony Trollope, with his want of discretion in this particular. In a digression, a parenthesis or an aside, he concedes to the reader that he and this trusting friend are only "making believe." He admits that the events he narrates have not really happened, and that he can give his narrative any turn the reader may like best. Such a betrayal of a sacred office seems to me, I confess, a terrible crime; it is what I mean by the attitude of apology, and it shocks me every whit as much in Trollope as it would have shocked me in Gibbon or Macaulay. It implies that the novelist is less occupied in looking for the truth (the truth, of course I mean, that he assumes, the premises that we must grant him, whatever they may be) than the historian, and in doing so it deprives him at a stroke of all his standing-room. To represent and illustrate the past, the actions of men, is the task of either writer, and the only difference that I can see is, in proportion as he succeeds, to the honour of the novelist, consisting as it does in his having more difficulty in collecting his evidence, which is so far from being purely literary. It seems to me to give him a great character, the fact that he has at once so much in common with the philosopher and the painter; this double analogy is a magnificent heritage.

It is of all this evidently that Mr. Besant is full when he insists upon the fact that fiction is one of the *fine* arts, deserving in its turn of all the honours and emoluments that have hitherto been reserved for the successful profession of music, poetry, painting, architecture. It is impossible to insist too much on so important a truth, and the place that Mr. Besant demands for the work of the novelist may be represented, a trifle less abstractly, by saying that he demands not only that it shall be reputed artistic, but that it shall be reputed very artistic indeed. It is excellent that he should have struck this note, for his doing so indicates that there was need of it, that his proposition may be to many people a novelty. One rubs one's eyes at the thought; but the rest of Mr. Besant's essay confirms the revelation. I suspect in truth that it would be possible to confirm it still further, and that one would not be far wrong in saying that in addition to the people to whom it has never occurred that a novel

ought to be artistic, there are a great many others who, if this principle were urged upon them, would be filled with an indefinable mistrust. They would find it difficult to explain their repugnance, but it would operate strongly to put them on their guard. "Art," in our Protestant communities, where so many things have got so strangely twisted about, is supposed in certain circles to have some vague injurious effect upon those who make it an important consideration, who let it weigh in the balance. It is assumed to be opposed in some mysterious manner to morality, to amusement, to instruction. When it is embodied in the work of the painter (the sculptor is another affair!) you know what it is: it stands there before you, in the honesty of pink and green and a gilt frame; you can see the worst of it at a glance, and you can be on your guard. But when it is introduced into literature it becomes more insidious —there is danger of its hurting you before you know it. Literature should be either instructive or amusing, and there is in many minds an impression that these artistic preoccupations, the search for form, contribute to neither end, interfere indeed with both. They are too frivolous to be edifying, and too serious to be diverting; and they are moreover priggish and paradoxical and superfluous. That, I think, represents the manner in which the latent thought of many people who read novels as an exercise in skipping would explain itself if it were to become articulate. They would argue, of course, that a novel ought to be "good," but they would interpret this term in a fashion of their own, which indeed would vary considerably from one critic to another. One would say that being good means representing virtuous and aspiring characters placed in prominent positions; another would say that it depends on a "happy ending," on a distribution at the last of prizes, pensions, husbands, wives, babies, millions, appended paragraphs, and cheerful remarks. Another still would say that it means being full of incident and movement, so that we shall wish to jump ahead, to see who was the mysterious stranger, and if the stolen will was ever found, and shall not be distracted from this pleasure by a tiresome analysis or "description." But they would all agree that the "artistic" idea would spoil some of their fun. One would hold it accountable for all the description, another would see it revealed in the absence of sympathy. Its hostility to a happy ending would be evident, and it might even in some cases render any ending at all impossible. The "ending" of a novel is, for many persons, like that of a good dinner, a course of dessert and ices, and the artist in fiction is regarded as a sort of meddlesome doctor who forbids agreeable aftertastes. It is therefore true that this conception of Mr. Besant's of the novel as a superior form encounters not only a negative but a positive indifference. It matters little that as a work of art it should really be as little or as much of its essence to supply happy endings, sympathetic characters, and an objective tone, as if it were a work of mechanics: the association of ideas, however incongruous, might easily be too much for it if an eloquent voice were not sometimes raised to call attention to the fact that it is at once as free and as serious a branch of literature as any other.

Certainly this might sometimes be doubted in presence of the enormous number of works of fiction that appeal to the credulity of our generation, for it might easily seem that there could be no great character in a commodity so quickly and easily produced. It must be admitted that good novels are much compromised by bad ones, and that the field at large suffers discredit from overcrowding. I think, however, that this injury is only superficial, and that the superabundance of written fiction proves nothing against the principle itself. It has been vulgarised, like all other kinds of literature, like everything else to-day, and it has proved more than some kinds accessible to vulgarisation. But there is as much difference as there ever was between a good novel and a bad one: the bad is swept with all the daubed canvases and spoiled marble into some unvisited limbo, or infinite rubbish-yard beneath the back-windows of the world, and the good subsists and emits its light and stimulates our desire for perfection. As I shall take the liberty of making but a single criticism of Mr. Besant, whose tone is so full of love of his art, I may as well have done with it at once. He seems to me to mistake in attempting to say so definitely beforehand what sort of an affair the good novel will be. To indicate the danger of such an error as that has been the purpose of these few pages; to suggest that certain traditions on the subject, applied *a priori,* have already had much to answer for, and that the good health of an art which undertakes so immediately to reproduce life must demand that it be perfectly free. It lives upon exercise, and the very meaning of exercise is freedom. The only obligation to which in advance we may hold a novel, without incurring the accusation of being arbitrary, is that it be interesting. That general responsibility rests upon it, but it is the only one I can think of. The ways in which it is at liberty to accomplish this result (of interesting us) strike me as innumerable, and such as can only suffer from being marked out or fenced in by prescription. They are as various as the temperament of man, and they are successful in proportion as they reveal a particular mind, different from others. A novel is in its broadest definition a personal, a direct impression of life: that, to begin with, constitutes its value, which is greater or less according to the intensity of the impression. But there will be no intensity at all, and therefore no value, unless there is freedom to feel and say. The tracing of a line to be followed, of a tone to be taken, of a form to be filled out, is a limitation of that freedom and a suppression of the very thing that we are most curious about. The form, it seems to me, is to be appreciated after the fact; then the author's choice has been made, his standard has been indicated; then we can follow lines and directions and compare tones and resemblances. Then in a word we can enjoy one of the most charming of pleasures, we can estimate quality, we can apply the test of execution. The execution belongs to the author alone; it is what is most personal to him, and we measure him by that. The advantage, the luxury, as well as the torment and responsibility of the novelist, is that there is no limit to what he may attempt as an executant —no limit to his possible experiments, efforts, discoveries, successes. Here it is especially that he works, step by step, like his brother of the brush, of whom we may always say that he has painted his picture in a manner best known to himself. His manner is his secret, not necessarily a jealous one. He cannot disclose it as a general thing if he would; he would be at a loss to teach it to others. I say this with a due recollection of having insisted on the community of method of the artist who paints a picture and the artist who writes a novel. The painter *is* able to teach the rudiments of his practice, and it is possible, from the study of good work (granted the aptitude), both to learn how to paint and to learn how to write. Yet it remains true, without injury to the *rapprochement*, that the literary artist would be obliged to say to his pupil much more than the other, "Ah, well, you must do it as you can!" It is a question of degree, a matter of delicacy. If there are exact sciences, there are also exact arts, and the grammar of painting is so much more definite that it makes the difference.

I ought to add, however, that if Mr.

Besant says at the beginning of his essay that the "laws of fiction may be laid down and taught with as much precision and exactness as the laws of harmony, perspective, and proportion" he mitigates what might appear to be an extravagance by applying his remark to "general" laws, and by expressing most of these rules in a manner with which it would certainly be unaccommodating to disagree. That the novelist must write from his experience, that his "characters must be real and such as might be met with in actual life"; that "a young lady brought up in a quiet country village should avoid descriptions of garrison life," and "a writer whose friends and personal experiences belong to the lower middle-class should carefully avoid introducing his characters into society"; that one should enter one's notes in a commonplace book; that one's figures should be clear in outline; that making them clear by some trick of speech or of carriage is a bad method, and "describing them at length" is a worse one; that English Fiction should have a "conscious moral purpose"; that "it is almost impossible to estimate too highly the value of careful workmanship —that is, of style"; that "the most important point of all is the story," that "the story is everything": these are principles with most of which it is surely impossible not to sympathise. That remark about the lower middle-class writer and his knowing his place is perhaps rather chilling; but for the rest I should find it difficult to dissent from any one of these recommendations. At the same time, I should find it difficult positively to assent to them, with the exception, perhaps, of the injunction as to entering one's notes in a commonplace book. They scarcely seem to me to have the quality that Mr. Besant attributes to the rules of the novelist—the "precision and exactness" of "the laws of harmony, perspective, and proportion." They are suggestive, they are even inspiring, but they are not exact, though they are doubtless as much so as the case admits of: which is a proof of that liberty of interpretation for which I just contended. For the value of these different injunctions—so beautiful and so vague—is wholly in the meaning one attaches to them. The characters, the situation, which strike one as real will be those that touch and interest one most, but the measure of reality is very difficult to fix. The reality of Don Quixote or of Mr. Micawber is a very delicate shade; it is a reality so coloured by the author's vision that, vivid as it may be, one would hesitate to propose it as a model: one would expose one's self to some very embarrassing questions on the part of a pupil. It goes without saying that you will not write a good novel unless you possess the sense of reality; but it will be difficult to give you a recipe for calling that sense into being. Humanity is immense, and reality has a myriad forms, the most one can affirm is that some of the flowers of fiction have the odour of it, and others have not; as for telling you in advance how your nosegay should be composed, that is another affair. It is equally excellent and inconclusive to say that one must write from experience; to our suppositious aspirant such a declaration might savour of mockery. What kind of experience is intended, and where does it begin and end? Experience is never limited, and it is never complete; it is an immense sensibility, a kind of huge spider-web of the finest silken threads suspended in the chamber of consciousness, and catching every air-borne particle in its tissue. It is the very atmosphere of the mind; and when the mind is imaginative—much more when it happens to be that of a man of genius—it takes to itself the faintest hints of life, it converts the very pulses of the air into revelations. The young lady living in a village has only to be a damsel upon whom nothing is lost to make it quite unfair (as it seems to

me) to declare to her that she shall have nothing to say about the military. Greater miracles have been seen than that, imagination assisting, she should speak the truth about some of these gentlemen. I remember an English novelist, a woman of genius, telling me that she was much commended for the impression she had managed to give in one of her tales of the nature and way of life of the French Protestant youth. She had been asked where she learned so much about this recondite being, she had been congratulated on her peculiar opportunities. These opportunities consisted in her having once, in Paris, as she ascended a staircase, passed an open door where, in the household of a *pasteur,* some of the young Protestants were seated at table round a finished meal. The glimpse made a picture; it lasted only a moment, but that moment was experience. She had got her direct personal impression, and she turned out her type. She knew what youth was, and what Protestantism; she also had the advantage of having seen what it was to be French, so that she converted these ideas into a concrete image and produced a reality. Above all, however, she was blessed with the faculty which when you give it an inch takes an ell, and which for the artist is a much greater source of strength than any accident of residence or of place in the social scale. The power to guess the unseen from the seen, to trace the implication of things, to judge the whole piece by the pattern, the condition of feeling life in general so completely that you are well on your way to knowing any particular corner of it—this cluster of gifts may almost be said to constitute experience, and they occur in country and in town, and in the most differing stages of education. If experience consists of impressions, it may be said that impressions *are* experience, just as (have we not seen it?) they are the very air we breathe. Therefore, if I should certainly say to a novice, "Write from experience and from experience only," I should feel that this was rather a tantalising monition if I were not careful immediately to add, "Try to be one of the people on whom nothing is lost!"

I am far from intending by this to minimise the importance of exactness—of truth of detail. One can speak best from one's own taste, and I may therefore venture to say that the air of reality (solidity of specification) seems to me to be the supreme virtue of a novel—the merit on which all its other merits (including that conscious moral purpose of which Mr. Besant speaks) helplessly and submissively depend. If it be not there they are all as nothing, and if these be there, they owe their effect to the success with which the author has produced the illusion of life. The cultivation of this success, the study of this exquisite process, form, to my taste, the beginning and the end of the art of the novelist. They are his inspiration, his despair, his reward, his torment, his delight. It is here in very truth that he competes with life; it is here that he competes with his brother the painter in his attempt to render the look of things, the look that conveys their meaning, to catch the colour, the relief, the expression, the surface, the substance of the human spectacle. It is in regard to this that Mr. Besant is well inspired when he bids him take notes. He cannot possibly take too many, he cannot possibly take enough. All life solicits him, and to "render" the simplest surface, to produce the most momentary illusion, is a very complicated business. His case would be easier, and the rule would be more exact, if Mr. Besant had been able to tell him what notes to take. But this, I fear, he can never learn in any manual; it is the business of his life. He has to take a great many in order to select a few, he has to work them up as he can, and even the guides and philosophers who might have most to say to him must leave him alone when it comes to the application of precepts, as we leave the painter in communion with his palette. That his characters "must be clear in outline" as Mr. Besant says—he feels that down to his boots; but how he shall make them so is a secret between his good angel and himself. It would be absurdly simple if he could be taught that a great deal of "description" would make them so, or that on the contrary the absence of description and the cultivation of dialogue, or the absence of dialogue and the multiplication of "incident," would rescue him from his difficulties. Nothing, for instance, is more possible than that he be of a turn of mind for which this odd, literal opposition of description and dialogue, incident and description, has little meaning and light. People often talk of these things as if they had a kind of internecine distinctness, instead of melting into each other at every breath, and being intimately associated parts of one general effort of expression. I cannot imagine composition existing in a series of blocks, nor conceive, in any novel worth discussing at all, of a passage of description that is not in its intention narrative, a passage of dialogue that is not in its intention descriptive, a touch of truth of any sort that does not partake of the nature of incident, or an incident that derives its interest from any other source than the general and only source of the success of a work of art—that of being illustrative. A novel is a living thing, all one and continuous, like any other organism, and in proportion as it lives will it be found, I think, that in each of the parts there is something of each of the other parts. The critic who over the close texture of a finished work shall pretend to trace a geography of items will mark some frontiers as artificial, I fear, as any that have been known to history. There is an old-fashioned distinction between the novel of character and the novel of incident which must have cost many a smile to the intending fabulist who was keen about his work. It appears to me as little to the point as the equally celebrated distinction between the novel and the romance—to answer as little to any reality. There are bad novels and good novels, as there are bad pictures and good pictures; but that is the only distinction in which I see any meaning, and I can as little imagine speaking of a novel of character as I can imagine speaking of a picture of character. When one says picture one says of character, when one says novel one says of incident, and the terms may be transposed at will. What is character but the determination of incident? What is incident but the illustration of character? What is either a picture or a novel that is not of character? What else do we seek in it and find in it? It is an incident for a woman to stand up with her hand resting on a table and look at you in a certain way; or if it be not an incident I think it will be hard to say what it is. At the same time it is an expression of character. If you say you don't see it (character in *that—allons donc!*), this is exactly what the artist who has reasons of his own for thinking he does see it undertakes to show you. When a young man makes up his mind that he has not faith enough after all to enter the Church as he intended, that is an incident, though you may not hurry to the end of the chapter to see whether perhaps he doesn't change once more. I do not say that these are extraordinary or startling incidents. I do not pretend to estimate the degree of interest proceeding from them, for this will depend upon the skill of the painter. It sounds almost puerile to say that some incidents are intrinsically much more important than others, and I need not take this precaution after having professed my sympathy for the major ones in remarking that the only classification of the novel that I can

understand is into that which has life and that which has it not.

The novel and the romance, the novel of incident and that of character—these clumsy separations appear to me to have been made by critics and readers for their own convenience, and to help them out of some of their occasional predicaments, but to have little reality or interest for the producer, from whose point of view it is of course that we are attempting to consider the art of fiction. The case is the same with another shadowy category which Mr. Besant apparently is disposed to set up—that of the "modern English novel"; unless indeed it be that in this matter he has fallen into an accidental confusion of standpoints. It is not quite clear whether he intends the remarks in which he alludes to it to be didactic or historical. It is as difficult to suppose a person intending to write a modern English as to suppose him writing an ancient English novel: that is a label which begs the question. One writes the novel, one paints the picture, of one's language and of one's time, and calling it modern English will not, alas! make the difficult task any easier. No more, unfortunately, will calling this or that work of one's fellow-artist a romance—unless it be, of course, simply for the pleasantness of the thing, as for instance when Hawthorne gave this heading to his story of *Blithedale.* The French, who have brought the theory of fiction to remarkable completeness, have but one name for the novel, and have not attempted smaller things in it, that I can see, for that. I can think of no obligation to which the "romancer" would not be held equally with the novelist; the standard of execution is equally high for each. Of course it is of execution that we are talking—that being the only point of a novel that is open to contention. This is perhaps too often lost sight of, only to produce interminable confusions and cross-purposes. We must grant the artist his subject, his idea, his *donnée:* our criticism is applied only to what he makes of it. Naturally I do not mean that we are bound to like it or find it interesting: in case we do not our course is perfectly simple—to let it alone. We may believe that of a certain idea even the most sincere novelist can make nothing at all, and the event may perfectly justify our belief; but the failure will have been a failure to execute, and it is in the execution that the fatal weakness is recorded. If we pretend to respect the artist at all, we must allow him his freedom of choice, in the face, in particular cases, of innumerable presumptions that the choice will not fructify. Art derives a considerable part of its beneficial exercise from flying in the face of presumptions, and some of the most interesting experiments of which it is capable are hidden in the bosom of common things. Gustave Flaubert has written a story about the devotion of a servant-girl to a parrot, and the production, highly finished as it is, cannot on the whole be called a success. We are perfectly free to find it flat, but I think it might have been interesting; and I, for my part, am extremely glad he should have written it; it is a contribution to our knowledge of what can be done—or what cannot. Ivan Turgeniéff has written a tale about a deaf and dumb serf and a lap-dog, and the thing is touching, loving, a little masterpiece. He struck the note of life where Gustave Flaubert missed it—he flew in the face of a presumption and achieved a victory.

Nothing, of course, will ever take the place of the good old fashion of "liking" a work of art or not liking it: the most improved criticism will not abolish that primitive, that ultimate test. I mention this to guard myself from the accusation of intimating that the idea, the subject, of a novel or a picture, does not matter.

It matters, to my sense, in the highest degree, and if I might put up a prayer it would be that artists should select none but the richest. Some, as I have already hastened to admit, are much more remunerative than others, and it would be a world happily arranged in which persons intending to treat them should be exempt from confusions and mistakes. This fortunate condition will arrive only, I fear, on the same day that critics become purged from error. Meanwhile, I repeat, we do not judge the artist with fairness unless we say to him, "Oh, I grant you your starting-point, because if I did not I should seem to prescribe to you, and heaven forbid I should take that responsibility. If I pretend to tell you what you must not take, you will call upon me to tell you then what you must take; in which case I shall be prettily caught. Moreover, it isn't till I have accepted your data that I can begin to measure you. I have the standard, the pitch; I have no right to tamper with your flute and then criticise your music. Of course I may not care for your idea at all; I may think it silly, or stale, or unclean; in which case I wash my hands of you altogether. I may content myself with believing that you will not have succeeded in being interesting, but I shall, of course, not attempt to demonstrate it, and you will be as indifferent to me as I am to you. I needn't remind you that there are all sorts of tastes: who can know it better? Some people, for excellent reasons, don't like to read about carpenters; others, for reasons even better, don't like to read about courtesans. Many object to Americans. Others (I believe they are mainly editors and publishers) won't look at Italians. Some readers don't like quiet subjects; others don't like bustling ones. Some enjoy a complete illusion, others the consciousness of large concessions. They choose their novels accordingly, and if they don't care about your idea they won't *a fortiori,* care about your treatment."

So that it comes back very quickly, as I have said, to the liking: in spite of M. Zola, who reasons less powerfully than he represents, and who will not reconcile himself to this absoluteness of taste, thinking that there are certain things that people ought to like, and that they can be made to like. I am quite at a loss to imagine anything (at any rate in this matter of fiction) that people ought to like or to dislike. Selection will be sure to take care of itself, for it has a constant motive behind it. That motive is simply experience. As people feel life, so they will feel the art that is most closely related to it. This closeness of relation is what we should never forget in talking of the effort of the novel. Many people speak of it as a factitious, artificial form, a product of ingenuity, the business of which it is to alter and arrange the things that surround us, to translate them into conventional, tradition moulds. This, however, is a view of the matter which carries us but a very short way, condemns the art to an external repetition of a few familiar *clichés,* cuts short its development, and leads us straight up to a dead wall. Catching the very note and trick, the strange irregular rhythm of life, that is the attempt whose strenuous force keeps Fiction upon her feet. In proportion as in what she offers us we see life without rearrangement do we feel that we are touching the truth; in proportion as we see it with rearrangement do we feel that we are being put off with a substitute, a compromise and convention. It is not uncommon to hear an extraordinary assurance of remark in regard to this matter of rearranging, which is often spoken of as if it were the last word of art. Mr. Besant seems to me in danger of falling into the great error with his rather unguarded talk about "selection." Art is essentially selection, but it is a selection whose main care is

to be typical, to be inclusive. For many people art means rose-colored window-panes, and selection means picking a bouquet for Mrs. Grundy. They will tell you glibly that artistic considerations have nothing to do with the disagreeable, with the ugly; they will rattle off shallow commonplaces about the province of art and the limits of art till you are moved to some wonder in return as to the province and the limits of ignorance. It appears to me that no one can ever have made a seriously artistic attempt without becoming conscious of an immense increase—a kind of revelation— of freedom. One perceives in that case— by the light of a heavenly ray—that the province of art is all life, all feeling, all observation, all vision. As Mr. Besant so justly intimates, it is all experience. That is a sufficient answer to those who maintain that it must not touch the sad things of life, who stick into its divine unconscious bosom little prohibitory inscriptions on the end of sticks, such as we see in public gardens—"It is forbidden to walk on the grass; it is forbidden to touch the flowers; it is not allowed to introduce dogs or to remain after dark; it is requested to keep to the right." The young aspirant in the line of fiction whom we continue to imagine will do nothing without taste, for in that case his freedom would be of little use to him; but the first advantage of his taste will be to reveal to him the absurdity of the little sticks and tickets. If he have taste, I must add, of course he will have ingenuity, and my disrespectful reference to that quality just now was not meant to imply that it is useless in fiction. But it is only a secondary aid; the first is a capacity for receiving straight impressions.

Mr. Besant has some remarks on the the question of "the story" which I shall not attempt to criticise, though they seem to me to contain a singular ambiguity, because I do not think I understand them. I cannot see what is meant by talking as if there were a part of a novel which is the story and part of it which for mystical reasons is not—unless indeed the distinction be made in a sense in which it is difficult to suppose that any one should attempt to convey anything. "The story," if it represents anything, represents the subject, the idea, the *donnée* of the novel; and there is surely no "school"—Mr. Besant speaks of a school—which urges that a novel should be all treatment and no subject. There must assuredly be something to treat; every school is intimately conscious of that. This sense of the story being the idea, the starting-point, of the novel, is the only one that I see in which it can be spoken of as something different from its organic whole; and since in proportion as the work is successful the idea permeates and penetrates it, informs and animates it, so that every word and every punctuation-point contribute directly to the expression, in that proportion do we lose our sense of the story being a blade which may be drawn more or less out of its sheath. The story and the novel, the idea and the form, are the needle and thread, and I never heard of a guild of tailors who recommended the use of the thread without the needle, or the needle without the thread. Mr. Besant is not the only critic who may be observed to have spoken as if there were certain things in life which constitute stories, and certain others which do not. I find the same odd implication in an entertaining article in the *Pall Mall Gazette*, devoted, as it happens, to Mr. Besant's lecture. "The story is the thing!" says this graceful writer, as if with a tone of opposition to some other idea. I should think it was, as every painter who, as the time for "sending in" his picture looms in the distance, finds himself still in quest of a subject—as every belated artist not fixed about his theme will heartily agree. There are some sub-

jects which speak to us and others which do not, but he would be a clever man who should undertake to give a rule—an *index expurgatorius*—by which the story and the no-story should be known apart. It is impossible (to me at least) to imagine any such rule which shall not be altogether arbitrary. The writer in the *Pall Mall* opposes the delightful (as I suppose) novel of *Margot la Balafrée* to certain tales in which "Bostonian nymphs" appear to have "rejected English dukes for psychological reasons." I am not acquainted with the romance just designated, and can scarcely forgive the *Pall Mall* critic for not mentioning the name of the author, but the title appears to refer to a lady who may have received a scar in some heroic adventure. I am inconsolable at not being acquainted with this episode, but am utterly at a loss to see why it is a story when the rejection (or acceptance) of a duke is not, and why a reason, psychological or other, is not a subject when a cicatrix is. They are all particles of the multitudinous life with which the novel deals, and surely no dogma which pretends to make it lawful to touch the one and unlawful to touch the other will stand for a moment on its feet. It is the special picture that must stand or fall, according as it seem to possess truth or to lack it. Mr. Besant does not, to my sense, light up the subject by intimating that a story must, under penalty of not being a story, consist of "adventures." Why of adventures more than of green spectacles? He mentions a category of impossible things, and among them he places "fiction without adventure." Why without adventure, more than without matrimony, or celibacy, or parturition, or cholera, or hydropathy, or Jansenism? This seems to me to bring the novel back to the hapless little *role* of being an artificial, ingenious thing—bring it down from its large, free character of an immense and exquisite correspondence with life. And what is adventure when it comes to that, and by what sign is the listening pupil to recognize it? It is an adventure—an immense one—for me to write this little article; and for a Bostonian nymph to reject an English duke is an adventure only less stirring, I should say, than for an English duke to be rejected by a Bostonian nymph. I see dramas within dramas in that, and innumerable points of view. A psychological reason is, to my imagination, an object adorably pictorial; to catch the tint of its complexion—I feel as if that idea might inspire one to Titianesque efforts. There are few things more exciting to me, in short, than a psychological reason, and yet, I protest, the novel seems to me the most magnificent form of art. I have just been reading, at the same time, the delightful story of *Treasure Island*, by Mr. Robert Louis Stevenson, and, in a manner less consecutive, the last tale from M. Edmond de Goncourt, which is entitled *Chérie*. One of these works treats of murders, mysteries, islands of dreadful renown, hairbreadth escapes, miraculous coincidences and buried doubloons. The other treats of a little French girl who lived in a fine house in Paris, and died of wounded sensibility because no one would marry her. I call *Treasure Island* delightful, because it appears to me to have succeeded wonderfully in what it attempts; and I venture to bestow no epithet upon *Chérie*, which strikes me as having failed deplorably in what it attempts—that is in tracing the development of the moral consciousness of a child. But one of these productions strikes me as exactly as much of a novel as the other, and as having a "story" quite as much. The moral consciousness of a child is as much a part of life as the islands of the Spanish Main, and the one sort of geography seems to me to have those "surprises" of which Mr. Besant speaks quite as much as the other. For myself (since it comes back in the last

resort as I say, to the preference of the individual), the picture of the child's experience has the advantage that I can at successive steps (an immense luxury, near to the "sensual pleasure" of which Mr. Besant's critic in the *Pall Mall* speaks) say Yes or No, as it may be, to what the artist puts before me. I have been a child in fact, but I have been on a quest for a buried treasure only in supposition, and it is a simple accident that with M. De Goncourt I should have for the most part to say No. With George Eliot, when she painted that country with a far other intelligence, I always said Yes.

The most interesting part of Mr. Besant's lecture is unfortunately the briefest passage—his very cursory allusion to the "conscious moral purpose" of the novel. Here again it is not very clear whether he be recording a fact or laying down a principle; it is a great pity that in the latter case he should not have developed his idea. This branch of the subject is of immense importance, and Mr. Besant's few words point to considerations of the widest reach, not to be lightly disposed of. He will have treated the art of fiction but superficially who is not prepared to go every inch of the way that these considerations will carry him. It is for this reason that at the beginning of these remarks I was careful to notify the reader that my reflections on so large a theme have no pretention to be exhaustive. Like Mr. Besant, I have left the question of the morality of the novel till the last, and at the last I find I have used up my space. It is a question surrounded with difficulties, as witness the very first that meets us, in the form of a definite question, on the threshold. Vagueness, in such a discussion, is fatal, and what is the meaning of your morality and your conscious moral purpose? Will you not define your terms and explain how (a novel being a picture) a picture can be either moral or immoral? You wish to paint a moral picture or carve a moral statue: will you not tell us how you would set about it? We are discussing the Art of Fiction; questions of art are questions (in the widest sense) of execution; questions of morality are quite another affair, and will you not let us see how it is that you find it so easy to mix them up? These things are so clear to Mr. Besant that he has deduced from them a law which he sees embodied in English Fiction, and which is "a truly admirable thing and a great cause for congratulation." It is a great cause for congratulation indeed when such thorny problems become as smooth as silk. I may add that in so far as Mr. Besant perceives that in point of fact English Fiction has addressed itself preponderantly to these delicate questions he will appear to many people to have made a vain discovery. They will have been positively struck, on the contrary, with the moral timidity of the usual English novelist; with his (or with her) aversion to face the difficulties with which on every side the treatment of reality bristles. He is apt to be extremely shy (whereas the picture that Mr. Besant draws is a picture of boldness), and the sign of his work, for the most part, is a cautious silence on certain subjects. In the English novel (by which of course I mean the American as well), more than in any other, there is a traditional difference between that which people know and that which they agree to admit that they know, that which they see and that which they speak of, that which they feel to be a part of life, and that which they allow to enter into literature. There is the great difference, in short, between what they talk of in conversation and what they talk of in print. The essence of moral energy is to survey the whole field, and I should directly reverse Mr. Besant's remark and say not that the English novel has a purpose, but that it has a diffidence. To what degree a purpose in a

work of art is a source of corruption I shall not attempt to inquire; the one that seems to me least dangerous is the purpose of making a perfect work. As for our novel, I may say lastly on this score that as we find it in England today it strikes me as addressed in a large degree to "young people," and that this in itself constitutes a presumption that it will be rather shy. There are certain things which it is generally agreed not to discuss, not even to mention, before young people. That is very well, but the absence of discussion is not a symptom of the moral passion. The purpose of the English novel—"a truly admirable thing, and a great cause for congratulation"—strikes me therefore as rather negative.

There is one point at which the moral sense and the artistic sense lie very near together; that is in the light of the very obvious truth that the deepest quality of a work of art will always be the quality of the mind of the producer. In proportion as that intelligence is fine will the novel, the picture, the statue partake of the substance of beauty and truth. To be constituted of such elements is, to my vision, to have purpose enough. No good novel will ever proceed from a superficial mind; that seems to me an axiom which, for the artist in fiction, will cover all needful moral ground: if the youthful aspirant take it to heart it will illuminate for him many of the mysteries of "purpose." There are many other useful things that might be said to him, but I have come to the end of my article, and can only touch them as I pass. The critic in the *Pall Mall Gazette*, whom I have already quoted, draws attention to the danger, in speaking of the art of fiction, of generalising. The danger that he has in mind is rather, I imagine, that of particularising, for there are some comprehensive remarks which, in addition to those embodied in Mr. Besant's suggestive lecture, might without fear of misleading him be addressed to the ingenuous student. I should remind him first of the magnificence of the form that is open to him, which offers to sight so few restrictions and such innumerable opportunities. The other arts, in comparison, appear confined and hampered; the various conditions under which they are exercised are so rigid and definite. But the only condition that I can think of attaching to the composition of the novel is, as I have already said, that it be sincere. This freedom is a splendid privilege, and the first lesson of the young novelist is to learn to be worthy of it. "Enjoy it as it deserves," I should say to him; "take possession of it, explore it to its utmost extent, publish it, rejoice in it. All life belongs to you, and do not listen either to those who would shut you up into corners of it and tell you that it is only here and there that art inhabits, or to those who would persuade you that this heavenly messenger wings her way outside of life altogether, breathing a superfine air, and turning away her head from the truth of things. There is no impression of life, no manner of seeing it and feeling it, to which the plan of the novelist may not offer a place; you have only to remember that talents so dissimilar as those of Alexandre Dumas and Jane Austen, Charles Dickens and Gustave Flaubert have worked in this field with equal glory. Do not think too much about optimism and pessimism; try and catch the colour of life itself. In France today we see a prodigious effort (that of Emile Zola, to whose solid and serious work no explorer of the capacity of the novel can allude without respect), we see an extraordinary effort, vitiated by a spirit of pessimism on a narrow basis. M. Zola is magnificent, but he strikes an English reader as ignorant; he has an air of working in the dark; if he had as much light as energy, his results would be of the highest value. As for the aberrations of a shallow optimism, the ground (of English fiction especially) is strewn with their brittle particles as with broken glass. If you must indulge in conclusions, let them have the taste of a wide knowledge. Remember that your first duty is to be as complete as possible— to make as perfect a work. Be generous and delicate and pursue the prize."

James T. Farrell
✳ 1904-

After Theodore Dreiser, whose patient realism in SISTER CARRIE *and* AN AMERICAN TRAGEDY *he has admired and defended, James T. Farrell is perhaps our most consistently successful contemporary naturalist. Farrell is intent on setting down objective, sometimes almost reportorial, representations of urban life in America, but is skilled also in expressing the groping bewilderment within the minds of young men like Studs Lonigan and Danny O'Neill who dream of being what circumstances can not allow them to be. His discussion of "Social Themes in American Realism" is reprinted from a collection of essays published in 1947 on* LITERATURE AND MORALITY.

Social Themes in American Realism

Since the 1890's, American writers of the realistic tradition have been trying to tell the story of the human consequences of the advance of American civilization. As is well known, a pioneer in this tradition was Theodore Dreiser. A significant distinction can be made between his work and that of such writers as Henry James, Stephen Crane, and Harold Frederic. While these writers differ greatly from one another, they were all concerned with the same theme of self-development, of awareness. This theme is even involved in the manner in which James creates suspense. Crane's *The Red Badge of Courage* is not merely a war novel. Using the setting of war, he tells the story of how a boy becomes a man. Frederic's *The Damnation of Theron Ware* also deals with the theme of awareness or development, though negatively Theron Ware becomes aware of values superior to, and more sophisticated than, those embodied in his ministerial education and in his life as a minister in a small community in upstate New York. His "damnation" or disintegration is the result of his inability to live by these superior values.

With Dreiser, the conditions of life and the ideals of success in America are thematic: the motif of development or awareness, when treated by him, is secondary to these. His characters usually take on the color of their environment. Failure and tragedy in his novels are to be interpreted as consequences of the pitiless force of circumstances. His heroes and heroines are seeking to rise socially, to change their class status. If they fail, it is because of the circumstances of their lives—a lack of education, a lack of physical magnetism, or a lack of control of the levers of social power, most notably, money. Money provides the means for wielding power and, if it is gained, the individual is in a better position to satisfy desire. Human beings—for instance, Roberta Alden, in *An American Tragedy*, or Jennie Gerhardt—are sacrificed in the interests of success and social prestige in a society dominated by those who control because they are rich or, at least, well off. And only those who are born into the upper classes, or those who are particularly strong-willed, magnetic, shrewd, or lucky, can escape the alternative fates of tragedy and failure or apathetic mediocrity. In the Dreiserian

world, the emotional capacities of men and women for affection and the powers of the individual will are weaker than the forces of social circumstance. In this sense, Dreiser wrote realistic novels about the conditions of American life.

2

In recent years the cultural climate provided by the "New Deal" has had a manifest influence on American writing. In a political speech, the late President Franklin D. Roosevelt said: "Always the heart and soul of our country will be the heart and soul of the common man—the men and women who never have ceased to believe in democracy, who never have ceased to love their families, their homes, and their country." The faith of America, he declared, is the faith of the common man. The New Deal cultural climate which evolved in America during the 1930's, and which was patently exemplified in many motion pictures, radio plays, and novels of the war period, helped to produce a pseudo-populist literature of the common man. This neo-populist art and literature emphasizes the concept of Americanism as a means of unifying all races, creeds, and classes. Instead of a literature which penetratingly describes class differences and which also reveals the consequences of the conditions of life that thwart the boy and girl of plebeian origin in the struggle for success and growth, as Dreiser did, this literature has generally stressed and sentimentalized the theme that the common man is human; it has also used the theme that the rich are Americans, too, and that they are like the common man.

The cultural influence of populism, like its political influence, cannot be interpreted in the same way for the 1940's as for the nineteenth century. The agrarian populist movement, reaching its political height with the rise of William Jennings Bryan, played a profound

role in the shaping of American literature and in influencing American social
thinking. It is one of the social, political,
economic developments which stand behind twentieth-century literature. One
of the best illustrations of the populist influence can be found in Frank Norris,
a major initiator of modern American
literature. His books are democratic, popular, anti-snobbish. In his essay "The Responsibilities of the Novelist," he argues
that the novelist must accept the responsibility of writing truthfully for the large
mass of the people. *The Octopus,* Volume I of Norris' uncompleted trilogy,
An Epic of the Wheat, portrays economic
struggle and class relationships on the
level of personal experience. It recounts
the conflict between independent wheat-
growers of the West and the railroad
"octopus." Although the former think of
themselves as the "people," they are independent capitalists who are producing
wheat on a capitalist basis and with the
use of the most advanced machinery of
the time; thus, while they think they are
fighting the battles of the people against
the railroad, they are also reducing
smaller producers to the status of tenants
or of agricultural laborers. A poet character, Pressley, speaks in these pages for
the author; he formalizes and generalizes
this populist theme by conceiving it in
terms of the interests of the people as a
whole. In this sense *The Octopus* can be
called "populist." However, populism is
not introduced as a vehicle for rhetorical
persuasiveness; rather, it is implanted in
the novel as a conviction which is in-
tegral in the narrative; it is socially
rooted and empirically developed as part
of the story.

In contrast to this, recent works of a
"populist" character are tendentiously
organized and rely for conviction on the
author's editorializations. A most notable
example of this is to be seen in the radio
plays of Norman Corwin. This difference
is important, both artistically and socio-
logically. Some recent works that grew
out of the New Deal cultural climate present life in America on the level of newspaper editorials, oversimplifying character and situation. Oversimplification of
this kind is to be found, for instance, in
such books as *The Grapes of Wrath.*

3

The American realistic novel has
treated the American Way of Life in
terms of the human costs of American
success and expansion. Dreiser's "successful" characters do not find inner harmony. This is exemplified by his finan-
cier, Cowperwood, and by Carrie Meeber of *Sister Carrie.* The most notable
characters who fail, Hurstwood and Clyde
Griffiths, suffer a terrible and tragic
end. Sherwood Anderson, influenced by
Dreiser, wrote principally of the little
man of the lower middle class, the man
on the level of the handicraftsman. Many
of his characters have already lost their
social identity before the stories com-
mence or are in the process of losing it as
the stories progress. With capitalist relationships conquering in the small town
—in fact, all over the country—types
such as these which Anderson describes
are declassed. Anderson deals, then, with
the consequences of such a development.
This is even seen in his emphasis on
hands—on working with one's hands.
And the feeling of human need in his
writings is seen in the need for contacts,
physical contacts. Through contacts,
need will be satisfied, and some sense of
personal and social identity will be re-
gained. The Andersonian emphasis on
sex grows out of this; sex is a way out of
confusion, a form of intimate contact
which might make more happy the lot of
the confused child of a confused world.

Dreiser presents more formally the result of conflict between the need for
sexual expression and the repressions imposed by the Puritan moral code. David
Graham Phillips also does this in his

novel, *Susan Lennox: Her Fall and Rise.* His heroine, Susan, is presented as a superior and attractive girl. However, she is socially ostracized because she was born out of wedlock. She is socially punished because of her mother's "sin." Both Dreiser and Phillips (the latter in a more sentimentally romantic vein) reveal social aspects of class relationships and class differences through their treatment of sex. As a result of social ostracism, Susan is driven out of her class; she is made a victim of the sexual appetites of men of a superior class. This is the essence of her "fall" in the first portions of this work. Dreiser's heroines, Carrie Meeber and Jennie Gerhardt, also have lovers who are of a social class superior to the one from which they come. Jennie is punished for her sin. Here, class injustice is involved in the punishment which society metes out to the girl who "sins." Sex in works of this kind serves as a focus which permits the author to reveal social consequences rooted in class differentiation. At the same time, we are shown the social snobbery, the social hypocrisy, and the double standard prevalent in the upper classes.

4

In the literature of the 1920's, leisure and consumption are of growing thematic importance. Also, the commodity and commodity values become either an open or a concealed theme. Babbitt's shallowness, for instance, is related to the fact that his social life and his inner world are controlled by commodities and cash values. Even his pleasures are bought, and a cash value placed on them. His thoughts and his life are governed to a great extent by the fact that he must impress those who are impressing him with cost prices. Childish display and ostentation are dominating factors in his life. Babbitt is living on the other side of the success dream. In a small way, he has become a success. But

his individuality has been lost. In a time of standardized commodities, he is a standardized man. This suggests the major criticism Sinclair Lewis makes of American civilization. The representative American, Babbitt, does not know how to use and enjoy his leisure, does not, with his success and greater leisure, learn how to *consume* more civilized and more sophisticated cultural values.

Other writers of this period, for instance F. Scott Fitzgerald, Hemingway, and Ring Lardner, also deal with the theme of leisure. Fitzgerald describes the social disillusionments and ballroom romanticism of the young people of the upper classes and the loneliness of Gatsby, who gives large parties and has an extensive social life; yet he is lonely, and his guests scarcely know him. Hemingway's characters live in a tourist world, and one of their major problems is that of consuming time itself. It is interesting to observe that his works are written from the standpoint of the spectator. His characters are usually people who are looking—looking at bull fights, scenery, and at one another across café tables. Ring Lardner's satire is directed against the snobbery and stupidity of people who are trying to enjoy themselves and do not know how. Most of his characters are seen in their leisure. If we see them at work, it is at some occupation concerned with the amusement or entertainment of others. Thus he shows us baseball players, prize fighters, a golf caddy, and songwriters at work. Leisure as a theme in such works is treated in terms of satire and social disillusionment.

5

After the Depression, with the entry of a new generation into literature, we can observe another thematic change in realistic American fiction. By and large, the plebeian classes, the lower class, and special groups of the American population were not centrally treated in American fiction before the end of the Twenties. But suddenly we can observe the change. It is mirrored in the racial backgrounds of writers, in the themes, in the subjects, and in the conditions of life which are treated. The orphan asylum, the streets of the city, poolrooms, lower-class homes and family life, the backward sections of America, such as parts of Georgia or the decaying sections of New England, hobo life—all this is introduced into the American novel and short story, and introduced from the inside rather than the outside. At the same time, first- and second-generation Americans of diverse racial and national backgrounds become characters in the American novel and short story.

With this, the problems of lower-class childhood are carefully and realistically introduced into the American novel. The burden placed on the child in society which is gradually becoming more stratified is dealt with more painfully and in greater detail than was usually the case in earlier fiction. One of the first books suggesting the new trend was *Bottom Dogs,* by Edward Dahlberg, a novel dealing with the life of a boy in an orphan asylum and his subsequent migratory existence. One could use the title of this novel to suggest the new emphasis. A bottom-dog literature, in the social sense, began to develop.

An important feature of this literature is that social snobbery—thematically dealt with in earlier realistic novels (like those of Dreiser and Phillips)—is revealed here as ugly racial prejudice. There should be nothing surprising in this fact. Snobbery and prejudice find different outlets on different levels of society. The snobbery of the upper classes is pressed down on the lower classes. The lower classes are undefended in the face of a class educational system which favors the sons and daughters of the upper classes. Possession of money and

the sense of security it usually provides can easily give a tone, a veneer, a seeming graciousness to upper-class life. Prejudice in such circles is a matter of excluding others, of not inviting them to one's home or social functions. Toward the bottom of the social ladder there is more interracial contact. The burden of all social problems weighs down most heavily on the areas of lower-class life. The personal psychological frustrations of those in the lower classes are additionally emphasized by economic frustration. Just as life here is less secure, it often happens that the personality, also, is less secure. This lack of security commonly exacerbates tempers. The struggle for place, money, and social position on the upper rungs is often transformed into the naked struggle of the individual vanities on the lower plane. This is all revealed in the violence described in some of the realistic writings of American plebeian writers. A clear example can be found in the short stories of Richard Wright, in *Uncle Tom's Children,* where we can see lynch violence breaking out or threatening to break out over seeming coincidences or accidents. Thus, a white woman sees a colored boy naked after he has been swimming. Coincidences such as these, in a society of acute class and racial tensions, flare into the social tragedy of violence.

Two of the dominant notes in the best of this literature are tension and violence—inner tension, expressed in frustration, frequently that of children, and violence on the physical plane. The class, group, and racial tensions in American society produce frustration and violence when there is a world or society of isolated and more-or-less estranged individuals who express their natures in a savage personal struggle of vanities. When you do not express your vanity through money and social position, you do it by your fists, by your sexual conquests, and by your language of insult and aggression. Even the dialogue of this literature is frequently sharp and violent.

This bottom-dog literature, a literature that is sharply realistic and that depicts conditions of dirt, physical misery, and inner frustration, is also a literature that introduces the plebeian classes on a more human level than was the case (with perhaps a few exceptions) in American writings before the late 1920's and early 1930's. It implicitly asserts the humanity of its characters; this constitutes its most positive value. It boldly introduces men and women and boys and girls of the lowest social stratum as human beings whose problems and whose feelings demand the urgent attention of the serious reading public of America. The boy on the street, the uneducated Negro, the sharecropper, the worker, and many others are here introduced, irrevocably, into the consciousness of America.

And with *Black Boy*, by Richard Wright, the problem of awareness, of development, is shown to be as important among the lower strata of American society as in the world of Henry James. This bottom-dog literature has now begun to combine a treatment of awareness with an account of conditions of life in America.

In this new literature, characterizations are developed without acceptance of prevailing stereotypes. Just as earlier realistic writing turned upside down the attitudes and editorial affirmations of the American dream, so this literature has done away with the stereotypes of the stage Irishman, the stage Negro, the stage Jew of earlier popular writing. One of the social implications or meanings of this work is that it breaks—in fact, it tears to ribbons—the earlier stereotypes associated with the American melting pot. By and large, this literature is one of realistic statement. It states social problems, not in terms of generalizations but rather in terms of direct characterization, of the immediacy of life de-

scribed on the printed page. If we define social causation as the more deeply influential economic and social forces in a society, which affect all the members in that society, we can then say that, in this literature, social causation is translated into individual motivation and into immediacy of action, thought, dream, and word. This literature deals concretely and directly with the major phases of American life which now seriously interest scores of sociologists, social workers, psychiatrists, criminologists, jurists, and others. It seeks to present in the more humanizing terms of literature much of what the newspapers sensationalize and view with alarm. Often it tells us what the quality of life is really like among "one-third of the nation."

It is easy to confuse such writings with neo-populist works on "the common man" that sentimentalize poverty and point up an editorialized national unity and a verbally formalized affirmation of democracy that exudes snobbery when evidence daily substantiates the conclusion that American class society is torn apart and exacerbated by class, group, and racial tensions. If one sees the pertinence in the obvious point that, in order to make men better, you must first tell them what they are like, it is easier to make distinctions between these two types of writing. There is always a gap between conventional images of life and life as it is lived. Realistic writing has constantly sought to narrow that gap. Earlier in the present century, American realistic writing had the effect of tearing away conventional images of the American dream, of sex, and of the social snobbery of the upper classes; in the last decade and a half, a major impact of American realistic writing has been the tearing apart of conventional images of life among the lower strata. Thus the realistic writers of America have contributed to social thinking by setting down in fictional form material that can help to create wider consciousness of what life is like in America.

If this literature is appreciated as a fictional account of the quality of many American lives, it may then be a little easier to tear aside the conventional false images: it will be possible to make people try to see more directly, more clearly. Literature is not, in itself, a means of solving problems: these can be solved only by action, by social and political action. But realistic literature can and should serve as a means of helping people discover more about themselves and about the conditions of life around them. And the best of American realistic literature can be shown to have contributed toward this effort. This analysis (necessarily sketchy because of the limitation of space) is an attempt to show in what way we should approach the problem of evaluating American literature by seeing it as a body of works that reveal how American realists have struggled to pin down important aspects of the realities of living in America, here and now.

Richard Chase

✳ 1914-

Richard Chase, who teaches literature at Columbia University, is known to students of American writings as author of studies on Herman Melville, Emily Dickinson, and Walt Whitman. He has broken new paths in these and in THE DEMOCRATIC VISTA *of 1958, which is a dialogue on attitudes toward our achievement in literature, but he discovers vitalizing suggestions along older paths also. "The Broken Circuit" appeared in its present form in the* ANCHOR REVIEW *for 1957 and, slightly revised and expanded, in 1959 as the first chapter of* THE AMERICAN NOVEL AND ITS TRADITION, *which speaks at greater length than Simms and Hawthorne on subjects which they had introduced.*

The Broken Circuit: Romance and the American Novel

The imagination that has produced much of the best and most characteristic American fiction—that of Charles Brockden Brown, Cooper, Hawthorne, Melville, Henry James, Mark Twain, Frank Norris, Faulkner, and Hemingway, among others —has been shaped by the contradictions and not by the unities and harmonies of our culture. In a sense this may be true of all literatures of whatever time and place. Nevertheless there are some literatures which take their form and tone from polarities, opposites, and irreconcilables, but are content to rest in and sustain them, or to resolve them into unities, if at all, only by special and limited means. The American novel tends to rest in contradictions and among extreme ranges of experience. When it attempts to resolve contradictions, it does so in oblique, morally equivocal ways. As a general rule it does so either in melodramatic actions or in pastoral idyls, although intermixed with both one may find the stirring instabilities of "American humor." These qualities constitute the uniqueness of that branch of the novelistic tradition which has flourished in this country. They help to account for the strong element of "romance" in the American "novel."

Briefly, and hence dogmatically, the contradictions which have vivified and excited the American imagination seem traceable to these historical facts. First, there is the dual allegiance of the American, who in his intellectual culture belongs both to the old world and the new.

Second, there is the solitary position man has been placed in in this country, vis-à-vis the state and mankind in general—a position enforced, as Tocqueville points out, by the very institutions of democracy as those evolved in the eighteenth and nineteenth centuries. In aristocratic societies there was a shared body of inherited habits, attitudes, and institutions that stood in a mediating position between the individual and the state. But when democratic man contemplates his situation, as Tocqueville says, he is conscious of the stark, unmediated opposition between himself and "the immense form of society" and "the still more imposing aspect of mankind." The ingrained tendency to conceive reality as involving irreconcilable contradictions was enforced also by New England Puritanism, which starkly opposed the individual to his God, and perhaps by the frontier experience, which opposed the individual to the immense form, not of society, but of nature.

Third, there is the special character of New England Puritanism, which not only harshly confronted man with his God but which took on a positively Manichaean quality. It is this quality which affects writers like Hawthorne and Melville and enters deeply into the national consciousness, reappearing, for example, in the mythology of Populism. From the historical point of view, New England Puritanism was a backsliding in religion as momentous in shaping the imagination as the cultural reversion Cooper studied on the frontier (see especially Chapter VI of *The Prairie*). For, at least as apprehended by the literary imagination, New England Puritanism—with its grand metaphors of election and damnation, its opposition of the kingdom of light and the kingdom of darkness, its eternal and autonomous contraries of good and evil—seems to have recaptured the Manichaean sensibility. The American imagination, like the New

England Puritan mind itself, seems less interested in redemption than in the melodrama of the eternal struggle of good and evil, less interested in incarnation and reconciliation than in alienation and disorder. If we may suppose ourselves correct in tracing to this origin the prevalence in the American novel of the symbols of light and dark, we may doubtless suppose also that this sensibility has been enhanced by the racial composition of our people and by the Civil War that was fought, if more in legend than in fact, over the Negro.

In contrast to the American novel, the English novel has followed a middle way. It is notable for its great practical sanity, its powerful, engrossing composition of wide ranges of experience into a moral centrality and equability of judgment. Oddity, distortion of personality, dislocations of normal life, recklessness of behavior, malignancy of motive—these the English novel has included. Yet the profound poetry of disorder we find in the American novel is missing, with rare exceptions, from the English. Radical maladjustments and contradictions are reported but are seldom of the essence of form in the English novel, and although it is no stranger to suffering and defeat or to triumphant joy either, it gives the impression of absorbing all extremes, all maladjustments and contradictions into a normative view of life. In doing so, it shows itself to derive from the two great influences that stand behind it—classic tragedy and Christianity. The English novel has not, of course, always been strictly speaking, tragic or Christian. Often it has been comic, but often, too, in that superior form of comedy which approaches tragedy. Usually it has been realistic or, in the philosophical sense of the word, "naturalistic." Yet even its peculiar kind of gross poetic naturalism has preserved something of the two great traditions that formed English literature. The English novel, that is, follows the tendency of tragic art and Christian art, which characteristically move through contradictions to forms of harmony, reconciliation, catharsis, and transfiguration.

Judging by our greatest novels, the American imagination, even when it wishes to assuage and reconcile the contradictions of life, has not been stirred by the possibility of catharsis or incarnation, by the tragic or Christian possibility. It has been stirred, rather, by the aesthetic possibilities of radical forms of alienation, contradiction, and disorder.

The essential difference between the American novel and the English will be strongly pointed up to any reader of F. R. Leavis' *The Great Tradition.* Mr. Leavis' "great tradition" of the novel is really Anglo-American, and it includes not only Jane Austen, George Eliot, Conrad, and Henry James but, apparently, in one of its branches Hawthorne and Melville. The American novel is obviously a development from the English tradition. At least it was, down to 1880 or 1890. For at that time our novelists began to turn to French and Russian models and the English influence has decreased steadily ever since. The more extreme imagination of the French and Russian novelists has clearly been more in accord with the purposes of modern American writers than has the English imagination. True, an American reader of Mr. Leavis' book will have little trouble in giving a very general assent to his very general proposition about the Anglo-American tradition. Nevertheless, he will also be forced constantly to protest that there is another tradition of which Mr. Leavis does not seem to be aware, a tradition which includes most of the best American novels.

Ultimately, it does not matter much whether one insists that there are really *two* traditions, the English and the American (leaving aside the question of what writers each might be said to com-

prise) or whether one insists merely that there is a radical divergence within one tradition. All I hold out for is a provisional recognition of the divergence as a necessary step towards understanding and appreciation of the American novel. The divergence is brought home to an American reader of Mr. Leavis' book when, for example, he comes across the brief note allotted to the Brontës. Here is Mr. Leavis' comment on Emily Brontë:

I have said nothing about *Wuthering Heights* because that astonishing work seems to me a kind of sport . . . she broke completely, and in the most astonishing way, both with the Scott tradition that imposed on the novelist a romantic resolution of his themes, and with the tradition coming down from the eighteenth century that demanded a plane-mirror reflection of the surface of 'real' life. Out of her a minor tradition comes, to which belongs, most notably, *The House with the Green Shutters.*

Of course Mr. Leavis is right; in relation to the great tradition of the English novel, *Wuthering Heights* is indeed a sport. But suppose it were discovered that *Wuthering Heights* was written by an American of New England Calvinist or southern Presbyterian background. The novel would be astonishing and unique no matter who wrote it or where. But if it were an American novel it would not be a sport; it has too close an affinity with too many American novels, and among them some of the best. Like many American fictions *Wuthering Heights* proceeds from an imagination that is essentially melodramatic, that operates among radical contradictions and renders reality indirectly or poetically, thus breaking, as Mr. Leavis observes, with the traditions that require a surface rendering of real life and a resolution of themes, "romantic" or otherwise.

Those readers who make a dogma out of Mr. Leavis' views are thus proprietors of an Anglo-American tradition in which many of the most interesting and original and several of the greatest American novels are sports. Charles Brockden Brown's *Wieland* is a sport, and so are *The Scarlet Letter* and *The Blithedale Romance, Moby Dick, Pierre,* and *The Confidence Man, Huckleberry Finn, The Red Badge of Courage, McTeague, As I Lay Dying, The Sun Also Rises*—all are eccentric, in their differing ways, to a tradition of which, let us say, *Middlemarch* is a standard representative. Not one of them has any close kinship with the massive, temperate, moralistic rendering of life and thought we associate with Mr. Leavis' "great tradition."

The English novel, one might say, has been a kind of imperial enterprise, an appropriation of reality with the high purpose of bringing order to disorder. By contrast, as Lawrence observed in his *Studies in Classic American Literature*, the American novel has usually seemed content to explore, rather than to appropriate and civilize, the remarkable and in some ways unexampled territories of life in the new world and to reflect its anomalies and dilemmas. It has not wanted to build an imperium but merely to discover a new place and a new state of mind. Explorers see more deeply, darkly, privately, and disinterestedly than imperialists, who must perforce be circumspect and prudential. The American novel is more profound and clairvoyant than the English novel, but by the same token it is narrower and more arbitrary, and it tends to carve out of experience brilliant, highly wrought fragments rather than massive unities.

In the history of the American novel, the tradition of romance is major, whereas in the history of the English novel it is minor. True, nothing is to be gained by trying to separate too sharply the romance from the novel. One of their chief advantages is that, as literary forms go, they are relatively loose and flexible. But especially in discussing American literature, these terms have to be defined closely enough to distinguish between them, even though the distinction itself may sometimes be meaningless as applied to a given book and even though, following usage, one ordinarily uses the word "novel" to describe a book like Cooper's *The Prairie* which might more accurately be called a "romance" or a "romance-novel."

Doubtless the main difference between the novel and the romance is the way in which they view reality. The novel renders reality closely and in comprehensive detail. It takes a group of people and sets them going about the business of life. We come to see these people in their real complexity of temperament and motive. They are in explicable relation to nature, to each other, to their social class, to their own past. Character is more important than action and plot, and probably the tragic or comic actions of the narrative will have the primary purpose of enhancing our knowledge of and feeling for an important character, a group of characters, or a way of life. The events that occur will usually be plausible, given the circumstances, and if the novelist includes a violent or sensational occurrence in his plot, he will introduce it only into such scenes as have been (in the words of Percy Lubbock) "already prepared to vouch for it." Historically, as it has often been said, the novel has served the interests and aspirations of an insurgent middle class.

By contrast the romance, following distantly the medieval example, feels free to render reality in less volume and detail. It tends to prefer action to character, and action will be freer in a romance than in a novel, encountering, as it were, less resistance from reality. (This is not always true, as we see in what might be called the static romances of Hawthorne, in which the author uses the allegorical, rather than the dramatic, possibilities of the form.) The romance can flourish without providing much intricacy of relation. The characters, probably rather two-dimensional types, will not be complexly related to each other or to society or to the past. Human beings will on the whole be shown in ideal relation—that is, they will share emotions only after these have become abstract or symbolic. To be sure, characters may become profoundly involved in some way, as in Hawthorne or Melville, but it will be a deep and narrow, an obsessive, involvement. In American romances it will not matter much what class people come from, and where the novelist would arouse our interest in a character by exploring his origin, the romancer will probably do so by enveloping it in mystery. Character itself becomes, then, somewhat abstract and ideal, so much so in some romances that it seems to be merely a function of plot. The plot we may expect to be highly colored. Astonishing events may occur, and these are likely to have a symbolic or perhaps ideological, rather than a realistic, plausibility. Being less committed to the immediate rendition of reality than the novel, the romance will more freely veer toward mythic, allegorical, and symbolistic forms.

Although some of the best works of American fiction have to be called, for purposes of criticism, romances rather than novels, we would be pursuing a chimera if we tried, except provisionally, to isolate a literary form known as the American prose romance, as distinguished from the European or the American novel. In actuality the romances of our literature, like European prose romances, are literary hybrids, unique only in their peculiar but widely differing amalgamation of novelistic and romance elements. Obviously, our fiction is historically a branch of the European tradition of the novel. And it is the better part of valor in the critic to understand the American romances as adaptations of traditional novelistic procedures to new cultural conditions and new aesthetic aspirations. It will not damage our appreciation of the originality and value of *Moby Dick* or *The Blithedale Romance* to say that they both seem to begin as novels but then veer off into the province of romance, in the one case making a supreme triumph, in the other, a somewhat dubious but interesting medley of genres and intentions. Speaking generally, one may say that when the American novelists depart from the novelistic tradition, they do so, with variations, by way of melodrama or pastoral idyl, often both.

Most of the American writers of fiction, from Brown and Cooper to Norris, have described themselves as romancers rather than novelists. In the Preface to *The Yemassee* (1835), for example, William Gilmore Simms dwells at length on this distinction. Echoing Cooper and Scott, as well as Aristotle's *Poetics,* he describes "modern Romance" as the new form of epic. Epic turned out to be an important source of romance in American fiction, but, outside of *Moby Dick,* Cooper's *The Prairie,* and one or two other books, not a major source.

Hawthorne's brief prefaces to his longer works explain and defend for the first time the distinctively American art of romance. And it is in Hawthorne that some of the considerable psychological and intellectual possibilities of romance are first explored. As he sees the problem confronting the American author, it consists in the necessity of finding (in the words of the Introduction to *The Scarlet Letter*) "a neutral territory, somewhere between the real world and fairyland, where the Actual and the Imaginary may meet, and each imbue itself with the nature of the other." Romance is, as we see, a kind of "border" fiction, whether the field of action is in the neutral territory between civilization and the wilderness, as in the adventure tales of Cooper and Simms or whether, as in Hawthorne and later romancers, the field of action is conceived not so much as a place as a state of mind—the borderland of the human mind where the actual and the imaginary intermingle. Romance does not plant itself, like the novel, solidly in the midst of the actual. Nor when it is memorable, does it escape into the purely imaginary.

In saying, as he does in the preface to *The House of the Seven Gables*, that no matter what its extravagances romance must not "swerve aside from the truth of the human heart," Hawthorne was in effect announcing the definitive adaptation of romance to America. To keep fiction in touch with the human heart is to give it a universal human significance. But this cannot be done memorably in prose fiction, even in the relatively loose form of the romance, without giving it a local significance. The truth of the heart as pictured in romance may be more generic or archetypal than in the novel; it may be rendered less concretely; but it must still be made to belong to a time and a place. Surely Hawthorne's romances do. In his writings romance was made for the first time to respond to the particular demands of an American imagination and to mirror, in certain limited ways, the American mind.

Among others, Melville, James, Mark Twain, Norris, Faulkner, and Hemingway comprise the tradition of the romance-novel established by Cooper, Brown, Simms, and Hawthorne. But there is, it should be parenthetically noted, a second stream of romance. This is the stream, justly contemned by Mark Twain and James, which descends directly from Scott and includes John Esten Cooke's *Surry of Eagle's Nest* (1866), Lew Wallace's *Ben Hur* (1880), Charles Major's *When Knighthood Was in Flower* (1898), and later books like

Gone With the Wind and the historical tales of Kenneth Roberts. Although these works may have their points, according to the taste of the reader, they are, historically considered, the tag end of a European tradition that begins in the Middle Ages and has come down into our own literature without responding to the forms of imagination which the actualities of American life have inspired.

In the preceding pages I have tried to formulate preliminary definitions of "romance" and the "novel" and then to look briefly at the matter from a historical point of view. In order to amplify the discussion, both in the abstract and the concrete, it will be of value at this point to return, with the aid of Henry James' prefaces, to the question of definition. In doing so, I shall risk repeating one or two observations which have already been made.

The first four prefaces James wrote for the New York edition of his works set forth, or at least allude to, the main items of his credo as a novelist, and although they are perhaps well known, there may be some advantage in looking them over again before noticing what James had to say directly about the relation of the romance to the novel. The four prefaces are those to *Roderick Hudson*, *The American*, *The Portrait of a Lady*, and *The Princess Casamassima*.

We might take as a motto this sentence from the preface to *The Princess*: "Experience, as I see it, is our apprehension and our measure of what happens to us as social creatures." Although James himself does not overtly contrast his procedure with that of romance until he comes to the preface to *The American*, we shall be justified in ourselves making the contrast, since James is obviously seeking to show, among other things, how the imperfections of romance may be avoided. And thus we reflect that, in a romance, "experience" has less to do with human beings as "social creatures" than as individuals. Heroes, villains, victims, legendary types confronting other individuals or confronting mysterious or otherwise dire forces—this is what we meet in romances.

When James tells us that the art of the novel is the "art of representation," the practice of which spreads "round us in a widening, not in a narrow circle," we reflect on the relative paucity of "representation" in the older American romances and their tendency towards a concentrated and narrow profundity. Again we hear that "development" is "of the very essence of the novelist's process," and we recall how in romances characters appear really to be given quantities rather than emerging and changing organisms responding to their circumstances as these themselves develop one out of another. For if characters change in a romance, let's say as Captain Ahab in *Moby Dick* or the Reverend Dimmesdale in *The Scarlet Letter* changes, we are not shown a "development"; we are left rather with an element of mystery, as with Ahab, or a simplified and conventionalized alteration of character, as with Dimmesdale. Similarly, the episodes of romance tend to follow each other without ostensible causation; here too there is likely to be an element either of mystery or convention. To "treat" a subject, James says, is to "exhibit . . . relations"; and the novelist "is in the perpetual predicament that the continuity of things is the whole matter, for him, of comedy and tragedy." But in a romance much may be made of unrelatedness, of alienation and discontinuity, for the romancer operates in a universe that is less coherent than that of the novelist.

As for the setting, James says that it is not enough merely to report what it seems to the author to be, in however minute detail. The great thing is to get into the novel not only the setting but somebody's *sense* of the setting. We recall that in *The Scarlet Letter* the setting, although sketchy, is pictorially very beautiful and symbolically apropos. But none of the characters has a *sense* of the setting; that is all in the author's mind and hence the setting is never dramatized but remains instead a handsomely tapestried backdrop. In *Moby Dick* the setting is less inert; it becomes, in fact, a kind of "enveloping action." Still, only in some of the scenes do we have Ishmael's sense of the setting; during most of the book Ishmael himself is all but banished as a dramatic presence.

The whole question of the "point of command" or "point of view" or "center of intelligence" is too complicated to go into here. Suffice it to say that the allotment of awareness, the question of what character shall be specially conscious of the meaning of what happens to and around him so that we see events and people more or less through his eyes, thus gaining a sense of dramatic coherence—these questions are less and less pertinent as fiction approaches pure romance. Natty Bumppo need be conscious only of what the Indians are going to do next. Hawthorne's Chillingworth and Melville's Ahab are clairvoyantly conscious, but with a profoundly obsessive distortion of the truth. They are not placed in context in order to give concrete dramatic form to a large part of what the author sees, as is the "point of command" in a James novel; all we learn from them is how *they* see. And in *The Blithedale Romance,* the dyed-in-the-wool romancer Hawthorne merely proves that you mustn't have a central observer in your story, because if you do you simply point up the faults of romance and admit your incapacity to follow out a fully developed novelistic procedure. In the romance too much depends on mystery and bewilderment to risk a generally receptive intelligence in the midst of things. Too often the effect you are after depends on a universe that is felt to be irrational, contradictory, and melodramatic—whereas the effect of a central intelligence is to produce a sense of verisimilitude and dramatic coherence.

One or two further items from the prefaces may point up the contrast. A character, especially "the fictive hero," as James says, "successfully appeals to us only as an eminent instance, as eminent as we like, of our own conscious kind." He must not be "a morbidly special case"—but in romance he may well be. Again, says James, when economy demands the suppression of parts of the possible story they must not be merely "eliminated"; they must be foreshortened, summarized, compressed, but nevertheless brought to bear on the whole. But in the looser universe of the romance, we may think "elimination" will be less criminal, and unexplained hiatuses and discontinuities may positively contribute to the effect. To take an obvious case, in *Moby Dick* we are content to think the sudden elimination of Bulkington an interesting oddity rather than a novelistic blunder and we gladly draw on the poetic capital Melville makes of it.

As for the moral significance of the novel, James sees a "perfect dependence of the 'moral' sense of a work of art on the amount of felt life concerned in producing it." We must ask, he says, "is it valid, in a word, is it genuine, is it sincere, the result of some direct impression or perception of life." These questions bear less on the romance, one of the assumptions of which is that it need not contain a full amount of felt life, that life may be felt indirectly through legend, symbol, or allegory. Nor does the romance need the sincerity of the novel; indeed, as Lawrence points out, American romances, especially, tend to make their effect by a deep "duplicity" or ironic indirection.

To come finally to James's specific comments on the question we are considering. In the prefaces he follows his own advice as expressed twenty-odd years earlier in "The Art of Fiction"— he sees no reason, that is, why the practicing writer should distinguish between novel and romance. There are good novels and bad ones, novels that have life and those that haven't—and this, for the novelist, is the only relevant question. The implication is that the novelist will be also the romancer if the "life" he is rendering extends into the realm of the "romantic." But if we are not, except as critics and readers, to distinguish between novel and romance, we still have to distinguish, within the novel that may be also a romance, the "romantic" from the "real." And this James essays in his Preface to *The American.*

In rereading this early novel James found a large element of romance in the free and easy way in which he had made his semi-legendary hero Christopher Newman behave on his European travels. Particularly, James thought, the picture of the Bellegard family was "romantic." James had made them reject Newman as a vulgar manufacturer when actually common sense tells us that "they would positively have jumped at him." And James comments that "the experience here represented is the disconnected and uncontrolled experience—uncontrolled by our general sense of 'the way things happen'—which romance alone more or less successfully palms off on us." At the same time James finds an unexpected pleasure in rereading *The American,* which somewhat compensates for the lapses of verisimilitude. And his description of this pleasure makes a fair definition of the pleasure of romance— "the free play of so much unchallenged instinct . . . the happiest season of surrender to the invoked muse and the projected fable." [1]

"The disconnected and uncontrolled experience," then, is of the essence of romance, and any adequate definition must proceed from this postulate. First, however, one may clear out of the way certain conventional but inadequate descriptions of romance. It is not "a matter indispensably of boats, or of caravans, or of tigers, or of 'historical characters,' or of ghosts, or of forgers, or of detectives, or of beautiful wicked women, or of pistols and knives"—although one might perhaps be a little readier than James to think that these things might be of service. Yet one follows him assentingly when he decides that the common element in sensational tales is "the facing of danger" and then goes on to say that for most of us the danger represented by caravans and forgers is certainly benign or impotent compared with the "common and covert" dangers we face in our everyday existence, which may "involve the sharpest hazards to life and honor and the highest instant decisions and intrepidities of action."

The "romantic" cannot be defined, either, as "the far and the strange," since, as such, these things are merely "unknown," whereas the "romantic" is something we know, although we know it indirectly. Nor is a novel romantic because its hero or heroine is. "It would be impossible to have a more romantic temper than Flaubert's Madame Bovary, yet nothing less resembles a romance than the record of her adventures." Nor can we say the presence or absence of "cos-

tume" is a crucial difference, for "where . . . does costume begin or end?"

James then arrives at the following formulation:

The only *general* attribute of projected romance that I can see, the only one that fits all its cases, is the fact of the kind of experience with which it deals—experience liberated, so to speak; experience disengaged, disembroiled, disencumbered, exempt from the conditions that we usually know to attach to it and, if we wish so to put the matter, drag upon it, and operating in a medium which relieves it, in a particular interest, of the inconvenience of a *related*, a measurable state, a state subject to all our vulgar communities.

And James goes on in words that are particularly illustrative of his own art:

The greatest intensity may so be arrived at evidently—when the sacrifice of community, of the "related" sides of situations, has not been too rash. It must to this end not flagrantly betray itself; we must even be kept if possible, for our illusion, from suspecting any sacrifice at all.

In a fully developed art of the novel there is, as James says, a "latent extravagance." In men of "largest responding imagination before the human scene," we do not find only the romantic or only reality, but a "current . . . extraordinarily rich and mixed." The great novelist responds to the "need of performing his whole possible revolution, by the law of some rich passion in him for extremes."

To have a rich passion for extremes is to grasp both the real and the romantic. By the "real," James explains, he means "the things we cannot possibly *not* know, sooner or later, in one way or another." By the "romantic" he means "the things that, with all the facilities in the world, all the wealth and all the courage and all the wit and all the adventure, we never *can* directly know; the things that can

---

[1] Cf. Melville's plea to his reality-minded readers for latitude in the depiction of character and incident. The ideal reader, he says, will "want nature. . . ; but nature unfettered, exhilarated, in effect transformed. . . . It is with fiction as with religion: it should present another world, and yet one to which we feel the tie." (*The Confidence Man,* Chapter 33)

reach us only through the beautiful circuit and subterfuge of our thought and our desire."

We hear much in these prefaces of the novelist's rich and mixed "current," of the possible "revolution" of his mind among extremes, of the "circuit" of thought and desire. James speaks, too, of the "conversion" that goes on in the mind of the novelist's characters between what happens to them and their *sense* of what happens to them, and of "the link of connection" between a character's "doing" and his "feeling." In other words James thinks that the novel does not find its essential being until it discovers what we may call the circuit of life among extremes or opposites, the circuit of life that passes through the real and the ideal, through the directly known and the mysterious or the indirectly known, through doing and feeling.

Much of the best American fiction does not meet James' specifications. It has not made the circuit James requires of the "largest responding imagination." And the closer it has stuck to the assumptions of romance the more capital it has made, when any capital has been made, exactly by leaving the Jamesian circuits broken. That very great capital can be made in this way James does not acknowledge or know, and hence his own hostility and that of many of his followers, to the more extreme forms of American fiction—those we associate, for example, with Brockden Brown, Melville, and Faulkner.

In this trans-Jamesian realm of fiction there are certain special virtues. Among them are the "intellectual energy" that Brown prized, the profundity described by Melville as "the blackness of darkness," a certain intrepid and penetrating dialectic of action and meaning, a radical skepticism about ultimate questions, a certain rapidity, irony, and abstraction. By their use of these qualities the American novelists have made of romance something far more valuable than the escapism, fantasy, and sentimentality often associated with this form.

Nevertheless James' theory of the novel, his idea of the circuit of life which allows him to incorporate in his own novels so many of the attributes of romance, is the most complete and admirable theory, as at their best James' are the most complete and admirable novels yet produced by an American. And it is against James' theory and often, though certainly not always, his practice that we have to test the achievements of his compatriots. The danger is that in doing so we should lapse into an easy disapproval of that "rich passion . . . for extremes" which James praised on his own grounds but which may be seen operating to advantage on other grounds too.

PROSPECTS

Ralph Waldo Emerson

✳ 1803-1882

*Emerson's "Self-Reliance," which ap-
peared as the second essay in his first
collected volume in 1841, has been read
with enthusiastic response by many generations of readers. It is among the least
diffuse of his writings, directed toward
a single, central subject, which is a call
to every man to be himself: otherwise,
said Emerson, there can be no thinking,
no proper progress, no literature worth
reading. Imitation even of the thought of
Emerson, or of any man, is fatal. The
greatest peril therefore to a reader of
this essay is that he may believe it, or
that his approval of what is said will
tempt him to say just the same thing.*

Self-Reliance

"Ne te quæsiveris extra."

Man is his own star; and the soul that
    can
Render an honest and a perfect man,
Commands all light, all influence, all
    fate;
Nothing to him falls early or too late.
Our acts our angels are, or good or ill,
Our fatal shadows that walk by us still.

*Epilogue to Beaumont and Fletcher's
Honest Man's Fortune.*

Cast the bantling on the rocks,
Suckle him with the she-wolf's teat,
Wintered with the hawk and fox,
Power and speed be hands and feet.

I read the other day some verses written by an eminent painter which were
original and not conventional. The soul
always hears an admonition in such lines,
let the subject be what it may. The
sentiment they instil is of more value
than any thought they may contain. To
believe your own thought, to believe
that what is true for you in your private
heart is true for all men—that is genius.
Speak your latent conviction, and it shall
be the universal sense; for the inmost
in due time becomes the outmost, and
our first thought is rendered back to us
by the trumpets of the Last Judgment.
Familiar as the voice of the mind is to
each, the highest merit we ascribe to
Moses, Plato and Milton is that they set
at naught books and traditions, and
spoke not what men, but what *they*
thought. A man should learn to detect
and watch that gleam of light which
flashes across his mind from within, more
than the lustre of the firmament of bards
and sages. Yet he dismisses without notice his thought, because it is his. In
every work of genius we recognize our
own rejected thoughts; they come back
to us with a certain alienated majesty.
Great works of art have no more affecting lesson for us than this. They teach
us to abide by our spontaneous impression with good-humored inflexibility then
most when the whole cry of voices is on
the other side. Else to-morrow a stranger
will say with masterly good sense precisely what we have thought and felt all
the time, and we shall be forced to take
with shame our own opinion from another.

There is a time in every man's education when he arrives at the conviction
that envy is ignorance; that imitation is

283

suicide; that he must take himself for better for worse as his portion; that though the wide universe is full of good, no kernel of nourishing corn can come to him but through his toil bestowed on that plot of ground which is given to him to till. The power which resides in him is new in nature, and none but he knows what that is which he can do, nor does he know until he has tried. Not for nothing one face, one character, one fact, makes much impression on him, and another none. This sculpture in the memory is not without preëstablished harmony. The eye was placed where one ray should fall, that it might testify of that particular ray. We but half express ourselves, and are ashamed of that divine idea which each of us represents. It may be safely trusted as proportionate and of good issues, so it be faithfully imparted, but God will not have his work made manifest by cowards. A man is relieved and gay when he has put his heart into his work and done his best; but what he has said or done otherwise shall give him no peace. It is a deliverance which does not deliver. In the attempt his genius deserts him; no muse befriends; no invention, no hope.

Trust thyself: every heart vibrates to that iron string. Accept the place the divine providence has found for you, the society of your contemporaries, the connection of events. Great men have always done so, and confided themselves childlike to the genius of their age, betraying their perception that the absolutely trustworthy was seated at their heart, working through their hands, predominating in all their being. And we are now men, and must accept in the highest mind the same transcendent destiny; and not minors and invalids in a protected corner, not cowards fleeing before a revolution, but guides, redeemers and benefactors, obeying the Almighty effort and advancing on Chaos and the Dark.

What pretty oracles nature yields us on this text in the face and behavior of children, babes, and even brutes! That divided and rebel mind, that distrust of a sentiment because our arithmetic has computed the strength and means opposed to our purpose, these have not. Their mind being whole, their eye is as yet unconquered; and when we look in their faces we are disconcerted. Infancy conforms to nobody; all conform to it; so that one babe commonly makes four or five out of the adults who prattle and play to it. So God has armed youth and puberty and manhood no less with its own piquancy and charm, and made it enviable and gracious and its claims not to be put by, if it will stand by itself. Do not think the youth has no force, because he cannot speak to you and me. Hark! in the next room his voice is sufficiently clear and emphatic. It seems he knows how to speak to his contemporaries. Bashful or bold then, he will know how to make us seniors very unnecessary.

The nonchalance of boys who are sure of a dinner, and would disdain as much as a lord to do or say aught to conciliate one, is the healthy attitude of human nature. A boy is in the parlor what the pit is in the playhouse; independent, irresponsible, looking out from his corner on such people and facts as pass by, he tries and sentences them on their merits, in the swift, summary way of boys, as good, bad, interesting, silly, eloquent, troublesome. He cumbers himself never about consequences, about interests; he gives an independent, genuine verdict. You must court him; he does not court you. But the man is as it were clapped into jail by his consciousness. As soon as he has once acted or spoken with *éclat* he is a committed person, watched by the sympathy or the hatred of hundreds, whose affections must now enter into his account. There is no Lethe for this. Ah, that he could pass again into his neutrality! Who can thus avoid all pledges and, having observed, observe again from the same unaffected, unbiased, unbribable, unaffrighted innocence—must always be formidable. He would utter opinions on all passing affairs, which being seen to be not private but necessary, would sink like darts into the ear of men and put them in fear.

These are the voices which we hear in solitude, but they grow faint and inaudible as we enter into the world. Society everywhere is in conspiracy against the manhood of every one of its members. Society is a joint-stock company, in which the members agree, for the better securing of his bread to each shareholder, to surrender the liberty and culture of the eater. The virtue in most request is conformity. Self-reliance is its aversion. It loves not realities and creators, but names and customs.

Whoso would be a man, must be a nonconformist. He who would gather immortal palms must not be hindered by the name of goodness, but must explore if it be goodness. Nothing is at last sacred but the integrity of your own mind. Absolve you to yourself, and you shall have the suffrage of the world. I remember an answer which when quite young I was prompted to make to a valued adviser who was wont to importune me with the dear old doctrines of the church. On my saying, "What have I to do with the sacredness of traditions, if I live wholly from within?" my friend suggested—"But these impulses may be from below, not from above." I replied, "They do not seem to me to be such; but if I am the Devil's child, I will live then from the Devil." No law can be sacred to me but that of my nature. Good and bad are but names very readily transferable to that or this; the only right is what is after my constitution; the only wrong what is against it. A man is to carry himself in the presence of all opposition as if every thing were titular and ephemeral but he. I am ashamed to think how easily we capitulate to badges and names, to large societies and dead institutions. Every decent and well-spoken individual affects and sways me more than is right. I ought to go upright and vital, and speak the rude truth in all ways. If malice and vanity wear the coat of philanthropy, shall that pass? If an angry bigot assumes this bountiful cause of Abolition, and comes to me with his last news from Barbadoes, why should I not say to him, 'Go love thy infant; love thy wood-chopper; be good-natured and modest; have that grace; and never varnish your hard, uncharitable ambition with this incredible tenderness for black folk a thousand miles off. Thy love afar is spite at home.' Rough and graceless would be such greeting, but truth is handsomer than the affectation of love. Your goodness must have some edge to it—else it is none. The doctrine of hatred must be preached, as the counteraction of the doctrine of love, when that pules and whines. I shun father and mother and wife and brother when my genius calls me. I would write on the lintels of the door-post, *Whim*. I hope it is somewhat better than whim at last, but we cannot spend the day in explanation. Expect me not to show cause why I seek or why I exclude company. Then again, do not tell me, as a good man did to-day, of my obligation to put all poor men in good situations. Are they *my* poor? I tell thee, thou foolish philanthropist, that I grudge the dollar, the dime, the cent I give to such men as do not belong to me and to whom I do not belong. There is a class of persons to whom by all spiritual affinity I am bought and sold; for them I will go to prison if need be; but your miscellaneous popular charities; the education at college of fools; the building of meeting-houses to the vain end to which many now stand; alms to sots, and the thousand-fold Relief Societies; though I confess with shame I sometimes succumb and give the dollar, it is a wicked dollar, which by and by I shall have the manhood to withhold.

Virtues are, in the popular estimate, rather the exception than the rule. There is the man *and* his virtues. Men do what is called a good action, as some piece of courage or charity, much as they would pay a fine in expiation of daily non-appearance on parade. Their works are done as an apology or extenuation of their living in the world—as invalids and the insane pay a high board. Their virtues are penances. I do not wish to expiate, but to live. My life is for itself and not for a spectacle. I much prefer that it should be of a lower strain, so it be genuine and equal, than that it should be glittering and unsteady. I wish it to be sound and sweet, and not to need diet and bleeding. I ask primary evidence that you are a man, and refuse this appeal from the man to his actions. I know that for myself it makes no difference whether I do or forbear those actions which are reckoned excellent. I cannot consent to pay for a privilege where I have intrinsic right. Few and mean as my gifts may be, I actually am, and do not need for my own assurance or the assurance of my fellows any secondary testimony.

What I must do is all that concerns me, not what the people think. This rule, equally arduous in actual and in intellectual life, may serve for the whole distinction between greatness and meanness. It is the harder because you will always find those who think they know what is your duty better than you know it. It is easy in the world to live after the world's opinion; it is easy in solitude to live after our own; but the great man is he who in the midst of the crowd keeps with perfect sweetness the independence of solitude.

The objection to conforming to usages that have become dead to you is that it scatters your force. It loses your time and blurs the impression of your character. If you maintain a dead church, contribute to a dead Bible-society, vote with a great party either for the government or against it, spread your table like base housekeepers—under all these screens I have difficulty to detect the precise man you are: and of course so much force is withdrawn from your proper life. But do your work, and I shall know you. Do your work, and you shall reinforce yourself. A man must consider what a blindman's-buff is this game of conformity. If I know your sect I anticipate your argument. I hear a preacher announce for his text and topic the expediency of one of the institutions of his church. Do I not know beforehand that not possibly can he say a new and spontaneous word? Do I not know that with all this ostentation of examining the grounds of the institution he will do no such thing? Do I not know that he is pledged to himself not to look but at one side, the permitted side, not as a man, but as a parish minister? He is a retained attorney, and these airs of the bench are the emptiest affectation. Well, most men have bound their eyes with one or another handkerchief, and attached themselves to some one of these communities of opinion. This conformity makes them not false in a few particulars, authors of a few lies, but false in all particulars. Their every truth is not quite true. Their two is not the real two, their four not the real four; so that every word they say chagrins us and we know not where to begin to set them right. Meantime nature is not slow to equip us in the prison-uniform of the party to which we adhere. We come to wear one cut of face and figure, and acquire by degrees the gentlest asinine expression. There is a mortifying experience in particular, which does not fail to wreak itself also in the general history; I mean "the foolish face of praise," the forced smile which we put on in company where we do not feel at ease, in answer to conversation which does not interest us. The muscles, not spontaneously moved but moved by a low usurping wilfulness, grow tight about the outline of the face, with the most disagreeable sensation.

For nonconformity the world whips you with its displeasure. And therefore a man must know how to estimate a sour face. The by-standers look askance on him in the public street or in the friend's parlor. If this aversion had its origin in contempt and resistance like his own he might well go home with a sad countenance; but the sour faces of the multitude, like their sweet faces, have no deep cause, but are put on and off as the wind blows and a newspaper directs. Yet is the discontent of the multitude more formidable than that of the senate and the college. It is easy enough for a firm man who knows the world to brook the rage of the cultivated classes. Their rage is decorous and prudent, for they are timid, as being very vulnerable themselves. But when to their feminine rage the indignation of the people is added, when the ignorant and the poor are aroused, when the unintelligent brute force that lies at the bottom of society is made to growl and mow, it needs the habit of magnanimity and religion to treat it godlike as a trifle of no concernment.

The other terror that scares us from self-trust is our consistency; a reverence for our past act or word because the eyes of others have no other data for computing our orbit than our past acts, and we are loth to disappoint them.

But why should you keep your head over your shoulder? Why drag about this corpse of your memory, lest you contradict somewhat you have stated in this or that public place? Suppose you should contradict yourself; what then? It seems to be a rule of wisdom never to rely on your memory alone, scarcely even in acts of pure memory, but to bring the past for judgment into the thousand-eyed present, and live ever in a new day. In your metaphysics you have denied personality to the Deity, yet when the devout motions of the soul come, yield to them heart and life, though they should clothe God with shape and color. Leave your theory, as Joseph his coat in the hand of the harlot, and flee.

A foolish consistency is the hobgoblin of little minds, adored by little statesmen and philosophers and divines. With consistency a great soul has simply nothing to do. He may as well concern himself with his shadow on the wall. Speak what you think now in hard words and to-morrow speak what to-morrow thinks in hard words again, though it contradict every thing you said to-day.—'Ah, so you shall be sure to be misunderstood.' —Is it so bad then to be misunderstood? Pythagoras was misunderstood, and Socrates, and Jesus, and Luther, and Copernicus, and Galileo, and Newton, and every pure and wise spirit that ever took flesh. To be great is to be misunderstood.

I suppose no man can violate his nature. All the sallies of his will are rounded in by the law of his being, as the inequalities of Andes and Himmaleh are insignificant in the curve of the sphere. Nor does it matter how you gauge and try him. A character is like an acrostic or Alexandrian stanza; read it forward, backward, or across, it still spells the same thing. In this pleasing contrite wood-life which God allows me, let me record day by day my honest thought without prospect or retrospect, and, I cannot doubt, it will be found symmetrical, though I mean it not and see it not. My book should smell of pines and resound with the hum of insects. The swallow over my window should interweave that thread or straw he carries in his bill into my web also. We pass for what we are. Character teaches above our wills. Men imagine that they communicate their virtue or vice only by overt actions, and do not see that virtue or vice emit a breath every moment.

There will be an agreement in whatever variety of actions, so they be each honest and natural in their hour. For of one will, the actions will be harmonious, however unlike they seem. These varieties are lost sight of at a little distance, at a little height of thought. One tendency unites them all. The voyage of the best ship is a zigzag line of a hundred tacks. See the line from a sufficient distance, and it straightens itself to the average tendency. Your genuine action will explain itself and will explain your other genuine actions. Your conformity explains nothing. Act singly, and what you have already done singly will justify you now. Greatness appeals to the future. If I can be firm enough to-day to do right and scorn eyes, I must have done so much right before as to defend me now. Be it how it will, do right now. Always scorn appearances and you always may. The force of character is cumulative. All the foregone days of virtue work their health into this. What makes the majesty of the heroes of the senate and the field, which so fills the imagination? The consciousness of a train of great days and victories behind. They shed a united light on the advancing actor. He is attended as by a visible escort of angels. That is it which throws thunder into Chatham's voice, and dignity into Washington's port, and America into Adams's eye. Honor is venerable to us because it is no ephemera. It is always ancient virtue. We worship it to-day because it is not of to-day. We love it and pay it homage because it is not a trap for our love and homage, but is self-dependent, self-derived, and therefore of an old immaculate pedigree, even if shown in a young person.

I hope in these days we have heard the last of conformity and consistency. Let the words be gazetted and ridiculous henceforward. Instead of the gong for dinner, let us hear a whistle from the Spartan fife. Let us never bow and apologize more. A great man is coming to eat at my house. I do not wish to please him; I wish that he should wish to please me. I will stand here for humanity, and though I would make it kind, I would make it true. Let us affront and reprimand the smooth mediocrity and squalid contentment of the times, and hurl in the face of custom and trade and office, the fact which is the upshot of all history, that there is a great responsible Thinker and Actor working wherever a man works; that a true man belongs to no other time or place, but is the centre of things. Where he is, there is nature. He measures you and all men and all events. Ordinarily every body in society reminds us of somewhat else, or of some other person. Character, reality, reminds you of nothing else; it takes place of the whole creation. The man must be so much that he must make all circumstances indifferent. Every true man is a cause, a country, and an age; requires infinite spaces and numbers and time fully to accomplish his design; and posterity seem to follow his steps as a train of clients. A man Cæsar is born, and for ages after we have a Roman Empire. Christ is born, and millions of minds so grow and cleave to his genius that he is confounded with virtue and the possible of man. An institution is the lengthened shadow of one man; as, Monachism, of the Hermit Antony; the Reformation, of Luther; Quakerism, of Fox; Methodism, of Wesley; Abolition, of Clarkson. Scipio, Milton called "the height of Rome"; and all history resolves itself very easily into the biography of a few stout and earnest persons.

Let a man then know his worth, and keep things under his feet. Let him not peep or steal, or skulk up and down with the air of a charity-boy, a bastard, or an interloper in the world which exists for him. But the man in the street, finding no worth in himself which corresponds to the force which built a tower or sculptured a marble god, feels poor when he looks on these. To him a palace, a statue, or a costly book have an alien and forbidding air, much like a gay equipage, and seem to say like that, "Who are you, Sir?" Yet they all are his, suitors for his notice, petitioners to his faculties that they will come out and take possession. The picture waits for my verdict; it is not to command me, but I am to settle its claims to praise. That popular fable of the sot who was picked up dead-drunk in the street, carried to the duke's house, washed and dressed and laid in the duke's bed, and, on his waking, treated with all obsequious ceremony like the duke, and assured that he had been insane, owes its popularity to the fact that it symbolizes so well the state of man, who is in the world a sort of sot, but now and then wakes up, exercises his reason and finds himself a true prince.

Our reading is mendicant and sycophantic. In history our imagination plays us false. Kingdom and lordship, power and estate, are a gaudier vocabulary than private John and Edward in a small house and common day's work; but the things of life are the same to both; the sum total of both is the same. Why all this deference to Alfred and Scanderbeg and Gustavus? Suppose they were virtuous; did they wear out virtue? As great a stake depends on your private act today as followed their public and renowned steps. When private men shall act with original views, the lustre will be transferred from the actions of kings to those of gentlemen.

The world has been instructed by its kings, who have so magnetized the eyes of nations. It has been taught by this colossal symbol the mutual reverence that is due from man to man. The joyful loyalty with which men have everywhere suffered the king, the noble, or the great proprietor to walk among them by a law of his own, make his own scale of men and things and reverse theirs, pay for benefits not with money but with honor, and represent the law in his person, was the hieroglyphic by which they obscurely signified their consciousness of their own right and comeliness, the right of every man.

The magnetism which all original action exerts is explained when we inquire the reason of self-trust. Who is the Trustee? What is the aboriginal Self, on which a universal reliance may be grounded? What is the nature and power of that science-baffling star, without parallax, without calculable elements, which shoots a ray of beauty even into trivial and impure actions, if the least mark of independence appear? The inquiry leads us to that source, at once the essence of genius, of virtue, and of life, which we call Spontaneity or Instinct. We denote this primary wisdom as Intuition, whilst all later teachings are tuitions. In that deep force, the last fact behind which analysis cannot go, all things find their common origin. For the sense of being which in calm hours rises, we know not how, in the soul, is not diverse from things, from space, from light, from time, from man, but one with them and proceeds obviously from the same source whence their life and being also proceed. We first share the life by which things exist and afterwards see them as appearances in nature and forget that we have shared their cause. Here is the fountain of action and of thought. Here are the lungs of that inspiration which giveth man wisdom and which cannot be denied without impiety and atheism. We lie in the lap of immense intelligence, which makes us receivers of its truth and organs of its activity. When we discern justice, when we discern truth, we do nothing of ourselves, but allow a passage to its beams. If we ask whence this comes, if we seek to pry into the soul that causes, all philosophy is at fault. Its presence or its absence is all we can affirm. Every man discriminates between the voluntary acts of his mind and his involuntary perceptions, and knows that to his involuntary perceptions a perfect faith is due. He may err in the expression of them, but he knows that these things are so, like day and night, not to be disputed. My wilful actions and acquisitions are but roving; the idlest reverie, the faintest native emotion, command my curiosity and respect. Thoughtless people contradict as readily the statement of perceptions as of opinions, or rather much more readily; for they do not distinguish between perception and notion. They fancy that I choose to see this or that thing. But perception is not whimsical, but fatal. If I see a trait, my children will see it after me, and in course of time all mankind—although it may chance that no one has seen it before me. For my perception of it is as much a fact as the sun.

The relations of the soul to the divine spirit are so pure that it is profane to seek to interpose helps. It must be that when God speaketh he should communicate, not one thing, but all things; should fill the world with his voice; should scatter forth light, nature, time, souls, from the centre of the present thought; and new date and new create the whole. Whenever a mind is simple and receives a divine wisdom, old things pass away—means, teachers, texts, temples fall; it lives now, and absorbs past and future into the present hour. All things are made sacred by relation to it—one as much as another. All things are dissolved to their centre by their cause, and in the universal miracle petty and particular miracles disappear. If therefore a man claims to know and speak of God and carries you backward to the phraseology of some old mouldered nation in another

country, in another world, believe him not. Is the acorn better than the oak which is its fulness and completion? Is the parent better than the child into whom he has cast his ripened being? Whence then this worship of the past? The centuries are conspirators against the sanity and authority of the soul. Time and space are but physiological colors which the eye makes, but the soul is light: where it is, is day; where it was, is night; and history is an impertinence and an injury if it be any thing more than a cheerful apologue or parable of my being and becoming.

Man is timid and apologetic; he is no longer upright; he dares not say 'I think,' 'I am,' but quotes some saint or sage. He is ashamed before the blade of grass or the blowing rose. These roses under my window make no reference to former roses or to better ones; they are for what they are; they exist with God to-day. There is no time to them. There is simply the rose; it is perfect in every moment of its existence. Before a leaf-bud has burst, its whole life acts; in the full-blown flower there is no more; in the leafless root there is no less. Its nature is satisfied and it satisfies nature in all moments alike. But man postpones or remembers; he does not live in the present, but with reverted eye laments the past, or, heedless of the riches that surround him, stands on tiptoe to foresee the future. He cannot be happy and strong until he too lives with nature in the present, above time.

This should be plain enough. Yet see what strong intellects dare not yet hear God himself unless he speak the phraseology of I know not what David, or Jeremiah, or Paul. We shall not always set so great a price on a few texts, on a few lives. We are like children who repeat by rote the sentences of grandames and tutors, and, as they grow older, of the men of talents and character they chance to see—painfully recollecting the exact words they spoke; afterwards, when they come into the point of view which those had who uttered these sayings, they understand them and are willing to let the words go; for at any time they can use words as good when occasion comes. If we live truly, we shall see truly. It is as easy for the strong man to be strong, as it is for the weak to be weak. When we have new perception, we shall gladly disburden the memory of its hoarded treasures as old rubbish. When a man lives with God, his voice shall be as sweet as the murmur of the brook and the rustle of the corn.

And now at last the highest truth on this subject remains unsaid; probably cannot be said; for all that we say is the far-off remembering of the intuition. That thought by what I can now nearest approach to say it, is this. When good is near you, when you have life in yourself, it is not by any known or accustomed way; you shall not discern the footprints of any other; you shall not see the face of man; you shall not hear any name; the way, the thought, the good, shall be wholly strange and new. It shall exclude example and experience. You take tho way from man, not to man. All persons that ever existed are its forgotten ministers. Fear and hope are alike beneath it. There is somewhat low even in hope. In the hour of vision there is nothing that can be called gratitude, nor properly joy. The soul raised over passion beholds identity and eternal causation, perceives the self-existence of Truth and Right, and calms itself with knowing that all things go well. Vast spaces of nature, the Atlantic Ocean, the South Sea; long intervals of time, years, centuries, are of no account. This which I think and feel underlay every former state of life and circumstances, as it does underlie my present, and what is called life and what is called death.

Life only avails, not the having lived. Power ceases in the instant of repose; it resides in the moment of transition from a past to a new state, in the shooting of the gulf, in the darting to an aim. This one fact the world hates; that the soul *becomes;* for that forever degrades the past, turns all riches to poverty, all reputation to a shame, confounds the saint with the rogue, shoves Jesus and Judas equally aside. Why then do we prate of self-reliance? Inasmuch as the soul is present there will be power not confident but agent. To talk of reliance is a poor external way of speaking. Speak rather of that which relies because it works and is. Who has more obedience than I masters me, though he should not raise his finger. Round him I must revolve by the gravitation of spirits. We fancy it rhetoric when we speak of eminent virtue. We do not yet see that virtue is Height, and that a man or a company of men, plastic and permeable to principles, by the law of nature must overpower and ride all cities, nations, kings, rich men, poets, who are not.

This is the ultimate fact which we so quickly reach on this, as on every topic, the resolution of all into the ever-blessed One. Self-existence is the attribute of the Supreme Cause, and it constitutes the measure of good by the degree in which it enters into all lower forms. All things real are so by so much virtue as they contain. Commerce, husbandry, hunting, whaling, war, eloquence, personal weight, are somewhat, and engage my respect as examples of its presence and impure action. I see the same law working in nature for conservation and growth. Power is, in nature, the essential measure of right. Nature suffers nothing to remain in her kingdoms which cannot help itself. The genesis and maturation of a planet, its poise and orbit, the bended tree recovering itself from the strong wind, the vital resources of every animal and vegetable, are demonstrations of the self-sufficing and therefore self-relying soul.

Thus all concentrates: let us not rove; let us sit at home with the cause. Let us stun and astonish the intruding rabble of men and books and institutions by a simple declaration of the divine fact. Bid the invaders take the shoes from off their feet, for God is here within. Let our simplicity judge them, and our docility to our own law demonstrate the poverty of nature and fortune beside our native riches.

But now we are a mob. Man does not stand in awe of man, nor is his genius admonished to stay at home, to put itself in communication with the internal ocean, but it goes abroad to beg a cup of water of the urns of other men. We must go alone. I like the silent church before the service begins, better than any preaching. How far off, how cool, how chaste the persons look, begirt each one with a precinct or sanctuary! So let us always sit. Why should we assume the faults of our friend, or wife, or father, or child, because they sit around our hearth, or are said to have the same blood? All men have my blood and I all men's. Not for that will I adopt their petulance or folly, even to the extent of being ashamed of it. But your isolation must not be mechanical, but spiritual, that is, must be elevation. At times the whole world seems to be in conspiracy to importune you with emphatic trifles. Friend, client, child, sickness, fear, want, charity, all knock at once at thy closet door and say—'Come out unto us.' But keep thy state; come not into their confusion. The power men possess to annoy me I give them by a weak curiosity. No man can come near me but through my act. "What we love that we have, but by desire we bereave ourselves of the love."

If we cannot at once rise to the sanctities of obedience and faith, let us at least resist our temptations; let us enter into the state of war and wake Thor and Woden, courage and constancy, in our Saxon breasts. This is to be done in our smooth times by speaking the truth. Check this lying hospitality and lying affection. Live no longer to the expectation of these deceived and deceiving people with whom we converse. Say to them, 'O father, O mother, O wife, O brother, O friend, I have lived with you after appearances hitherto. Henceforward I am the truth's. Be it known unto you that henceforward I obey no law less than the eternal law. I will have no covenants but proximities. I shall endeavor to nourish my parents, to support my family, to be the chaste husband of one wife—but these relations I must fill after a new and unprecedented way. I appeal from your customs. I must be myself. I cannot break myself any longer for you, or you. If you can love me for what I am, we shall be the happier. If you cannot, I will still seek to deserve that you should. I will not hide my tastes or aversions. I will so trust that what is deep is holy, that I will do strongly before the sun and moon whatever inly rejoices me and the heart appoints. If you are noble, I will love you; if you are not, I will not hurt you and myself by hypocritical attentions. If you are true, but not in the same truth with me, cleave to your companions; I will seek my own. I do this not selfishly but humbly and truly. It is alike your interest, and mine, and all men's, however long we have dwelt in lies, to live in truth. Does this sound harsh to-day? You will soon love what is dictated by your nature as well as mine, and if we follow the truth it will bring us out safe at last.'—But so may you give these friends pain. Yes, but I cannot sell my liberty and my power, to save their sensibility. Besides, all persons have their moments of reason, when they look out into the region of absolute truth; then will they justify me and do the same thing.

The populace think that your rejection

of popular standards is a rejection of all standard, and mere antinomianism; and the bold sensualist will use the name of philosophy to gild his crimes. But the law of consciousness abides. There are two confessionals, in one or the other of which we must be shriven. You may fulfil your round of duties by clearing yourself in the *direct*, or in the *reflex* way. Consider whether you have satisfied your relations to father, mother, cousin, neighbor, town, cat and dog—whether any of these can upbraid you. But I may also neglect this reflex standard and absolve me to myself. I have my own stern claims and perfect circle. It denies the name of duty to many offices that are called duties. But if I can discharge its debts it enables me to dispense with the popular code. If any one imagines that this law is lax, let him keep its commandment one day.

And truly it demands something godlike in him who has cast off the common motives of humanity and has ventured to trust himself for a taskmaster. High be his heart, faithful his will, clear his sight, that he may in good earnest be doctrine, society, law, to himself, that a simple purpose may be to him as strong as iron necessity is to others!

If any man consider the present aspects of what is called by distinction *society*, he will see the need of these ethics. The sinew and heart of man seem to be drawn out, and we are become timorous, desponding whimperers. We are afraid of truth, afraid of fortune, afraid of death, and afraid of each other. Our age yields no great and perfect persons. We want men and women who shall renovate life and our social state, but we see that most natures are insolvent, cannot satisfy their own wants, have an ambition out of all proportion to their practical force and do lean and beg day and night continually. Our housekeeping is mendicant, our arts, our occupations, our marriages, our religion

we have not chosen, but society has chosen for us. We are parlor soldiers. We shun the rugged battle of fate, where strength is born.

If our young men miscarry in their first enterprises they lose all heart. If the young merchant fails, men say he is *ruined*. If the finest genius studies at one of our colleges and is not installed in an office within one year afterwards in the cities or suburbs of Boston or New York, it seems to his friends and to himself that he is right in being disheartened and in complaining the rest of his life. A sturdy lad from New Hampshire or Vermont, who in turn tries all the professions, who *teams it, farms it, peddles,* keeps a school, preaches, edits a newspaper, goes to Congress, buys a township, and so forth, in successive years, and always like a cat falls on his feet, is worth a hundred of these city dolls. He walks abreast with his days and feels no shame in not 'studying a profession,' for he does not postpone his life, but lives already. He has not one chance, but a hundred chances. Let a Stoic open the resources of man and tell men they are not leaning willows, but can and must detach themselves; that with the exercise of self-trust, new powers shall appear; that a man is the word made flesh, born to shed healing to the nations; that he should be ashamed of our compassion, and that the moment he acts from himself, tossing the laws, the books, idolatries and customs out of the window, we pity him no more but thank and revere him; and that teacher shall restore the life of man to splendor and make his name dear to all history.

It is easy to see that a greater self-reliance must work a revolution in all the offices and relations of men; in their religion; in their education; in their pursuits; their modes of living; their association; in their property; in their speculative views.

1. In what prayers do men allow

themselves! That which they call a holy office is not so much as brave and manly. Prayer looks abroad and asks for some foreign addition to come through some foreign virtue, and loses itself in endless mazes of natural and supernatural, and mediatorial and miraculous. Prayer that craves a particular commodity, anything less than all good, is vicious. Prayer is the contemplation of the facts of life from the highest point of view. It is the soliloquy of a beholding and jubilant soul. It is the spirit of God pronouncing his works good. But prayer as a means to effect a private end is meanness and theft. It supposes dualism and not unity in nature and consciousness. As soon as the man is at one with God, he will not beg. He will then see prayer in all action. The prayer of the farmer kneeling in his field to weed it, the prayer of the rower kneeling with the stroke of his oar, are true prayers heard throughout nature, though for cheap ends. Caratach, in Fletcher's "Bonduca," when admonished to inquire the mind of the god Audate, replies—

His hidden meaning lies in our endeavors;
Our valors are our best gods.

Another sort of false prayers are our regrets. Discontent is the want of self-reliance: it is infirmity of will. Regret calamities if you can thereby help the sufferer; if not, attend your own work and already the evil begins to be repaired. Our sympathy is just as base. We come to them who weep foolishly and sit down and cry for company, instead of imparting to them truth and health in rough electric shocks, putting them once more in communication with their own reason. The secret of fortune is joy in our hands. Welcome evermore to gods and men is the self-helping man. For him all doors are flung wide; him all tongues greet, all honors crown, all eyes follow with desire. Our love goes out to him and embraces him because he did not need it. We solicitously and apologetically caress and celebrate him because he held on his way and scorned our disapprobation. The gods love him because men hated him. "To the persevering mortal," said Zoroaster, "the blessed Immortals are swift."

As men's prayers are a disease of the will, so are their creeds a disease of the intellect. They say with those foolish Israelites, 'Let not God speak to us, lest we die. Speak thou, speak any man with us, and we will obey.' Everywhere I am hindered of meeting God in my brother, because he has shut his own temple doors and recites fables merely of his brother's, or his brother's brother's God. Every new mind is a new classification. If it prove a mind of uncommon activity and power, a Locke, a Lavoisier, a Hutton, a Bentham, a Fourier, it imposes its classification on other men, and lo! a new system. In proportion to the depth of the thought, and so to the number of the objects it touches and brings within reach of the pupil, is his complacency. But chiefly is this apparent in creeds and churches, which are also classifications of some powerful mind acting on the elemental thought of duty and man's relation to the Highest. Such is Calvinism, Quakerism, Swedenborgism. The pupil takes the same delight in subordinating every thing to the new terminology as a girl who has just learned botany in seeing a new earth and new seasons thereby. It will happen for a time that the pupil will find his intellectual power has grown by the study of his master's mind. But in all unbalanced minds the classification is idolized, passes for the end and not for a speedily exhaustible means, so that the walls of the system blend to their eye in the remote horizon with the walls of the universe; the luminaries of heaven seem to them hung on the arch their master built. They cannot imagine how you aliens have any right to see—how you can see; 'It must be somehow that you stole the light from us.' They do not yet perceive that light, unsystematic, indomitable, will break into any cabin, even into theirs. Let them chirp awhile and call it their own. If they are honest and do well, presently their neat new pinfold will be too strait and low, will crack, will lean, will rot and vanish, and the immortal light, all young and joyful, million-orbed, million-colored, will beam over the universe as on the first morning.

2. It is for want of self-culture that the superstition of Travelling, whose idols are Italy, England, Egypt, retains its fascination for all educated Americans. They who made England, Italy, or Greece venerable in the imagination, did so by sticking fast where they were, like an axis of the earth. In manly hours we feel that duty is our place. The soul is no traveller; the wise man stays at home, and when his necessities, his duties, on any occasion call him from his house, or into foreign lands, he is at home still and shall make men sensible by the expression of his countenance that he goes, the missionary of wisdom and virtue, and visits cities and men like a sovereign and not like an interloper or a valet.

I have no churlish objection to the circumnavigation of the globe for the purposes of art, of study, and benevolence, so that the man is first domesticated, or does not go abroad with the hope of finding somewhat greater than he knows. He who travels to be amused, or to get somewhat which he does not carry, travels away from himself, and grows old even in youth among old things. In Thebes, in Palmyra, his will and mind have become old and dilapidated as they. He carries ruins to ruins.

Travelling is a fool's paradise. Our first journeys discover to us the indifference of places. At home I dream that at Naples, at Rome, I can be intoxicated with beauty and lose my sadness. I pack my trunk, embrace my friends, embark on the sea and at last wake up in Naples, and there beside me is the stern fact, the sad self, unrelenting, identical, that I fled from. I seek the Vatican and the palaces. I affect to be intoxicated with sights and suggestions, but I am not intoxicated. My giant goes with me wherever I go.

3. But the rage of travelling is a symptom of a deeper unsoundness affecting the whole intellectual action. The intellect is vagabond, and our system of education fosters restlessness. Our minds travel when our bodies are forced to stay at home. We imitate; and what is imitation but the travelling of the mind? Our houses are built with foreign taste; our shelves are garnished with foreign ornaments; our opinions, our tastes, our faculties, lean, and follow the Past and the Distant. The soul created the arts wherever they have flourished. It was in his own mind that the artist sought his model. It was an application of his own thought to the thing to be done and the conditions to be observed. And why need we copy the Doric or the Gothic model? Beauty, convenience, grandeur of thought and quaint expression are as near to us as to any, and if the American artist will study with hope and love the precise thing to be done by him, considering the climate, the soil, the length of the day, the wants of the people, the habit and form of the government, he will create a house in which all these will find themselves fitted, and taste and sentiment will be satisfied also.

Insist on yourself; never imitate. Your own gift you can present every moment with the cumulative force of a whole life's cultivation; but of the adopted talent of another you have only an extemporaneous half possession. That which each can do best, none but his Maker can teach him. No man yet knows what it is, nor can, till that person has exhibited it. Where is the master who could have taught Shakespeare? Where is the master who could have instructed Franklin, or Washington, or Bacon, or Newton? Every great man is a unique. The Scipionism of Scipio is precisely that part he could not borrow. Shakespeare will never be made by the study of Shakespeare. Do that which is assigned you, and you cannot hope too much or dare too much. There is at this moment for you an utterance brave and grand as that of the colossal chisel of Phidias, or trowel of the Egyptians, or the pen of Moses or Dante, but different from all these. Not possibly will the soul, all rich, all eloquent, with thousand-cloven tongue, deign to repeat itself; but if you can hear what these patriarchs say, surely you can reply to them in the same pitch of voice; for the ear and the tongue are two organs of one nature. Abide in the simple and noble regions of thy life, obey thy heart, and thou shalt reproduce the Foreworld again.

4. As our Religion, our Education, our Art look abroad, so does our spirit of society. All men plume themselves on the improvement of society, and no man improves.

Society never advances. It recedes as fast on one side as it gains on the other. It undergoes continual changes; it is barbarous, it is civilized, it is christianized, it is rich, it is scientific; but this change is not amelioration. For every thing that is given something is taken. Society acquires new arts and loses old instincts. What a contrast between the well-clad, reading, writing, thinking American, with a watch, a pencil and a bill of exchange in his pocket, and the naked New Zealander, whose property is a club, a spear, a mat and an undivided twentieth of a shed to sleep under! But compare the health of the two men and you shall see that the white man has lost his aboriginal strength. If the traveller tell us truly, strike the savage with a broadaxe and in a day or two the flesh shall unite and heal as if you struck the blow into soft pitch, and the same blow shall send the white to his grave.

The civilized man has built a coach, but has lost the use of his feet. He is suported on crutches, but lacks so much support of muscle. He has a fine Geneva watch, but he fails of the skill to tell the hour by the sun. A Greenwich nautical almanac he has, and so being sure of the information when he wants it, the man in the street does not know a star in the sky. The solstice he does not observe; the equinox he knows as little; and the whole bright calendar of the year is without a dial in his mind. His notebooks impair his memory; his libraries overload his wit; the insurance-office increases the number of accidents; and it may be a question whether machinery does not encumber; whether we have not lost by refinement some energy, by a Christianity, entrenched in establishments and forms, some vigor of wild virtue. For every Stoic was a Stoic; but in Christendom where is the Christian?

There is no more deviation in the moral standard than in the standard of height or bulk. No greater men are now than ever were. A singular equality may be observed between the great men of the first and of the last ages; nor can all the science, art, religion, and philosophy of the nineteenth century avail to educate greater men than Plutarch's heroes, three or four and twenty centuries ago. Not in time is the race progressive. Phocion, Socrates, Anaxagoras, Diogenes, are great men, but they leave no class. He who is really of their class will not be called by their name, but will be his own man, and in his turn the founder of a sect. The arts and inventions of each period are only its costume and do not invigorate men. The harm of the improved machinery may compensate its good. Hudson and Behring accomplished so much in their fishing-boats as to astonish Parry and Franklin, whose equipment exhausted the resources of science and art. Galileo, with an opera-glass, discovered a more splendid series of celestial phenomena than any one since. Columbus found the New World in an undecked boat. It is curious to see the periodical disuse and perishing of means and machinery which were introduced with loud laudation a few years or centuries before. The great genius returns to essential man. We reckoned the improvements of the art of war among the triumphs of science, and yet Napoleon conquered Europe by the bivouac, which consisted of falling back on naked valor and disencumbering it of all aids. The Emperor held it impossible to make a perfect army, says Las Casas, "without abolishing our arms, magazines, commissaries and carriages, until, in imitation of the Roman custom, the soldier should receive his supply of corn, grind it in his hand-mill and bake his bread himself."

Society is a wave. The wave moves onward, but the water of which it is composed does not. The same particle does not rise from the valley to the ridge. Its unity is only phenomenal. The persons who make up a nation to-day, next year die, and their experience dies with them.

And so the reliance on Property, including the reliance on governments which protect it, is the want of self-reliance. Men have looked away from themselves and at things so long that they have come to esteem the religious, learned and civil institutions as guards of property, and they deprecate assaults on these, because they feel them to be assaults on property. They measure their esteem of each other by what each has, and not by what each is. But a cultivated man becomes ashamed of his property, out of new respect for his nature. Especially he hates what he has if he see that it is accidental—came to him by inheritance, or gift, or crime; then he feels that it is not having; it does not belong to him, has no root in him and merely lies there because no revolution or no robber takes it away. But that which a man is, does always by necessity acquire; and what the man acquires, is living property, which does not wait the beck of rulers, or mobs, or revolutions, or fire, or storm, or bankruptcies, but perpetually renews itself wherever the man breathes. "Thy lot or portion of life," said the Caliph Ali, "is seeking after thee; therefore be at rest from seeking after it." Our dependence on these foreign goods leads us to our slavish respect for numbers. The political parties meet in numerous conventions; the greater the concourse and with each new uproar of anouncement, The delegation from Essex! The Democrats from New Hampshire! Tho Whigs of Maine! the young patriot feels himself stronger than before by a new thousand of eyes and arms. In like manner the reformers summon conventions and vote and resolve in multitude. Not so, O friends! will the God deign to enter and inhabit you, but by a method precisely the reverse. It is only as a man puts off all foreign support and stands alone that I see him to be strong and to prevail. He is weaker by every recruit to his banner. Is not a man better than a town? Ask nothing of men, and, in the endless mutation, thou only firm column must presently appear the upholder of all that surrounds thee. He who knows that power is inborn, that he is weak because he has looked for good out of him and elsewhere, and, so perceiving, throws himself unhesitatingly on his thought, instantly rights himself, stands in the erect position, commands his limbs, works miracles; just as a man who stands on his feet is stronger than a man who stands on his head.

So use all that is called Fortune. Most men gamble with her, and gain all, and lose all, as her wheel rolls. But do thou leave as unlawful these winnings, and deal with Cause and Effect, the chancellors of God. In the Will work and acquire, and thou hast chained the wheel of Chance, and shall sit hereafter out of fear from her rotations. A political victory, a rise of rents, the recovery of your sick or the return of your absent friend, or some other favorable event raises your spirits, and you think good days are preparing for you. Do not believe it. Nothing can bring you peace but yourself. Nothing can bring you peace but the triumph of principles.

Abraham Lincoln

✳ 1809-1865

Abraham Lincoln spoke only ten sentences at the dedication of the National Cemetery at Gettysburg on November 19, 1863. He talked, not of literature, but of the subject of literature, which is the spirit of man. His sentences survive because they continue to speak to and of that spirit. It is difficult to think of any others which do their work so simply and well.

The Gettysburg Address

Fourscore and seven years ago our fathers brought forth on this continent a new nation, conceived in liberty, and dedicated to the proposition that all men are created equal.

Now we are engaged in a great civil war, testing whether that nation, or any nation so conceived and so dedicated, can long endure. We are met in a great battlefield of that war. We have come to dedicate a portion of that field as a final resting-place for those who here

gave their lives that that nation might live. It is altogether fitting and proper that we should do this.

But, in a larger sense, we cannot dedicate—we cannot consecrate—we cannot hallow—this ground. The brave men, living and dead, who struggled here, have consecrated it far above our poor power to add or detract. The world will little note or long remember what we say here, but it can never forget what they did here. It is for us, the living, rather, to be dedicated here to the unfinished work which they who fought here have thus far so nobly advanced. It is rather for us to be here dedicated to the great task remaining before us—that from these honored dead we take increased devotion to that cause for which they gave the last full measure of devotion; that we here highly resolve that these dead shall not have died in vain; that this nation, under God, shall have a new birth of freedom; and that government of the people, by the people, for the people, shall not perish from the earth.

Logan Pearsall Smith

✳ 1865-1946

Logan Pearsall Smith was a Quaker from New Jersey who as a young man knew and befriended Walt Whitman. Educated at Haverford College and then at Oxford, he spent most of his adult life in England as a bibliophile who amused his friends and himself with such collections of aphoristic essays as TRIVIA *in 1902 and* MORE TRIVIA *in 1921. He wrote infrequently and without robust power, but with concentration on saying exactly what he had in mind. "The Prospects of Literature" appeared in 1927 as a* pamphlet printed by the Hogarth Press of Smith's friends Leonard and Virginia Woolf.

The Prospects of Literature

. . . Literature is not a branch of philosophy or of social science; it is an art, and the arts blossom freely—and how rarely they blossom with freedom!—under certain technical conditions, and when their material, their medium happens to be in a state favorable to their right development. Great thoughts seem only able to produce great literature when they happen to coincide with a special condition of the means of expression, with what I may call, perhaps, a certain plastic state of language. This plastic state is due either to the unhackneyed freshness of an unexploited idiom, full of unconscious poetry, and with the dew of the morning, so to speak, upon it —and an unexhausted form of speech like this, as with the Greeks, the Romans and the Elizabethan English, has formed the medium of the supremest literature; or it may be due, as in the Romantic period, to what is called linguistic renovation, to the vigor borrowed from popular speech, and to the revival of an old vocabulary which had fallen out of use. So important is this need of an unhackneyed, expressive diction to give to thought an enduring form, or at least so important does it seem to me (but I am perhaps a faddist on the subject), that I should hardly consider it a paradox to regard what we call the great imaginative periods of literature as being, in fact, linguistic phenomena—incidents, not so much in the history of man's mind, as in that of his language.

Of the preoccupation with language, the verbal precosity and experiment which absorbed so much attention in the age of Ronsard in France, and in that of Shakespeare in England, or of that search for a renewed vocabulary which inaugurated the Romantic revivals in those countries,—of any of this kind of linguistic ferment, which is the surest sign of a revival of letters, I can see, however, little or no evidence today. Almost all our younger writers appear to be perfectly content with the common and current vocabulary; save for a few almost grotesque aberrations, the diction and style of each of them is indistinguishable, to me at least, from the diction and style of any of the others.

The very conditions, moreover, which I have already mentioned as being apparently so full of encouragement—the widespread interest in literature, the large reading public, the prompt recognition of merit,—all these things are hardly as favorable as they might seem to the development of literary talent. Enduring excellence in any art is not at all a necessary result—it would seem indeed to be more like an accidental by-product—of artistic activity, and a general interest in the art, and enthusiasm for it, often tends, by making it fashionable, to hamper and impede, rather than to foster it. And is not this what is happening today? A large number of people who would do well to concern themselves with other things are now led by fashion to take an intelligent, or semi-intelligent, interest in new books; they form enthusiastic cliques, so eager to welcome and make notorious any novelty, that the clever young writer is able to attain recognition much too easily. Success is, indeed, as Trollope says somewhere, a necessary poison; but they are fortunate, he wisely adds, to whom it comes late in life and in small doses.

The effects of this easy success—and of the many dangers in the path of the would-be artist, premature success is probably the most dangerous,—the results of this quickly won popularity are not difficult to observe all about us. As soon as any glimmering of talent, any freshness of originality, makes its appearance, it is immediately noted and exploited. Editors of the weekly and even the daily papers seize upon it; they have acquired, one may almost say of them, the habits of cannibals or ogres; they suck the brains of young writers, and then replace them by a new levy of adolescent talent. Their victims find it easy at the outstart to make money; even the fashion-papers pay them large sums for their little essays; they acquire expensive habits; they are introduced by benevolent patrons into what is called good society, and losing before long, as journalists are apt to lose, the power of reading and of nourishing their minds by disinterested study, they soon exhaust their little stock of originality: they have nothing more to say; their contributions are no longer wanted; a new set of beginners supplants them, to be soon exhausted and supplanted in their turn.

I do not mean to suggest that journalism, the habit of rapid composition for the press, is always inimical to talent. Often, indeed, to men of matured minds it is a fortunate incentive, which compels them, as it compelled Hazlitt for instance, to give the world their accumulated treasures of reading and meditation, to pour out the richness of their minds upon paper. But to the young, the inexperienced, the immature, how can this marketing of unripe fruit, be anything but injurious?

Publishers also compete nowadays with editors in killing the goose whose golden eggs they live on. As soon as a young author makes a success his publisher urges him to repeat it at once; other publishers are eager to win his patronage, and he is not infrequently offered a fixed income on the condition that he shall regularly provide one or two volumes a year. It is difficult for the impecunious young to refuse these offers; but they stimulate, they indeed

necessitate, that kind of hasty and abundant composition which must be harmful to any young writer, unless indeed he is endowed with the supremest talent. A great genius, it is true, born in a great age of literary creation, and finding ready at hand a plastic medium in which to embody his imagination, is sometimes able to produce abundant masterpieces, one after the other, and to write down without care pages which are destined to endure for ever. But these fortunate epochs occur so rarely, and these great unscrupulous artists who, like Shakespeare or Molière, can cater for the market without harm, and blamelessly worship the golden calf on the highest peak of Parnassus, are so divinely gifted and so exceptional, that they are quite outside all the ordinary rules.

It would be invidious to mention names, but in following the careers of the more recent writers whose first books have charmed me, I almost invariably find that their earliest publications, or at least their earliest successes, are their best achievements; their promise ripens to no fulfillment; each subsequent work tends to be a feeble replica and fainter echo of the first. In recent years, and especially since the war, similar conditions have prevailed in France and in America; in these countries, as in England, the number of miscarriages of talent, the rate of infant mortality among gifts of promise, seems to be ever increasing. And, indeed, with all the advertisement and premature publicity of our time, where can we hope to find that leisurely ripening of talent in the shade of obscurity, that slow development by experiment and failure, by which it can best be mellowed and matured?

No; the old, hard conditions were surely better. It was much better to stone the prophets than to crown them, as we now crown them at once, with roses. They are stifled by the roses, but the stones in the old days of stoning only drove them out into the desert to meditate on their mission and perfect their gifts, so that they might return at last to take their revenge on the world which had scorned them.

Van Wyck Brooks

✳ 1886-

Since 1909 when in WINE OF THE PURITANS *he pointed to the stultifying effect of our barren seventeenth century on all subsequent American culture, Van Wyck Brooks has spoken often with authority on matters of literary history and in criticism of the writings of his time. His search for a usable past, by which he means a native tradition on which American writers can build with profit, resulted in books on Mark Twain, Henry James, and Emerson. But best known now among his writings is the "Makers and Finders" series which in five volumes published between 1936 and 1952 surveys the history of literary activity in the United States from the time of Washington Irving to the first World War. "On Literature Today" was first presented as an address at Hunter College in 1940 and appeared in* LITERATURE TODAY *in the next year.*

On Literature Today

I have been asked to speak on the state of our literature today. We live in a very unhappy world at present, a time of great confusion, and the public has a right to expect from its poets and thinkers some light on the causes of our problems and the way to a better future. Few writers, I think, at present, are living up to these expectations. But still the belief in literature persists, because so many writers in the past have performed their true public function. "In literature alone," said Leopardi, "the regeneration of our country can have a substantial beginning." This may seem a large claim, and yet there is some truth in it, for, as Ibsen said, "Except as afterwards invented"—invented, that is, by thinking minds—"the conscious guiding principle is never present in the general sentiment of the people." The world can only be changed by desires, but we are always desiring things, and only ideas can make desires effective; and so the minds that invent and express have a powerful influence over us. What then is literature doing for us in these perplexing times? And if it is not doing more and better, what are the reasons for this?

Literature at all times is a very complex phenomenon. When you see it in perspective, historically, it seems simple enough. We know what we call the Victorian age. As it appears in the histories, it is like the map of a country, all one colour, with novelists, poets and essayists of various sizes, corresponding to towns and cities, dotted over the surface, united by currents of thought as clearly represented as rivers and railroads. But if one had lived in that age, it would all have seemed very different. An age is a chaos while one is living in it, and the past would be a chaos also if it were not interpreted for us. Besides, it is difficult to understand living writers because they are involved in our problems, which we cannot solve for ourselves. To generalize about the present is therefore a hazardous undertaking, although we are compelled to undertake. All manner of writers are living in the world, and if, confining oneself to America, one thinks of talent, and even genius, the present seems to me beyond all question one of the brilliant epochs. In literary capacity, in vigour of style, in the number of our novelists, poets and critics, we are obviously in the midst of a revival; and I am only quoting foreign writers, English, Irish, French, Scandinavian, Russian, when I say that never before, outside this country, wherever books are read, have American writers been so influential. But, aside from this question of talent, there is another question, implied in my quotations from Leopardi and Ibsen. Among these brilliant writers, where does one find the "conscious guiding principle"? How far do they contribute to "regenerate the country"? Let the Russian writer Chekhov reply to these questions. "Lift the robe of our muse and you will find within an empty void." Chekhov said this fifty years ago, and perhaps it expresses your feeling about our current literature. You may agree with a further observation which I have found in Chekhov's Letters: "Let me remind you that writers who, we say, are for all time, or are simply good, and who intoxicate us, have one common and very important characteristic. They are going towards something and are summoning you towards it, too, and you feel, not with your mind, but with your whole being, that they have some object. . . . The best of them are realists and paint life as it is, but, through every line's being soaked in the consciousness of an object, you feel, besides life as it is, the life which ought to be, and that captivates you. And we? We paint life as it is, but beyond that—nothing at all. We have neither immediate nor remote aims, and in our soul there is a great empty space."

I quote this long passage because it suggests the dominant note of our epoch. We have, to be sure, many writers who do not convey this impression, writers who make us feel what ought to be and for whom life is noble and important. In Robert Frost, in Lewis Mumford, to mention two of these, one feels a joyous confidence in human nature, an abounding faith in the will, a sense of the heroic in the human adventure, good will, the leaven of existence. All good things seem possible as one reads these writers. I remember a remark of John Butler Yeats, the father of the Irish poet. Thirty years ago, in New York, I used to see him every day, and one day he spoke of an old friend of his in Dublin, a judge who had retired from the bench. When someone asked this judge what remained in his mind, what had most deeply impressed him, during his fifty years in the criminal courts, his answer was, "The goodness of human nature." The grand old Yeats, who also loved his species, quoted this with a smile of agreement, for although he did not take an easy view of life, he felt that a seasoned magistrate knew whereof he spoke. I have never forgotten this remark, and I have always felt that literature, if it is to carry out its function, must contain this germ of faith, and that the greatest literature has always done so. The writers who retain this faith are what we call idealists. Robert Frost and Lewis Mumford—let me repeat their names, and there are many others—stand in our time for this position. In them one feels the power of the healthy will. Whenever I think of them, I remember Whitman's line, "Allons, the road is before us."

This mood of health, will, courage, faith in human nature, is the dominant mood in the history of literature. It was the mood of Homer, and writers will always return to it, as water rises to the level of its source. It is the warp of literature—the rest is the woof. But this is not the mood of the last two decades, and it seems as if these writers had lost the day, as if the poet Yeats were right in saying (although perhaps in quite a different sense),—

The best lack all conviction, while the worst Are full of passionate intensity.

A mood of desperate unhappiness reigns in the world, and this is marked especially in most of the writers. Have you thought how strange it is that so much of the world swallowed Spengler whole? —and I do not deny that Spengler was a very great genius, I do not deny the reality of his intuitions. The temperamental cards of our time are all stacked in favour of despair, and a somewhat sterile despair. One error that an optimist makes destroys his whole case, while a pessimist can get away with murder. It seems as if our writers passively wallowed in misery, calling it fate; as if the most powerful writers, from James Joyce to Hemingway, from Eliot of *The Waste Land* to Eugene O'Neill and Theodore Dreiser, were bent on proving that life is a dark little pocket. Influence in literature goes with intensity. The intense minds, good or evil, are those that wield the power; and the genius that has moulded the mind of the present is almost wholly destructive; and even where, as in many cases, these writers are fighting for social justice, they still picture life as hardly worth the trouble of fighting for it. Their tone is cynical, bleak, hard-boiled, hard-bitten, and life for them is vain, dark and empty, the plaything, in Theodore Dreiser's phrase, of "idle rocking forces" or currents of material interest. What did Joyce's *Ulysses* say if not that life is a bad joke? What do our novelists say if not that nothing good exists, that only the ugly is real, the perverted, the distorted? You know the picture of life you find in the novels of William Faulkner, Dos Passos, James T. Farrell and so many others, who carry the day with their readers because they are writers of great power. They seem to delight in kicking their world to pieces, as if civilization were all a pretence and everything noble a humbug. There are teachers and psychologists who back them up. Only the other day I was reading a well-known psychologist who made two statements that he took for granted: 1, Men have always known that the romantic picture of love

is false; 2, That which portrays the neurotic and defeated in human nature is closer to truth than that which pictures the aspirations of men. Love is a lie, in short, and the only realities are defeat and failure. This mood of incredulity and despair has penetrated millions of minds, and one finds it in the most unexpected places. There are people, educated people, who really think that Plutarch's heroes were humbugs, that Plutarch was pulling the wool over his readers' eyes when he pretended that heroes had ever existed. For these people, and they are many, all the closets are full of skeletons, for them even Diogenes was optimistic. What a gullible fellow Diogenes was—imagine wasting one's time, going about with a lantern, looking for an honest man, as if such a thing were to be conceived of! Not long ago I was talking with a distinguished professor about Eugene O'Neill's play *Mourning Becomes Electra*. He said that O'Neill had given the only truthful picture of New England, the New England not only of the present but of the past—that Cambridge and Concord a hundred years ago were just like this village in the play, whited sepulchres, full of dead men's bones. As for the old New England writers, they were all hypocrites and liars. So far has this iron of incredulity entered into the modern soul.

What this all means is seldom discussed in the critical writing of the present. Most of our critical writing deals with technical questions, and technical novelty, as it seems to me, is almost the only virtue it demands or praises. Not whether a writer contributes to life, but whether he excels in some new trick, is the question that is usually asked. It is their formal originality that has given prestige to writers like Joyce, Eliot and Gertrude Stein; and perhaps this is natural in an age of technics. But how can we ignore the larger questions involved in this drift of the modern mind? It seems to me it represents the "death-drive," as certain psychologists call it, the will to die that is said to exist side by side in our minds with the will to live. Defeat and unhappiness can reach a point where we accept them and embrace them and rejoice in our enervation and disintegration. And whether we rejoice in it or not, this literature is disintegrating. "All that is ugly," Nietzsche said, "weakens and afflicts man. It reminds him of deterioration, of danger and of impotence. He actually suffers loss of power by it. The effect of ugliness," Nietzsche continues, "can be measured by the dynamometer. Whenever man is depressed, he has a sense of the proximity of something ugly. His sense of power, his will to power, his courage, his pride—they decrease with the ugly, they increase with the beautiful." That is what I mean by suggesting that all these writers represent the death-drive. And if, with their technical virtues, they destroy our faith, our will to make the world worth living in, we cannot let their influence go unchallenged.

Now, I have an instinctive will to believe in writers. Deep down below the level where I agree or disagree with them, I like and respect them because they are writers. In less expansive moods, I admit that there are rattlesnake writers, rhinoceros, hyena, jackal writers. There are literary Hitlers and Mussolinis, who are as useful to the race as a large and active copperhead in August. But writers, as a class, as I have known them, are sensitive, scrupulous men, lovers of justice and full of good will for other people. They are almost all idealists by instinct. And so, when I see great numbers of writers bent, as they seem to be, on destroying life, I ask myself, What are the reasons for it? Why do they see only the ugly in life? Why are they so cynical and fatalistic? And are they to blame for this, or are we to blame—we, all of us, society, the world we live in?

Creative minds, of all minds, are those that naturally love life most. Obviously, these writers have been disappointed.

It is a commonplace that all these writers have expressed the state of mind of a world between wars. Thirty years ago, when I began to write, the future was an exciting and hopeful vista. Everyone believed in evolution, as a natural social process. We took the end for granted. Mankind was marching forward, and the only questions were of ways and means. I do not need to say how far the first world-war destroyed this happy vista. The young and sensitive minds who grew up in its shadow were utterly disillusioned by what they saw. They felt they had been betrayed, and, as evil triumphed, they came to feel that nothing else was real. This was the case all over our world, and the triumph of reactionary forces, in the years that followed, has gone very far to confirm this impression. We have witnessed every day the success of the powers of evil, that have bragged and bullied their way towards the rule of the world. Everything good has been pushed to the wall, and even five years ago Bertrand Russell, speaking of England, said that no one could think of reform any longer, no one could think of anything but the approaching menace, the threat of these conquering forces that have darkened the world. If, in this respect, we are relatively fortunate, our writers have shared this world-depression; and their cynicism has other local causes. The optimistic picture of our life that prevailed in the last generation led to a reaction that was automatic. It was too good to be true; and as Howells, for instance, could not bear to look at the ugly things in life, the ugly things in life became an obsession with the novelists who followed. A similar reaction took place in the sphere of language. The obscenity and profanity of many of our writers seems to me as childish as the prudery of Howells; but Howells was prudish, and much of his generation was prudish, and this was bound to lead to what I call inverted prudery. Just so we had our "debunking" biographies, in reaction against the writers who drew the veil over the faults of their heroes; and in other ways too our civilization is reaping its whirlwinds. A few years ago, as a publisher's reader, I ran through a novel every day by some young man or woman who had grown up in the West or the South. They could not seem to forgive the towns they were born in— just to escape from these towns and tell the world how ugly, false and brutal they were seemed to be almost the motive of these writers in living. I think our generation will be remembered as the one in which everyone hated, often without visible reason, the town in which he was born. And the writers of whom I am speaking were obsessed with ugly memories, ugly as to material things and mostly as to spiritual. And I thought, Well, these towns were not founded with sensitive types in view. They were founded by aggressive men who were seeking an outlet for their primitive forces, and now the sensitive types have appeared and demanded their place in the sun, and their world is not ready to receive them. You know how Thomas Wolfe describes his country: "More land, more wooden houses, more towns, hard and raw and ugly. . . . Ugly disorder and meanness." The moral of his novel is the moral of hundreds of other American novels: "The great masculine flower of gentleness, courage and honour died in a foul tangle." We are getting in this generation the reports of writers who have seen nothing else but this rawness and hardness. And we are getting also the reports of the excluded, the children of our newly arrived foreign population, many of whom have seen little else in all their lives but the slums and mean streets of monstrous cities, who have

often known here little but slights and indignity. How far, for them, has America been the promised land of which we heard so much before the war?

It is the reports of all these classes that we are getting in our fiction—the excluded, the disinherited and the hypersensitive types who have grown up in our less developed regions. Worst of all, we have been getting the reports of expatriates, whose prestige of late has been immense. And when I say expatriates, I mean the word in our sense—not the sense it has come to have in connection with refugee intellectuals. The expatriates to whom I refer are those who have broken with their group-life, by choice, on grounds of taste and taste alone. The prestige of Henry James rose with that of Ezra Pound, Gertrude Stein, Eliot and various others. These writers, as writers, have great integrity, and they have made discoveries, both literary and psychological, that entitle them to much of their position; and you may say that where one lives is a purely personal question. Is it possible to lay down rules about it? Certainly many writers have lived outside their country and served their country or the world better by so doing. Ibsen lived for forty years abroad, and he said he had never seen his home so clearly as from a distance and during his absence. But I do not think this is true for Americans, perhaps because our roots are not so deep as the roots of men of older countries. When we leave our country we are apt to leave our roots behind us, and we fail to develop roots in any other country; and what this means is that we miss the deeper experiences that give us a mature point of view. Missing these experiences, we live on the surface, and, having evaded life because we cannot master it, we end by denying its importance—we end by denying the importance of all the primary things of life. You know how all these writers ridicule provinciality. But much of what they

call provincial is basic in every civilization. No country could survive for six
months without it. To escape from provinciality is good, provided we make distinctions; but, besides provinciality of
place, there is also "time-provinciality,"
as Professor Whitehead calls it. This is
the illusion that to be modern is worth
all the other virtues; and the great effort of these writers is to represent the
last minute, as if to keep up with the
mode were more important than any of
the great realities of life and death. They
make much of technical questions because they have little to say otherwise,
and they sneer at the great writers of
the past, as Henry James used to say that
Tolstoy was not worth reading, as Eliot
prefers to Milton a dozen obscure metaphysical poets. To exalt the inferior over
the great, in the name of their technical
virtues, is a way of defending their own
weakness; and Gertrude Stein has reduced their position to the last absurdity.
In her theory of æsthetics, neither
thought nor feeling matters. Nothing
counts but the word-pattern, and the
greatest thing in life is a nursery-jingle.

You know this is infantile, and in fact
it seems to me that most of our current
literature is written by adolescent minds.
Mencken has remained a boy. The brag
and bluster of Hemingway speak for a
boy,—certainly a very gallant boy; so do
Thomas Wolfe's poetic gropings; so does
the cult of *Huckleberry Finn,* uniquely a
book of boys, for boys, by a boy. Our
novelists seldom picture developed
types; and, if Eliot exalts the minor poets
over the major poets, is it not because
he does not feel the major emotional
problems? If this is the case, what is the
reason but a lack of the sort of attachments, to the family, to the soil, to public life, that develop the sense of responsibility and, with this, maturity of
mind? Let me add that the writers I
have mentioned have felt this problem;
they have all, in one way or another,

struggled with it, and that is why, among
us, they are eminent writers. But even
if they, the eminent, are adolescent—because of the conditions of our time—
what shall we say of the rank and file,
who are boys without the genius? The
great cry of this age is that we should
"face life"; but facing life means in many
cases evading the most important elements of life. The world has seemed so
difficult to writers, it has seemed so
sinister and fearful, that to keep their
personalities alive they have thrown the
cargo over to save the ship. Their lives
have been narrowed and desiccated, and
they have remained emotionally shallow.

But, to return to their cynicism, does
it really deny ideals? Is it not properly
seen, rather, as a desperate affirmation
of them? The depth of the despair of the
present is the measure of its defeated
expectation. It demands, it presupposes,
the things it denies. Our writers like to
say that "free will" is played out. They
think they are determinists, but they always turn out to be fatalists, and that is
quite a different matter. William James
marked the distinction. "The fatalistic
argument," he said, "is really no argument for simple determinism. There runs
through it the sense of a force which
might make things otherwise from one
moment to another, if it were only strong
enough to breast the tide. A person who
feels the *impotence* of free effort in this
way has the acutest notion of what is
meant by it, and of its possible independent power. How else could he be so
conscious of its absence and of that of
its effects? But genuine determinism occupies a totally different ground: not the
impotence, but the *unthinkability* of free
will is what it affirms." There is the
Asiatic attitude, and one could never
imagine an Asiatic writing as Faulkner
writes, or as Dos Passos, or Dreiser, or
Hemingway or any of our writers. It
takes long generations of disappointment,
hundreds and thousands of years of dis-

illusion, to produce the deterministic frame of mind. The determinist is one who has never had any expectations, but our American fatalism presupposes hope. It does not argue that free will does not exist; it merely affirms that the will is not effective. It pays the highest tribute to the will, for it says that life is meaningless and empty precisely because of this negation. The only unthinkable thing, for American minds, is that the will should not exist; and that is the reason why, when it is not effective, its impotence seems to Americans so overwhelming.

So it appears that the mood of these writers is a kind of inverted idealism. Their harsh incredulity is the measure of their potential faith; and when I think of the loose talk about "high ideals" that governed the general mind when I was a boy, and that went hand in hand with so many abuses, it seems to me that this turn of thought should prove in the end beneficial, creative of all that it misses. The ideal has often been maintained by those who have denied it in their youth; and, while there are no Saint Augustines in my generation, or any John Bunyans that I know of, I think the mind of the country, as a whole, has had its adolescence in our time—old as the sections were, the South, New England. It has gone through terrible growing pains, but the nation will be, in consequence, more mature. It is a good thing, surely, that young people now are so exacting, so wary of hypocrisy and humbug. And is there not a visible reaction against the defeatist mind, and against these parasites and air-plants, who have thriven in a discouraged world, as Spanish moss thrives on decaying trees? I see on all sides a hunger for affirmations, for a world without confusion, waste or groping, a world that is full of order and purpose, and for ourselves, in America, a chance to build it. When Europe too had its chance, and Americans were

hankering for Europe, William James wrote, "Europe has been made what it is by men staying in their homes and fighting stubbornly, generation after generation, for all the beauty, comfort and order they have got. We must abide and do the same." Europe still has its chance, no doubt; but Europe is reaping whirlwinds far worse than ours and has lost the charm for us that it once possessed. It has thrown us back upon ourselves, and America has risen immensely in its power to charm us. Thousands of novels, biographies and histories, published in recent years, have shown us what multifarious strivings and failures and what multifarious victories lie behind us; and young writers now are settling in the remotest regions, determined to find them interesting or make them so. You never hear now of Greenwich Village, which used to be a haven for the exiles from Alabama and Kansas, the West and the South; and the reason you never hear of it is that the exiles have gone back to Alabama and to Kansas. They are founding schools in Iowa City and writing novels about Montana, and some are poet-farmers in Vermont. They are cultivating their roots where the seeds were sown, and where they are sure to yield their flowers and fruit.

William Barrett

✳ 1913-

William Barrett, who teaches philosophy at New York University, is a former editor of the PARTISAN REVIEW *and author of* IRRATIONAL MAN: A STUDY IN EXISTENTIAL PHILOSOPHY *(1958). The following essay is reprinted from the* NEW YORK TIMES BOOK REVIEW *of May 10, 1959.*

We're on the Road: American Writing in the Cold War

Some months ago I made my first automobile trip across country from California to New York. For a provincial Easterner the effect was both exalting and humbling, somewhat as if I were taking out first citizenship papers in the country in which I had been born but which I had always taken so much (and without really knowing how much) for granted.

A few days after getting back, I visited an old friend, an anti-Communist of the oldest vintage, scarred and tired by the political wars but capable still of soaring into political argument with that old high theoretical passion of the Nineteen Thirties. Our talk turned naturally to politics, where because I had been out of touch I rather expected him to have the good word. I got it, too, and quickly: "America," he declared somberly, "has already lost the war." Well, I could concede without too much difficulty that we had not exactly been winning the Cold War; but no, he shook his head, he meant just what he said, America had slipped back into a position where it could no longer recover the initiative. And he went on to proofs and instances, retailing point by point a long decade of chances missed, actions not taken, Russian advances. A grim game at chess that he seemed to leave with the caption: Red to play and mate in ten moves.

Of course, life and chess are not exactly the same game, and I could recall many prognoses like this one by political intellectuals before World War II that had looked so solid and turned out so fragile against the rock of historical events. But instead of arguing back, I found myself remembering my trip. While my friend talked, I was looking at mental pictures—of the land with its

people through which I had just driven. Probably I could not have put my hand on any better argument at the time, and now I'm convinced there isn't any better.

The reader may get some idea of the violent contrast here if he imagines the conversation staged à la television: two men talking against the sliding background of mountains, farms, rivers, towns and factories; in the foreground the dialogue of defeat and in the background the unreeling picture of a land and its people that do not have at all the look of defeat.

This contrast, in all its violence, I offer here as a key to much of our literature since World War II. In my own mind, at any rate, the two experiences—my trip and the talk—have rather merged to symbolize the two compelling realities in the background of our American writing during these years: (1) the image of the land and (2) the presence of the Cold War. Let us take them up in order.

The big land with its overwhelming variety, raw and not yet humanized as Europe is by the hands of history and peasantry—"unstoried, unenhanced and artless," as Robert Frost puts it—has always been at once a challenge and an escape for our writers. There it is, rolling immensely and beckoningly westward, or eastward if you are a Californian, or on both sides of you if you grew up in the Middle West. You can always escape into it from your present place and problems.

Even more than as this direct lure into travel, the land haunts the American writer as an inner image from which he cannot quite escape. It rolls immensely in the mind, too. The land is a peculiarly American archetype, and as such has been a reality in our literature from the start. Why bring it in then as a special characteristic of our recent literature? Well, old archetypes have a way of boiling over suddenly like old volcanoes, and in recent years this one has been kicking up in new and virulent ways.

There is nothing immemorial, on the other hand, about the Cold War. It is a very present fact, grimly so, and the one above all others that has given the decisive stamp to our period.

However lush our domestic prosperity, we have not been able to enjoy it without the international threat. The human atmosphere engendered by the Cold War has been one of such sullen stalemate and total threat that we all begin to feel as if we were living on the slopes of Vesuvius. Thus we can hardly expect from our writers now the exuberant sense of personal liberation that the Twenties knew. It is a fateful and heavy thing to live in a period when the future of human liberty may be decided.

Naturally enough, this atmosphere of the Cold War can be expected to sour the disposition of literary critics, too. Thus a rather damp mist of literary disparagement has been injected steadily into the air. The tone was rather set some years ago by John Aldridge in his "After the Lost Generation" (though Mr. Aldridge later changed to a more benevolent attitude). Despair at our present period has been a staple of the literary quarterlies ever since the post-war period got under way. And when the poor writers have not been catching it from the highbrows, they get it from Mr. J. Donald Adams. And then one of the most brilliant writers of the period, Randall Jarrell, in his very clever spoof, "The Age of Criticism" (in his book, "Poetry and the Age"), put his hatchet to the very mentality of the time: the way we are going, Jarrell argued, we shall soon be incapable of any spontaneous and first-hand response to literature at all.

All this is rather tough on the writers. They are hardly helped by being convinced even before they sit down to write that nothing good can come out of this time. Whether this critical disparagement has been an unconscious

transfer of pessimism over politics, I cannot say; but I should like here to suggest an opposite judgment: that the literature of these years has been one of considerable variety and power, and, whatever its shortcomings, is bound to occupy a distinct and valuable place in our literary history. Some day Americans, looking back on this post-war period, may even conclude that they have been better served by their writers than their politicians.

First of all, is it really such a wise habit we Americans have got into of counting our literary history by decades? Webster defines a generation as spanning thirty-three years; we with our penchant for speed would like to cram at least three literary "generations" into that stretch. The habit got started by the neat way in which history and the calendar fell together in the division between our Roaring Twenties and Depression Thirties—two decades that had their own distinct human and literary physiognomies and were neatly separated by the crash of 1929.

Then the war ended the Thirties in 1939, and one was tempted to carry this counting habit on to the Forties and Fifties. But here things become much less clear. What was the literary character of the Forties? of the Fifties? History does not tally here so neatly with the calendar, and the artificiality of doling out literary history by the decade becomes obvious.

Since 1939, in literature at least, things rather blur together. If we want to mark out any clear-cut period in the years just past, we have to go over to politics—another indication, if we needed it, that politics rules our lives nowadays—and the period straddles both Forties and Fifties. It began with the conclusion of the war in the summer of 1945 and ended with the launching of the first sputnik in the fall of 1957. Only twelve years, but these years are a clear-cut period within history, and their inner unity is the grim fact of a peripety, or reversal, in American political fortunes.

World War II ended with a situation of unparalleled power for the United States; sharing still the amity of a wartime alliance with Russia, with all its forces mobilized and in the field, it also enjoyed (if that can ever be the word) exclusive possession of the most powerful instrument of war, the atomic bomb. As the period went on, these advantages were lost one by one: the alliance with Russia turned into the Cold War, and before long Russia had the hydrogen bomb and launched the first sputnik. To vary our opening image from chess to poker: one of the players sat down to the game holding three aces, and then somehow in the discard managed to lose them all.

Seen against this background of receding political fortunes for America, the achievement of our writers does not look at all bad. The usual gambit in denigrating them is a comparison with the Twenties. We have not, it is argued, produced a new Hemingway, Fitzgerald or Faulkner; no single works of the period can stand beside "The Great Gatsby," "The Sun Also Rises" or "The Sound and the Fury."

Suppose this is true, why should we expect masterpieces to be produced on demand and as regularly as clockwork? It looks like rather backhand praise for Hemingway, Fitzgerald or Faulkner to cry out with bustling importunity, Where are their likes today? For if they are as good as critics who use them as sticks to beat the present generation seem to think, then we ought not to expect their equal to be automatically delivered up by the bare machinery of time every decade.

I remember being accosted by one of the younger and more impatient literati in 1950. "Here it is more than four years since the end of the war," he complained, "and by 1922 *they* had 'Ulysses' and 'The Waste Land.'" I could only suggest that we Americans did have a genius for mass production but could hardly expect it to work the same miracles in literature as in industry.

We forget that a great work of art *happens,* like a gift of grace, and is not produced on schedule in some invisible assembly-line of history. A masterpiece is a peculiar marriage of genius and luck. The conditions that made the writing of the Twenties what it was cannot be duplicated today.

Hemingway, for example, came along at a peculiar juncture of influences where he had both the luck and the genius to be able to make a breakthrough into new regions of the American language for prose fiction. This language has now become permanently engrafted upon our fiction, imitated so often that we begin to take the imitations merely as instances of a now native American style. The American language, of course, is inexhaustible; but we would hardly seem to need new discoveries within this language now when so much of our fiction is still assimilating Hemingway—in some cases, alas, regurgitating him.

This note of assimilation strikes the right key for our period. Where the Twenties experimented and discovered, ours has been a period not of breakthrough but of consolidation of forces. Necessarily so, and valuably so. Assimilation, however, is not idle repetition, and requires good writers to carry it out. There has been an abundance of talent in this period: J. D. Salinger, Saul Bellow, James Jones, Norman Mailer, Truman Capote, Mary McCarthy, Jean Stafford, Louis Auchincloss, Ralph Ellison, James Baldwin; in the theatre Tennessee Williams and Arthur Miller. I leave out critics, poets, and older writers that were still flourishing during these years, but quite clearly this list does not suggest anything like literary impoverishment.

What is remarkable here is that all these names are known—try as I did, I could come up with no sleepers on this list. No unknown writers have been waiting around for discovery or their just due; the writers of the period, good and bad alike, got recognized, rewarded, were given prizes, fellowships, stipends, jobs. As it was not an age of experiment, so neither was it the age of the starving genius.

An age of assimilation is also one of dissemination; and so, quite in key, the revolution in publishing that took place in this period was the paperback book. Americans now have more good books available than ever before. The Twenties may have had brighter spots of light, but ours is more evenly diffused. Our general literate audience seems to me much more knowledgeable than that of the Twenties.

Since its task was to absorb the revolutionary works of modern literature into its own bloodstream, our age has had to be one of criticism. The title of Jarrell's essay is right for our time, as is also a great deal of his satire; but he failed to observe that the most important critical job of this "age of criticism" has been done, not by the critics, but by the novelists and poets themselves in following out the impetus of earlier styles and experiments. Jarrell's own poetry is profoundly critical in this sense, since it continues, and attempts to digest, so many modern influences.

More than criticism, we have here a kind of rite of literary communion in which the body and blood of the dead master are eaten and drunk in order that his life-giving spirit may pass into his descendants. When the influence of that great mastodonic hulk, James Joyce's "Finnegans Wake," is metamorphosed almost magically into some of the more eerie and exquisite pieces of James Thurber, we are present at an act of critical assimilation more significant for the lifestream of literature than any solemn and scholarly exegesis of the original leviathan.

What has really been wrong with our postwar literature? I am not Pollyanna enough not to know that the disparagers do have their points—there is always something wrong with every period. The trouble with our postwar literature, to put it somewhat paradoxically, is that it has been good enough to have been even much better. When we review its impressive array of talent, we feel somehow that the period should add up to more than it does. Literary power, vitality, energy—these things have been abundant; but the writers have lacked a center somewhere, they have been without great and central themes. The power without purpose in some American writing makes us think sometimes of all that useless horsepower in the big American automobile.

Why this should be so, why the great themes have been lacking, has surely been due in part to the cramping and inhibiting atmosphere of the Cold War. But the rootlessness, the lack of center, of much of our good literary talent has to do also with the American's relation to the land. I come back thus to the two facts—the Cold War and the American land—with which I began this article. It would be another article to explore in detail this influence of the image of the land, but I can't close this one without suggesting the lines along which an answer to our question may be found.

Our history has been from the start a curious dialogue with the land, and mainly with the land as a stranger. "The land was ours before we were the land's," says Robert Frost; and in the rest of the poem adds that Americans found their salvation from this colonial status only by surrendering themselves at last to the land. But is this really so? Have Americans really given themselves to the land? The big land, to be sure, is always something into which one can escape, riding back and forth across country like the members of the Beat Generation. But that is hardly to belong to the land.

Kerouac's "On the Road" would do as a title for a large slice of American literature. This literature has been on the road since the start: the theme of so many of our classics is the American quest for experience—Whitman, Melville, Twain, Wolfe; and Henry James and Hemingway merely did the switch of taking this quest to Europe. The big exception is Faulkner, our most deeply regional writer; and the point of the whole Faulkner corpus is that it is in the end a saga of the land—a saga in which the tragedy of the Faulknerian hero is that in separating himself from the land he also becomes separated from his own human center.

Great as has been the literature written around this American quest for experience, we have to ask ourselves whether this theme can pay off as richly now as it once did. Since the war, with its vast shifts of industries and population, Americans have become everywhere more mobile—and more rootless. The Beat Generation merely opens up an old sore in the American psyche. Kerouac and his pals ought to be useful to us precisely because of their naïveté, for what all those frantic flights across country dramatize so painfully is the perpetually centrifugal tendency of American experience. Fix your gaze hypnotically on experience as an ever widening circle, and the center may drop out of sight. The mind itself becomes all circumference and no center.

Yet these failings are, clearly, not unique to this period, and even as failings they do illumine the traditional problem of the American writer before the vastness and variety of the American experience. This so-called "age of Criticism" has at least raised the level of our literary consciousness all along the line. We know more now about our national resources and liabilities in literature than we ever did.

William Faulkner
* 1897-

In his simple, almost Biblical affirmation of the dignity and spiritual tenacity of man spoken on the occasion of his receiving the Nobel Prize for literature in 1950, William Faulkner provided comfort to many among the apprehensive of his generation. If man is to be blown to extinction or blighted to sterility, even as he sails in capsule to the moon, he can, while he exists, remain man, compassionate, human, in spirit close to immortality. It is old and, to some, cold comfort, but it seems to be, Mr. Faulkner seems to say, all we have, and enough.

The Stockholm Address

I feel that this award was not made to me as a man, but to my work—a life's work in the agony and sweat of the human spirit, not for glory and least of all for profit, but to create out of the materials of the human spirit something which did not exist before. So this award is only mine in trust. It will not be difficult to find a dedication for the money part of it commensurate with the purpose and significance of its origin. But I would like to do the same with the acclaim too, by using this moment as a pinnacle from which I might be listened to by the young men and women already dedicated to the same anguish and travail, among whom is already that one who will some day stand here where I am standing.

Our tragedy today is a general and universal physical fear so long sustained by now that we can even bear it. There are no longer problems of the spirit. There is only the question: When will I be blown up? Because of this, the young man or woman writing today has forgotten the problems of the human heart in conflict with itself which alone can make good writing because only that is worth writing about, worth the agony and the sweat.

He must learn them again. He must teach himself that the basest of all things is to be afraid; and, teaching himself that, forget it forever, leaving no room in his workshop for anything but the old verities and truths of the heart, the old universal truths lacking which any story is ephemeral and doomed—love and honor and pity and pride and compassion and sacrifice. Until he does so, he labors under a curse. He writes not of love but of lust, of defeats in which nobody loses anything of value, of victories without hope and, worst of all, without pity or compassion. His griefs grieve on no universal bones, leaving no scars. He writes not of the heart but of the glands.

Until he relearns these things, he will write as though he stood among and watched the end of man. I decline to accept the end of man. It is easy enough to say that man is immortal simply because he will endure: that when the last ding-dong of doom has clanged and faded from the last worthless rock hanging tideless in the last red and dying evening, that even then there will still be one more sound: that of his puny inexhaustible voice, still talking. I refuse to accept this. I believe that man will not merely endure: he will prevail. He is immortal, not because he alone among creatures has an inexhaustible voice, but because he has a soul, a spirit capable of compassion and sacrifice and endurance. The poet's, the writer's, duty is to write about these things. It is his privilege to help man endure by lifting his heart, by reminding him of the courage and honor and hope and pride and compassion and pity and sacrifice which have been the glory of his past. The poet's voice need not merely be the record of man, it can be one of the props, the pillars to help him endure and prevail.

William Faulkner visited Japan during the summer of 1955 and there at Nagano met with a seminar of Japanese professors of American literature and spoke before several student groups. The following is a transcript, reprinted from FAULKNER AT NAGANO, *published in Tokyo in 1956, of remarks made on one of the latter occasions.*

To the Youth of Japan

A hundred years ago, my country, the United States, was not one economy and culture, but two of them, so opposed to each other that ninety-five years ago they went to war against each other to test which one should prevail. My side, the South, lost that war, the battles of which were fought not on neutral ground in the waste of the ocean, but in our own homes, our gardens, our farms, as if Okinawa and Guadalcanal had been not islands in the distant Pacific but the precincts of Honshu and Hokkaido. Our land, our homes were invaded by a conqueror who remained after we were defeated: we were not only devastated by the battles which we lost, the conqueror spent the next ten years after our defeat and surrender despoiling us of what little war had left. The victors in our war made no effort to rehabilitate and reestablish us in any community of men or of nations.

But all this is past; our country is one now. I believe our country is even stronger because of that old anguish since that very anguish taught us compassion for other peoples whom war has injured. I mention it only to explain and show that Americans from my part of America at least can understand the feeling of the Japanese young people of today that the future offers him nothing but hopelessness, with nothing anymore to hold or believe in. Because the young people of my country during those ten years must have said in their turn: "What shall we do now? Where shall we look for the future? Who can tell us what to do, how to hope and believe?"

I would like to think that there was someone there at that time too, to speak to them out of what little experience and knowledge a few more years might have added to what he had, to reassure them that man is tough, that nothing, nothing —war, grief, hopelessness, despair—can last as long as man himself can last; that man himself will prevail over all his anguishes, provided he will make the effort to; make the effort to believe in man and in hope—to seek not for a mere crutch to lean on, but to stand erect on his own feet by believing in hope and in his own toughness and endurance.

I believe that is the only reason for art—for the music, the poetry, the painting—which man has produced and is still ready to dedicate himself to. That art is the strongest and most durable force man has invented or discovered with which to record the history of his invincible durability and courage beneath disaster, and to postulate the validity of his hope.

I believe it is war and disaster which remind man most that he needs a record of his endurance and toughness. I think that that is why after our own disaster there rose in my country, the South, a resurgence of good writing, writing of a good enough quality that people in other lands began to talk of a "regional" Southern literature until even I, a countryman, have become one of the first names in our literature which the Japanese people want to talk to and listen to.

I believe that something very like that will happen here in Japan within the next few years—that out of your disaster and despair will come a group of writers whom all the world will want to listen to, who will speak not a Japanese truth but a universal truth.

Because man's hope is in man's freedom. The basis of the universal truth which the writers speak is freedom in which to hope and believe, since only in liberty can hope exist—liberty and freedom not given man as a free gift but as a right and a responsibility to be earned if he deserves it, is worthy of it, is willing to work for it by means of courage and sacrifice, and then to defend it always.

And that Freedom must be complete freedom for all men; we must choose now not between color and color nor between kind and kind nor between ideology and ideology. We must choose simply between being slave and being free. Because the day is past now when we can choose a little of each. We cannot choose a freedom established on a hierarchy of freedom, on a caste system of degree of equality like military rank. We think of the world today as being a helpless battleground in which two mighty forces face each other in the form of two irreconcilable ideologies. I do not believe they are two ideologies. I believe that only one of them is an ideology because the other is simply a human belief that no government shall exist immune to the check of the consent of the governed;

that only one of them is a political state or ideology, because the other one is simply a mutual state of man mutually believing in mutual liberty, in which politics is merely one more of the clumsy methods to make and hold good that condition in which all men shall be free.

A clumsy method, until we have found something better, as most of the mechanics of social democracy creak and rattle. But until we find a better, democracy will do, since man is stronger and tougher and more enduring than even his mistakes and blundering.

Bibliography

Probably the most consistently attractive informal essays appear regularly today in the *New Yorker,* in the "Accent on Living" section of the *Atlantic Monthly,* and the "After Hours" section of *Harper's Magazine,* though essays of all varieties are of course to be found elsewhere in abundance. Such annual or occasional publications as *New World Writing, Discovery,* the *Avon Book of Modern Writing,* and the *Anchor Review* include essays which are usually more formally addressed to contemporary problems. The following brief bibliography presents only some of the collections of essays currently available. Those starred are paperback editions. Those marked with a dagger contain informal essays. An eye kept on the display shelves of any bookstore will discover many more.

INDIVIDUAL AUTHORS: THE NINETEENTH CENTURY AND BEFORE

*†CRÈVECOEUR, HECTOR ST. JOHN, *Letters from an American Farmer.* Everyman's Library, E. P. Dutton & Co., Inc.

*†EMERSON, RALPH WALDO, *Complete Essays and Other Writings.* Modern Library, Random House, Inc.

*——, *Five Essays on Man and Nature,* ed. Robert E. Spiller. Crofts Classics, Appleton-Century-Crofts, Inc.

*†FRANKLIN, BENJAMIN, *Autobiography and Other Writings.* Riverside Editions, Houghton Mifflin Co.

*†HOLMES, OLIVER WENDELL, *The Autocrat of the Breakfast Table.* American Century Series, Sagamore Press, Inc.

HOWELLS, WILLIAM DEAN, *Criticism and*

Fiction, ed. Clara M. and Rudolf Kirk. New York: New York University Press, 1959.

*†IRVING, WASHINGTON, *Selected Writings.* Modern Library, Random House, Inc.

*JAMES, HENRY, *The American Essays of Henry James,* ed. Leon Edel. Vintage Books, Alfred A. Knopf, Inc.

*——, *The Art of the Novel,* ed. R. P. Blackmur. Charles Scribner's Sons.

*——, *Literary Views and Reviews,* ed. Albert Mordell. Evergreen Books, Grove Press, Inc.

*†LONGSTREET, A. B., *Georgia Scenes.* American Century Series, Sagamore Press, Inc.

*†MARK TWAIN, *The Portable Mark Twain,* ed. Bernard de Voto. The Viking Press, Inc.

*†THOREAU, HENRY DAVID, *Walden and Other Writings.* Modern Library, Random House, Inc.

*——, *Selected Writings,* ed. Lewis Leary. Crofts Classics, Appleton-Century-Crofts, Inc.

*WHITMAN, WALT, *Complete Poetry and Selected Prose,* ed. James E. Miller, Jr. Riverside Editions, Houghton Mifflin Co.

INDIVIDUAL AUTHORS: THE TWENTIETH CENTURY

*BLACKMUR, R. P., *Form and Value in Modern Poetry.* Doubleday Anchor Books, Doubleday & Company, Inc.

*BROOKS, CLEANTH, *The Well Wrought Urn.* Harvest Books, Harcourt, Brace & Co., Inc.

*COWLEY, MALCOLM, *The Literary Situa-*

316

tion. Compass Books, The Viking Press, Inc.

*CHASE, RICHARD, *The American Novel and the Tradition.* Doubleday Anchor Original, Doubleday & Company, Inc.

*†EDMAN, ERWIN, *Philosopher's Holiday.* Compass Books, The Viking Press, Inc.

ELIOT, T. S., *Selected Essays.* New York: Harcourt, Brace & Co., Inc., 1950.

*†HUNEKER, JAMES G., *Ivory, Apes, and Peacocks.* American Century Series, Sagamore Press, Inc.

* JARRELL, RANDALL, *Poetry and the Age.* Vintage Books, Alfred A. Knopf, Inc.

†KRUTCH, JOSEPH WOOD, *The Twelve Seasons: A Perpetual Calendar for the Country.* New York: William Sloane Associates, Inc., 1949.

LEVIN, HARRY, *The Power of Blackness.* New York: Alfred A. Knopf, Inc., 1958.

MACLEISH, ARCHIBALD, *Poetry and Opinion.* Urbana: University of Illinois Press, 1940.

MACY, JOHN, *The Spirit of American Literature.* New York: Boni and Liveright, 1913.

MATTHIESSEN, F. O., *The Responsibilities of a Critic: Essays and Reviews.* New York: Oxford University Press, Inc., 1952.

*†MENCKEN, H. L., *Prejudices: A Selection,* ed. James T. Farrell. Vintage Books, Alfred A. Knopf, Inc.

MORE, PAUL ELMER, *Selected Shelburne Essays.* New York: Oxford University Press, Inc., 1935.

MORRIS, WRIGHT, *The Territory Ahead.* New York: Harcourt, Brace & Co., Inc., 1957.

*RAHV, PHILIP, *Image and Idea: Twenty Essays on Modern Literature.* New Directions.

*REISMAN, DAVID, *Selected Essays from Individualism Reconsidered.* Doubleday Anchor Books, Doubleday & Company, Inc.

*†SANTAYANA, GEORGE, *Dialogues in Limbo.* Ann Arbor Paperbacks, University of Michigan Press.

*————, *Interpretations of Poetry and Religion.* Harper Torchbooks, Harper & Brothers.

TATE, ALLAN, *Reactionary Essays on Poetry and Ideas.* New York: Charles Scribner's Sons, 1936.

*†TRILLING, LIONEL, *A Gathering of Fugitives.* Beacon Press, Inc.

*————, *The Liberal Imagination.* Doubleday Anchor Books, Doubleday & Company, Inc.

*WARREN, AUSTEN, *Rage for Order: Essays in Criticism.* Ann Arbor Paperbacks, University of Michigan Press.

*†WILLIAMS, WILLIAM CARLOS, *In the American Grain.* New Directions.

*WILSON, EDMUND, *Axel's Castle.* Charles Scribner's Sons.

*————, *Eight Essays.* Doubleday Anchor Books, Doubleday & Company, Inc.

*————, *A Literary Chronicle, 1920–1950.* Doubleday Anchor Books, Doubleday & Company, Inc.

*†————, *A Piece of My Mind.* Doubleday Anchor Books, Doubleday & Company, Inc.

†WHITE, E. B., *One Man's Meat.* New York: Harper & Brothers, 1942.

GENERAL COLLECTIONS

BROWN, CLARENCE A., ed., *The Achievement of American Criticism.* New York: The Ronald Press Company, 1954.

†FIEDLER, LESLIE, ed., *The Art of the Essay.* New York: Thomas Y. Crowell Company, 1958.

*FEIDELSON, CHARLES, AND PAUL BRODTKORD, eds., *Interpretations of American Literature.* Galaxy Books, Oxford University Press.

†HICKS, GRANVILLE, ed., *The Living Novel: A Symposium.* New York: The Macmillan Co., 1957.

*RAHV, PHILLIP, ed., *Literature in America: An Anthology of Literary Criticism.* Meridian Books, Inc.

*†SCHORER, MARK, ed., *Selected American Prose, 1814–1900*. Rinehart Editions, Rinehart & Company, Inc.

*SHAPIRO, CHARLES, ed., *Twelve Original Essays on Great American Novels*. Wayne State University Press.

*†SHAW, CHARLES B., ed., *American Essays*. Pelican Mentor Books, New American Library.

STOVALL, FLOYD, ed., *The Development of American Literary Criticism*. Chapel Hill: University of North Carolina Press, 1955.

ZABEL, MALCOLM, ed., *Literary Opinion in America*. New York: Harper & Brothers, 1951.

BIBLIOGRAPHIES

JOHNSON, THOMAS H., ed., *Literary History of the United States: Bibliography*. New York: The Macmillan Co., 1948.

LEARY, LEWIS, ed., *Articles on American Literature, 1900–1950*. Durham: Duke University Press, 1954.

———, *Contemporary Literary Scholarship: A Critical Review*. New York: Appleton-Century-Crofts, Inc., 1958.

STOVALL, FLOYD, ed., *Eight American Authors: A Review of Research and Criticism*. New York: The Modern Language Association of America, 1956.

Concord Days (1872)	Amos Bronson Alcott (1799-1888)
Birds and Poets (1877)	John Burroughs (1837-1921)
Critical Essays and Literary Notes (1880)	Bayard Taylor (1825-1878)
The Science of English Verse (1880)	Sidney Lanier (1842-1881)
Medical Essays (1883) *Over the Teacups* (1891)	Oliver Wendell Holmes (1809-1894)
Poets of America (1885)	Edmund Clarence Stedman (1833-1908)
Books and Men (1888) *Counter Currents* (1916)	Agnes Repplier (1858-1950)
Partial Portraits (1888) *Notes on Novelists* (1914)	Henry James (1843-1916)
Criticism and Fiction (1891) *Literature and Life* (1902)	William Dean Howells (1837-1920)
Crumbling Idols (1894)	Hamlin Garland (1860-1940)
Gray Days and Gold (1894)	William Winter (1836-1917)
Fenimore Cooper's Literary Offenses (1895)	Mark Twain [Samuel Clemens] (1835-1910)
The Relation of Literature to Life (1896)	Charles Dudley Warner (1829-1900)
Emerson and Other Essays (1898)	John Jay Chapman (1862-1933)
The Future of the American Negro (1899)	Booker T. Washington (1859-1915)
The Rise of the Short Story (1899)	Bret Harte (1836-1902)
Strategems and Spoils (1901)	William Allen White (1868-1944)
Trivia (1902) *Afterthoughts* (1931)	Logan Pearsall Smith (1865-1946)
The Development of the Drama (1903)	Brander Matthews (1852-1929)
The Responsibilities of the Novelist (1903)	Frank Norris (1870-1902)
The Friendship of Art (1904)	William Bliss Carman (1861-1929)
Shelburne Essays (1904/35)	Paul Elmer More (1864-1937)
The Education of Henry Adams (1907)	Henry Adams (1835-1918)
America's Coming of Age (1915) **On Literature Today** (1941)	Van Wyck Brooks (1886-)
Tendencies in Modern American Poetry (1917)	Amy Lowell (1874-1925)
Shandygaff (1918) *Tales from a Rolltop Desk* (1921)	Christopher Morley (1890-1957)
Prejudices (1919/27) *Notes on Democracy* (1926)	H. L. Mencken (1880-1956)
Character and Opinion in the United States (1920)	George Santayana (1863-1952)